MW00781213

*Whitehead's Metaphysics of Extension
and Solidarity*

SUNY Series *in Philosophy*
Robert C. Neville, Editor

Whitehead's Metaphysics of Extension and Solidarity

Jorge Luis Nobo

State University of New York Press

Published by
State University of New York Press, Albany

Printed in the United States of America

For information, address State University of New York
Press, State University Plaza, Albany, N.Y., 12246

Library of Congress Cataloging in Publication Data

Nobo, Jorge Luis, 1940–
   Whitehead's metaphysics of extension and solidarity.

   (SUNY series in philosophy)
   Bibliography: p.
   Includes index.
   1. Whitehead, Alfred North, 1861–1947—Contributions
in metaphysics.   2. Whitehead, Alfred North, 1861–
1947—Contributions in ontology.   3. Metaphysics.
4. Ontology.   I. Title.   II. Series.
B1674.W354N63   1986   110'.92'4   85-25040
ISBN 0-88706-261-X
ISBN 0-88706-262-8 (pbk.)

10 9 8 7 6 5 4 3 2 1

A la memoria de mi padre, y a mi madre—juntos me enseñaron el amor a la sabiduría y la sabiduría del amor.

Contents

List of Abbreviations

The influence of the journal *Process Studies* has helped to standardize the abbreviations for Alfred North Whitehead's major books. The standard abbreviations, with one addition, are here used in all citations and also in the text after the full title of a book has appeared at least once. But, except as noted below, I have not followed the recent practice, by *Process Studies*, of citing *Process and Reality* by a double-reference to the Corrected Edition of 1978 and the original edition of 1929. Since the Corrected Edition parenthetically incorporates the pagination of the original edition, citing the latter (original) edition alone saves space without sacrificing information. I do cite both editions, however, when quoting a corrected passage. To achieve conformity with my text and modern philosophical practice, I have taken the liberty, when quoting from Whitehead's works, of placing any punctuation that follows an emphatic use of single quotation marks outside the closing quotation mark.

AI   *Adventures of Ideas.* New York: Macmillan, 1933.

CN   *The Concept of Nature.* Cambridge: Cambridge University Press, 1964.

CPR *Process and Reality, The Corrected Edition,* New York: Free Press, 1978.

ESP *Essays in Science and Philosophy.* New York: Philosophical Library, 1947.

FR   *The Function of Reason.* Boston: Beacon Press, 1958.

IS   *The Interpretation of Science.* Indianapolis: Bobbs-Merrill, 1961.

MT   *Modes of Thought.* New York: Macmillan, 1938.

PNK *An Enquiry Concerning the Principles of Natural Knowledge.* Cambridge: Cambridge University Press, 1919.

PR   *Process and Reality.* New York: Macmillan, 1929.

R   *The Principle of Relativity.* Cambridge: Cambridge University Press, 1922.

RM   *Religion in the Making.* New York: Macmillan, 1926.
S   *Symbolism, Its Meaning and Effect.* New York: Capricorn, 1959.
SMW   *Science and the Modern World.* New York: Macmillan, 1925.

Preface

Whether the metaphysical ideas underlying Alfred North Whitehead's philosophy of organism are conceptually coherent, logically consistent, and empirically adequate is rightfully a matter for continuing philosophical debate. But the general importance of those ideas for philosophy, science, theology, religion, art, and civilization is now more than sufficiently well-established. Witness, in this respect, the variety and sheer bulk of the secondary Whiteheadian literature. Witness, too, the vitality and growing influence of Whiteheadian-based process theology. Witness, finally, the significant number of scientists—such as Charles Birch, David Bohm, Karl Pribram, Ilya Prigogine, Henry Pierce Stapp, and W. H. Thorpe—who find Whitehead's metaphysical ideas significantly relevant to their own specialized investigations, or whose own philosophical speculations exhibit remarkably Whiteheadian overtones.

The general agreement concerning the importance of Whitehead's philosophy has not led, unfortunately, to a comparable agreement regarding how best to understand, develop, and apply the metaphysical ideas at the base of that philosophy. The received interpretations of Whitehead's metaphysics are many; the areas of agreement in those interpretations are few, particularly so when the discussion goes beyond paraphrasing vague doctrinal generalities. Admittedly, the novelty and complexity of Whitehead's metaphysical doctrines go a long way towards explaining the number, extent, and depth of the received disagreements. But there are, I think, other reasons.

One such reason, perhaps the most important, is the general neglect of the fundamental vision of reality that, as I will argue, Whitehead's metaphysical conceptuality was designed to convey and elucidate. Accordingly, this book reflects my conviction that the difficult tasks of correctly interpreting, constructively criticizing, coherently developing, and systematically appplying Whitehead's metaphysical ideas presuppose, one and all, a truly adequate understanding, not heretofore achieved, of

Whitehead's most fundamental vision of the ultimate nature of reality. The vision in question is the vision of universal solidarity: that the entire universe is somehow to be found within each of its ultimate concrete components or, equivalently, that the final real actualities of which the universe is composed are each in all and all in each.

The solidarity of the universe is the fundamental thesis of Whitehead's metaphysical philosophy. Achieving an adequate elucidation of that thesis is the chief goal of this book. But in order to fulfill that goal, I have found it necessary to develop a number of metaphysical doctrines that Whitehead neglected to make sufficiently explicit in his published writings, but which are truly central to the philosophy of organism. Chief among those neglected doctrines is the organic theory of eternal, or metaphysical, extensive continuity. Thus, this book derives its title from the conjunction of the fundamental organic vision of reality and the fundamental organic doctrine intended to elucidate that vision.

By the solidarity of the universe, Whitehead ultimately understood the holistic functioning of the universe in each of its concrete constituents. Accordingly, this book's investigation of solidarity indirectly underscores the relevance of Whitehead's metaphysics to the holistic conception of reality, and to the attendant holographic paradigm, that a small but growing number of scientists seems increasingly to favor. But I have found it neither possible nor desirable here to explore the implications of my discussion for what some see as the emerging science of wholeness. Whenever possible, however, I have tried to present my interpretation and development of Whitehead's basic metaphysical principles in a manner suggestive of those implications.

My attempt to be suggestive in this last respect is but a special case of my more general attempt to develop the elucidation of solidarity in a manner strongly suggestive of new ways and new areas in which Whitehead's metaphysical conceptuality may be successfully employed. For I would like this book to serve not only as a point of departure for my subsequent philosophical efforts, but also, for those interested readers persuaded by its arguments, as a sort of prolegomenon to their own future interpretation, criticism, development, and employment of Whitehead's metaphysics. To paraphrase Whitehead, then, the ideas here put forth may have been born privately, but they are intended to have public careers. To the extent they do, I will have partially repaid the immense debt I owe to those without whose help I would have never completed this book.

I owe the greatest immediate debt to Lewis S. Ford, who strongly encouraged me to write this book, which expands and revises themes I first treated in my doctoral dissertation, and who recommended it to SUNY Press. Given our many differences in respect to the approach to, and the interpretation of, Whitehead's philosophy, Ford's efforts on behalf of this book's publication are all the more significant of his nobility of character and fairness of mind. No irritable philosopher he but, in the words of Robert C. Neville, "a critic of great mind and soul and without ego."

Less immediate but more extensive and deeply rooted is the debt I owe to my philosophical mentors, Douglas Browning, Charles Hartshorne, and the late David L. Miller. As my teachers, all three provided personal and professional inspiration, guided my philosophical development, gave impetus to my interest in metaphysics, and facilitated my initial understanding of Whitehead. My interpretation of Whitehead's metaphysics now differs significantly from theirs, but the years have lessened neither the influence of these men nor my admiration for them.

I am indebted to my employer, Washburn University of Topeka, for awarding me an academic sabbatical in the Spring semester of 1984, which gave me the free time needed to write much of this book, and also for a research grant to cover the cost of word-processing the manuscript's final draft. I am particularly grateful for the encouragement and support provided by Provost Sheldon Cohen, Dean Paul Salter, and by my chairman and good friend, Harold J. Rood.

My thanks to Vivian McCormick and Rhonda Boose, who shared the task of word-processing the text, to Michelle Hubach for typing the notes and bibliography, and to LaJean Rinker for typing this preface, other front matter, and the index. The last two and Dr. Rood also helped with the tedious task of proofreading the galleys, as did Pam Griebat and Vickie Jacobs. I am grateful also to William Eastman, Director of SUNY Press, for his trust and infinite patience, and to Peggy Gifford, Production Editor, for her expert and cheerful assistance. Finally, I am greatly indebted to my wife, Pat, for preparing the bibliography, for proofreading the book's manuscript, and for her constant support.

Jorge Luis Nobo
Topeka, Kansas
February 17, 1986

Acknowledgements

I am grateful to Lewis S. Ford, editor of *Process Studies*, and to Vincent G. Potter, S.J., editor of *International Philosophical Quarterly*, for permission to incorporate in this book materials which first appeared as articles in their journals. The articles in question are "Whitehead's Principle of Process," *Process Studies*, 4 (1974), 275–84; "Whitehead's Principle of Relativity," *Process Studies*, 8 (1978), 1–20; and "Transition in Whitehead: A Creative Process Distinct from Concrescence," *International Philosophical Quarterly*, 19 (1979), 265–83.

ONE

Solidarity and the Categories

The fundamental thesis of Alfred North Whitehead's philosophy of organism is that the final actualities of the universe cannot be abstracted from one another because each actuality, though individual and discrete, is internally related to all other actualities. This mutual involvement of discrete actualities is what Whitehead meant by the *solidarity* or *connectedness* of the universe.[1] Whitehead's thesis appears to be logically inconsistent, for it posits final actualities that are at once mutually transcendent, as entailed by their discreteness and individuality, and mutually immanent, as required by their reciprocal internal relations. Most interpreters of Whitehead have avoided this problem by conveniently interpreting the solidarity of actualities to mean simply that earlier actualities are immanent in later ones. Any other sense of immance—such as that of later actualities in earlier ones, or of contemporaries in each other—they tend either to ignore altogether, or to explain away by the claim that Whitehead was being careless whenever he spoke of the mutual, or reciprocal, immanence of the universe's final actualities.[2]

This last claim, I hold, is entirely without justification. I am quick to admit, even insist, that Whitehead was a far from careful writer. But we are not talking here of an occasional phrase or passing remark. Rather, numerous explicit references to the mutual immanence of the universe's final actualities are to be found in each of Whitehead's metaphysical works. One book, *Adventures of Ideas*, even devotes almost an entire chapter (Ch. XII) to discussing the immanence of later actualities in earlier ones and of contemporaries in each other. Thus, to ignore or to explain away Whitehead's pronouncements on the mutual immanence of discrete actualities is a tacit admission that no one has yet made complete sense of the fundamental metaphysical vision animating the philosophy of organism. For that vision, I shall argue, is that *any* two actualities, regardless of their temporal relationship, are internally related to each other by reason of their immanence in one another. Accordingly, one major goal of this essay is to elucidate Whitehead's thesis of universal solidarity, while recognizing its paradoxical nature but also trying to exonerate it from charges of logical inconsistency.

1.   Solidarity and the organic categoreal scheme

Let me begin by emphasizing the central role that the doctrine of solidarity plays in the organic philosophy. This can be done by inspecting a few passages taken from Whitehead's writings and from his lectures at Harvard. To understand the full import of these passages, however, two things must be borne in mind. First, for Whitehead the final actualities of the world—what he terms *actual entities*, *actual occasions*, or *events*—are, one and all, happenings or events having all the necessary or metaphysical characters of occasions of experience (AI 284, 303). Second, to say that actual entities, or occasions of experience, are the final actualities is to say that whatever exists in the universe *by way of actuality* is an actual entity, a constituent aspect of an actual entity, or an interrelated group—technically termed a *nexus* or *society*—of actual entities (PR 27–30).

  With those two observations in mind, let us first examine Victor Lowe's account of what Whitehead took to be the six basic principles of his metaphysics. Since these principles jointly provide a bird's-eye view of Whitehead's philosophy, I quote in its entirety the account Lowe gives of them:

> I can also report what Whitehead gave out in his regular Harvard lectures of 1926–27 as "the six main principles of my metaphysics". These were the principles of Solidarity (every actual entity requires all other entities in order to exist), Creative Individuality (every actual entity is a process and its issue comes from its own limitations), Efficient Causation, the Ontological Principle (the character of Creativity is derived from its own creatures, and expressed by its own creatures), Aesthetic Individuality (every actual entity is an end in itself and for itself, involving its own measure of individual self-satisfaction), and Ideal Comparison (every creature involves in its constitution an ideal reference to ideal creatures in ideal relationships to each other, and in comparison with its own satisfaction). Whitehead added that these principles apply to all actualities, including God.[3]

When Whitehead says that every actuality requires all other entities for
its existence, we must understand him to mean that all other entities are
constituents of that actuality. This follows necessarily from the hypothesis that the final actualities have the metaphysical properties of occasions
of experience; for, as construed by Whitehead, "experience is not a
relation of an experient to something external to it, but is itself the
'inclusive whole' which is the required connectedness of 'many in one'"
(AI 299). Accordingly, for Whitehead, "every item of the universe, including all the other actual entities, are constituents in the constitution of
any one actual entity" (PR 224).

The problem posed by the thesis of solidarity now becomes obvious:
How can the universe, or world, be composed of actual entities and yet be
itself contained in each of its component actualities? Whitehead, however,
is fully aware of the problem; indeed, he makes it explicit in more than a
few passages of his works, referring to it sometimes simply as 'the problem
of solidarity' and at other times as 'the paradox of the connectedness of
things' (PR 88; AI 293). To cite but one example, in *Modes of Thought* we
find Whitehead saying that

> there is a dual aspect to the relationship of an occasion of experience as
> one relatum and the experienced world as another relatum. The
> world is included within the occasion in one sense, and the occasion is
> included in the world in another sense. (MT 224)

This bond between world and occasion, Whitehead immediately admits,
is a "baffling antithetical relation" (MT 224); but, for him, when we
examine our everyday experience of the world, or when we inquire into
the presuppositions of common practice, into the presuppositions of the
natural sciences, or into the presuppositions of basic epistemic claims, we
run again and again into this paradoxical relation of mutual immanence
(MT 218–27):

> For example, consider the enduring self-identity of the soul. The soul
> is nothing else than the succession of my occasions of experience,
> extending from birth to the present moment. Now, at this instant, I
> am the complete person embodying all these occasions. They are
> mine. On the other hand it is equally true that my immediate occasion
> of experience, at the present moment, is only one among the stream of
> occasions which constitutes my soul. Again, the world for me is
> nothing else than how the functionings of my body present it for my
> experience. The world is thus wholly to be discerned within those
> functionings. Knowledge of the world is nothing else than an analysis
> of the functionings. And yet, on the other hand, the body is merely

> one society of functionings within the universal society of the world.
> We have to construe the world in terms of the bodily society, and the
> bodily society in terms of the general functionings of the world.
> (MT 224–25)

This compelling character of human experience—that it is a constituent
of the universe and that the universe is a constituent of it—suggests to
Whitehead that the togetherness of all final actualities somehow involves
their mutual immanence: "In some sense or other, this community of the
actualities of the world means that each happening is a factor in the nature
of every other happening" (MT 225). By thus generalizing what is manifest in our experience of the world into a necessary feature of every final
actuality, Whitehead arrives at what I have termed the thesis of solidarity
(MT 227). The thesis maintains that "any set of actual occasions are united
by the mutual immanence of occasions, each in the other" (AI 254). It
asserts, in effect, that any two actual entities, regardless of their temporal
relationship (AI 254), are at once mutually transcendent and mutually
immanent. The problem is to find a sense of 'mutual immanence' wholly
consistent with the discrete individuality of actual entities.

It is precisely in respect to this problem that the importance of the
solidarity thesis—its pivotal role in Whitehead's philosophy—can be made
fully evident; for it is no exaggeration to say that the organic philosophy is
devoted to the elucidation of the mutual immanence of discrete actualities.
That this is so becomes evident when we examine the following three
passages taken from *Process and Reality* and *Adventures of Ideas*:

> The [categoreal] scheme should [develop] all those generic notions
> adequate for the expression of any possible interconnection of things.
> (PR vii)

> The coherence which the system seeks to preserve, is the discovery
> that the process, or concrescence, of any one actual entity involves the
> other actual entities among its components. In this way the obvious
> solidarity of the world receives its explanation. (PR 10)

> The world within experience is identical with the world beyond
> experience, the occasion of experience is within the world and the
> world is within the occasion. The categories have to elucidate this
> paradox of the connectedness of things:—the many things, the one
> world without and within. (AI 293)

Clearly, the solidarity, or connectedness, of the world is the thesis whose
truth the organic categoreal scheme is designed to convey and demonstrate.

The importance of connectedness is also made evident by Whitehead's assertion that it was with a view toward its elucidation that he chose the working hypothesis of his philosophy—namely, that the final actualities of the world have the necessary features of acts or occasions of experience (AI 284; PR 65, 217). It is instructive, in this regard, to first consider the manner in which, in the following passage, Whitehead takes Cartesian philosophy to task:

> [If] we hold the Cartesian doctrine of substantial souls with many adventures of experience, and of substantial material bodies, then on that hypothesis the relations between two occasions of experience qualifying one soul are no evidence as to the connectedness of two such occasions respectively qualifying two different souls, and are no evidence as [to] the connectedness of a soul and a material body, and are no evidence as to the connectedness of two occasions of agitation of one material body, or of two such occasions respectively belonging to different material bodies. (AI 283–84)

Surely, the gist of Whitehead's criticism is that the central hypothesis of Cartesian philosophy precludes outright any possibility of doing justice to the connectedness of nature. In marked contrast, the advantage of the organic working hypothesis, that which makes it attractive to Whitehead, is precisely its capacity to suggest categories applicable to the connectedness of things. Thus, immediately after the passage just quoted, Whitehead writes:

> But if we hold, as for example in *Process and Reality*, that all final individual actualities have the metaphysical character of occasions of experience, then on that hypothesis the direct evidence as to the connectedness of one's immediately present occasion of experience with one's immediately past occasions, can be validly used to suggest categories applying to the connectedness of all occasions in nature. (AI 284)

Thus the organic philosophy's basic working hypothesis, as well as its categoreal scheme, is intended to help illuminate the paradoxical connectedness of occasions.

What needs to be illuminated, it must be added, is "the solidarity of individuals with each other" (PR 532). For, in the organic philosophy, actual entities are not only the final constituents, but also the final *individuals*, of the universe. In this regard, it is important to notice that Whitehead borrowed the term 'solidarity' from H. Wildon Carr's Presidential Address ("The Interaction of Body and Mind") to the Aristotelian Society, Session 1917–18 (PR 65, fn. 3), and that, for Carr, the term solidarity meant "that diverse, even divergent, activities together bring to pass a single common result to which all the activities contribute without sacrificing their individual integrity."[4] It follows that the problem posed by the *solidarity* of actual entities is not to be solved at the expense of the *individuality* of actual entities (PR 22; AI 54; IS 200–01; MT 98).

The preceding considerations establish beyond any reasonable doubt the fundamental role that the thesis of solidarity is intended to play in the organic philosophy; they also strongly suggest that any attempt to solve the problem posed by that thesis should do so through an examination of the organic categories that were meant to shed light on it. This is the approach taken in this essay. Accordingly, my first task is to attempt to isolate, so far as this is possible, those organic categories that have an immediate bearing on the connectedness of occasions. To achieve this end, I will shortly analyze an instance of mnemonic experience in order to take advantage of Whitehead's suggestion that the analysis of the obvious connection between one's own successive occasions of experience yields categories applicable to the connectedness of all occasions. When this presystematic analysis of an act of remembering is completed, I will then seek those organic doctrines or categories that closely correspond to, or are presupposed by, the factors and processes yielded by that analysis.

The need to isolate as soon as possible those categories which are relevant to the explanation of the world's solidarity is dictated by the complexity and opacity of the organic categoreal scheme. As formulated in PR, the scheme consists of one Category of the Ultimate, eight Categories of Existence, twenty-seven Categories of Explanation and nine Categoreal Obligations. And this scheme, Whitehead himself tells us, "is practically unintelligible" when taken by itself (PR v). Its categories become meaningful only through their use in the elaboration and discussion of the organic cosmology, that is, by their "confrontation with the various topics of experience" (PR vii). To avoid having to consider the entire organic cosmology, therefore, it is imperative that I differentiate the categories more immediately pertinent to the task at hand from the less relevant ones.

In one sense, however, all the organic categories are relevant to the elucidation of the connexity of occasions. At least this is what one should expect, given the criteria that according to Whitehead any scheme of metaphysical categories should meet. We must remember in this regard that, for Whitehead, metaphysics or speculative philosophy "is the endeavour to frame a coherent, logical, necessary system of general ideas in terms of which every element of our experience can be interpreted" (PR 4). Now, in respect to this definition, 'coherence'

> means that the fundamental ideas, in terms of which the scheme is developed, presuppose each other so that in isolation they are meaningless. This requirement does not mean that they are definable in terms of each other; it means that what is indefinable in one such notion cannot be abstracted from its relevance to the other notions. It is the ideal of speculative philosophy that its fundamental notions shall not seem capable of abstraction from each other. (PR 5)

To the extent that this ideal is fulfilled by the organic philosophy, this essay's final elucidation of the thesis of solidarity will be deficient precisely in those respects having to do with those notions, or categories, that will have been considered either perfunctorily or not at all. These shortcomings, however, should be outweighed by the depth of interpretive analysis obtained in other more basic respects. This essay, then, should be judged by how well it enables us to understand what Whitehead meant by the solidarity of occasions, not by how much of the organic categoreal scheme it brings to that task.[5]

2.   Concerns, limitations, and plan of this essay

The elucidation of the solidarity thesis is this essay's pivotal concern, but it is not its only concern. It cannot be its only concern because the mutual relevance of the solidarity thesis and the categoreal scheme necessitates that the elucidation of the thesis go hand in hand with the interpretation and development of the scheme. After all, the very fact that the organic scheme of metaphysical principles is intended to illuminate the solidarity of actual entities implies that no major organic principle can be deemed to be adequately understood unless its relevance to the solidarity of actual entities has been duly demonstrated.

It is precisely in this last regard, I maintain, that the major received interpretations of Whitehead's metaphysics are flawed. They have failed to capture the full sweep of Whitehead's profound metaphysical vision because they have either ignored or underestimated the importance of achieving an adequate understanding of the solidarity or connectedness of actual entities. Moreover, because they have overlooked the mutual relevance of the solidarity thesis and the scheme of categoreal principles, the received interpretations have often misrepresented—sometimes grossly so—many of the most fundamental organic principles, including, for example, the Category of the Ultimate and the principles of relativity, process and ontology (*i.e.*, the fourth, ninth, and eighteenth Categories of Explanation). Accordingly, our concern with interpreting and developing the organic principles most relevant to the elucidation of solidarity is necessitated also by the fact that we cannot rely on the received interpretations of those principles.

So far as they miss the full import of the metaphysical principles most relevant to the solidarity of the universe, the major received interpretations endanger significant areas of the *applicability* of Whitehead's organic metaphysics.[6] At risk, to mention a few, are, first, the theories of perception and cognition; second, the reconciliation of deterministic efficient causation with autonomous final causation; third, the relevance of God to the concrete course of universal history; and fourth, the development of a metaphysically grounded existentialist anthropology. An additional concern of this essay is to suggest the increased range and depth of applicability gained by the organic metaphysical scheme when its most basic principles are interpreted in accord with the demands of the solidarity thesis.

In this regard, no more than a suggestive treatment of the relevant metaphysical doctrines is possible because the central task of elucidating the fundamental organic thesis is too complex and time-consuming to allow extended explorations of the specialized applications of the organic conceptuality. Moreover, the sustained employment of Whitehead's metaphysical scheme in any special field of interest requires, to my mind, more critical evaluation and improvement of that scheme than is compatible with the immediate purpose of this essay. For the same reason, the essay can only suggest that when the thesis of solidarity has been properly understood the affinities between Whitehead's speculative thought and that of philosophically-minded contemporary scientists, such as David Bohm, Karl Pribram, Ilya Prigogine and Henry Pierce Stapp, will be seen as greater than is usually acknowledged.[7]

All this is by way of stating the concerns and the limitations of this essay. It does not attempt to explain the whole of Whitehead's metaphysical theory, to critically evaluate it, or to explore the empirical applications of its principles. For all those tasks presuppose an adequate understanding of the basic organic thesis, and achieving that understanding is itself a task of no small proportions. Accordingly, the elucidation of the thesis of solidarity is the sole immediate aim and the unifying concern of this essay. I do confess an underlying aim to place the interpretation, criticism, development, and application of Whitehead's philosophy of organism on a radically new foundation, one that takes seriously the vision of universal solidarity animating all of Whitehead's speculative thought.

For the moment, the task at hand is the interpretation and development of the solidarity thesis. To that end, the remainder of this chapter seeks to identify, and to begin the discussion of, the organic categories and doctrines that are most immediately relevant to the elucidation of solidarity. Indeed, the chapter seeks to present in microcosm the ideas, principles, and doctrines which the rest of the essay presents in macrocosm. For the sake of readers less than familiar with Whitehead's philosophy, the chapter gradually introduces the basic organic ideas and technical terms used in the subsequent discussion. Thus, the initial presentation of the relevant terms, principles, and doctrines will enable us, in Section 12, to further explain the problem posed by the solidarity thesis, as well as to anticipate the crucial elucidatory role played in that respect by the metaphysical theory of extensive continuity that is implicit, I will argue, in Whitehead's speculative writings. A brief preview of the remaining chapters concludes the present one.

3.   Memory: a key to the relevant categories

My immediate task is to locate and examine the organic categories in terms of which the connectedness of nature is to be elucidated. A key to these categories is to be found in a presystematic analysis of the connection between one's own successive occasions of experience. For, as we saw earlier, Whitehead maintains that such an analysis can be validly used to suggest categories applicable to the connectedness of all occasions— provided, of course, that we assume the truth of his working hypothesis. Therefore, it is to be assumed, as over against the traditional doctrine of substantial souls, that a man's soul is nothing else than the coordinated stream of his experiences, and that the stream is ultimately composed of discrete but interconnected occasions of experience, no two of which originate in unison.

According to Whitehead, whenever we remember a definite moment of our antecedent experiences, the act of remembering and its relation to the remembered experience are such that they cannot be intelligibly analyzed without the introduction of four interrelated notions, which he terms respectively 'repetition', 'immediacy', 'becoming', and 'being' (PR 205–08). In order to see how these four notions function in presystematic or pre-categoreal analyses of instances of remembering, let us consider one such instance. Let the experience to be remembered be something as relatively simple as a quick glance at an issue of *The New Yorker* lying on the floor, a foot or so to the right of the desk where I am presently writing. Let me glance at the magazine only long enough to notice that its cover depicts a harbor scene. Now let me return to my original position at the desk, and let me immediately try to remember what I have just done and seen. What salient features of this act of remembering may be considered, according to Whitehead, as essential to all such acts?

One such feature, Whitehead would hold, is the indubitable feeling that some contents of my present experience are somehow effecting a *repetition* of my earlier experience. I find myself experiencing once more the kinesthetic sensations of turning my head to one side and downward; I feel again the previous orientation of my body, particularly of my head, in respect to the magazine on the floor; finally, I have once again before me the magazine's cover painting, and I even grasp, albeit dimly, some of its details—a solitary sailboat in the harbor, the cluster of houses in the foreground, and the sun half-hidden behind a group of clouds. Now these are all contents of my present experience, yet one and all have stamped on their foreheads, as it were, this character—that they are repeating in and for my present experience the contents of my earlier experience.

Another prominent feature of my act of remembering, Whitehead would maintain, is its *immediacy*. I am remembering my earlier experience, but I am remembering it *now*. The earlier experience, as repeated in, and for, my present experience, has a second-hand character about it. However, my present experience has an essential over-all character of first-handedness. This first-handedness involves my feeling or entertainment of those contents of my present experience that are repeating contents of my earlier experience. These repetitive contents constitute *what* I am feeling or entertaining, but other present contents express *how* I am feeling them. Thus, even as I am remembering the painting on the magazine's cover, I begin to wonder who painted it and whether it represents an actual harbor. Curiosity, then, is an additional factor of my experience, expressing the manner in which I entertain or feel the repetitive contents. My curiosity is ultimately about the painting itself; nevertheless, as it arises in my present experience, it is concerned directly only with the memory-image. It arises with the act of remembering and not with the original perception. In any case, the total configuration of curiosity spurred by, and directly referring to, a memory-image constitutes the first-handedness or immediacy of my present experience.

Actually, the total configuration of my present experience is more complex than that. The manner in which I entertain my memory-image of the painting on the magazine's cover is only one concrete component of my present experience, albeit the focal one. In the periphery of my experience, so to speak, there is a slight pain in my neck, which I associate with the memory of having turned my head too quickly a brief moment ago; these additional contents I entertain respectively with annoyance and regret. Also lurking in my experiential background are auditory, visual, tactile, and kinesthetic sensations expressing, no matter how vaguely, the fact that I am sitting at my desk, in this room, this particular afternoon. Each of these contents I feel in some manner or other, and the manners in which I feel them ultimately coalesce into a unified feeling of myself-in-the-world-at-this-moment. This unified feeling is, properly speaking, the total configuration of my present experience—abstracting, of course, from the ongoingness of the self-emergence of that experience. The unified feeling and the process of its emergence constitute the immediacy of my present experience. Thus, as Whitehead puts it,

> 'immediacy', or 'first-handedness', is another element in experience. Feeling overwhelms repetition; and there remains the immediate, first-handed fact, which is the actual world in an immediate complex unity of feeling. (PR 206)

A third essential trait of my present experience, Whitehead would say, is precisely the ongoingness of its emergence. It is something that *becomes*, and, presently at least, it is just its own *becoming*. In this respect, it should be obvious that the notions of 'repetition' and 'immediacy' involve the notion of 'becoming'. My act of remembering first repeats, though not necessarily in all its details, my earlier experience; then it overwhelms that repetition through feeling, and is on the whole a novel, fresh, immediate fact of experience. Clearly, this is evidence for the ongoingness of my experience—its repetitive contents becoming first, and the feelings whereby these contents are overwhelmed becoming afterwards. Two phases of becoming are thus distinguished; but they are phases of my one present moment of experience, inasmuch as the later phase presupposes, refers to, and includes within itself, the earlier phase. In other words, the creative operations of the second phase take into account the product of the creative operations of the first phase.

A fourth essential feature of my present experience, according to Whitehead, is its ultimate reference to the *being* of my earlier experience.

Thus, in the background of my experience there is the vague but insistent feeling that my earlier experience endures in a fashion of its own. If this be doubted, consider the notion that some contents of my present experience effect a repetition of my earlier experience. This notion presupposes the continued endurance, or being, of my earlier experience, not merely as repeated in my present experience, but, as I intend to show, in itself. For just as it would make no sense to speak of an artist painting a replica of a masterpiece, unless that masterpiece were there to serve as a model, so, for the same reason, it would make no sense to speak of my present experience repeating my earlier one, unless the earlier one were in some sense also there, serving as a model.

But in what sense can the earlier experience be there? In what sense can it endure or be? Surely, it cannot endure as its own process of becoming; that is, it cannot endure as something which is happening. For the direct deliverance of my present experience is that I am remembering something which was happening a brief moment ago, but which is definitely not happening now. Therefore, if what endures cannot be my earlier experience considered as the process of its becoming, then the only alternative is to posit that what endures is the experience considered as the product or outcome of that process.

This may be put in another way. My earlier experience is no longer happening; yet it is not on that account mere nothingness. Nor is it something merely because I remember it. Its being something in its own right is a presupposition of my remembering it, and not the other way around. What then is it? Since it cannot be a process, I am led to the idea, by no means far-fetched, that its process terminated in an enduring product, and that it is this product which serves as the datum from which derive, and to which refer, certain contents of my present experience. I am also led to the idea of the enduring product somehow giving witness to the process whereby it came to be. Otherwise, the product would not provide a basis for the reconstruction of its becoming effected by and within my present experience.

The upshot of this line of thought is that the intelligible analysis of my act of remembering, considered as a *becoming* or experience-process, requires the endurance of the remembered experience, considered as a *being* or experience-product. It may be objected that this is not so. Thus, one may try to argue that the relation between my present and earlier experiences can be adequately explained in terms of the neurophysiological functionings with which they are associated. On this approach, some such present functioning is held to be identical with, or similar to, some earlier functioning. The functionings in question are assumed to give rise to identical or similar contents in the experiences with which they are respectively associated. But it is only to the extent that the present functioning is identical with, or similar to, the earlier one, that I experience a feeling of familiarity with some contents of my present experience. Roughly speaking this is all that is needed, it could be argued, to account for the nature of my present act of remembering, at least insofar as it has the character of repeating contents of my earlier experience.[8]

But surely this explanation of memory is circular. For how would I know that some of my present neurophysiological functionings are identical or similar to some of my earlier ones? Do I remember the earlier functionings? Are they somehow still available, so that I can compare them with my present neurophysiological functionings? Clearly, either this explanation is circular or it is forced to posit some manner of endurance for the earlier functionings. This is not to deny, however, that these functionings play an important role in our acts of remembering. What one is questioning is whether such functionings can account for the ultimate character of our mnemonic experiences—that they are presently repeating something which occurred earlier.

In any case, we are not presently interested in the problem of memory *per se*. We are merely using a Whiteheadian (presystematic) analysis of my act of remembering to familiarize ourselves with certain features of that act which Whitehead takes to be essential to all such acts and which suggest to him categories applicable to the connectedness of nature. That my earlier experience endures and that my present experience is a novel becoming have emerged as two such features. For Whitehead, this means that we

> have certainly to make room in our philosophy for the two contrasted notions, one that every actual entity endures, and the other that every morning is a new fact with its measure of change. (PR 207)

Another pertinent observation, in this regard, is that the analysis of my act of remembering also presupposes the endurance of that act *qua* experience-product. For in fact the analysis of that act was carried out in, and by, experiences subsequent to it. Hence, it was analyzed only to the extent that it was remembered or reconstructed in and by those subsequent experiences. For this reason, my mnemonic act itself must be construed as an ephemeral becoming, involving repetition and immediacy and terminating in an enduring being that somehow gives witness to the process which was its becoming.

In addition to the notions already considered, a Whiteheadian, pre-categoreal analysis of mnemonic experience involves two other notions that are worth mentioning at this point, for they will be incorporated in organic doctrines directly relevant to the connectedness or solidarity of the universe. I will term these notions 'anticipation' and 'succession'. Both of them functioned implicitly in the foregoing analysis of an act of remembering.

The first notion has to do with the fact that my remembered experience, as well as my experience of remembering, involved an element of anticipation. Thus, my reason for glancing at the magazine on the floor was so that, in a subsequent experience, I could remember taking that glance. Also, my reason for remembering the experience of glancing at the magazine was so that, in subsequent experiences, I could analyze my experience of remembering and thus provide an example of a Whiteheadian, pre-categoreal analysis of mnemonic experience. In both cases, I anticipated that my then present moment of experience would terminate and thus give way to a new experience; also in both cases I anticipated that my then present experience would somehow be an object for my subsequent experiences. It seems, therefore, that each experience involves the anticipation of the fact that what it is as a process will terminate with the achievement of what it is to be as a product, and involves also the anticipation that this product can be taken into account by subsequent experiences. It should be noted, in passing, that each experience takes into account the general potentiality for subsequent experiences.

The second notion has to do with the fact that the remembering occasion succeeded the remembered occasion, and it was in turn succeeded by the occasions which effected its analysis. Also, in the becoming of the remembering occasion there was a succession of phases—the first phase involved repetition; the second, immediacy. Thus succession is intrinsic to the occasion, as well as extrinsic. But in this context 'succession' is misleading, for what we are alluding to is not *mere* succession. The act of remembering succeeds the remembered act and takes it into account. Also, the act of remembering is succeeded and taken into account by the acts which effect its analysis. Finally, the phase of immediacy succeeds and takes into account the phase of repetition. Thus the relata of 'succession' are also the relata of 'taking into account'. We shall see that this twofold notion of succession, intrinsic and extrinsic, gives rise to one of the truly important categories of Whitehead's organic philosophy.

Our presystematic analysis of memory has involved six basic notions: *becoming, being, repetition, immediacy, succession,* and *anticipation*. The first four of these are explicitly generalized by Whitehead into essential features of all occasions of experience. This move permits Whitehead to summarize these four notions

> in the statement that *experience* involves a *becoming*, that *becoming* means that *something becomes* [*i.e.*, that an experience-product comes to be ⁹], and that *what becomes* involves *repetition* transformed into *novel immediacy*. (PR 207)

It is implicit in this passage that *succession* is also essential to an occasion of experience. This is obvious, for, as we have seen, what is repeated, albeit under an abstraction, is the occasion or occasions that the experience in question is succeeding. Moreover, it is evident that the passage from the phase of mere repetition to the phase of novel immediacy involves the succession of the one by the other, even though the former, or rather its product, may remain as a component of the latter. Finally, though the notion of *anticipation* is not implicit in the passage just quoted, Whitehead does say elsewhere that the experience-process of an actual occasion is in essence a passage from repetition, or *re-enaction*, to *anticipation* (AI 248; IS 243). In short, all six notions considered in the analysis of mnemonic experience denote essential features of every actual occasion.

Accordingly, my next task is to provide a first look at the organic categories or doctrines suggested by, or giving expression to, these six presystematic notions. For those doctrines or categories should prove to be the organic principles most useful for, and most pertinent to, the elucidation of the connectedness of all occasions—the elucidation, that is, of the thesis of solidarity. To the extent that this is true, their claim on our attention is fully warranted.

4. Becoming and being: the actual entity as subject-superject

Whitehead incorporates the distinction between 'becoming' and 'being' in the doctrine that every actual entity is to be construed as a 'subject-superject', where in each case 'subject' refers to the actual entity considered as a becoming, and 'superject' to the actual entity considered as a being (PR 57). For any given actual entity, therefore, the subject is that entity considered in respect to its existence while in the process of becoming, and the superject is that same entity considered in respect to its existence as the product or outcome of that becoming (PR 71, 369, 390). The *subject* is the 'actuality in attainment', whereas the *superject* is the 'attained actuality' (PR 326–27).

The relation of subject to superject, therefore, is that of creative process to created product. It must be emphasized, however, that we do not have two different entities, the one creating the other. On the contrary, we have but one entity, first existing as in the process of realizing itself, and then existing as the static outcome of that process of self-realization. The one entity is both the process of self-realization and the self-realized product. "An actual entity is at once the subject of self-realization, and the superject which is self-realized" (PR 340). An actual entity, however, is not literally at once both subject and superject, both creative process and created product. The product is the final outcome of the creative process; hence, the existence of the product marks the end of, and is subsequent to, the existence of the process. In other words, an actual entity first exists as subject, and then as superject. Both modes of existence cannot belong to it at once.

Nevertheless, *in regard to its complete history*, an actual entity is both process *and* product, both becoming *and* being, both subject *and* superject. This is one reason why an actual entity is not to be construed merely as subject or merely as superject but is to be construed always as subject-superject. "An actual entity is at once the subject experiencing and the superject of its experiences. It is subject-superject, and neither half of this description can for a moment be lost sight of" (PR 43). Achieving a complete description of an actual occasion is not a matter of juxtaposing two otherwise independent descriptions: the one of the occasion's subjective existence, the other of its superjective existence. On the contrary, the two partial descriptions are not independent of one another, since they convey the analyses of two modes of existence that presuppose each other for their ultimate intelligibility.

Thus, on the one hand, the analysis of what an occasion is *qua* subject requires a reference to what that same occasion will be *qua* superject; for the subject is not an aimless creative process but is guided by its ideal of what the superject or outcome of that process is to be (PR 130). "The enjoyment of this ideal," writes Whitehead, "is the subjective aim, by reason of which the actual entity is a determinate process" (PR 130). The subjective aim, then, is the final cause of the occasion entertaining it. But what the occasion *qua* subject is aiming at is the realization of itself *qua* superject. The ideal superject is the final determinateness at which the subject aims. Accordingly, what happens during the occasion's process of becoming is, in part at least, "merely the outcome of the subjective aim of the subject, determining what it is integrally to be, in its own character of the superject of its own process" (PR 369). In this respect, therefore, the superject is already present (ideally or conceptually) as a condition determining how the process conducts itself (PR 341). For this reason, any explanation of the character of the subjective process involves a reference to the character of the superjective product either as aimed at in, or as achieved by, that process.

On the other hand, any explanation of the character of the superjective product requires a reference to the character of the subjective process; for the superject is what it is partly by reason of the genetic process that produced it. Indeed, to understand the structure of the superject, it is necessary to reconstruct the process of which it is the outcome. How this is done need not concern us at this time. What should be emphasized now is that, for Whitehead, the analysis of the superject can be deemed successful only if it allows for the reconstruction of the genetic process. If the reconstruction is not possible, then the analysis of the superject has been faulty (PR 359–60).

An occasion's existence as subject and its existence as superject, we must conclude, cannot be intelligibly divorced from one another; but this is not to say that an occasion exists simultaneously as subject and superject. The attainment of the subjective aim halts the creative process; but since the process *is* the subject, the subject has ceased to exist; what remains is the completed occasion—the superject. The actuality in attainment has given way to the attained actuality.

The superject is the actual entity as fully made and is, for that reason, also termed the *satisfaction*, in the root sense of that word (PR 71, 129–30). The satisfaction "is the actual entity as a definite, determinate, settled fact, stubborn and with unavoidable consequences" (PR 336). The superjective satisfaction can have consequences because once it exists it never ceases to exist (PR 44). Moreover, it has consequences in virtue of being repeated, or reproduced, in every actuality whose becoming finds that satisfaction already in existence. In the organic philosophy, we shall argue throughout this essay, attained actuality is construed as being both cumulative and reproducible (PR 365). Moreover, what is already accumulated must be reproduced in and for each new actuality in attainment. Thus the becoming of each actual entity constitutes an expansion of what the universe is by way of actuality (PR 438). Thus, too, the creative advance of actuality is irreversible (PR 363). Metaphysically, there is no undoing what has been done, and every deed impresses its identity on all deeds beyond itself.

5. *Repetition and immediacy: objectification and subjective form*

The notion of repetition gives rise to, and is incorporated in, Whitehead's theory of (causal) *objectification*. This theory generalizes the repetition of the past that is evident in conscious mnemonic occasions of human experience into a feature of all actual occasions, human and non-human. Thus, the "doctrine of objectification is an endeavor to express how what is settled in actuality is repeated under limitations, so as to be 'given' for immediacy" (PR 208). The objectification of a completed occasion abstracts from its qualitative essence, or *definiteness*, but it does not abstract from that occasion's relational essence, or *position*. Since, as we shall argue later, the particular identity of an occasion is primarily a function of its position, this means that a completed occasion and any one of its objectifications in later occasions are *two and the same particular*. That a completed actual occasion can be repeated without losing its self-identical particularity is so paradoxical and revolutionary a doctrine that Whitehead's interpreters heretofore have been unable to accept it literally.[10] But accept it literally we must if we are to do justice to the thesis of solidarity. It follows that a substantial portion of our essay will be devoted to the elucidation of the interrelated notions of objectification, position, and self-identity.

The notion of novel immediacy gives rise to, and is incorporated in, Whitehead's theory of *subjective form* (AI 227; PR 354). This theory generalizes what is novel in an act of remembering—the 'manner' of entertaining, or of responding to, the past as given for it—into a feature of all actualities. According to it, every nascent occasion responds to each past occasion objectified in it by generating some novel quality or other to define its own manner of taking that objectified occasion into account, and thereby to partly define itself (PR 354–56). In this way, the occasion contributes to its own determination as it responds to every past occasion given, or objectified, for it (PR 234). Each resulting instance of self-definition is termed a *subjective form* because the occasion as self-determining—or, equivalently, as self-functioning—is the occasion as *subject* (PR 38). Thus the subject is the occasion as in its own immediacy of self-realization (PR 38). "But the subjective form is the immediate novelty; it is how *that* subject is feeling that objective datum" (PR 354).

The theories of (causal) objectification and of subjective form combine to form the broader theory of *physical prehensions* or, equivalently, of *physical feelings*. Physical prehensions contrast with *conceptual* ones, which we shall discuss shortly. For the moment, let us notice that the *physical prehension* "of one actual entity by another actual entity is the complete transaction, analysable into the objectification of the former entity as one of the data for the latter, and into the fully clothed feeling whereby the datum is absorbed into the subjective satisfaction—'clothed' with the various elements of its 'subjective form'" (PR 82). This formulation of the nature of a physical prehension begins to make evident, the majority of Whitehead's interpreters notwithstanding, that the subjective activity of an actual occasion is subsequent to the activity whereby the past actualities are objectified, or repeated, in the novel occasion and are in that fashion data for the novel occasion's subjective activity. The objectifications, in other words, are data derived, by means of a reproductive activity, from the novel occasion's correlative universe of completed, or settled, actualities. But the subjective activity of the novel occasion is in no way involved in the derivation or production of the objectifications. The subject does not create the objectifications; it merely reacts to them. This is one reason why the completed actualities are always said by Whitehead to be objectified *for*, rather than *by*, the novel subject.

The activity of objectification, I am contending, *precedes* the activity of self-determining immediacy, even though the products of the former activity are absorbed into, or subordinated to, the products of the latter. We have to distinguish, in other words, between the becoming of the datum *for* subjective immediacy and the becoming which *is* the subjective immediacy (PR 228). True, the two becomings are only successive stages in the becoming of one and the same actual occasion; nonetheless, to lose sight of this distinction is to eradicate the organic philosophy's distinction between efficient causation and final causation or, equivalently, between the process of transition and the process of concrescence.

6. *Objectification, immanence, and the extensive continuum*

Before examining how the presystematic contrast between repetition and immediacy is incorporated into the systematic contrast between transition and concrescence, we need to take a closer look at the organic doctrine of objectification. For that doctrine plays a truly crucial role in the elucidation of the solidarity thesis. Notice, in this regard, that, *as objectified*, the universe is *included* in each of its constituent occasions; whereas, *in itself*, the universe is also *outside* each occasion (PR 347–48). The universe, then, is both inside and outside every occasion. In this manner, the notion of repetition, as incorporated in the doctrine of objectification, begins to throw some light on the "paradox of the connectedness of things:—the many things, the one world without and within" (AI 293). The world without and the world within, it now begins to appear, are numerically different; yet they are the same world, in a sense of 'same' to be gradually explained.

It must be emphasized at this time that the notion of objectification is broader than the notion of repetition. If it were not, the doctrine of mutually immanent occasions would have to be abandoned for two reasons. First, according to Whitehead the notion of repetition is tied up with the notion of *efficient causation*—that is, if one occasion is repeated within another, then the former is a cause of the latter; therefore, since for him mutually contemporary occasions are causally independent of one another, it follows that they cannot directly repeat one another; nevertheless, in the organic philosophy, contemporary occasions do objectify one another, and the one sense in which these objectifications are direct implies the mutual immanence, in some sense or other, of the occasions involved. Second, for Whitehead, anticipation implies the objectification of the future; but such an objectification cannot involve the repetition of occasions (though it may involve the anticipation of repetition) because there are no actual occasions in the future, and thus there is nothing to be repeated. Repetition, then, must be construed as an aspect of the peculiar mode of objectification—the *causal* mode—by which an occasion becomes immanent in occasions later than itself. But there are two other modes of objectification—having to do, respectively, with contemporary occasions and with the potentiality for future occasions—which do not involve repetition.

The existence of these two other modes of objectification forces me to look beyond the notion of repetition in my attempt to explain the thesis of solidarity. The repetition, or *causal objectification*, of an earlier occasion in a later one may account for the immanence of the past in the future, but it cannot account for the immanence of the future in the past nor for the mutual immanence of occasions contemporary with one another. To account for these other modes of immanence, indeed to fully account for the causal mode also, we must turn to the organic doctrine of the *extensive continuum*. In that doctrine, as we shall see, lies the solution to the paradox of solidarity.

These last remarks are not intended to serve as an explanation of the doctrines of objectification and mutual immanence; they only intimate such an explanation. They are intended, however, to forestall objections of the sort raised by Hartshorne to an earlier version of this essay.[11] As

Hartshorne saw it, the doctrine of mutual immanence is to be repudiated on the grounds that inheritance must be an asymmetrical relation. But to raise this objection is to assume that immanence and inheritance are one and the same thing. This is not true for Whitehead. Indeed, for him inheritance entails immanence, but immanence does not entail inheritance.

It is along these lines, in fact, that Whitehead distinguishes the notion of a *nexus* of actual entities from that of a *society* of actual entities. 'Nexus' and 'society' signify two types of order among occasions. The first type implies only the mutual immanence, in some sense or another, of the occasions involved, so that *any* set of occasions constitutes a nexus. "Thus the term Nexus does not presuppose any special type of order, nor does it presuppose any order at all pervading its members other than the *general metaphysical obligation of mutual immanence* (AI 258–59; italics mine). For this reason, we must construe the actual universe, at any stage in its history, as a nexus of occasions. The second type of order, however, in addition to implying the mutual immanence of the occasions involved, also implies that, among the occasions involved, some are earlier than others, and that the later ones inherit from the earlier ones a *common* character, which is in effect the defining characteristic of *that* society (AI 260–61; PR 50–52). It follows that all societies are nexūs, but not all nexūs are societies. It should be noted that a group of mutually contemporary occasions constitute a nexus that cannot be a society, though it may be part of a society (AI 261).

In respect to Hartshorne's objection, then, we must emphasize that Whitehead is well aware of the asymmetry of inheritance, *i.e.*, that whereas a later occasion can inherit from an earlier one, the earlier one cannot inherit from the later. But Whitehead is also aware of the asymmetry of anticipation—the earlier can anticipate the later, but not the other way around. For him, nevertheless, these two asymmetrical relations— inheritance and anticipation—equally presuppose the mutual immanence, in some sense as yet to be explained, of the relata they involve.

Furthermore, according to Whitehead, contemporary occasions are mutually immanent, though they neither inherit from nor anticipate one another. In fact, for him, the relation of mutual immanence is symmetrical in *all* respects only when the actual occasions serving as relata are contemporary with one another (AI 278). When the occasions are not contemporaries, *i.e.*, where one is in the past of the other, the relation of mutual immanence still obtains, *but it is not a symmetrical relation in all respects*; for the earlier is immanent in the later in the mode of causal efficacy, whereas the later is immanent in the earlier in the mode of anticipation. But though two different modes of immanence are involved, it remains true that the occasions in question are mutually immanent. On this, Whitehead is quite explicit:

> Any set of actual occasions are united by the mutual immanence of occasions, each in the other. To the extent that they are united they mutually constrain each other. Evidently, this mutual immanence and constraint of a pair of occasions is not in general a symmetric relation. For, apart from contemporaries, one occasion will be in the future of the other. Thus, the earlier will be immanent in the later according to the mode of efficient causality, and the later in the earlier according to the mode of anticipation. (AI 254)

The relation of mutual immanence, then, need not be symmetrical in all respects, but it must be symmetrical in at least one respect, or Whitehead is indeed talking nonsense. What has yet to be explained, of course, is this one respect in which immanence is mutual for all occasions.

The one respect in which immanence is symmetrical is to be understood in terms of the *extensive* character of actual occasions. Actual occasions are extensive because each occupies or embodies a unique region of what Whitehead variously terms 'extension', 'the receptacle', 'the extensive scheme', or 'the extensive continuum'. Here, it should be noted, 'extension' does not mean the same as 'physical space'; nor for that matter does the organic notion of 'creative advance' mean the same as 'physical time'. In the organic philosophy, physical time and physical space are modifications of extension brought about by the becoming of actual occasions; the modifications are significant of the relationships that actual occasions bear to one another.

The notion of extension will be amply treated later. At present I need emphasize only that it is in regard to, and by virtue of, their extensiveness that actual occasions are in one sense mutually transcendent and in another sense mutually immanent. The aim of this essay, of course, is to show that this is so.

My immediate claim, then, is that there can be little understanding of the doctrine of objectification and even less understanding of the thesis of solidarity without recourse to an adequate interpretation of the role that extension plays in the organic philosophy. In support of the first part of this claim we find Whitehead saying that "if we take the doctrine of objectification seriously, the extensive continuum at once becomes the primary factor in objectification" (PR 118). The second part is supported by the following passage from PR:

It is evident that if the solidarity of the physical world is to be relevant to the description of its individual actualities, it can only be by reason of the fundamental internality of the relationships in question. On the other hand, if the individual discreteness of the actualities is to have its weight, there must be an aspect in these relationships from which they can be conceived as external, that is, as bonds between divided things. The extensive scheme serves this double purpose. (PR 470–71)

Further considerations in support of the basic role that extension plays in the organic philosophy will be advanced later in this chapter. But the passages just quoted make it sufficiently evident that the doctrine of extension addresses itself to the problem raised by the thesis of world solidarity, since extension has the double purpose of explaining how actual entities can be at once mutually immanent and mutually transcendent.

The study of extension and the elucidation, in terms of it, of both objectification and solidarity will be made in the final four chapters of this essay. There we shall see that the extensive scheme is crucial in explaining how a superject and each of its causal objectifications can be *numerically different instances of the same particular*. But the extensive scheme, we shall also see, plays an essential role in all modes of objectification, not just the causal one.

The fact that causal objectification cannot by itself account for the mutual immanence of occasions has led me to adumbrate the all-important doctrine of the extensive continuum. But I must now return to the consideration of the organic doctrines suggested by the notions of repetition and immediacy. In particular, in order to explain the contrast between transition and concrescence, I must insist that the objectification of past actualities is *not* produced by the immediate subjective activity of the actuality in which they are objectified.

7. Repetition and immediacy: some relevant categoreal terms

I maintain, with regard to the precedence of immediacy by objectification, that the first stage of the creative process begetting a new occasion also repeats within that occasion all the superjects already in existence relative to the origination of that process. As repeated, the already existing superjects not only become constituents of the novel occasion within which they are repeated but they are also given for the next stage of becoming of the novel occasion, the stage of immediacy. This means that the given for the stage of immediacy—what Whitehead often refers to simply as 'the datum'—is the product of an earlier stage of the occasion's becoming. Accordingly, what is given for the stage of immediacy must be distinguished from what is given for the stage of repetition. The given for the stage of repetition is the settled universe of already existing superjects; the given for the stage of immediacy is the objectifications, or reproductions, of those superjects. Thus, the former datum is composed of the accumulated attained actualities as their *original* selves; whereas the latter datum is composed of the attained actualities as their *reproduced* selves.

As their own original selves, the attained actualities are what Whitehead sometimes terms 'the absolutely initial data' relative to the becoming of a new actual occasion (PR 44). As their own reproduced selves, the attained actualities compose what Whitehead sometimes terms 'the objective content' of an actual occasion (PR 230). In keeping with this terminological distinction, the terms 'initial datum' and 'objective datum' are used frequently by Whitehead to refer respectively to a single attained actuality and to its reproduced self in another occasion (PR 361–65). The initial datum is thus the satisfied occasion *in* itself and, in a sense to be gradually explained, *beyond* all other occasions. The objective datum is the satisfied occasion existing *for* another, later, occasion and, in a sense also to be gradually explained, *within* the other for which it exists. The activity of causal objectification is thus the creative process by which an attained actuality becomes a constituent of a new actuality, and is, in that guise, an objective datum for the prehensive activity of the new actuality. More generally, causal objectification is the creative process whereby the attained universe, or *actual world*, into which an occasion is born becomes an immanent constituent of that occasion, and is, in that guise, a complex datum for the immediate experience enjoyed by the occasion in question.

Causal objectification is repetition, and repetition, we have seen, is second-handedness. Immediacy, however, is first-handedness. Accordingly, the mere givenness of objectified occasions for the second stage of an occasion's becoming does not constitute immediacy. We must look to the creative process of the second stage for the generation of true novelty. As Whitehead says:

> It is by reference to feelings that the notion of 'immediacy' obtains its meaning. The mere objectification of actual entities by eternal objects lacks 'immediacy'. It is 'repetition', and this is contrary to 'immediacy'. But 'process' is the rush of feelings whereby second-handedness attains subjective immediacy; in this way, subjective form overwhelms repetition, and transforms it into immediately felt satisfaction; objectivity is absorbed into subjectivity. (PR 234–35)

The passage just cited is important for two reasons: first, it clearly asserts that the *activity* of repetition is over when the subjective activity begins, even though the *product* of repetition is absorbed into the subjective immediacy; second, it makes use of important organic notions—'eternal objects', 'feelings', 'process', and 'immediately felt satisfaction'—the elucidation of which is indispensable for the understanding of the stage of novel immediacy. Let us now briefly examine each of these notions.

Eternal objects are the real universals of the organic philosophy. A particular shade of red, a given sound, a certain pain, a determinate geometric figure, are all examples of eternal objects. The correct understanding of the nature and function of eternal objects is essential to the understanding of solidarity; hence, I shall have to devote considerable attention to them at a later time. For the moment, however, the following remarks must suffice.

An eternal object instantiated in a particular actual entity is said to be *ingressed* in the actuality in question. Through their ingressions, eternal objects are involved not only in the determination of objectifications, but also in the determination of subjective forms. An eternal object ingressed as a determinant of either the objective datum, or the subjective form, of a physical prehension is said to be *unrestrictedly* ingressed into the occasion to which the physical prehension belongs (PR 445). Unrestricted ingressions are also termed *physical* ingressions. Eternal objects unrestrictedly ingressed into an occasion so as to specify *how* earlier occasions are objectified for it are said to be functioning *datively* (PR 249). However, as I shall amply explain later, the dative functioning of eternal objects is a necessary, but definitely *not* a sufficient, condition for the objectification of earlier occasions in later ones. For, by themselves, the datively ingressed eternal objects would constitute reproductions of characters exhibited by the earlier occasions, but would not constitute reproductions of the earlier occasions themselves. I thus again adumbrate the indispensable role which the extensiveness of the universe plays in the objectification of its creatures.

Eternal objects unrestrictedly ingressed so as to determine the subjective forms of an actual occasion are said to be functioning *subjectively* (PR 249, 446). As subjectively ingressed, eternal objects express both how the subject feels its data—*i.e.*, the manner in which it reacts to them or entertains their significance—and how it integrates its simpler feelings into more complex ones. This subjective activity at once absorbs the objective data into the subjective immediacy and defines the emerging individuality of the subject. Thus, the *definiteness* of an actual entity is its subjective instantiation of a selection of eternal objects (PR 38). Indeed, it is precisely because they constitute the definiteness of the actuality *qua* subject, that the subjectively ingressed eternal objects, *qua* those particular ingressions, are properly construed as the subjective forms of the actuality in question. According to the thirteenth Category of Explanation, "there are many species of subjective forms, such as emotions, valuations, purposes, adversions, aversions, consciousness, etc." (PR 35).

This brief treatment of eternal objects enables us to expand our understanding of Whitehead's theory of *feelings* or, more generally, of *prehensions*. Of immediate interest is the distinction between a *physical* prehension, which is one whose datum involves objectified actual entities, and a *conceptual* or mental prehension, which is one whose datum involves eternal objects other than those conveying the determinateness of objectified actualities (PR 35). If the datum of a prehension, or feeling, involves only objectified actualities, it is said to be a *pure physical feeling* (PR 375). If the datum involves only eternal objects, the feeling is said to be a *pure conceptual* one (PR 48–49). If a feeling integrates feelings of the two pure types, it is said to be an *impure* feeling. Since 'impurity' here applies to the integration of physical with conceptual feelings, it follows that an impure physical feeling is the same thing as an impure conceptual feeling. Impure feelings are at times labeled 'physical' and at other times 'mental'; but this, Whitehead tells us, is only to direct "attention in the discussion concerned" (PR 49).

An eternal object serving as the objective datum of a pure conceptual feeling is said to have a *restricted* ingression in the occasion to which the feeling belongs (PR 445). Restricted ingressions are also termed *mental*. Restrictedly ingressed eternal objects play a variety of extremely important roles in an occasion's experience; but their primary role is to express ways in which the subjectivity of the occasion may become definite. However, a restrictedly ingressed eternal object does *not* confer definiteness on the occasion prehending it unless it is unrestrictedly ingressed by the occasion in a later stage of its becoming. It should be noted, in this respect, that an occasion's subjective aim is a conceptual feeling having for its datum a complex group of eternal objects whose particular germaneness to the occasion's objective content makes them specially suitable for unrestricted ingression as determinants of the occasion's subjectivity. Thus, the self-realization of the occasion involves the unrestricted ingression of some, but not all, of the eternal objects constituting the complex datum of its subjective aim (PR 131).

The clarification must now be made that *not* all prehensions are feelings; rather, feelings are but one species of the genus of creative operations termed 'prehensions'. A *prehension*, in general, is the manner in which the subject appropriates, or makes use of, a particular datum, thus establishing a fully determinate bond with that datum (PR 335). There are, however, two species of prehension, *positive* and *negative*, reflecting the two basic ways in which the subject may utilize any one of its data. Feelings are positive prehensions and as such must be distinguished from negative prehensions.

To distinguish between these two species of prehensions, we must first notice that Whitehead construes the stage of immediacy of an occasion's becoming as involving a *real* succession of creative phases of experience, these phases progressively leading to the realization of the occasion's subjective aim (PR 337). Thus, the subjective immediacy "is a process proceeding from phase to phase towards the completion of the thing in question" (PR 327). In this process, the product of an earlier phase serves as a datum for, as well as a basis of, a later phase. Accordingly, the prehensions realized in an earlier phase are themselves data for, and are integrated by, the prehensions realized in a later phase (PR 337). The process terminates in one final prehension, the satisfaction, which integrates all antecedent prehensions (PR 337). Because of this integration, or growing together, of many prehensions into one final prehension, the stage of immediacy is said to be a process of concrescence, or simply a *concrescence*.

The difference between a positive and a negative prehension now may be understood in terms of the respective roles they play in an occasion's process of concrescence. Thus, in the twelfth Category of Explanation, we read:

> (xii) That there are two species of prehensions: (a) 'positive prehensions' which are termed 'feelings', and (b) 'negative prehensions' which are said to 'eliminate from feeling'. Negative prehensions also have subjective forms. A negative prehension holds its datum as inoperative in the progressive concrescence of prehensions constituting the unity of the subject. (PR 35)

And, in the twenty-seventh Category of Explanation, we are told that:

> (xxvii) In a process of concrescence, there is a succession of phases in which new prehensions arise by integration of prehensions in antecedent phases. In these integrations 'feelings' contribute their 'subjective forms' and their data to the formation of novel integral prehensions; but 'negative prehensions' contribute only their 'subjective

> forms'. The process continues till all prehensions are components in
> the one determinate integral satisfaction. (PR 39)[12]

The final integral prehension, it should be noted, is always positive. The
satisfaction *is* a feeling (PR 38).

Another important clarification must be made at this time. The term
'feeling' is used ambiguously by Whitehead, but deliberately so:

> The conventionalized abstractions prevalent in epistemological theory
> are very far from the concrete facts of experience. The word 'feeling'
> has the merit of preserving this double significance of subjective form
> and of the apprehension of an object. It avoids the *disjecta membra*
> provided by the abstraction. (AI 299)

Thus, the term 'feeling' means, on the one hand, the same as 'subjective
form', and, on the other, the complete creative operation whereby a
subject takes account of, reacts to, and appropriates an objective datum
(PR 215). The feeling is also the finished product of the operation.

Since a feeling, in the sense of *subjective form*, is a component of a
feeling, in the sense of *positive prehension*, the ambiguity of this term does
cause some problems for the interpretation of many of Whitehead's pronouncements on the nature of feelings, their generation, and their
synthesis.[13] Consider, for example, Whitehead's attempt to provide a
definition of 'positive prehension': "The 'positive prehension' of an entity
by an actual entity is the complete transaction analysable into the ingression, or objectification, of that entity as a datum for feeling, and into the
feeling whereby this datum is absorbed into the subjective satisfaction"
(PR 82). Given that 'feeling' can mean 'positive prehension', is Whitehead
here defining 'positive prehension' in terms of itself? Is the ingressed, or
objectified, entity a datum for subjective form? or a datum for positive
prehension? Clearly, Whitehead's meaning is not clear. However, if forewarned is indeed forearmed, we should be able as our essay progresses to
determine Whitehead's intended meaning in this and in similar passages.

The definition just cited, like the definition of 'positive prehension'
cited earlier, employs the phrase 'subjective satisfaction' to mean the same
as 'subjectively felt satisfaction'. Since Whitehead explicitly asserts that a
subject *cannot* feel its own satisfaction (PR 129–30), we have here a second
instance (we shall uncover many others) of the carelessness with which
Whitehead develops and employs the technical terminology of his philosophy. To make sense of his inconsistent uses of the term 'satisfaction' we
have carefully to distinguish between the satisfaction which a subject can

and must feel, the *subjective* satisfaction, and the satisfaction which a subject *cannot* feel—what I have previously referred to as the *superjective* satisfaction. The subjective satisfaction is the final *creative* phase of an actual occasion. It is the occasion in its final and ephemeral moment of experiential and creative immediacy. In that moment, the second-hand data are completely absorbed into the occasion's first-hand immediacy. Thus, in keeping with the presystematic analysis of memory in which this notion has its roots, the immediately felt satisfaction—the *subjective* satisfaction—is "the immediate, first-handed fact, which is the actual world in an immediate complex unity of feeling" (PR 206). The *superjective* satisfaction, on the other hand, is the occasion in its final, everlasting, *created* phase of existence. The superjective satisfaction is the satisfaction proper; for it is the occasion as completely determinate or fully made. The satisfaction proper, then, is the occasion as a fully determinate being, utterly devoid of experiential and creative immediacy (PR 44, 71, 129, 336). It is the occasion as stubborn fact, with unavoidable consequences.

8. Repetition and immediacy: transition and concrescence

What has been said so far about the organic doctrines of eternal object, feeling and satisfaction, and, more generally, about the creative process associated with subjective immediacy, is sufficient to enable us to provide a preliminary account of the systematic counterpart of the presystematic contrast between repetition and immediacy. In this respect, when Whitehead says in the passage quoted earlier that " 'process' is the rush of feelings whereby second-handedness attains subjective immediacy" (PR 235), his unqualified use of the term 'process' is misleading. I say this because the process by which subjective forms overwhelm the objective data is neither the *same* process, nor the same *kind* of process, as the one whereby the objective data come to be. There are two processes involved and, as Whitehead makes abundantly clear elsewhere (PR 227–29, 232, 317–28), they represent two radically different *species* of creative process. In other words, the creative process whereby subjective forms are realized and integrated differs *numerically* and *specifically* from, and is—in a non-temporal sense of 'subsequent' soon to be explained—*subsequent* to, the creative process whereby the objectification of settled actualities is achieved.

In the creation of an actual occasion, the earlier type of process effects the transition from the universe of attained actualities to the novel actuality in attainment (PR 326–27, 320). Hence, this species of process is termed the *process of transition*. Transition at once creates the new occasion and objectifies in it the superjects already in existence. This is why each actual occasion forever bears the stamp of the state of the universe from which it arose. In this respect, the state of the universe relative to a new occasion is, in part at least, a settlement of attained actualities. Each new occasion arises from a unique settlement; or, conversely, each particular settlement gives birth to a particular occasion. This latter way of putting it makes evident that, for the organic philosophy, there is in the universe a creative factor that accounts for the addition to what is settled of what is not yet settled. The ultimate principle of the organic philosophy—*the category of creativity*—is thus introduced. By virtue of the reality of creativity, the universe as a whole is actively involved in the creation of each new occasion. "Each creative act is the universe incarnating itself as one, and there is nothing above it by way of final condition" (PR 375). Thus, the process of transition is also known as the *macroscopic process* since it involves the entire universe construed as a macroscopic organism (PR 326–27, 254, 196).

The outcome of transition is a novel but incomplete occasion that contains within itself the objectification of its correlative universe. The second species of process takes rise from this partially completed occasion; indeed, this process is nothing more than the already existing occasion as engaged in the activity of *completing* itself (PR 373, 423, 524). *The creature is created as the final creator of itself.* From the basis of its given character, the creature goes on to fashion its own ultimate character. Accordingly, the second species of process must be construed as the occasion itself originating the subjective forms, or rush of feelings, whereby the objectified universe is absorbed into subjective immediacy. This process terminates with the achievement of a total synthesis of objective content and subjective reaction. It is a growing together of diverse elements and, as we have already seen, is for that reason called *concrescence* (PR 320). But Whitehead also calls this process the *microscopic process*, apparently because it only involves the occasion itself as an individual microcosm (PR 326–27, 254; RM 100). Concrescence, then, is the self-fashioning of an organism—an organism that may be said to be *microscopic* in relation to the sense in which the universe may be said to be *macroscopic* (PR 254, 196).

Since concrescence is the process by which an occasion attains its subjective immediacy, or, more properly, since a process of concrescence is nothing but an occasion as self-realizing, and since Whitehead tells us that an occasion "is called the 'subject' of its own immediacy" (PR 38), it follows that the terms 'concrescence', 'microscopic process', 'immediacy', 'subject', and 'subjective immediacy' are synonymous with one another or nearly so. But if the interpretation of transition and concrescence just adumbrated is correct, it also follows that these terms cannot be construed as referring to the *whole* of an occasion's becoming; for the becoming of each actual occasion involves a process of transition as well as a process of concrescence. Moreover, from the correctness of that interpretation, it would also follow that the subjective existence of an occasion coincides exclusively with the microscopic process, though it presupposes and includes the outcome of the macroscopic process.

It is important to stress the importance of correctly understanding the contrast between the processes of transition and concrescence. For that contrast subsumes under itself, or is part and parcel of, a number of parallel contrasts that are each essential for understanding the generic essence and the solidarity of all actual entities. First, there is the contrast between *efficient* causation and *final* causation: transition *is* the process of efficient causation whereby a new occasion is begotten and partly determined by its correlative universe of attained actualities, whereas concrescence *is* the process of teleological self-determination whereby the already begotten occasion autonomously completes itself. Second, there is the contrast between the *repetitive* phases and the *originative* phases of an occasion's becoming. Third, there is the contrast between the *objective* functioning and the *formal* functioning of actual entities. Finally, there is the contrast between the determinate *position* and the determinate *definiteness* of an actuality: the former is the *relational* aspect, whereas the latter is the *qualitative* aspect, of the actuality's individual essence.

I shall closely examine each of these contrasts as this essay unfolds, but it will prove helpful to preview immediately the contrast between phases repetitive and phases originative. The repetitive phases are the first three phases in the becoming of an occasion. They are analytical of the process of transition to that occasion, and, in the order in which they emerge, are (i) a *dative* phase composed primarily, but not exclusively, of the causal objectifications of all past occasions; (ii) a phase of *conformal physical feelings*, that is, of feelings whose subjective forms re-enact, or repeat, the qualities exemplified in the subjective forms of the objectified occasions; and (iii) a phase of *conformal conceptual feelings* whereby the eternal objects exemplified in the conformal physical feelings are conceptually reproduced and evaluated. According to this analyis, the process of transition begets not only the occasion's complex objective content but also its initial conformal subjectivity.

The subject begotten by transition is the autonomous master of its remaining phases of becoming. The autonomous phases are the truly originative phases and are analytical of the process of concrescence. In the order of their emergence, they are (i) a phase of conceptual novelty; (ii) a finite number of successive phases of integrative feelings; and (iii) the subjective satisfaction, which is the ultimate autonomous origination and unification of subjective forms made by the subject in response to the operative datum provided by the penultimate phase of concrescence. "This final reaction completes the self-creative act by putting the decisive stamp of creative emphasis upon the determinations of efficient cause" (PR 75). The originative phases of concrescence are thus intermediate between the threefold product of transition and the superjective satisfaction.

I am aware that much of what I have said here is at odds with, or simply foreign to, the received interpretations of transition and concrescence. In fact, most interpreters of Whitehead collapse the process of transition into the process of concrescence and thereby destroy, albeit unknowingly, Whitehead's profoundly important theory of *genuine* efficient causation: causation which *really produces* its effect; causation which *really determines* its effect in part, though not in whole; and causation which—*in addition, and not merely*—*conditions* the subsequent self-determining phases of the effect it has produced. In place of Whitehead's theory of efficient causation, but still under the same, if now undeserved, title, most received interpretations give us what in the end is no more than a theory of *material causation*, a theory where the already-attained actualities are the material, but in no sense the efficient, causes of the actualities in attainment.

That Whitehead's theory of efficient causation, and the doctrine of transition under which it is subsumed, should come to be so radically misunderstood is all the more surprising because the contrast between transition and concrescence, and thus also that between efficient causation and final causation, is developed by Whitehead with unusual clarity and explicitness (PR 317–28, 228–29). The received misunderstanding of transition, or of efficient causation, becomes much less surprising, however, when we realize that it is aided and abetted by the received misconceptions of the most basic of Whitehead's metaphysical doctrines—the principles of creativity, ontology, relativity, and process. The latter misconceptions, I maintain, result largely from the general neglect by most of Whitehead's interpreters of the bearing which the thesis of solidarity and the organic categoreal scheme have on each other.

9. The principles of creativity, relativity, ontology, and process

Among the explicitly formulated principles of the organic philosophy, four stand out as claiming to be more fundamental than the rest; they are, as I have just intimated, the principle of *creativity*, the principle of *relativity*, the principle of *ontology*, and the principle of *process*. In their most succinct formulations they assert, respectively: that "the many become one, and are increased by one" (PR 32); that "it belongs to the nature of every 'being' that it is a potential for every 'becoming'" (PR 71); that "actual entities are the only *reasons*" (PR 37); and that "*how* an actual entity *becomes* constitutes *what* that actual entity *is*" (PR 34). Unless the full import of each of these four principles is correctly and completely understood, it is impossible to do justice to transition and efficient causation. Moreover, these four principles, not by accident, are of paramount importance for the proper understanding of the thesis of solidarity. In fact, the principles of relativity and ontology are explicitly linked by Whitehead to the elucidation of solidarity (PR 65, 336), and the principle of creativity merely provides, I shall soon argue, an alternative formulation of the thesis, one emphasizing that the solidarity of the universe is a dynamic affair, ever renewing itself in the creative advance from attained actuality to actuality in attainment. As for the principle of process, I will show in the last three chapters that it signals a broader sense of solidarity than we have yet discussed—one requiring that the determinateness of an actual entity result from contributions made by *all* actualities, *itself included*.

My point, then, is that the doctrine of transition and the thesis of solidarity alike require for their elucidation that the principles of creativity, relativity, ontology, and process be properly construed. Unfortunately, the received interpretations of Whitehead's philosophy misconstrue in part or in whole one or more of these principles, often all four. Accordingly, achieving a correct understanding of each of these principles is this essay's first major task. In particular, since my views on the first three principles differ significantly from all the received views, it will be necessary to argue carefully and extensively for them. This I shall do in the next two chapters. My interpretation of the process principle, on the other hand, is shared by a growing number of Whiteheadian scholars, and thus requires less rigorous and extensive consideration. For that reason, and also because its correct understanding facilitates the elucidation of the other three principles, I will consider it immediately in the next section.

Before considering the principle of process, however, it may be instructive to preview briefly my understanding of the other three principles. I take the principle of creativity to assert that every actual entity synthesizes within itself not the already completed actualities *per se*, but only their reproduced selves. Appropriately, I understand the principle of relativity to maintain, in effect, that every completely determinate entity, including every superject, is repeatable. Finally, I construe the ontological principle as asserting that each actual entity is partly the outcome of a process of efficient causation and partly the outcome of a process of final causation.

10. Becoming and being: 'actuality' and the principle of process

The full import of the principles of creativity, relativity, and ontology will never be adequately understood unless it is first established that completed occasions exist as such in addition to, and presupposed by, their causal objectifications in occasions later than themselves. In this respect, if we ignore differences of detail, the most prevalent view among Whiteheadian scholars seems to be that each actual occasion ceases to exist when its becoming comes to an end, except to the extent that some element of its terminal character is reproduced within later occasions.[14] On that view, then, as opposed to mine, all that remains of the completed occasion is the reproduced character; the occasion as such has ceased to exist.[15]

The view under attack rests, in part if not wholly so, on a misunderstanding of what Whitehead means by 'actual'. I am alluding to the widespread belief that 'actuality' can be properly predicated only of processes of concrescence.[16] To be actual, most Whiteheadian scholars would hold, is to be a subject. But this, I maintain, is not quite accurate. It would be better to say: to be actual is either to be, or to have been, a subject. For a completed occasion is no longer a subject, it is a superject; nonetheless, it is an *actual* occasion.

In this respect, the distinction Whitehead makes between an actuality in attainment and an attained actuality clearly indicates that for him 'actuality' has a twofold meaning (PR 326–27). Whitehead gives systematic expression to this double meaning of 'actuality', or of 'actual', when he says:

> An actuality is self-realizing, and whatever is self-realizing is an actuality. An actual entity is at once the subject of self-realization, and the superject which is self-realized. (PR 340)

One thing Whitehead is telling us here is that an incomplete occasion, or subject, is actual in the sense that it is still involved in the process of self-realization. But Whitehead is also telling us here that a completed occasion, or superject, is actual in the sense that it is a self-realized entity, even though it is no longer a self-realizing entity. Hence, in the general sense in which the notion of actuality is tied to the notion of self-realization, the superjective existence of an occasion is as actual as its subjective existence.

In Whitehead's writings, it is generally recognized, there are numerous references to the continuing existence of completed occasions, of occasions that are past relative to some new occasion still in the process of becoming. Thus Whitehead speaks again and again of 'entities already actual', of 'entities already become', of 'already constituted actual entities', of 'settled actualities', and, more generally, of 'the world already actual'.[17] But if this is so, and if, as we have just seen, there is abundant evidence that Whitehead intended to predicate actuality of superjects as well as of subjects, then why balk at the notion that completed occasions continue to exist, continue to be actual, even though they are no longer engaged in their own process of self-realization? In other words, why do so many interpreters of Whitehead hold that a completed occasion cannot actually exist because it is no longer a process? Why do they want to say that all that remains of a completed occasion is some element of its character as reproduced in occasions that are now still becoming, in occasions that are *truly* actual?

Perhaps the single most important reason for holding this view is to be traced to a rather widespread misunderstanding of the ninth Category of Explanation, the principle of process. According to Whitehead, this "principle states that the *being* of a *res vera* is constituted by its 'becoming'" (PR 252). Now, as it is most frequently interpreted, the principle of process is held to equate actual existence with becoming.[18] In other words, Whitehead is supposed to be contending that the being of an actual entity *is* its becoming.[19] But notice that to arrive at this understanding of the principle we must assume that the verb 'to constitute' is functioning as a copula—that it merely links the grammatical subject to a predicate nominative, thus establishing the identity of 'being' and 'becoming'. Only if we so construe the verb in question can we read the principle of process to mean that the existence of an actuality is its process of becoming.

However, to interpret the principle of process in this manner, one must remain blind to the context in which it appears, and blind also to the many meanings of the verb 'to constitute'. Also, one must overlook the specific directions which Whitehead gives for the interpretation of the principle under discussion.

In regard to general context, a careful reading of PR, particularly of its first two Parts, reveals that Whitehead never uses 'becoming' and 'being' as synonyms. Rather, these terms express the essential nature of subjects and superjects, respectively. Indeed in the Abstract of Part II, Chapter I, Section III, we find the notions of subject and superject explicitly correlated with the notions of becoming and being (PR 57). Moreover, if the becoming and the being of an actual entity were one and the same thing, Whitehead would be repeating himself needlessly when he says that the "positive doctrine of . . . [his] lectures is concerned with the becoming, the being, and the relatedness of 'actual entities' " (PR viii).

In respect to the relevant meaning of 'to constitute', we must admit that Whitehead frequently uses that verb as a copula; but we must also point out that, just as frequently, he uses it in the sense of 'to produce' or 'to create'. Consider, in this connection, the following passages from his writings:

> [An actual entity appropriates] for the foundation of its own existence, the various elements of the universe out of which it arises. . . . The ultimate elements of the universe, thus appropriated, are the *already-constituted* actual entities, and the eternal objects. (PR 335; italics mine)

> The various particular occasions of the past *are in existence*, and are severally functioning as objects for prehension. . . . But there are no actual occasions in the future, *already constituted*. (AI 250–51; italics mine)

> The regulative principle is derived from the novel unity which is imposed on [the subjective forms] by the novel creature in process of *constitution*. (PR 328; italics mine)

> It is only by reason of the categories of subjective unity, and of subjective harmony, that the process *constitutes* the character of the product, and that conversely the analysis of the product discloses the process. (PR 390; italics mine)

In each of these passages, Whitehead is obviously using 'to constitute' in the sense of 'to create'. For example, in the first two passages, he is telling us that past occasions exist as already-created but that there are no occasions in the future, already-created. Even more important, in the last passage quoted, Whitehead is clearly saying that the process creates the character of the product and that the analysis of the product somehow reveals the process by which it was created.

If in the principle of process Whitehead is using 'to constitute' to mean the same as 'to create', he is saying that the subject creates or produces the superject. Thus, Whitehead is asserting what we should indeed expect him to be asserting, namely, that the subject is the genetic process whereby the superjective product, or satisfaction, comes to be. That this is what is being asserted in the principle of process, or ninth Category of Explanation, Whitehead himself makes explicit when, in the context of explaining how the genetic process can be reconstructed from an analysis of the satisfaction, he says: "This relation between the satisfaction and the genetic process is expressed in the eighth and ninth categories of explanation . . ." (PR 360).

In light of this last statement, it is evident that the principle of process should always be interpreted in relation to the eighth Category of Explanation. These two categories are formulated as follows:

> (viii) That two descriptions are required for an actual entity: (a) one which is analytical of its potentiality for 'objectification' in the becoming of other actual entities, and (b) another which is analytical of the process which constitutes its own becoming. . . .
> (ix) That *how* an actual entity *becomes* constitutes *what* that actual entity *is;* so that the two descriptions of an actual entity are not independent. Its 'being' is constituted by its 'becoming'. This is the 'principle of process'. (PR 34–35)

It can now be argued that these two categories simply give systematic expression to Whitehead's conception of the actual entity as subject-superject. In this connection, we should keep in mind two statements by Whitehead, already quoted: the one, to the effect that whatever is actual is either self-realizing or self-realized; the other, to the effect that an actual entity is both the subject experiencing and the superject of its experiences, and that neither half of that description should be lost sight of. We should also bear in mind that, as we saw earlier, the two partial descriptions of an actual entity are not independent of one another because the subject, or process, is guided by the ideal of what the superject, or product, of that process is to be.

If these points are kept in mind, it need hardly be argued that the two descriptions referred to in the eighth Category of Explanation are those of the satisfaction and subject, respectively. The subject is the genetic process; and the satisfaction, as Whitehead tells us elsewhere, is the completed actual entity "considered as a creative determination, by which the objectifications of the entity beyond itself are settled" (PR 130). These two descriptions, then, are the two halves of an actual entity's total description.

As for the ninth Category of Explanation, it simply asserts that the two partial descriptions of an actual entity are interdependent because the actuality *qua* being, the superject or satisfaction, is created by the actuality *qua* becoming, the subject or genetic process. Indeed, to read straightforwardly the principle of process in this manner we have only to substitute 'creates' for 'constitutes' in its categoreal formulation. The relevant text would then read as follows:

> That *how* an actual entity *becomes* creates *what* that actual entity *is;* so that the two descriptions of an actual entity are not independent. Its 'being' is created by its 'becoming'.

In other words, each attained actuality is what it is because its process of becoming was what it was. Had the process been different, the product would have been different.[20] To truly understand the nature of a particular superject, therefore, it is necessary to reconstruct the particular process which was its becoming. This is one reason (we have seen another) why the two descriptions of an actual entity are not independent.

Apart from its establishment of the interdependence of the two partial descriptions of an actual entity, however, the true significance of the principle is this; that the final definiteness of an actual entity is determined or created by *how* the subject conducts its process.[21] This is why, elsewhere, Whitehead speaks of the subject as "determining what it is integrally to be, in its own character of the superject of its own process" (PR 369). This is also why Whitehead says, in another place, that the "actual entity, in becoming itself, also solves the question as to *what* it is to be" (PR 227). Finally, the principle of process is again the reason why Whitehead in still another place says, "The point to be noticed is that the actual entity, in a state of process during which it is not fully definite, determines its own ultimate definiteness" (PR 390).

The evidence, then, is clear: the principle of process, far from supporting the view that an occasion can be actual only as process, establishes instead that what an occasion is as actual product is dependent on what it was as actual process. But the occasion, let us always remember, "is both process and outcome" (PR 129). An actual entity is a subject-superject.[22]

Some clarification of what Whitehead means by 'being' is now in order. To say that an occasion as subject is a becoming and not a being, is not to deny in any way the existence of the subject. Rather *becoming* and *being* are to be understood as two modes of existence. An actual occasion ceases to exist in the former mode only to continue existing in the latter mode. Its being presupposes its becoming. However, given the manner in which Whitehead uses the term 'being', it is not for him true that every being was once a becoming. It thus becomes necessary to distinguish actual beings from non-actual ones.

A superject is an actual being because it is a self-realized entity. But the organic philosophy's universe is also populated by other real entities that are not self-realized. Now, since they are not self-realized, these other entities are not actual in the peculiar Whiteheadian sense which we have been studying; but they are *real* beings, nonetheless. More specifically, they are non-actual entities or non-actual beings. These non-actual things either are in all respects eternal, and hence not self-realized, or are in all respects other-realized, that is, their realization is parasitic on the becoming of actual entities. Under the former heading are included the eternal objects. Under the latter heading are included subjective forms, contrasts, propositions, prehensions, and nexūs. Under both headings we are dealing with entities that are real, but not actual.

There are, of course, derivative senses of 'actual', such that we may speak of an actual world, or an actual nexus, or even an actual prehension. But with strict regard to the definition of the actual as whatever is either self-realizing or self-realized, the conclusion is that, in the organic philosophy, whatever is actual is also real, but not everything real is also actual. The real, then, includes not only actual becomings and actual beings, but also non-actual beings.

Of these three modalities of the real, however, actual becomings are in an important sense *the* fundamental realities. For 'being', whether actual or non-actual, is ultimately defined in terms of actual becomings, in terms, that is, of experiencing occasions. This definition of 'being'—and of its organic synonynms, 'entity' and 'thing'—is precisely what is undertaken in the fourth Category of Explanation, the principle of relativity:

> (iv) That the potentiality for being an element in a real concrescence of many entities into one actuality, is the one general metaphysical character attaching to all entities, actual and non-actual; and that every item in its universe is involved in each concrescence. In other words, it belongs to the nature of a 'being' that it is a potential for every 'becoming'. This is the 'principle of relativity'. (PR 33)

Whitehead's own comments on the significance of this category will help to further our understanding of it:

> . . . 'potentiality for process' is the meaning of the more general term 'entity' or 'thing' . . . . (PR 68)

> The fourth category . . . asserts that the notion of an entity means 'an element contributory to the process of becoming'. (PR 43)

> [The 'effects' of an actual entity] are all to be described in terms of its 'satisfaction'. The 'effects' of an actual entity are its interventions in concrescent processes other than its own. Any entity, thus intervening in processes transcending itself, is said to be functioning as an 'object'. According to the fourth Category of Explanation it is the one general metaphysical character of all entities of all sorts, that they function as objects. (PR 336)

These three comments have a twofold value relative to the present task: first they make abundantly clear the near synonymity of the terms 'being', 'entity' and 'thing', as used by Whitehead; and second, they introduce us to the systematic meaning which Whitehead attaches to the notion of 'functioning'.

According to Whitehead, "the determinateness and self-identity of one entity cannot be abstracted from the community of the diverse functioning of all entities" (PR 38). This is but another way of stating the thesis of solidarity. An entity *functions* in an actual occasion to the extent that it contributes to the determinateness of that occasion (PR 38). Every eternal object, and every occasion already actual, is a potential contributing to the determination of an occasion that is becoming. "They are, like all entities, potentials for the process of becoming" (PR 44). This is what Whitehead means when he says that every being is a potential for every becoming (PR 71). The functioning of one actual occasion in the becoming of another actual occasion is termed the 'objectification' of the former in the latter (PR 38). The functioning of an eternal object in the becoming of an actual occasion is termed the 'ingression' of the former in the latter (PR 38, 69). In this respect, the whole point of the thesis of solidarity is that the determinateness of an actual occasion cannot be divorced from the ingression within itself of a select group of eternal objects, and it cannot be divorced from the causal objectification within itself of all the completed actualities in its universe. By virtue of this fact, the determinateness of an actual occasion is analyzable into its *definiteness* and *position*, "where 'definiteness' is the illustration of select eternal objects and 'position' is relative status in a nexus of actual entities" (PR 38).

In respect to a completely determinate occasion, therefore, eternal objects function in it as determinants of its definiteness (PR 44). This is obvious. Less obvious is the fact that the actual entities causally objectified in a given occasion are determinants of the latter's position. That this is so I shall argue in Chapter Six, for the notion of position is of paramount importance to the thesis of solidarity. Unfortunately, it cannot be adequately elucidated until the category of extension has been considered at length.

For the moment, let us notice that eternal objects and other actual occasions can be determinants of a given actual occasion only if, in some sense or another, they are constituents of it. But to function in an actual entity is not only to be an element of its constitution; it is also to be an object for that actuality—an *object* for it, that is, so long as that actuality is a subject. For this reason, this kind of functioning is termed 'objective functioning' (PR 128, 340), and any entity which so functions "is said to be functioning as an 'object' " (PR 336, 371).

All entities of all sorts alike have objective functioning. This is what the principle of relativity so far comes to. But if an actual occasion has objective functioning, and if, as we contend, each actual occasion is immortal in respect to its superjective existence, then the objective functioning of an occasion in occasions later than itself must also be immortal. With each new occasion that comes to be, the completed occasion gains a new objective functioning; and there is no end to this process, assuming, of course, that there will always be new occasions coming into being. This, I maintain, is what Whitehead meant by the 'objective immortality' of an actual entity.

With this in mind, we may now look at still another passage wherein Whitehead equates the *being* of an actual entity with its existence as superject. Thus, immediately after discussing "the doctrine of the emergent unity of the superject," Whitehead says:

> An actual entity is to be conceived both as a subject presiding over its own immediacy of becoming, and a superject which is the atomic creature exercising its function of objective immortality. It has become a 'being'; and it belongs to the nature of every 'being' that it is a potential for every 'becoming'. (PR 71)

Accordingly, it is primarily in respect to its superjective existence that an actual entity is subsumed under the principle of relativity (PR 128).

I say that the objective functioning of an actual entity is due *primarily* to its superjective existence, and not *exclusively* so, because the thesis of solidarity requires that, in any given occasion, even those occasions that are in its future, or that are contemporary with it, must function objectively in it. But the objective functioning of those occasions cannot depend on their superjective existence. I shall argue in due course that their objective functioning depends on the extensive character which they already have, or will have; in fact, I shall argue that the objective functioning of *all* occasions—past, present, and future—depends on their extensive character, though *how* they function depends on whether they are past, contemporary, or inexistent (future) relative to the occasions in which they function. If my meaning here is obscure, this is unavoidable at this time. Until the theory of the extensive continuum has been considered, I can only hint at how the objective functioning of contemporary and future occasions is to be explained. In any case, aside from the general objective functioning of its extensive character, the objective functioning of an actual entity *is* due to its superjective existence (PR 128). Indeed, if we are talking about the objective functioning of an actual entity *qua* completely determinate particular, we can say without further qualification that it is due to its existence as superject.

Now, in respect to its being, or superjective existence, the functioning of an actual entity does not differ from that of any other entity. However, by reason of its subjective existence, an actual entity enjoys a mode of functioning which is not open to any other entity. For to function is to contribute to the determination of an actual entity—*any* actual entity; hence, under the functioning of an actual entity must be included the contributions that it makes toward its own determination. An actual entity is self-determining to the extent that, as subject, it makes autonomous decisions that are creative of its own ultimate definiteness. Thus, an actual entity functions in respect to itself. Its self-realization is its self-functioning. The subject is the actual entity as self-functioning (PR 38).

Moreover, since only actual entities are self-realizing, no other entity of any other sort can be self-functioning. For this reason it is possible to define 'actuality' in terms of 'self-functioning'. This Whitehead undertakes in the twenty-first Category of Explanation:

> (xxi) An entity is actual when it has significance for itself. By this it is meant that an actual entity functions in respect to its own determination . . . . (PR 38)

In other words, an entity is to be deemed actual if, and only if, it enjoys self-functioning. But this, it should be noted, is not to deny actuality to the superject. For to say, as Whitehead does say, that to be actual is to be either self-realizing or self-realized, is also to say, if in somewhat clumsier terms, that to be actual is to be either self-functioning or self-functioned. The superject is the self-functioned entity; and there is no entity of any other sort of which this might be said. Being self-functioned (or self-realized), therefore, is a sufficient criterion for distinguishing actual from non-actual beings.

It should be noticed, furthermore, that if actual entities were actual only while they were subjects, they would have only one mode of functioning open to them—that of self-functioning. The superjects, whatever else they might be, would *not* be actual entities. In other words, if only subjects were actual, then *actual* entities as such would not have objective functioning. But this is contrary to what Whitehead explicitly says; for him, the peculiarity of an actual entity is that it is both self-functioning and other-functioning; or, to put it in terms which Whitehead borrows from Descartes, the peculiarity of an actual entity is that it functions both *formally* and *objectively* (PR 335-36).

The point I have been trying to make is that if completed occasions were not actual the principle of relativity would not apply to actual entities. But actual entities do fall under the principle of relativity; therefore, the view in question must be false. The correct view is that for Whitehead an entity is not actual unless it is, *or has been*, self-realizing. But this is compatible with saying that an entity which is actual is actual regardless of whether its present existence is that of a subjectively functioning process or that of an objectively functioning product. As Whitehead says:

> To be actual must mean that all actual things are alike objects, enjoying objective immortality in fashioning creative actions; and that all actual things are subjects, each prehending the universe from which it arises. (PR 89)

Clearly, then, an occasion is actual *both* when it is functioning as object, *and* when it is functioning as subject.

In view of these considerations, it is difficult to understand why so many of Whitehead's commentators have contended that an occasion ceases to be actual with the attainment of its satisfaction. We have studied one major cause of this mistaken contention—the ambiguous statement of the principle of process. Perhaps another major reason for the prevalence of this misunderstanding is Whitehead's unfortunate use of the term 'perishing' in connection with the termination of an occasion's becoming. For Whitehead does say that "in the organic philosophy an actual entity has 'perished' when it is complete" (PR 126). But in so saying, Whitehead has no intention of denying either existence or actuality to the completed occasion. Thus, only one sentence after the passage just quoted he adds, "The creature perishes *and* is immortal." Therefore, Whitehead's intended meaning, when he thus speaks, is far from elusive. An actual entity does perish in the sense that with the attainment of its satisfaction it ceases to exist subjectively; but it does not cease on that account to exist or to be actual; it continues to exist everlastingly as an actual superject with objective functioning (PR 44). The completion of an actual occasion, then, is the perishing of its subjective immediacy but not of its existence (PR 130).[23]

11.   *Succession and anticipation: supersession and the future*

In the presystematic analysis of mnemonic experiences, we found (i) that the remembered experience is succeeded by the remembering experience; (ii) that the remembering experience is succeeded by the experiences which effect its analysis; and (iii) that the remembering experience is itself a succession of stages, the earlier stage merely reproducing something of the experience being remembered, and the later stage reacting to the reproductive content given to it by the earlier stage. This notion of threefold succession is incorporated in the organic category of *supersession*. Thus, according to Whitehead, "supersession is a three-way process. Each occasion supersedes other occasions, it is superseded by other occasions, and it is internally a process of supersession, in part potential and in part actual" (IS 241).

Supersession is not merely another name for succession. The relata of supersession are either actual occasions or phases in the becoming of an actual occasion. In the former case we may speak of *extrinsic* supersession, since the occasions which supersede, or are superseded by, a given occasion are in some sense *beyond* it. In the latter case we may speak of *intrinsic* supersession, since the relata are phases *within* the becoming of one and the same occasion. But in both cases of supersession, extrinsic and intrinsic, the earlier relatum remains in existence as a condition for the later relatum. Moreover, in both cases the later relatum takes into account, or in some way reacts to, the earlier relatum. Finally, also in both cases the later relatum does not abolish the existence of the earlier relatum but rather, in some sense, incorporates it within itself (PR 225–26). Thus, accumulation, condition, taking into account, and integration, as well as creative succession, are among the basic notions embodied in the organic doctrine of supersession. Accordingly, though supersession involves succession, it is never to be construed as mere succession.

Supersession is not another creative process over and above the creative processes of transition and concrescence. On the contrary, to speak of the process of supersession is merely to emphasize that the processes of transition and concrescence generate real products that are really sequentially related to one another. In other words, transition to and from a given occasion *is* extrinsic supersession; and concrescence *is* intrinsic supersession. Thus, if *A*, *B*, and *C* are three successive occasions, the transition from *A* to *B* is the creative process whereby *B* comes into existence as superseding *A*. Similarly, the transition from *B* to *C* is the process whereby *B* is superseded by *C*. Finally, *B*'s process of concrescence is but another name for the supersession of creative phases by which *B*, starting from the datum produced by transition, attains its individual satisfaction.[24]

Very little can be said about supersession that is not in fact about transition and concrescence, the creative processes it subsumes as a genus subsumes its species. Since transition and concrescence will be amply discussed in subsequent chapters, what needs to be said now is mostly by way of clarifying what we are to understand by *intrinsic* supersession. For Whitehead has said explicitly, but much to the confusion of no small number of his interpreters, that the supersession of the phases of concrescence is *not* temporal (PR 380, 434; IS 241).

In this regard, the question raised by Whitehead's interpreters is this: If one phase of concrescence is not temporally prior to another, then in what sense is the one prior to the other? One answer has been to deny that there is any real succession of phases, and to assert that the division of concrescence into phases is one of logical, and not ontological, sequence.[25] In other words, one phase of concrescence is logically prior to another in the same sense as the simple parts of a complex whole are logically prior to the whole itself. For according to this view, the whole occasion is created all at once. A second answer to the problem of non-temporal supersession holds that the succession of phases of concrescence is real but *sui generis*—a polite way of saying that Whitehead's doctrine of intrinsic supersession is unintelligible.[26]

But intrinsic supersession *is* an intelligible doctrine. To avoid misconstruing it along the lines of either of the two interpretations just mentioned, we must first realize that both modes of supersession, extrinsic and intrinsic, must have something in common, or Whitehead would not have given them the same name. What they have in common is, first, that one relatum of the supersessional relation is always in existence before the other; second, that when the later relatum is in existence, the earlier relatum is also in existence; and third, that the earlier relatum is always, in some sense, incorporated in the later relatum. Thus, supersession, whatever else it may be, and whatever the relata involved, is *cumulative succession incorporative of the earlier in the later*.

I need not defend this thesis in connection with extrinsic supersession; for every interpreter of Whitehead holds that, in some sense or another, earlier occasions are constitutive of later ones; and this, of course, amounts to holding that the superseded occasions are constituents of the superseding occasions. The only immediate issue, then, is whether what is true of extrinsic supersession is also true of intrinsic supersession. Now, unless Whitehead is perversely misleading us, the following passages strongly support an affirmative answer:

> [An actual entity] is a process proceeding from phase to phase, each phase being the real basis from which its successor proceeds towards the completion of the thing in question. (PR 327)

> Eternal objects express *how* the predecessor-phase is absorbed into the successor-phase without limitation of itself, but with additions necessary for the determination of an actual unity in the form of individual satisfaction. (PR 225/CPR 149)

> The process of concrescence is divisible into an initial stage of many feelings, and a succession of subsequent phases of more complex feelings integrating the earlier simpler feelings, up to the satisfaction which is one complex unity of feeling. (PR 337)

But if both modes of supersession involve a real cumulative and incorporative succession of relata, then the pertinent question to ask is: What does Whitehead mean by 'temporal', given that he applies the term to extrinsic, but not to intrinsic, supersession? To answer correctly this question we must bear in mind that Whitehead came to metaphysics by way of relativitiy physics. Therefore, we should expect the modern physicist's conception of temporal relations to color Whitehead's use of terms such as 'temporal', 'in time', and 'temporally earlier'. If this is so, we can expect that Whitehead will not construe an entity as being temporally earlier than another unless the former entity is an efficient cause of the latter.

This is precisely what we find when we examine Whitehead's philosophy at the metaphysical level. Thus, one actual occasion is earlier than another actual occasion if and only if the former is causally objectified in the latter. But since an actual occasion is causally objectified only when it is complete—that is, when it is in its final but immortal stage, the satisfaction—it follows that an actual occasion cannot function as an efficient cause while it is in the process of becoming. Hence, neither the phases of becoming occurring between the dative phase and the satisfaction, nor the dative phase itself, can function *by themselves* as efficient causes. Of course, the dative phase and the creative results of the intermediate phases are subordinate components of the satisfaction, so to that extent they do have causal efficacy. But the fact remains that an actual occasion in any phase of its existence other than the superjective phase is not the efficient cause of anything.

In addition to an actual occasion being wholly devoid of causal efficacy until it is complete, it is also the case that such an occasion is the result of efficient causes only in respect to its initial phases of existence, the dative and conformal phases. Beyond the conformal phases, the concrescing occasion is entirely a teleological process of self-formation or self-completion. This means, moreover, that we cannot construe an earlier phase of concrescence as the efficient cause of a later phase. Instead, we must construe each phase of concrescence as a creative step toward the progressive attainment of the subjective aim guiding the occasion's process of self-completion. Thus, the relation of the earlier to the later phases of concrescence is not that of cause to effect but of means to end. To be sure, the partial achievement of an earlier phase does condition the subsequent phases, but such conditioning is of the nature of material causation and not of efficient causation. Indeed, beyond the conditions imposed on it by the dative and conformal phases, by the earlier concrescent phases, if any, and by the subjective aim, every phase of the subjective concrescence makes originative decisions which are not determined by those conditions (PR 75). So much is entailed by the freedom which Whitehead ascribes to the occasion in its subjective existence (PR 41–42).

From these considerations we must conclude that the phases of becoming, other than the dative and conformal phases, are not relata of efficient causation. For, *in themselves*, they are not determined by efficient causes, nor are they the efficient causes of anything, nor, finally, are they related to one another as cause to effect. Therefore, given Whitehead's identification of temporal relations with relations of causal efficacy, it follows that the intrinsic supersession of phases of concrescence cannot be construed as temporal. But this signifies a restriction on the meaning of 'temporally earlier' and not a restriction on the meaning of 'supersessionally earlier'.

Thus one occasion is both supersessionally and temporally earlier than another occasion; but one phase of concrescence is merely supersessionally earlier than another phase.

There is more to Whitehead's doctrine of temporal or extrinsic supersession than is possible to explain at this time.[27] The reason is that the temporal character of an occasion is tied up with the region of the extensive continuum which it embodies and with the relation which that region bears to the extensive regions embodied by other occasions. We must therefore postpone any further treatment of extrinsic supersession, indeed of supersession in general, until we have studied the metaphysical doctrine of the extensive continuum.

A similar problem faces us in regard to the categoreal notion of anticipation. For without recourse to the metaphysical properties of the extensive continuum—the receptacle wherein actual occasions come to be and whereby they have an extensive character—there is no possibility of understanding how an actual occasion can anticipate its supersession by, and its immanence in, occasions later than itself. Nevertheless, we can at this time examine how the notion of anticipation, which we found to be implicit in the presystematic analysis of memory, is incorporated in Whitehead's doctrine of the subject-superject.

In setting up the analysis of memory, I anticipated that my experience of looking at the magazine on the floor would become, when completed, an object for a subsequent act of remembering; and I also anticipated that there would be a subsequent experience of remembering, and that the remembering experience, when completed, would be an object for the subsequent experiences that would carry out its analysis. Now, at the metaphysical level of Whitehead's philosophy this element of anticipation comes to this: first, that each actual occasion takes into account, or feels, the general potentiality for the becoming of occasions that will be future relative to itself; and second, that each occasion feels the necessity, grounded in the ultimate metaphysical character of the universe, that it be, when completed, a constituent of, and an object for, all subsequent occasions (AI 246–51).

Put in more technical terms, this means that each occasion experiences, through anticipatory feelings, the necessity of its involvement in the macroscopic, or extrinsic, processes productive of the occasions that will supersede it (IS 242–44). Thus if A is an actual occasion, then, according to Whitehead, "A prehends in its concretion objectification of occasions X, Y, Z, . . . which must supersede A but, as in A, have not the actuality of determinate concretions. Thus the objectification of its own supersession belongs to the real essence of A" (IS 243; italics mine).

Let me hasten to add that Whitehead is not saying that occasions X, Y, and Z exist antecedently to the termination of A's becoming. On the contrary, for him:

> In the present, the future occasions, as individual realities with their measure of absolute incompleteness, are non-existent. Thus the future must be immanent in the present in some different sense [sic] to the objective immortality of the individual occasions of the past. (AI 247)

The problem, however, is to render intelligible the sense in which the future is immanent in the present. My contention, in this regard, is that the related facts of anticipation and of the immanence of the future cannot be understood without reference to extension and creativity as real and eternal factors of the universe—factors which jointly express the potentiality for the becoming, the being, and the objective immortality of mutually immanent occasions. That, at any rate, is what I intend to demonstrate at a later moment of this essay.

Until that moment comes, however, the following statements by Whitehead must suffice to indicate that anticipation and the objective reality of the future are essential elements in the constitution of every actual occasion:

> It belongs to the essence of [the] subject that it pass into objective immortality. Thus its own constitution involves that its own activity in *self*-formation passes into its activity of *other*-formation. It is by reason of the constitution of the present subject that the future will embody the present subject and will reenact its patterns of activity. (AI 248)
>
> The final phase of anticipation is a propositional realization of the essence of the present-subject, in respect to the necessities which it lays upon the future to embody it and to re-enact it so far as compatibility may permit. (AI 248)
>
> What is objective in the present is the necessity of a future of actual occasions, and the necessity that these future occasions conform to the conditions inherent in the essence of the present occasion. (AI 251)
>
> An 'object' is a transcendent element characterizing that *definiteness* to which our 'experience' has to conform. In this sense, the future has *objective* reality in the present, but no *formal* actuality. For it is inherent in the constitution of the immediate, present actuality that a future will supersede it. Also conditions to which that future must conform, including real relationships to the present, are really objective in the immediate actuality. (PR 327)

The problem of anticipation, it is now evident, is of a piece with the problem of the immanence of the future in the present, and is thus of a piece with the problem posed by the thesis of solidarity. Accordingly, we cannot expect to solve the one problem without also solving the other.

We have now completed an initial study—far from exhaustive, despite its length—of organic doctrines suggested by a presystematic analysis of memory. If my understanding of those doctrines and of the other organic principles introduced in their study is correct, they should prove their worth when, in the later chapters of this essay, I bring them to bear on the elucidation of the world's solidarity.

12. *Solidarity, the extensive continuum, and the formative elements*

Before bringing this chapter to its conclusion, some further remarks on the thesis of solidarity are in order. These remarks would not have been intelligible prior to the considerations of the last nine sections, and they are made now with five ends in mind: first, to provide as explicit a rendering of the problem of solidarity as is possible at this time; second, to emphasize that the key to this problem's solution lies in Whitehead's metaphysical theory of extensive continuity; third, to examine briefly what Whitehead construes as the three formative elements of the temporal world—creativity, eternal objects, and God's primordial nature—and to unveil my contention that the metaphysical extensive continuum is to be construed as a fourth formative element; fourth, to specify the general requirements which any adequate interpretation of the thesis of solidarity must fulfill; and fifth, to state the most general reasons for my dissatisfaction with the received interpretations of this puzzling thesis.

By the solidarity of actualities we are to understand that any two actualities, regardless of their temporal relation, are mutually immanent. To be sure, the mode of immanence does vary according to the temporal relation that each actuality bears to the other: there is the mode of efficient causality, or of causal objectification, which is how the earlier is immanent in the later (PR 91); there is the mode of anticipation, or of anticipatory objectification, which is how the later is immanent in the earlier (PR 424–25; AI 247–52; IS 243); and finally there is the mode of contemporaneity, or of presentational objectification, which is how one actuality is immanent in another actuality contemporary with it (PR 91; AI 251–53). Thus, aside from contemporaries, the solidarity of actualities is *not* a reciprocal relation in respect to the *modes* of immanence involved. But the solidarity of occasions *is* a reciprocal relation in respect to the general fact of *immanence.* This is why, for Whitehead, "no two actualities can be torn apart: each is all in all" (PR 529).

The doctrine that all actual occasions are mutually immanent appears even more paradoxical when we remember that actual occasions are held to be discrete individuals; each occasion must be, in some sense, separate and distinct from all other occasions. The solidarity of occasions, then, is a paradoxical doctrine because it boldly asserts that any two actualities are at once mutually transcendent and mutually immanent. It maintains, on the one hand, that "if the individual discreteness of the actualities is to have its weight," then the relationships that all actualities bear to one another must be construed "as bonds between divided things" (PR 470–71). It also maintains, on the other hand, that "any set of occasions are united by the mutual immanence of occasions, each in the other" (PR 254). The problem is: If actual occasions are discrete individuals— that is, if they are divided from one another—what sense are we to make of their mutual immanence?

Lest it be thought that I have misinterpreted Whitehead at some point, let me emphasize once more that Whitehead is aware of the problem posed by the doctrine of solidarity and that he construes this problem in exactly the same manner as I have construed it above. The problem, according to Whitehead, is how

> to express the interconnection of facts, each with its measure of self-sufficiency. Each fact is just that limited thing that it is. How then do facts require each other? (MT 138)

Therefore, if Whitehead adopts the thesis of solidarity, it is not because he is ignorant of the problem it raises, but because for him (as we saw earlier) the mutual immanence of all final actualities is the necessary presupposition of the character of even our most ordinary experiences. It follows that we do not even begin to understand what Whitehead meant by the solidarity of the universe unless we realize that the mutual immanence of discrete occasions posed a real problem for him, one requiring a radically new metaphysical system for its solution. It also follows that any adequate elucidation of the thesis of solidarity must address itself to this problem, and must provide systematic and compatible meanings for the notions of 'mutual transcendence' and 'mutual immanence'.

In addition, any adequate explication of solidarity must explain both the mutual transcendence and the mutual immanence of occasions in terms of the organic doctrine of *the extensive continuum*, as it is called in PR, or of *the Receptacle*, as it is called in AI. There can be no doubt that it is to this doctrine that we must look for the key to Whitehead's solution to the problem of solidarity. The evidence for that conclusion is overwhelming. We have already seen the passage where Whitehead tells us that the extensive scheme "serves the double purpose" of explaining the discreteness of occasions and the fundamental internality of their relationships; to that passage we must now add the following ones:

> The extensive scheme is that general relational element in experience whereby the actual entities experienced, and that unit experience itself, are united in the solidarity of the one common world. (PR 112)

> [The extensive continuum is] the primary factor in objectification. It provides the general scheme of extensive perspective which is exhibited in all the mutual objectifications by which actual entities prehend each other. (PR 118)

> The Receptacle, as discussed in the *Timaeus*, is the way in which Plato conceived the many actualities of the physical world as components in each other's natures. . . . It is Plato's doctrine of the medium of intercommunication. (PR 172)

> [The Receptacle's] sole function is the imposition of a unity upon the events of Nature. These events are together by reason of their community of locus, and they obtain their actuality by reason of emplacement within this community. (AI 241)

> The general common function exhibited by any group of actual occasions is that of mutual immanence. In Platonic language, this is the function of belonging to a common Receptacle. (AI 258)

The passages cited speak for themselves; the organic theory of the extensive continuum must, in some truly fundamental manner, provide the solution to the problem of solidarity. For this reason, any adequate interpretation of the thesis of solidarity must show that in an essential sense the mutual immanence of discrete occasions is a function of their emplacement in the extensive continuum.

The term 'extensive continuum' has a variety of interrelated meanings in Whitehead's philosophy, only one of which is the requisite metaphysical meaning presupposed by the thesis of solidarity. For that reason, one major task of this essay is to separate the term's relevant metaphysical meaning from its various empirical or cosmological meanings. Suffice it to say for now that in its metaphysical sense the term signifies a continuum of extension which is presupposed by the becoming, the being, and the solidarity of actual occasions, but which *does not itself become*. Thus, the metaphysical continuum of extension is *eternal*, and it is not to be confused with the spatio-temporal continuum posited both by relativity physics and by Whitehead's organic cosmology.

The latter continuum, as I shall explain in Chapter Five, is *not* eternal; rather, it results from the fact that the actualities composing our familiar temporal world constitute an expanding *plenum* of actualized eternal exten-sion—*i.e.*, a plenum of extensive regions embodied and structured by actualities. In this way, the spatio-temporal continuum is derivative from the becoming and the being of the actual occasions forming that *portion* of the universal nexus—or that *cosmic epoch*, to use Whitehead's term—whose detailed investigation is the topic of empirical cosmology. As the cosmic epoch grows through the creative advance from occasion to occasion, the spatio-temporal continuum expands by the addition of newly structured, or newly spatio-temporalized, extensive quanta—each quantum being the determinate extensive standpoint of a particular subject-superject. In the organic philosophy, then, the spatio-temporal continuum is understood as an abstraction from the spatio-temporalization, actual or potential, of eternal extension that is produced by the actual occasions constituting our cosmic epoch (PR 112, 442).

The metaphysical extensive continuum, on the other hand, is under-stood as a factor or aspect of the universe's eternal potentiality for the becoming, the being, and the solidarity of actual occasions. As such it is, to use Whitehead's term, a *formative element* of the temporal world. But this last claim raises a problem for my interpretation of solidarity because Whitehead does not include the extensive continuum in the apparently exhaustive list of formative elements that he presents and discusses in *Religion in the Making.* The formative elements there listed and discussed are:

> 1.   The creativity whereby the actual world has its character of temporal passage to novelty.
> 2.   The realm of ideal entities, or forms, which are in themselves not actual, but are such that they are exemplified in everything that is actual, according to some proportion of relevance.
> 3.   The actual but non-temporal entity whereby the indetermina-tion of mere creativity is transmuted into a determinate freedom. This non-temporal actual entity is what men call God—the supreme God of rationalized religion. (RM 90)

Strictly speaking, the third formative element is not God but an ab-stract aspect of God's concrete actuality. This abstract aspect is what in PR is termed the *primordial nature of God.* But God has in addition a *consequent nature*, which is derivative from the objectification in God of the completed occasions of the temporal world, and a *superjective nature*, which is the objective functioning of God in the temporal actualities. Here is how Whitehead summarizes God's threefold nature:

> (i) The 'primordial nature' of God is the concrescence of a unity of conceptual feelings, including among their data all eternal objects. The concrescence is directed by the subjective aim, that the subjective forms of the feelings shall be such as to constitute the eternal objects into relevant lures of feeling severally appropriate for all realizable basic conditions. (ii) The 'consequent nature' of God is the physical prehension by God of the actualities of the evolving universe. His primordial nature directs such perspectives of objectification that each novel actuality in the temporal world contributes such elements as it can to a realization in God free from inhibitions of intensity by reason of discordance. (iii) The 'superjective nature' of God is the character of the pragmatic value of his specific satisfaction qualifying the transcendent creativity in the various temporal instances. (PR 134–35/CPR 87–88)

The primordial nature of God, the eternal objects, and the creativity are thus the three formative elements explicitly discussed by Whitehead in RM. However, an examination of the presuppositions of the solidarity thesis will reveal that the creativity is *not* the ultimate reality posited by the organic philosophy but is, instead, an *aspect* of that reality. At any rate, that is what I shall argue in Chapters Five and Six. I shall argue, in fact, that terms such as 'the creativity', 'the extensive continuum', and 'the Receptacle' designate an ultimate reality which is extensive as well as creative. It will then follow that the list of formative elements presented in RM—and, for that matter, the categoreal scheme presented in PR— already includes, albeit only implicitly, the notion of an eternal extensive continuum. In other words, the eternal continuum is an aspect of that ultimate reality of which the creativity is another aspect. The two aspects are distinguishable but inseparable; in their unity, they constitute an eternal extenso-creative matrix which is the ultimate metaphysical ground for the becoming, the being, and the solidarity of all actual entities. It is one major contention of this essay that there can be no adequate elucidation of the solidarity of all actual existence until the nature and function of the matrix's extensiveness is fully understood.

An adequate elucidation of the solidarity of occasions has one other major requirement to fulfill: it must explain how, and in what sense, earlier occasions are repeated, or 'causally objectified', in later occasions.

For the peculiarity of the immanence of the earlier in the later is that it involves an essential reference to the notion of repetition—in addition to involving, as all modes of immanence do, a reference to the notion of extension. We have already seen in this regard that an attained actuality is repeated in another actuality so as to be given for the immediacy of the latter actuality (PR 208, 211). This is the reason why for Whitehead each novel actuality "is the reproduction of the many actual entities of the past" (PR 364).

Three major requirements that an adequate interpretation of the thesis of solidarity must fulfill have now been considered; we may summarize these requirements as follows: first, an adequate interpretation must provide systematic and compatible meanings for the notions of 'mutual transcendence' and 'mutual immanence' as relations applicable to the same relata, where the relata are any pair of actual occasions or subject-superjects; second, it must explain the mutual immanence of discrete occasions as primarily a function of their belonging to a common continuum of extension; third, it must explain the immanence of earlier occasions in later ones in terms of the causal objectification, or abstractive repetition, of the former in the latter, as well as in terms of the properties of the extensive continuum. My general dissatisfaction with the received interpretations of Whitehead's philosophy, so far as they address or fail to address the problem of solidarity, can now be stated in terms of these requirements.

Of the major interpreters of Whitehead's metaphysics, only Christian has attempted to approach the problem of solidarity in a manner even remotely similar to the approach undertaken in this essay. Christian does not usually speak of the doctrine of solidarity as such; but his influential book, *An Interpretation of Whitehead's Metaphysics*, is in large part devoted to the elucidation of the senses in which actual entities are 'socially transcendent' and 'socially immanent'—his terms for the notions of 'mutual transcendence' and 'mutual immanence', respectively. Thus, we do find in Christian's interpretation of solidarity an attempt—ultimately unsuccessful—to fulfill the first of the requirements listed above.

Christian maintains that any two actual occasions transcend one another in two basic respects.[28] First, any two actual occasions are mutually transcendent in respect to their subjective immediacies—that is to say, no actual occasion *qua* subject includes another actual occasion *qua* subject.[29] Second, any two actual occasions transcend one another in respect to the extensive regions which they occupy, each its own.[30] Christian spells out his views on the mutual transcendence of extensive regions as follows:

1. An actual occasion is extensive.
2. The region of an actual occasion is definite.
3. The regions of actual occasions form an extensive plenum.
4. No two actual occasions have the same region.
5. The region of any two actual occasions are nonoverlapping.[31]

My only objection to Christian, in regard to these five propositions, is that number three is true for our cosmic epoch, but is not, according to Whitehead, a necessary or metaphysical feature of the universe (I shall give detailed treatment of this matter in Chapter Five). But, apart from this objection, I agree with Christian's basic claim that the extensive regions occupied by any two occasions are mutually transcendent. I also agree with him that there can be no mutual immanence of subjective immediacies as such; but this, by the way, does not prevent me from holding that something of the essential character of a subject is immanent in other subjects contemporary with it.

Of interest to us is the fact that Christian has made use of the extensive continuum to explain how the relations between actual occasions are bonds between divided things. This brings his interpretation of solidarity to the halfway mark of fulfilling the second of the three requirements we have been considering. Unfortunately, Christian's interpretation remains at this halfway mark; it does not go the full distance. For Christian, having found a way in which the extensive continuum has a bearing on the mutual transcendence of occasions, makes no attempt to find how the extensive continuum also has a bearing on the mutual immanence of occasions. In view of Whitehead's repeated assertions to the effect that the extensive continuum or Receptacle must account for the mutual immanence of occasions, this is no minor oversight on Christian's part. On the basis of this shortcoming alone, Christian's interpretation of the solidarity of actual occasions must be rejected as inadequate.

Not having recourse to the extensive continuum for the explanation of mutual immanence, Christian finds no direct connection between occasions, except when one occasion is in the immediate past of another. He then construes the immanence of the earlier in the later as the ingression in the later occasion of an eternal object also ingressed in the earlier occasion.[32] My earlier discussion of objectification by itself offers strong grounds for rejecting Christian's interpretation. Later I shall reject this aspect of Christian's interpretation on the additional grounds that he confuses the doctrine of *conformation*, which involves the reproduction of eternal objects *qua* determinants of subjective form, with the doctrine of *causal objectification*, which involves the repetition of superjects, that is, of particulars.[33] Moreover, Christian construes causal objectification to be the result of the subjective concrescence; whereas Whitehead, I shall argue later, holds that causal objectification is the result of the macroscopic transition, and is a datum *for* the microscopic concrescence.[34] Thus, Christian's interpretation of solidarity also fails in this last respect.

None of the other major interpreters of Whitehead have been as systematically concerned with the notions of mutual transcendence and mutual immanence as Christian has. In general, their concern with the solidarity of occasions is limited to investigating in what way actual occasions transcend each other and in what way earlier occasions are immanent in later ones.[35] In respect to the first of these concerns, it may be safely said that all major interpreters agree that the subjective immediacies of any two occasions are mutually transcendent. This meaning of 'mutual transcendence' is valid enough; but it is not the meaning requisite for the elucidation of solidarity. For to understand 'mutual transcendence' exclusively in terms of the subjective immediacies of occasions is to fail to notice that the doctrine of solidarity does not discriminate between actual occasions existing as subjects and actual occasions existing as superjects. The doctrine holds, in effect, that all actual occasions—*i.e.*, that all subject-superjects—are discrete entities. It also asserts, therefore, that there is a sense in which every subject-superject transcends all other subject-superjects. For the purposes of this doctrine, then, *any* two actual occasions, whatever their mode of existence, must be in some sense mutually exclusive. This must be true when the occasions are both superjects, as well as when they are both subjects. It must also be true when one occasion is a subject and the other a superject. Accordingly, the mutual transcendence of subjective immediacies has by itself little or no bearing on the doctrine of solidarity.

In respect to the immanence of earlier occasions in later ones, the major interpreters of Whitehead divide into two groups. One group asserts the *literal* immanence, without repetition, of earlier occasions in later ones; the other group maintains that there is immanence only to the extent that an eternal object characterizing the subjective form of an earlier occasion is repeated in a later occasion so as to characterize also the latter's subjective form. Since I hold that an earlier occasion is included in a later one only *qua* repeated particular, my charge against the interpreters of the first group is that they take the immanence of the past too literally, whereas my charge against those of the second group is that they do not take the immanence of the past literally enough. That there is a middle ground between these two extremes is what I intend to prove in this essay. The main thrust of my interpretation of the thesis of solidarity, however, is aimed at showing how the extensive continuum at once accounts for the mutual transcendence and the mutual immanence of any two occasions. To the best of my knowledge, this is something that no interpreter of Whitehead has ever attempted to do. Nevertheless, it is now evident that this is what Whitehead himself suggests must be done if we are to solve the riddle of solidarity.

13. Brief preview of remaining chapters

The problem posed by the thesis of solidarity, the relation that the organic categories bear to the solution of this problem, and the inadequacies of the received attempts to interpret this difficult aspect of the organic philosophy have now been made sufficiently clear. The task of explaining this paradoxical thesis, however, lies ahead. The path that I will follow in attempting to fulfill this task must now be briefly indicated.

In Chapter Two, I examine the principle of relativity and the role of repetition in the becoming and being of each subject-superject.

In Chapter Three, I interpret the principles of ontology and creativity, paying particular attention to the organic theories of efficient and final causation.

In Chapter Four, I examine the three formative elements explicitly identified by Whitehead and elucidate their immediate bearing on the thesis of solidarity.

In Chapter Five, I recover, reconstruct, and develop the theory of eternal extension that is implicit in Whitehead's metaphysical and cosmological writings.

In Chapter Six, I explore the relevance of the metaphysical theory of extensive continuity to the organic doctrines of objectification, position, definiteness, self-identity, self-diversity, autonomy, and, of course, solidarity.

In Chapter Seven, I present a detailed examination of the emergence and nature of an occasion's dative phase and exhibit how all elements of the occasion's correlative universe play an essential function in the begetting of the occasion's dative phase. In addition, I there explain how the metaphysical properties of extension necessitate, establish, and immortally preserve the internal relatedness of the occasion to its correlative universe, and how those properties are presupposed by both the genetic and the coordinate analysis of the occasion. The extensional solidarity of the universe is thus elucidated.

Finally, in Chapter Eight, I show how the extensive structure of actual occasions is presupposed by the organic theories of perceptual and cognitive experience, and I distinguish and develop three interrelated senses of 'solidarity'—extensional, objective, and functional. Three major interpretive theses thus emerge: (i) that without extensional solidarity there would be neither occasions, nor nexūs of occasions; (ii) that without objective solidarity there would be no common world of perception and knowledge; and (iii) that the functional solidarity of the universe is its essential reconciliation of the interrelatedness of all actual existence with the autonomous individuality of all actual existence.

Although they focus on different doctrines of Whitehead's philosophy, these seven chapters reflect each the others because of their interrelated bearing on the elucidation of solidarity, and because of their successive treatments of a number of recurring themes. The different discussions of a given theme are intended to complement and supplement one another; for that reason, any one discussion of a particular theme may repeat aspects of earlier discussions of it and may also anticipate aspects of discussions of it yet to come. Thus, the general form of this essay, in respect to the mutual relevance of its chapters, exhibits some of the very features of solidarity that its contents seek to illuminate.

TWO

The Principle of Relativity

More than half a century after the publication of PR, process scholars have yet to recognize that the principle of relativity—the principle on which Whitehead founded his metaphysical system (PR 76)—asserts, in effect, the repeatability of all entities of all sorts: the repeatability, that is, of particulars as well as of universals. They have recognized, to be sure, that Whitehead intended the relativity principle, together with the ontological principle, to "blur the sharp distinction between what is universal and what is particular" (PR 76). They have recognized also that actual entities and eternal objects are the closest analogues, in Whitehead's metaphysics, to particulars and universals, respectively (PR 76). But the idea of particulars having multiple instances is so paradoxical and revolutionary that even Whitehead's most sympathetic interpreters have been unable to take him literally when he says, and he says it frequently, that earlier actual entities are repeated in later ones (*e.g.*, PR 208, 224, 347, 364).[1] In one way or another, the interpreters have avoided the conclusion that Whitehead blurred the traditional distinction between universals and particulars with his doctrine that actual entities as well as eternal objects are repeatable. They have, to that extent, missed the full import of the relativity principle.

Missing the full import of the doctrine of relativity is a matter of no small consequence; for Whitehead, it must be remembered, strove with considerable success to have his metaphysical principles presuppose each the others (PR 5, 9). Accordingly, any error or misapprehension in the interpretation of the relativity principle can be expected to visit itself on, and thus vitiate, the interpretation of other important organic principles. The ontological principle, the causal objectification of earlier occasions in later ones, the mutual immanence of discrete occasions, and even the Category of the Ultimate, are all, I maintain, organic doctrines presupposing the repetition of completed actual occasions. Hence, insofar as the major interpreters of Whitehead do not acknowledge the repetition of particulars, their accounts of these four doctrines severely distort, or truncate, the meaning Whitehead intended them to have. Moreover, to the degree they are accepted as being completely accurate, those accounts stand in the way of many genuine applications of Whitehead's conceptuality—applications as basic and important as the elucidation of memory and perception. Suffice it to note, in this last regard, that the reformed subjectivist principle, on which Whitehead based his metaphysical theory of memory, perception, and knowledge, was for him "merely an alternative statement of the principle of relativity" (PR 252). At issue in the interpretation of the relativity principle, therefore, is the applicability, as well as the coherence, of the metaphysics of organic process.

In this chapter, the interpretation of this fundamental principle is developed with a limited but basic objective: to argue that the doctrine of relativity implies the repeatability of all entities, including actual entities, and to begin to exhibit the extent to which Whitehead's philosophy of organism is built on the tenet that even particulars are repeatable. To achieve this twofold objective, I shall argue, through a series of textual considerations, that the relativity principle must be understood as asserting that to be an entity is both to have a *potentiality* for being repeated and to have that potentiality *realized* in every actual occasion whose becoming finds that entity already existing as a fully determinate being. I shall argue also that the principle, thus understood, implies that every completed occasion in the universe of a novel occasion is reproduced in and for that occasion. This reproduction of earlier occasions in later ones, I shall show, is what Whitehead meant by the objectification of the former in the latter. In the next chapter, I shall further argue for my interpretation of the relativity principle by bringing it to bear on the ontological principle, on the creativity principle, and, more generally, on the doctrine of solidarity. It will then be seen that actual entities must be repeatable if these three doctrines are each to be prevented from issuing in either a conceptual incoherence or an outright logical contradiction.

1. To be is to be repeatable

In the categoreal scheme of PR, the relativity principle is listed as the fourth Category of Explanation and reads as follows:

(iv) That the potentiality for being an element in a real concrescence of many entities into one actuality, is the one general metaphysical character attaching to all entities, actual and non-actual; and that every item in its universe is involved in each concrescence. In other words, it belongs to the nature of a 'being' that it is a potential for every 'becoming'. This is the 'principle of relativity'. (PR 33)

In this formulation of the principle, its ultimate meaning is not yet made clear. Certainly the formulation contains no explicit assertion of the repeatability of all entities. Indeed, no meaning is apparent in it other than this: every entity in the universe of a concrescing actuality must be involved in the actuality, so that to be an entity in *that* universe is to be involved in *that* concrescence. But the nature of the involvement, or the meaning of 'being a potential for every becoming', is not at all obvious.

Fortunately, throughout PR Whitehead makes frequent and illuminating references to the principle of relativity. Through a careful interpretation of those references, the true meaning and import of the principle can be gradually ascertained. For example, many of those references make clear that Whitehead construed 'thing', 'entity', 'being', and 'object' as synonymous, or nearly synonymous, with one another (PR 68, 336, 366, 371; see also 31). They are but nearly synonymous because, for Whitehead, an actuality in process of attainment is an entity or thing, but it is not yet a being or object. To be a being or object the actuality must be complete or already become, *i.e.*, it must be an attained actuality—the superject or satisfaction, rather than the subject or genetic process. This is why Whitehead says of the completed actuality or superject: "It has become a 'being'; and it belongs to the nature of every 'being' that it is a potential for every 'becoming'" (PR 71). Given that the superject is the fully determinate occasion, this statement also suggests that an entity is a being if, and only if, it is completely determinate; entities that are still in the process of becoming fully determinate are not yet beings. Hence, an occasion *qua* subject is an entity but it is not a being. Nonetheless, though 'entity' and 'being' do not have exactly the same connotation or intension, they do have the same denotation or extension; for the actuality as in process of attainment and the actuality as attained are one and the same entity (PR 326–28). "It is subject-superject, and neither half of this description can for a moment be lost sight of" (PR 43). My point is that for Whitehead all entities are, or are destined to be, beings or objects. Hence, all entities fall, or are destined to fall, under the scope of the relativity principle.[2]

From other passages where Whitehead discusses the principle of relativity, we can safely infer that what all entities have in common—and thus what 'entity', 'being', 'object', and 'thing' connote in common—is their *capacity* to contribute determination to every actuality whose becoming finds *those* entities already existing (PR 366, 371, 392). In this manner, it becomes evident that 'being a *potential* for every becoming' means the same thing as 'being a *capacity* for being a realized determinant of every becoming' (PR 366, 371). To have the capacity is to *be* an object and to exercise it is to *function* as an object. But the capacity must be exercised in one way or another; for "every item in its universe is involved in each concrescence." Therefore, "according to the fourth Category of Explanation it is the one general metaphysical character of all entities of all sorts, that they function as objects" (PR 336).

The objective functioning of entities turns out to be one of two species of functioning distinguished by Whitehead. The generic meaning common to both species is set out in the twentieth Category of Explanation, where we are told that "to 'function' means to contribute determination to the actual entities in the nexus of some actual world" (PR 38). The next four Categories of Explanation jointly establish a distinction between the functioning of one entity in respect to another and the functioning of one entity in respect to itself. All entities of all sorts function in respect to other entities. But only actual entities function each in respect to itself. For that reason, self-function or self-realization constitutes a sufficient criterion of actuality (PR 38). To be an actual entity is to be, or to have been, self-realizing. "An actuality is self-realizing, and whatever is self-realizing is an actuality. An actual entity is at once the subject of self-realization, and the superject which is self-realized" (PR 340). The self-realization of the actuality is what Whitehead terms its formal functioning (PR 81, 336). But the self-realized superject is the actuality as completed or already become; it is a being and, like all other beings, it must function objectively in the becoming of actualities later than itself. "The peculiarity of an actual entity is that it can be considered both 'objectively' and 'formally'" (PR 336).

According to the twenty-fourth Category of Explanation, the "functioning of one actual entity in the self-creation of another actual entity is the 'objectification' of the former for the latter actual entity" and the "functioning of an eternal object in the self-creation of an actual entity is the 'ingression' of the eternal object in the actual entity" (PR 38). But in the eighth Category of Explanation we are told that the objectification of one actuality in another is the particular mode in which the potentiality (or capacity) of the former is realized (or exercised) in the latter, and in the seventh Category of Explanation we are told that the ingression of an eternal object into an actuality is the particular mode in which the potentiality (or capacity) of the eternal object is realized (or exercised) in the actuality (PR 34). This latter way of characterizing the objectification of actual entities and the ingression of eternal objects has the advantage, for our purposes, of emphasizing the distinction Whitehead makes between an entity or object *qua* capacity for being a realized determinant and that same entity or object *qua* realized determinant. This distinction provides an important clue to the meaning of the principle of relativity.

Whitehead explicitly contrasts the object as capacity and the object as realized determinant in terms of the object's transcendence and immanence relative to the actuality in which it functions: "Immanence and transcendence are the characteristics of an object: as a realized determinant it is immanent; as a capacity for determination it is transcendent; in both roles it is relevant to something not itself" (PR 366–67). What sense is to be made of this contrast? How can the same object be at once immanent and transcendent relative to the same actuality?

In the case of eternal objects, a possible answer immediately suggests itself. As ingressed in a particular actuality, a particular eternal object is just another instance of itself. It contributes its unique individual essence to the determination of the actuality. No other eternal object can make that contribution. But that *same* eternal object must make exactly the *same* contribution to any actuality or occasion in which it is ingressed. Thus, the individual essence

> of an eternal object is merely the eternal object considered as adding its own unique contribution to each actual occasion. This unique contribution is identical for all such occasions in respect to the fact that the object in all modes of ingression is just its identical self. But it varies from one occasion to another in respect to the differences of its mode of ingression. (SMW 222)

These different modes of ingression are a function of the eternal object's relational essence, that is, of its patience for being jointly ingressed with other eternal objects having the requisite relational essence (SMW 222–24). But the point to emphasize now is that any eternal object is just itself in whatever mode of ingression it is involved (SMW 240). Hence, as ingressed in a particular occasion, a particular eternal object is an exact replica of every other instance of itself. It becomes a realized determinant of the particular occasion by being reproduced within the occasion. Moreover, as eternally ingressed in God's primordial nature, each eternal object is, relative to the temporal actualities, a transcendent capacity for their determination. In this manner, the same eternal object can be both immanent and transcendent relative to the same occasion.

Can this explanation be extended to include the functioning of one actuality in another? Does an earlier actuality function in a later one by being reproduced in it? Is the earlier actuality in itself the transcendent capacity? Is its reproduction within the later actuality the realized determinant? To pave the way for affirmative answers to these questions, I now turn to one of Whitehead's most illuminating characterizations of the fourth Category of Explanation:

> The principle of universal relativity directly traverses Aristotle's dictum, '(A substance) is not present in a subject'. On the contrary, according to this principle an actual entity *is* present in other actual entities. In fact if we allow for degrees of relevance, and for negligible relevance, we must say that every actual entity is present in every other actual entity. The philosophy of organism is mainly devoted to the task of making clear the notion of 'being present in another entity'. This phrase is here borrowed from Aristotle: it is not a fortunate phrase, and in subsequent discussion it will be replaced by the term 'objectification'. (PR 79–80)

'Being present in another entity', when the entities in question are both actual entities, means the same as 'being objectified in another entity'— that much is evident. But elsewhere Whitehead equates 'being objectified' with 'being repeated': "In the organic philosophy the notion of repetition is fundamental. The doctrine of objectification is an endeavor to express how what is settled in actuality is repeated under limitations, so as to be 'given' for immediacy" (PR 208). Accordingly, 'being present in another entity' means 'being repeated in another entity'. In other words, it is as repeated—*i.e.*, as another instance of itself—that the one entity is present in the other.

In this regard, it must be emphasized that whatever is given for the immediate experience of an actuality must be immanent in, and a constituent of, the actuality; for, in the organic philosophy, "experience is not a relation of an experient to something external to it, but is itself the 'inclusive whole' which is the required connectedness of 'many in one'" (AI 299). This is why for Whitehead "every item of the universe, including all the other actual entities, are constituents in the constitution of any one actual entity" (PR 224). But each item in the universe of an actual entity becomes a constituent of that entity by being repeated in it. It is only as thus repeated that the items are given for the experience of the actuality. "Tear 'repetition' out of 'experience' and there is nothing left" (PR 206).

By the repetition, or causal objectification, of an earlier occasion in a later one, let me hasten to add, Whitehead did not mean what many of his interpreters have erroneously taken him to mean, merely that some eternal object ingressed in the earlier occasion is also ingressed in the later occasion. Causal objectification is the repetition of an earlier particular in a later one, and no mere repetition of universals can ever count as the repetition of a particular. An actual occasion embodies other actual occasions (*qua* reproduced), and hence its make-up cannot be reduced to its embodiment of ingressed eternal objects. Thus, "an actual entity cannot be described, even inadequately, by universals; because other actual entities do enter into the description of any one actual entity" (PR 76). To reduce causal objectification, and thereby the immanence of the earlier in the later, to a mere repetition of eternal objects, is to make the repetition of occasions a sham repetition. It is simply to refuse to take Whitehead at his word, and what Whitehead says, in effect, is that each superject is repeated *in* every occasion whose origination is subsequent to the existence of that superject (PR 208, 211, 364).

But can Whitehead really mean that actual occasions, as well as eternal objects, are repeatable entities? If the following passage from PR is at all significant, the answer must be that that is *precisely* what Whitehead means: "The oneness of the universe, and the oneness of each element in the universe, repeat themselves to the crack of doom in the creative advance from creature to creature, each creature including in itself the whole of history and exemplifying the self-identity of things and their mutual diversities" (347–48). Surely, whatever else Whitehead is saying here, he is saying that actual occasions are repeated (*qua* superjects only, never *qua* subjects), for among the 'elements' in the universe relative to the origination of a novel creature are all those occasions which have already completed their becoming, *i.e.*, those which are already superjects; hence, every superject accumulated in the wake of the universe's creative advance is repeated *within* each novel creature at the utmost verge of that advance. In themselves, the superjects are *transcendent capacities* for the determination of the novel creature; as their own reproductions, however, they are *immanent determinants* of the creature.

Whitehead is also saying, in the passage just quoted, that *all* elements in the universe are repeated in each novel occasion. The property of being repeatable belongs to all organic entities and not just to eternal objects and actual entities. This, after all, is what we should expect, given that eternal objects and actual entities are the fundamental types of entities in Whitehead's ontology and that "the other types of entities only express how all entities of the two fundamental types are in community with each other, in the actual world" (PR 37). My point is that the repetition of entities of the fundamental types necessarily carries with it the repetition of entities of the derivative types. For example, a nexus is repeated if, and only if, its constituent actualities are repeated; also, if an actuality is repeated at least some element of its subjective form is also repeated.

Accordingly, all entities, actual and non-actual, achieve objective functioning in a given occasion by virtue of their reproduction within the occasion. But what needs to be emphasized now is that actual entities, when they are completely attained, share with eternal objects the property of being repeatable. It is in virtue of this property that actual entities and eternal objects alike have the capacity for being realized determinants of processes of becoming. Both types of entities contribute to the becoming of actual entities, and what the entities of either type contribute is themselves as *repeated*, i.e., as *objectified* or as *ingressed*, respectively. To that extent, actual entities and eternal objects behave in an identical manner. This is one reason (it is not the only one) why Whitehead refuses to identify 'universal' with 'eternal object': "The term 'universal' is unfortunate in its application to eternal objects; for it seems to deny, and in fact it was meant to deny, that actual entities also fall within the scope of the principle of relativity. If the term 'eternal objects' is disliked, the term 'potentials' would be suitable" (PR 226). The point is that the realization of *potentials* involves repetition—repetition either in the guise of ingression or in the guise of objectification. But if my interpretation is correct, and if being repeatable is made the criterion for being a universal, then it follows that eternal objects and actual entities are alike universals or, in Whitehead's terms, are alike potentials.

Moreover, since potentials are repeated *within* actualities, it follows that if being present in a subject, or actuality, is made the criterion for being a universal, then again actual entities and eternal objects are alike universals. This explains how the principle of relativity was meant to "blur the sharp distinction between what is universal and what is particular" (PR 76). As Whitehead put it:

> The notion of a universal is of that which can enter into the description of many particulars; whereas the notion of a particular is that it is described by universals, and does not itself enter into the description

of any other particular. According to the doctrine of relativity which is the basis of the metaphysical system of the present lectures, both these notions involve a misconception. An actual entity cannot be described, even inadequately, by universals; because other actual entities do enter into the description of any one actual entity. Thus every so-called 'universal' is particular in the sense of being just what it is, diverse from everything else; and every so-called 'particular' is universal in the sense of entering into the constitution of other actual entities. (PR 76)

To understand correctly the meaning of Whitehead's statement, we need only keep in mind that every so-called particular enters into the constitution of other particulars by being reproduced in them. But the same is true of every so-called universal. Thus, every entity contributes its own particularity to the determination of each novel actuality; thus, too, every entity contributes itself as repeated; and thus, finally, every entity in its objective functioning transcends itself—it is repeated beyond itself so as to be immanent in, and given for the immediacy of, each novel actuality (PR 324, 327, 336, 366).

My contention that the relativity principle implicitly asserts the repeatability of *all* entities, including actual entities, has now received its initial substantiation. It will receive additional support when in this chapter, and in later ones also, I examine how the relativity principle bears on, and is borne upon by, other metaphysical doctrines of the organic philosophy. But it should be obvious already that the repeatability of all entities is a necessary, though not a sufficient, condition for the universal solidarity of actual entities.[3] Indeed, this connection between the relativity principle and the solidarity thesis is made explicit by Whitehead when he says that, "according to the fourth Category of Explanation, it is the one general metaphysical character of all entities of all sorts, that they function as objects. It is this metaphysical character which constitutes the solidarity of the universe" (PR 336). To what extent this metaphysical character—*i.e.*, the repeatability of all entities—constitutes a presupposition of experience is the topic of the next seven sections. Two additional sections explore further the doctrine of causal objectification.[4]

2. Repetition in experience

Whitehead's claim that there is nothing left if we tear repetition out of experience is both illuminating and misleading. It is illuminating because it alerts us to the importance of repetition in his conception of experience; it is misleading because experience, as he conceives it, is not reducible to its repetitive elements. Novel immediacy is another essential element in experience. Accordingly, I take Whitehead's remark to be hyperbolic for the sake of emphasis. It is a reminder of the importance of repetition—of the importance, in other words, of the relativity principle. It thus serves as a corrective to the emphasis, at times just as exaggerated, which so many of Whitehead's statements place on novelty.

In truth, experience is the weaving together of elements repetitional and elements original. It is the synthesis of the old and the new. My immediate concern, however, is with the old or repetitive elements of experience. I want to examine them closely so as to exhibit the importance of the relativity principle and its bearing on the thesis of solidarity. But their examination turns out to be, for the most part, an explication of the three earliest phases in the becoming of an actual occasion. In other words, the repetitive aspects of an actual occasion are produced, in the main, by the three supersessionally earliest phases of its becoming. For this reason, the considerations that follow constitute a further development of the metaphysical doctrines suggested by the presystematic notions of repetition and succession.

According to Whitehead, the two earliest phases in the becoming of an actual occasion—the *dative* phase and the *responsive* phase—are *not* truly originative in their natures, except insofar as they constitute the earliest stages in the existence of a numerically new occasion (PR 179, 176). The occasion thus existing *is* new, but the components of its objective content are *old* and the characters defining its subjectivity are *second-hand*. Its phases of originative self-completion have yet to occur. As in these earliest phases, therefore, the occasion exists as a mere *receiver* of old content and second-hand character. Thus, these earliest phases in the occasion's existence are known also as its *receptive phases* (PR 179).

The components of the occasion's received objective content are, in their simplest concrete instances, the reproductions or objectifications of the already completed actualities in the occasion's correlative universe. The received characters of the occasion's newborn subjective immediacy are all re-enactments of characters defining the subjective forms of the received objectifications. Accordingly, in these earliest of phases, the make-up of an occasion is repetitive through and through. The occasion exists in the guise of a container receiving the reproductions of old objects and old characters.

But the language of reception is misleading. We do not have an occasion first existing and only subsequently receiving its objective content; rather, the occasion's first phase of existence and the occasion's objective content are one and the same thing. Nor do we have a subject first existing and only afterwards receiving its second-hand character; rather, the emergence of the newborn subject is one and the same thing as the occasion's acquisition of second-hand character. Moreover, the occasion's initial subjective immediacy emerges in virtue of a creative, but unoriginative, response to the concrete components of the objective content. This means that the objective content and the second-hand character are *two different components* of the nascent occasion, and that the production of the second-hand character is *supersessionally later* than the production of the objective content.

I am here explicating aspects of Whitehead's metaphysics—the related doctrines of causal objectification and conformal feeling—which are often misrepresented or confused in the received interpretations. Therefore, I must be careful and thorough in my treatment of the distinction between content received and character received. This distinction is of a piece with the distinction between the dative phase and the responsive phase of an occasion. To clarify the difference between these two phases, let me first emphasize that the dative phase is the occasion as in its first stage of existence. The dative phase, I shall argue in detail at later moments of this essay, is the occasion in the guise of being a finite extensive region within which the occasion's correlative universe has been reproduced or objectified (PR 101–05, 124). Accordingly, the dative phase is the occasion's correlative universe insofar as that universe, by reason of its reproductive immanence, has become a real potentiality for being felt in, and by, that occasion (PR 101). But in this phase there are as yet no feelings belonging to the new occasion. In other words, in this absolutely first phase of its existence the occasion is completely devoid of subjective immediacy. Therefore, the occasion *qua* dative phase, though really existing, is merely the potentiality for its own subjective immediacy.

This potentiality, let me next emphasize, begins to be realized in the responsive phase by which the dative phase is superseded. Thus, even though it is the occasion's *second phase of existence*, the responsive phase is the occasion's *first phase of subjective immediacy*. In this new phase, there is a creation of subjective forms in responsive conformity to the characters or qualities exhibited by the individual objectifications constituting the dative phase (PR 173). The subjective forms thus created constitute the initial definiteness of a new immediacy of subjective enjoyment. The immediacy of enjoyment is what the occasion is for itself. The occasion enjoys its own definiteness, but its definiteness, as in this first phase of subjective immediacy, is entirely made up of qualities that are mere repetitions of qualities in the individual components of the dative phase or objective content (AI 325–28). Moreover, the qualitative reproduction is not only *derived* from the individual components, but is also *dictated* by them (S 38). As Whitehead puts it, "each part of the total objective datum dictates its conformal qualitative reproduction in the subjective form" (AI 327). Thus, the datum provokes the conformal response, and the first phase of subjective immediacy is the enjoyment of the provoked response.

To appreciate fully the distinction between dative phase and responsive phase, we must recognize also that the supersessional process necessarily involves accumulation and integration, as well as conditioned creation. This means that in every instance of supersession, as we saw in the previous chapter, the superseding element not only reacts to, but in some fashion also integrates within itself, the superseded element (PR 225, 250). Accordingly, the responsive phase must be construed not only in its character of being a provoked response to the dative phase, but also in its character of being the integration of the provoking datum and the pro-voked response. When this integration is completed, the newly emerged phase is found to include the dative phase as its subordinate component. Precisely because of this subordination of the earlier to the later, it has been easy for many Whiteheadian commentators to lose sight of the fact that the dative phase is supersessionally earlier than the responsive phase.

To avoid losing sight of the supersessional order of phases in an occa-sion's becoming, as well as to capture the unique contribution each phase makes to the total constitution of the completed occasion, I analyze each phase into two subphases: a process-subphase and a product-subphase. Here by the process-subphase is meant the creative activity as in the very act of creating, and by the product-subphase is meant the immediate outcome of the creative subphase. When we consider a proper phase as in its process-subphase, the analytic emphasis is likely to fall on the emerging elements which are that phase's peculiar contribution to the emerging constitution of the occasion. When, on the other hand, we consider that same phase as in its product-subphase, the analytic emphasis is likely to fall on the achieved synthesis whereby the earlier phase has been incorpo-rated into the completed later phase. We are then emphasizing also the just completed phase in its character of being a datum for the next creative subphase (PR 327).

It should be evident that the complete analysis of a phase must do justice to both its creative process-subphase and its created product-subphase. Nonetheless, because the analysis of a phase is necessarily *post mortem*, the process-subphase often receives less attention than the product-subphase. This was obviously the case, for example, in my most recent characterization of the dative phase. On the other hand, the just given characterization of the responsive phase emphasized the creation of conformal subjective forms, but did not make explicit their synthesis with the individual components of the dative phase. Accordingly, in order to further the understanding of the repetitive elements in experience, let me now reconsider the dative and responsive phases so as to focus on the process-subphase of the former, and on the product-subphase of the latter.

3. Repetition in the dative phase

The first process-subphase in the becoming of an occasion is a creative action mediating between what is given for that subphase and what the subphase itself produces. What is *produced* by the subphase is its own product-subphase, more commonly known as the dative phase. What is *given for* the process-subphase is the universe itself, both in its character of being a community of occasions which are already become, and in its character of being a pure potentiality for the becoming of other occasions. About what the universe is by way of pure potentiality, I can say at this time only that it involves eternal extension and eternal creativity, as well as God and the eternal objects. Fortunately, my immediate concern is with what the universe is by way of actuality—that is, with the universe insofar as it is a nexus of actualities already attained. What the universe is by way of actuality relative to the becoming of an occasion is what Whitehead usually means by the *actual world* of that occasion (PR 351, 256, 42). Unfortunately, the term 'actual world' hides a systematic ambiguity which I must soon expose and explain. For the moment, let me say that, in one sense of the term, the actual world of an occasion is what is given for the first process-subphase in the becoming of that occasion.

In the organic philosophy, it is an ultimate fact that what the universe is by way of actuality always conditions and limits what the universe is by way of potentiality. This means that the pure potentiality for the becoming of an occasion is always conditioned and limited by the actual world of that occasion (PR 101). The thus limited and conditioned potentiality is the *real* or *natural* potentiality—Whitehead uses both terms indifferently—from which will spring the nascent occasion's successive phases of feeling (PR 101, 227; S 36). The transformation of the pure potentiality for an occasion into the real or natural potentiality for the occasion's own process of feeling is the creative achievement of the first process-subphase in the occasion's becoming. The subphase achieves this transformation by structuring a finite region of extension so as both to provide the region with a determinate boundary, and to reproduce within it every completed occasion already in existence relative to the origination of the bounded region (S 36). The region thus bounded, thus structured, and thus including the objectification of every past occasion, is the *real potentiality* for every subsequent phase of the occasion's becoming (PR 101, 124, 227, 441, 470). The region in question is also the first product-subphase in the occasion's becoming and is, therefore, the first phase of the occasion's existence. The occasion's first phase of existence *is* the real potentiality for all its subsequent phases of existence. It is both their *potentiality* and their *datum*.

The dative phase, I argue in later chapters, is the occasion's extensive standpoint of relativity (PR 202, 434–35); by it, the occasion is anchored to the state of the universe which gave it birth. The occasion's standpoint transcends, and is transcended by, the standpoints of the past actualities constituting its correlative actual world. To that extent, it also transcends, and is transcended by, the standpoint of its actual world, the latter standpoint being construed as the aggregate of the standpoints of the occasions constituting that actual world. In this sense, then, the occasion's actual world is *beyond*, or *without*, the occasion's standpoint. Nonetheless, by reason of the fact that each past occasion has been reproduced within the occasion's standpoint, the actual world is also *immanent*, or *within* that standpoint. Moreover, it is only as objectified within the occasion's standpoint that the actual world can be felt by the occasion. Accordingly, the standpoint, or datum, "which is the primary phase in the process constituting an actual entity, is nothing else than the actual world itself in its character of a possibility for the process of being felt" (PR 101).

This last characterization of the datum uncovers the systematic ambiguity attaching to the term 'actual world'. The ambiguity is systematic because it is a function of the twofold reality of every completed occasion. Thus, corresponding to what every completed occasion is as its own *original* self, there is a meaning of 'actual world' signifying what every actual world is as composed of the *original selves* of completed occasions. In the same manner, corresponding to what every completed occasion is as its own *reproduced* self, there is a meaning of 'actual world' signifying what every actual world is as composed of the *reproduced selves* of completed occasions. In respect to the first meaning, the actual world is a given for the first subphase of the creative process originating the new occasion correlative with that actual world. In respect to the second meaning, the actual world is a given for the first phase of feeling, and for all subsequent phases of feeling, in that same creative process. In the second sense of the term, *and only in that sense,* the actual world is the *real potentiality* for the conformal feelings generated by the responsive phase, and for the more original feelings generated by the phases of becoming subsequent to the responsive phase. Thus, the actual world, in the *second sense* of the term, is a real potentiality for creativeness beyond the standpoint of the actual world, in the *first sense* of the term.

According to this account of the twofold meaning of 'actual world', or, more accurately, of the twofold reality of actual worlds, "relative to any actual entity, there is a 'given' world of settled actual entities *and* a 'real' potentiality which is the datum for creativeness beyond that standpoint" (PR 101; italics mine). Given my interpretation of the full import of the relativity principle, there should be nothing surprising about the twofold reality of each actual world. An actual world, considered as a nexus of past occasions, is a *being.* Like any other being, the actual world *qua* its own original self is a *transcendent capacity* for the determination of its correlative actual occasion; and, like any other being, the actual world *qua* its re-produced self is a realized, *immanent determinant* of its correlative actual occasion. In its first role, the actual world is relevant to the creative process originating the dative phase of the occasion; in its second role, the actual world is relevant to the creative process originating the occasion's successive phases of feeling. In both roles, as Whitehead's conception of an object or being demands, the actual world "is relevant to something not itself" (PR 366–67). Thus, the twofold reality of an occasion's actual world "exemplifies the metaphysical principle that every 'being' is a potential for a 'becoming'" (PR 101).[5]

An occasion's actual world, in the second sense of the term, is the *objective content* of the occasion's experience (PR 101). The occasion's objective content, it can hardly be said too often, is the *datum* for the occasion's successive phases of feeling. Thus, the datum for feeling is made up of the objectifications, or reproductions, of the settled actualities constituting the actual world in the first sense of the term—constituting, that is, the actual world *qua* 'given' for the process-subphase begetting the dative phase or objective content. In Whitehead's own words, the "'given' world provides determinate data in the form of those objectifications of themselves which the characters of its actual entities can provide" (PR 101), and the thus provided "objectifications constitute the objective conditions from which an actual occasion . . . initiates its successive phases of feeling" (PR 489). Accordingly, the process-subphase that begets the dative phase may be construed as being the creative activity by which "what is settled in actuality is repeated under limitations, so as to be 'given' for immediacy" (PR 208). Therefore, the subjective immediacy, which first emerges with the responsive phase, always finds the objectifications as already in being, and is in no way involved in their production (PR 356, 234–35).

To sum up: The dative phase of an occasion is produced by the first process-subphase in the becoming of that occasion, and contains a reproduction, or objectification, of the actual world that was a given for that first process-subphase. As thus reproduced, and only as thus reproduced, the actual world is a datum for the subjective immediacy of the occasion. Since the dative phase is, for the most part, the actual world as a realized, immanent determinant of the occasion, it follows that the dative phase is both the aboriginal component of the occasion's constitution and the immediate datum for its experience. The occasion's phases of feeling start *from* that datum (S 86–87; PR 101, 117–18, 227, 232, 489; AI 269).

4. Repetition in the conformal phase

In keeping with the characterization of the dative phase just completed, we must construe the responsive phase as the *second* process-subphase in the becoming of an occasion. This new subphase is a creative action mediating between its datum and its product. Its datum is the occasion's dative phase; its product is the occasion's *first* phase of feeling. Each component feeling of this new product-subphase results from the fusion of an individual objectification in the datum with an individual subjective form produced by the responsive activity in conformation to the definiteness, or subjective form, of that objectification. The responsive phase, therefore, not only creates the conformal subjective forms, but also *incorporates* the dative phase into the first phase of feeling. By reason of this incorporation, the new occasion is now an individual immediacy of experience analyzable into *one* subject with *many* feelings. A new subject has been born, but with indeterminations awaiting its own subsequent activity of self-determination. The newborn subject, it must be noted, has arisen from, but also includes within itself, its own dative phase.

As the immediate product of the responsive phase, the newborn subject finds itself existing as in the act of severally feeling its data in ways imposed by, and conformal to, the data. The subject's many feelings are not yet integrated with one another, but each particular feeling is the synthesis of a particular objectification with a particular subjective form conformally derived from it. Thus, every particular feeling is a concrete relation whose particularity cannot be abstracted from the particularity of its relata. But this does not alter the fact that the objective and subjective components of each particular feeling are produced in two supersessionally successive stages: first, there is the production of the objective datum, which is the repetition of a past actuality; then, there is the production of conformal subjective form, which is the re-enactment of a quality characterizing the definiteness of the reproduced actuality. The latter product, however, absorbs the former into a synthetic union which is the particular feeling in question. Moreover, the emergence of the multiplicity of particular feelings and the emergence of the nascent subject are one and the same. There is no tearing the emerging subject and the emerging multiplicity of feelings from one another. Accordingly, the occasion's first phase of feeling is the occasion as in its first phase of subjective existence.

It would be difficult to exaggerate the importance of correctly understanding the production and nature of the initial feelings with which the subject is born. They play a basic role in the interrelated organic theories of efficient causation, of non-sensuous perception, of the irreversibility of time, and of the endurance of nature. Also, they are presupposed by all the other kinds of feelings posited by the organic philosophy. Yet these initial feelings are the ones most often misunderstood or misrepresented in the received interpretations. For example, the vast majority of Whiteheadian scholars take these feelings to be produced *by* the subject, and almost as many confuse the repetition involved in the objectification of past actualities with the repetition of qualitative definiteness involved in the conformation of subjective forms. It follows that we must examine the subject's initial feelings with the utmost care.

The feelings with which the occasion's subjective immediacy is born are referred to by Whitehead in a variety of ways: first, as 'conformal feelings', when he wishes to emphasize the *reproductive* character of their subjective forms (PR 173, 249, 364; AI 325–26); second, as 'causal feelings', when he wishes to stress that they constitute the machinery of *efficient causation* by which a new, but incomplete, subject is created (PR 361); third, as 'simple physical feelings' when he wants to emphasize that they have each the *simplest physical datum* possible, a single objectified actual entity, and that each is thereby an instance of the *simplest act of perception* possible (PR 361); and fourth, as 'primary physical feelings', when he wants to stress that they compose the *first* phase of physical feelings (PR 365). Each of these four ways of referring to the subject's initial feelings highlights a different aspect of their nature and function. Although my immediate concern is with the reproductive aspect of these feelings, it will prove helpful to consider the three other aspects as well.

In a conformal feeling, an eternal object already ingressed as characterizing the subjective form of an individual objectification in the dative phase of an occasion is reingressed as a character of the subjective form of the nascent subject's positive prehension of that objectification (PR 364, 446–47; AI 325–28). By reason of these two ingressions, the one eternal object is functioning both *datively* and *conformally* in the one self-same occasion (PR 249). In other words, the one eternal object, in virtue of its two ingressions, is functioning as a partial determinant of both the objective datum and the subjective form of one of the initial feelings with which the occasion's subjective immediacy is born (PR 364, 249; AI 235–36). If, for example, the ingressed eternal object constitutes an emotion, then the nascent subject "enjoys the emotion both *objectively* as belonging to the past, and also *formally* as continued in the present" (AI 236; italics mine). Thus, the whole point of the Doctrine of Conformation of Feeling, as Whitehead refers to it in AI, is that "there is a continuity between the subjective form of the immediate past occasion and the subjective form of its primary prehension in the origination of the new occasion" (AI 235).

We have now seen that each conformal feeling displays "a characteristic which has been variously described as 're-enaction', 'reproduction', and 'conformation'" (PR 364). But the description of the nature and function of the subject's initial feelings is not exhausted by this account of their conformal character. For the activity whereby an occasion's initial phase of feelings is created is the very same activity whereby the subject of those feelings is also created—created, that is, as in the first, partly indeterminate, stage of its existence. Therefore, the subject thus created cannot be the cause of the objectifications that are given for it, and cannot be the cause of the initial conformal definiteness of its subjective forms. My point is that when we consider the production of the occasion's two earliest phases, the dative phase and the conformal phase, we are dealing with the process of *efficient causation* by which an occasion is transcendentally begotten, and we are not dealing with the immanent process of *final causation* by which the already begotten occasion completes those aspects of its existence that were left indeterminate by its efficient causes. Accordingly, I must now examine the initial feelings of a subject in respect to those of their characteristics whereby each can be understood as an act of efficient causation.

The causal character of each initial feeling requires for its understanding an analysis involving: first, the earlier *attained actuality* whose objectification functions as the objective datum of the feeling in question; second, the *objectification* itself, which is an abstractive reproduction of the attained actuality, and which exhibits that actuality in the guise of being the subject of one of its component feelings; third, the *subjective form* whose fusion with the objectification constitutes the synthetic unity which is the initial feeling under surveyance; and fourth, the *novel subject* entertaining the initial feeling in question. Now, Whitehead leaves no doubt that he construes the earlier attained actuality as the *cause* of which the initial feeling is the *effect* (PR 361). This means that, in due time, I have to explain the earlier actuality in its function of constituting a transcendent decision in respect to how it is to be objectified in, and initially conformed by, a later actuality. At this time, however, the point to emphasize is that Whitehead construes the novel subject entertaining the initial feeling, or effect, as "the actual entity 'conditioned' by the effect" and that "this 'conditioned' actual entity will *also* be called the 'effect'" (PR 361; italics mine). Thus, the newborn subject itself, as well as each of its initial feelings, is an *effect produced by the attained actualities in its actual world*. In other words, in the conformal phase of its existence, an occasion is entirely the product of the efficient past, and is not in any way the cause of itself. Accordingly, each subject, through no choice of its own, is *thrown* into existence as conformally feeling its given actual world. The actual world both produces and conditions it.

To the conformal and causal characters of a subject's initial feelings, I must now add their perceptual character. The most primitive act of perception posited by the organic philosophy is a simple physical feeling (PR 361). Such a feeling "has as its datum only one actual entity, and this actual entity is objectified by one of its feelings" (PR 375). This definition of a simple physical feeling involves an implicit reference to the twofold reality of an attained actuality; there is a reference to the attained actuality as its own original self, and there is a reference to the attained actuality as its own objectified, or reproduced, self. To explain the perceptual nature and function of simple physical feelings, I must make explicit the twofold involvement of the earlier attained actualities serving in two ways as data for those feelings.

In the generation of a simple physical feeling, we first notice, an earlier attained actuality serves as the absolutely *initial datum* for the process generating that feeling. The objectification of that actuality, we notice also, is not only a component of the feeling generated, but is also a datum, an *objective datum*, for the generation of the feeling's other component, its conformal subjective form. The objective datum is itself the reproduction of a feeling entertained by the initial datum. This reproduced feeling, Whitehead tells us,

> is the 'objectification' of *its* subject for the subject of the simple physical feeling. The initial datum is objectified as being the subject of the feeling which is the objective datum: the objectification is the 'perspective' of the initial datum. (PR 361)

With this characterization of objectification as a perspective of the initial datum, Whitehead uncovers the aspects of a simple physical feeling whereby it may be understood as a primitive act of perception. In Whitehead's own words, "The actual entity which is the initial datum is the actual entity perceived, the objective datum is the 'perspective' under which that actual entity is perceived, and the subject of the simple physical feeling is the perceiver" (PR 361–62).

Of course, a simple physical feeling is not an example of sense perception, which for Whitehead is a derivative and more complex mode of perception, what he technically calls 'perception in the mode of presentational immediacy' (PR 474). Much less is it an example of conscious perception, which involves intellectual analysis as well as a synthesis of primitive and derivative modes of perception. Rather, a simple physical feeling is an instance of what Whitehead variously terms 'physical perception' (PR 365), 'physical memory' (PR 365; IS 244), 'non-sensuous perception' (AI 231–33), and, in a more technical vein, 'perception in the mode of causal efficacy' (PR 184, 246; S 43–49). A new subject is born as entertaining many such feelings, one for each actuality in its past. Thus, the subject's simple physical feelings constitute the first phase of its perceiving in the mode of causal efficacy. In the subsequent phases of its becoming, the subject's perception in the causal mode becomes increasingly more complex by reason of the integration of simple physical feelings with one another, and with conceptual feelings; but, as in the first phase of this mode of perception, the subject is one perceiver with *many* unintegrated perceptions of past actualities.

Let there be no doubt that what the subject perceives in each of its simple physical feelings *is* a past actuality. To be sure, what it perceives directly is the objectification of the past actuality. It perceives the objective datum and not the initial datum. But the objective datum and the initial datum are *two instances of the same particular actuality*. For although objectification abstracts from the full definiteness of the initial datum, it does not abstract from those elements of the initial datum on which its self-identity is predicated. Thus, the objective datum *is* the past actuality, albeit under an abstraction or perspective. The subject perceives the past actuality *qua* its objectification or reproduced self.

That the objective datum is a new instance of the initial datum is the main reason why Whitehead construes the objective datum, as well as the initial datum, as being a *cause* of the subject that prehends it (PR 364). Indeed, Whitehead makes it very clear that we are to construe the objectifications of past actualities as being the *efficient causes* out of which an actual occasion arises (PR 134). Moreover, the non-numerical identity of initial datum and objective datum is also a reason why the objectification of a past actuality is termed 'causal objectification'; for each such objectification is the repetition in a new occasion, which is the effect, of a past occasion, which is one of the efficient causes of that effect. The cause's *original self* transcends the new occasion; but the cause's *reproduced self* is immanent in it. Thus, the activity producing the objectification is a process of efficient causation whereby a transcendent cause of a new occasion becomes both an immanent constituent of, and an *object for*, the new occasion. This means that causal objectification is not only the first step in the production of the effect, but is also the *objectification of the cause for the effect*.

The non-numerical identity of an attained actuality with its causal objectification in another actuality explains the fact that 'efficient cause' has the same systematic ambiguity that attaches to all terms signifying repeatable entities. The attained actuality is a transcendent capacity for the efficient causation productive of a new occasion, and its causal objectification is the realized immanent efficient cause of the occasion in question. Moreover, as initial datum and objective datum, respectively, the attained actuality and its causal objectification are both causes of a conformal feeling belonging to the new occasion. The initial datum is the cause of the feeling's objective datum; and the objective datum is itself the cause of the feeling's conformal subjective form. However, since the initial datum and the objective datum are, in a non-numerical sense, the *same* entity, this means that the past actuality is the one efficient cause of the initial conformal feeling by which the new occasion feels the past actuality. This means also that causal objectifications "express the causality by which the external world fashions the actual occasion in question" (PR 489). But, since each causal objectification must be felt conformally, the causality fashions not only the objective content, but also the initial subjective form, of the new actual occasion. It fashions both the dative phase and the conformal phase of a new occasion. In short, it fashions a new subject as in the very first phase of its existence.

The experience of the subject thus fashioned is in every way repetitive. Its objective content is made up of 'old' occasions, abstractively repeated, and its subjective content is made up of 'second-hand' characters, re-productively derived from the objective content. It follows that the subject's initial conformal feelings are *not* the feelings Whitehead has in mind when he speaks of the rush of feelings through which repetition is over-whelmed by novel immediacy (PR 206–07, 234–35). On the contrary, conformal feelings are the metaphysically necessary instances of repetition in experience. Additional repetitive elements may appear in the later phases of an occasion's experience, but their appearance is not a meta-physical necessity. What are metaphysically necessary are the objectifica-tion of the past in the present and the conformation of the present's immediacy to the definiteness of the objectified past. However, although conformal feelings are *not* the feelings whereby "*repetition* [is] transformed into *novel immediacy*" (PR 207), they *are* the feelings which transform—or, as Whitehead puts it, which *merely* transform—"the objective content into subjective feelings" (PR 250). The point is that the subjective immediacy associated with conformal feelings is *not* novel except in a numerical sense. There is a new subject, but its immediacy is defined by second-hand qualities derived from an objective content which is also second-hand.

To sum up: The second process-subphase in the becoming of an occa-sion is an unoriginative, conformal response to the objectifications in the dative phase. Its product-subphase is what Whitehead refers to as the conformal phase of the occasion. The conformal phase is both the *second* product-subphase of the occasion's existence, and the *first* phase of the occasion's existence *qua* subject. But the completed conformal phase sub-sumes under itself the dative phase produced by the first process-sub-phase. Thus, by reason of the conformal response, the dative phase has been incorporated into a phase of simple physical feelings for which its component objectifications serve as objective data. The occasion *qua* sub-ject is born as the feeler of those feelings. In respect to each of its simple physical feelings, therefore, the newborn subject is the product of a two-stage act of efficient causation. First, a past actuality is objectified as the subject of one of its feelings so as to become, in that guise, a component of the dative phase for a new subject. Then, the new subject is born with the initial definiteness of its immediacy conformed to that objectification. Thus, the subject's initial physical feelings are at once causal, perceptual, and conformal. They are the means by which the subject is constituted and conditioned by its efficient *causes*, and they are also the means by which the subject *perceives* both its constituent causes and its own *conformation* to those causes. In other words, what the subject perceives, in its first phase of immediacy, is the efficacy of the objectifications in its dative phase in respect to the initial determination of the definiteness of its own subjective form. In short, for Whitehead, the "first phase in the immediacy of the new occasion is that of the conformation of feelings. The feeling as enjoyed by the past occasion is present in the new occasion as datum felt, with a subjective form conformal to that of the datum" (AI 235–36).

5. Repetition and novelty in the mental phases

The subject's conformal feelings are its *first* physical feelings. That is why Whitehead refers to them as the *primary* physical feelings. But they are primary in two additional senses. For all other physical feelings, which arise in the subject's later phases of becoming, involve the integration of these primary physical feelings, either with each other or with conceptual feelings. Moreover, the subject's first conceptual feelings are themselves derived from its primary physical feelings. It follows that the subject's conformal feelings are also primary in the sense of being its first feelings of any kind, and are primary, too, in the sense of being presupposed by all the subject's other feelings, either as their components or as the sources from which they derive.

My immediate concern is with the conceptual feelings that are immediately derived from the occasion's primary physical feelings; for they constitute the third phase in the occasion's becoming—and its third phase of a repetitive nature as well. It must be noted, in this regard, that there are three major supersessional stages in an occasion's process of feeling: first, the responsive or conformal stage, whose initial explanation I have just completed; second, the supplemental stage, which I must now begin to explain; and third, the satisfaction, which is the ultimate, all-encompassing feeling by which all the occasion's earlier feelings are finally integrated (PR 323, 249). But the process of feeling, as opposed to the final product of the process, lies in the conformal and supplemental stages.

The latter stage, which supersedes the former, "starts with two subordinate phases of conceptual origination, and then passes into phases of
integration, and of reintegration," in which additional feelings emerge
(PR 378). Thus, the two earliest phases of the supplemental stage are
concerned with the creation of conceptual feelings.

As it will turn out, there is a significant overlap between the two phases
of conceptual feelings; but, insofar as an order is discernible, the first
phase is termed the phase of 'conceptual reproduction', and the second,
the phase of 'conceptual reversion' (PR 380–81). The supersessional distinction between these two phases, if somewhat vague, is nonetheless
important; for the demarcation between them constitutes the dividing line
between the occasion's earlier, unoriginative phases and its later, originative phases. It constitutes in fact the dividing line between the old and the
new in an occasion of experience.

The generation of the phase of conceptual *reproduction* is governed by
the fourth Categoreal Obligation. In the categoreal scheme of PR, this
category reads as follows:

> (iv) *The Category of Conceptual Valuation.* From each physical feeling
> there is the derivation of a purely conceptual feeling whose datum is
> the eternal object determinant of the definiteness of the actual entity,
> or of the nexus, physically felt. (PR 39–40)

Thus, this category, as Whitehead reminds us, "concerns conceptual reproduction of physical feeling" (PR 40). Accordingly, we may posit a process-subphase whose datum is the phase of simple physical feelings, and
whose product-subphase is the phase of conceptual reproduction. By
reason of this new process-subphase, and in accord with the Category of
Conceptual Valuation, there is derived, from each simple physical feeling,
a conceptual feeling whose datum is the eternal object functioning not
only as a determinant of the definiteness of the physical feeling's objective
datum, but also as a determinant of the physical feeling's conformal
subjective form. Because the datum of each conceptual feeling merely
reproduces for its subject an eternal object already functioning as a determinant of both the objective content and the subjective form of that
subject, the conceptual feelings of this first supplemental phase introduce
nothing new into the subject's experience. Their sole initial function is to
register conceptually what the subject is feeling physically (PR 379). For
this reason, conceptual reproduction is also termed conceptual registration
(PR 380).

The difference between an object as a transcendent capacity for determination and that same object as an immanent realized determinant is the
only difference between an eternal object as the datum of a derivative
conceptual feeling, and that same eternal object as exemplified in the
objective datum and subjective form of the physical feeling from which
the conceptual feeling in question is derived. Here again the dual reality
which the principle of relativity attributes to all entities, or objects, is of
the utmost importance. Thus, when the subject feels the eternal object
conceptually, it is feeling it in respect to its "primary metaphysical character of being an 'object', that is to say, feeling its *capacity* for being a realized
determinant of process" (PR 366). The eternal object is *really* ingressed as
the datum of the conceptual feeling, but its ingression withholds the
immediate realization of its capacity to confer determination (PR 445).
Accordingly, as in its phase of conceptual reproduction the new occasion
does not exhibit any additional determination, let alone any *novel* determination. Therefore, although in this phase there is a conceptual registration of physical experience, nothing really new is experienced in it. But
the emergence of novelty is at hand.

The generation of the phase of conceptual *reversion* is governed by the
fifth Categoreal Obligation. In the categoreal scheme, this category reads
as follows:

(v) *The Category of Conceptual Reversion.* There is secondary origination
of conceptual feelings with data which are partially identical with,
and partially diverse from, the eternal objects forming the data in the
first phase of the mental pole. The diversity is a relevant diversity
determined by the subjective aim. (PR 40)

Thus, this category, as Whitehead reminds us, "concerns conceptual
diversity from physical feeling" (PR 40). But it also concerns diversity
from the data of the conceptual feelings of the first phase. Accordingly,
we may posit a process-subphase whose datum is the phase of conceptual
reproduction, and whose product-subphase is the phase of conceptual
reversion. Added together, the two product-subphases of conceptual feelings constitute what Whitehead refers to as the 'mental pole' of the
occasion. "Thus the first phase of the mental pole is conceptual reproduction, and the second phase is a phase of conceptual reversion" (PR 380–
81). Notice that in the first phase the eternal objects felt are all exemplified
in the actualities forming the past temporal world, whereas in the second
phase many of the eternal objects felt are *not* exemplified in the temporal

world. In its mental pole, therefore, the subject passes from prehending eternal objects as derivative from the temporal realm of actuality to prehending eternal objects as constitutive of the timeless realm of possibility. This passage has the nature of a *reversion* from realized possibilities to unrealized possibilities. Accordingly, as in its phase of conceptual reversion, the new subject is for the first time experiencing something which is truly *novel* in relation to the temporal world given for it. The strangle-hold of repetition has been broken, though only at the conceptual level.

In the subsequent phases of the occasion's supplemental stage, some of the conceptually prehended novelties will be admitted into immediate realization as determinants of the definiteness, or subjective form, of the occasion in question. Novelty will then have entered the subjective side of the occasion's physical constitution. Moreover, to the extent that the conceptual novelties are admitted into realization as determinants of certain feelings (*i.e.*, transmuted feelings) of presentational immediacy, novelty will also enter the objective side of the occasion's physical make-up. To avoid confusion in this regard, it is worth noting here, if only in passing, that, in the organic philosophy, the objective-subjective contrast does *not* correspond to the physical-mental contrast. Subjectively felt emotions, for example, are as physically real as are the physical organisms that provoke them. The felt fear is as physical as the roaring lion. But the former falls on the subjective side of experience, whereas the latter falls on the objective side. Indeed, at the level of inorganic occasions of experience, the emotional subjective forms are construed as scalar forms of physical energy. Similarly, the objective content of experience is construed as including conceptual prehensions, and other mental feelings, entertained by the objectified occasions. In fact, in the organic philosophy, the purely mental is to be equated only with the conceptual feelings of the mental pole.

I have digressed. The point to emphasize now is that novelty in physical realization derives from, and thus presupposes, novelty in conceptual realization. Therefore, the category of conceptual reversion "is the category by which novelty enters the world" (PR 381). Since this category becomes operative only in the occasion's phase of conceptual reversion, it follows that the occasion's three earlier phases of existence are devoid of novelty, whether physical or conceptual. This is why the dative phase, the conformal phase, and the phase of conceptual reproduction, are construed as unoriginative; they are really involved in the creation of a new occasion, but the content they give to that occasion—physical or conceptual—is *not* new. The truly originative phases are the supplemental phases that begin with the phase of conceptual reversion. Moreover, conceptual reversion is what makes possible the subsequent enrichment of the occasion's definiteness through the physical ingression of relevant novelties (PR 381). The second phase of the mental pole, we must conclude, is what makes possible the transformation of repetition into novel immediacy.

6. Conceptual novelty and God's primordial nature

So far, my analysis of an occasion's mental pole has made no mention of the metaphysical relevance of God's primordial nature. The reason for this is that I have been considering the mental pole solely in its relation to the temporal world, which is the non-divine component of the occasion's actual world (PR 377). In respect to that relation, conceptual reproduction is understood as the mental registering of eternal objects that are already physically realized in the temporal world, whereas conceptual reversion is understood as the mental grasping of eternal objects that are not yet physically realized in the temporal world, but which are proximately relevant to, and hence compatible for synthesis with, those that are already physically realized. The problem with this analysis is that it leaves unexplained the germaneness of the eternal objects felt in the phase of conceptual reversion. To provide an adequate explanation of their germaneness, it is necessary that the occasion's mental pole be considered in the light of the total actual world begetting the occasion—that is, it is necessary to consider the occasion in relation to the actual world as including both God's primordial nature and the temporal world.

Considering the relevance of God's primordial nature at once provides the required explanation and abolishes the Category, *but not the phase*, of Conceptual Reversion. Here is what Whitehead has to say on the issue:

The question, how, and in what sense, one unrealized eternal object can be more, or less, proximate to an eternal object in realized ingression—that is to say, in comparison with any other unfelt eternal object—is left unanswered by this category of reversion. In conformity with the ontological principle, this question can be answered only by reference to some actual entity. Every eternal object has entered into the conceptual feelings of God. Thus, a more fundamental account must ascribe the reverted conceptual feeling in a temporal subject to its conceptual feeling derived, according to Category IV, from the hybrid physical feeling of the relevancies conceptually ordered in God's experience. In this way, by the recognition of God's characterization of the creative act, a more complete rational explanation is attained. The category of reversion is then abolished; and Hume's principle of the derivation of conceptual experience from physical experience remains without any exception. (PR 381–82).

A more fundamental account of conceptually reverted feelings must now be given.

In respect to his primordial nature, the causal objectification of God in the dative phase of an occasion is effected in terms of the divine conceptual feeling whose data and subjective form are most relevant to the eternal objects exhibited in the temporal components of the occasion's dative phase. As thus objectified, God serves as the objective datum for one of the simple physical feelings constituting the occasion's first phase of subjective immediacy. Accordingly, the nascent subject's initial conformal feeling of God is a *hybrid* physical feeling.[6] Thus, in the primary phase of physical feelings, the new concrescent subject is feeling God

> in respect to God's conceptual feeling which is immediately relevant to the universe 'given' for that concrescence. There is then, according to the category of conceptual valuation, i.e. Categoreal Obligation IV, a derived conceptual feeling which reproduces for the subject the data and valuation of God's conceptual feeling. (PR 343)

This conceptual feeling derived from God is, on the one hand, an instance of conceptual reproduction, for it registers conceptually the occasion's hybrid physical feeling of God; but it is also, on the other hand, the first instance of conceptual reversion, for it feels many eternal objects that are not physically realized in the temporal world of its subject. Therefore, the occasion's first feeling of conceptual reversion is derived from one of its own physical feelings and not from one of its own conceptual feelings.

However, all of the occasion's subsequent feelings of conceptual reversion *are* derived from its first feeling of conceptual reversion. To understand the derivation of these other reverted feelings, we must note, first of all, that the conceptual feeling by which God's primordial nature is objectified in the occasion's dative phase is quite complex. In Chapter Four we shall see that, in this complex conceptual feeling, God is feeling what Whitehead terms 'an abstractive hierarchy of eternal objects'. For the moment, it is sufficient to notice that the complex conceptual feeling is itself the integration of many simpler conceptual feelings. The complex feeling integrates the subjective forms, *but not the data*, of the many simpler feelings. In other words, the complex feeling has one integral subjective form, but the eternal objects serving as its data remain uninte-grated, and thus are isolated from one another. The feeling's integral subjective form is a complex graduated appetition for the physical realiza-tion of the feeling's data, taken both singly and in sets.

Now, when a feeling of conceptual reproduction is derived from the temporal subject's hybrid feeling of God, what is reproduced for its subject are the data and the subjective form of the complex conceptual feeling by which God's primordial nature has been objectified. Accord-ingly, the subject's feeling of conceptual reproduction has a subjective form conformal with the subjective form of God's own conceptual feeling (PR 377). This means that the subject is feeling the eternal objects derived from God with an appetition for their physical realization. The question is, which of the eternal objects thus felt are to be physically realized? The answer can be provided only by the temporal subject itself as it autono-mously evaluates each of the eternal objects in question as possible con-tributors to its own definiteness. But each evaluation is itself a conceptual feeling having as its datum an eternal object derived from the initial conceptual reproduction of the subject's hybrid physical feeling of God. These new conceptual feelings, in other words, abstract their data from the initial conceptual reproduction derived from God. They are, there-fore, derivative feelings of conceptual reversion. Moreover, since the feeling from which they derive, though itself the very first instance of conceptual reversion, is a component of the phase of conceptual reproduc-tion, we must conclude that a phase involving many feelings of conceptual reversion does indeed follow, and is truly derived from, the phase of conceptual reproduction.

My point is that the abolition of the Category of Conceptual Reversion does not entail the abolition of the phase of conceptual reversion. Indeed, the Category is not so much abolished as it is *grounded* on the objective functioning of God's primordial nature. It can then be understood as covering the unique feeling of conceptual reproduction that is uniquely derived from a subject's hybrid physical feeling of God. It also covers all other conceptual feelings derived from this unique conceptual reproduc-tion. This feeling of conceptual reproduction is unique because it alone can introduce, for its subject, eternal objects that are not in any way exemplified in the subject's temporal world.[7] This is why the feeling in question may be construed also as the occasion's first feeling of conceptual reversion. But the subject's autonomous evaluation of the eternal objects provided by this unique conceptual feeling requires that there be derived from it additional, but simpler, feelings of conceptual reversion. The mental pole's phase of reverted feelings is thereby constituted. Thus, the true significance of the 'abolition' of the fifth Categoreal Obligation is to be sought not in the elimination of reverted feelings, for a phase of such feelings remains metaphysically necessary, but in the fact that conceptual novelty enters the temporal world only through the mediation of God's primordial nature (PR 377). This is the divine functioning by reason of which God is construed as "the ground of all order and of all originality" (PR 164).

7.   *Autonomy, physical novelty, and the integrative phases*

To further our understanding of reverted conceptual feelings, we must notice also that the conceptual feeling derived from a subject's hybrid physical feeling of God is the initial conceptual aim—or, as it is more frequently called, *the initial subjective aim*—which is to serve as the final cause guiding, but also being modified by, the subject's autonomous process of self-determination (PR 343). "In this sense God is the principle of concretion; namely, he is that actual entity from which each temporal concrescence receives that initial aim from which its self-causation starts" (PR 374). Thus, until the feeling of initial conceptual aim obtains, the subject is *not* self-causing, is *not* self-determining, is *not* autonomous. After this feeling obtains, however, the autonomy of the subject is ir-revocable and manifests itself in all subsequent phases of the occasion's becoming. This means that the subject's autonomous self-determination begins with the phase of conceptual reversion. The three earlier phases of the occasion's becoming—the dative phase, the conformal phase, and the phase of conceptual reproduction—are *not* phases of autonomous self-determination. Rather, they represent successive stages in the creative process by which the actual world begets, and partly determines, a new subject, which once it is thus begotten and until it reaches its satisfaction, "is the autonomous master of its own concrescence into subject-superject" (PR 374).

The autonomy of the subject does disturb or complete, as the case may be, the received content of the three earliest phases. Thus, the conceptual novelty introduced by the reverted feelings "disturbs the inherited 're-sponsive' adjustment of subjective forms" (PR 159). Thus, too, the auton-omy of the subject will affect the subjective forms, but not the data, of the conceptual reproductions derived from temporal occasions (PR 377). In other words, the datum of each conceptual reproduction is an eternal object derived, through no choice of the subject, from a conformal physical feeling; but the subjective form of the conceptual reproduction, though influenced and conditioned by the conformal feeling, is ultimately determined by the autonomous subject in accord with its initial subjective aim and its other reverted conceptual feelings. In this respect, then, the subject completes the final constitution of its conceptual reproductions in the light of its own conceptual reversions. But the converse is also true. For the subjective forms of all conceptual reproductions and all conceptual reversions are *valuations*, and, in accord with the Category of Subjective Harmony (the seventh Categoreal Obligation), "the valuations of conceptual feelings are mutually determined by the adaptation of those feelings to be contrasted elements congruent with the subjective aim" (PR 40–41; see also PR 389). This interplay between the reproductive and revertive phases of the mental pole is one of two reasons why they must be understood as partially overlapping. The other reason is that the first feeling of conceptual reversion, which is the initial subjective aim, belongs to the phase of conceptual reproduction.

Insofar as they do exhibit a discernible supersessional order, however, the phase of conceptual reproduction precedes, and is a datum for, the phase of conceptual reversion. To that extent, the earlier phase, provided we construe it as excluding the initial subjective aim, is the last purely *repetitive* phase in the occasion's becoming, whereas the later phase, provided we construe it as including the initial subjective aim, is the first phase in that becoming to involve *novelty* of content. But the content of the conceptually reverted feelings is novel only in relation to the temporal world. It is *not* novel in relation to the occasion's total actual world, which includes God's primordial nature. As a matter of fact, in the becoming of an actual occasion, the emergence of unqualified novelty is to be found only in the integrative phases of its supplemental stage. What emerges in those phases is a novelty of physical realization resulting from the subject's decision to realize a selection of the relevant conceptual novelties as immanent determinants of the definiteness of its subjective form, and of the integration of its primary feelings, physical and conceptual. Although such novelty is often negligible, so far as it does obtain in an actual occasion, it is an absolute novelty. It is something that has never been previously experienced in the universe, either by a temporal occasion or by God.

Since the emergence of physical novelty necessarily involves the physical ingression—and, therefore, the repetition—of eternal objects eternally entertained in God's primordial nature, it may seem a mistake to claim that the emerged physical realization is absolutely novel in relation to the total actual world, and not merely in relation to the temporal world. But the claim, though somewhat paradoxical, is in no way a mistake. I shall justify and explain it in Chapter Four. For now, it must suffice to say that, in God's primordial conceptual experience, eternal objects are isolated each from the others. Their capacity for joint physical ingression into the make-up of an actuality is prehended by God; but their conjoint ingression as immanent determinants is, for God's primordial nature, a pure possibility and in no way a realized fact. The primordial nature involves no feeling of eternal objects as really together. Thus, when two or more eternal objects are jointly ingressed, for the very first time in the universe, into the physical constitution of an actual occasion, something radically new has indeed emerged, something which has never been previously experienced, even by God. In fact, the enrichment of God's consequent nature results from the causal objectification in him of the temporal occasions with their novel physical achievements. Hence, just as God provides the temporal world with conceptual novelty, so too the temporal world provides God with physical novelty. "Either of them, God and the World, is the instrument of novelty for the other" (PR 529).

8. The ubiquity of repetition

The novelty of physical realization is not to be qualified in any manner. It may be negligible in importance, at least from a human perspective; but it is true, genuine, absolute novelty. It is something new in relation to the entire universe, not merely in relation to the temporal world of the occasion in which it emerges. Nonetheless, it is an inescapable fact that the realization of physical novelty involves the repetition of eternal objects. This last point is what I must emphasize at this time because our immediate concern in the past few sections has been with the role of repetition in experience. In that regard, we have considered five successive phases (or product-subphases) in the existence of an occasion: the dative phase, the conformal phase, the phase of conceptual reproduction, the phase of conceptual reversion, and (construing as one what are really many phases) the phase of integral feelings. All five phases, we have now seen, involve repetition.

My examination of these five phases constitutes, in effect, an analysis of the extent to which Whitehead spoke truly when he said that there is nothing left in experience if we tear repetition out of it. On the basis of that analysis we must conclude that this pronouncement, at least in respect to the internal coherence of the organic philosophy, is not much of an exaggeration. In fact, it *is* an exaggeration only because every actual occasion is numerically new and, more importantly, because every actual occasion involves some measure of physical novelty, however negligible. But in a more profound sense it is *not* an exaggeration at all, given that experience, as Whitehead construes it, would be impossible without the repetition of eternal objects and actual entities.

Consider in this respect the functioning of eternal objects in experience. Without the repetition of eternal objects involved in their physical ingressions as immanent determinants, no physical novelty is possible. Without their repetition as data for reverted conceptual feelings, the originative decisions of autonomous subjects become impossible. Without their repetition as data for the initial subjective aim, there would not even be an autonomous subject. Without their repetition as data for feelings of conceptual reproduction, there would be no mental registration of physical feelings. Finally, without their repetition, the subjective forms of simple physical feelings could not conform to the data of those feelings.

Consider next the functioning of earlier occasions and of God. Without the repetition of past actual occasions, there would be no objective world given for, or conformed to by, the initial subjective immediacy of a new actual occasion. Without the abstractive repetition of God's primordial nature, there would be no initial subjective aim to guide the subject's concrescence and no relevant conceptual novelties to lure the subject into originative activities.

In other words: Tear repetition out of experience and you will have torn from it the objectively real world that is both the first constituent of an occasion and the datum for its first phase of subjective immediacy. Tear repetition out of experience and there will be no conformation of present immediacies to past immediacies and hence no ground for the temporal endurance of nature. Tear repetition out of experience and there will be neither conceptual registration, nor conceptual novelty, nor any aim at novel self-definition. Tear repetition out of experience and physical novelty will evaporate. In short: tear repetition out of experience and there is nothing left!

9. Causal objectification, conformation, and self-formation

I have labored the role of repetition in experience for two main reasons: first, to exhibit the extent to which the organic metaphysical system is indeed based on the principle of relativity; and second, to begin a detailed explanation of a number of crucial organic doctrines that are variously misrepresented in most of the received interpretations. In respect to the first reason, my goal has been to demonstrate that the objective functioning of all entities presupposes, and is to be understood in terms of, their repeatability. To be is to be repeatable, and without the repetition of entities there could be no concrete relations between actualities—*that*, in a nutshell, is the whole point of the relativity principle. In respect to the second reason, my aim has been to provide a basis for the complete repudiation of a host of received misinterpretations regarding the closely related organic doctrines of efficient causation, causal objectification, and conformation. To that end, I have presented the first three phases of an occasion's existence in their true character of products of efficient causation; for I have shown that final causation begins only with the phase of conceptual reversion and is physically effective only in the subsequent phases of integration. To that same end, I have emphasized both the numerical difference between a past actual occasion and its causal objectification and the doctrinal difference between the causal objectification of actualities and the conformation of subjective forms.

The misrepresentations I wish to repudiate are well entrenched in the received interpretations. The ones requiring the most attention are enshrined in the commonplace, but erroneous, contention that an occasion's entire process of becoming is to be equated with its teleological process of concrescence. For this contention deprives the efficient process of transition of its genuine metaphysical function. Transition, I will argue in detail later, begets each novel occasion. In so doing it produces both the objectification of the past in the present and the initial conformation, physical and mental, of the present to the past. But if the becoming of an occasion is one and the same with its concrescence, then transition can have no constitutive function, and efficient causation must pass out of the picture. The activities of objectification and conformation must then be erroneously attributed to the autonomy of the novel subject.[8] On the basis of that attribution, it is then claimed that the past occasions are the efficient causes of the novel subject because it creates itself through its treatment of them and is thus affected by what they are. What is overlooked in this regard is that, if objectification and conformation issue from the subject's autonomous self-determination, the past occasions are the subject's *material* causes but are definitely not its *efficient* causes. Thus, the equation of becoming with concrescence either eliminates the doctrine of efficient causation altogether, or illegitimately replaces it with what in fact, if not in title, is no more than a doctrine of mere material causation.

The reduction of becoming to concrescence is but one of many dis-figurations suffered by Whitehead's complex doctrine of efficient causa-tion. Less widespread, but equally disfiguring, is the unwarranted identi-fication of causal objectification with physical conformation. But by far the most prevalent disfiguration results from the almost universal failure to recognize that the causal objectification of an actuality is the repetition of its self-identical particularity in and for, *but not by*, another actuality. Since the immanence of earlier actualities in later ones is produced by the efficient process of transition, these distortions of Whitehead's doctrine of efficient causation stand very much in the way of my attempt to elucidate the solidarity of actualities. Therefore, as my interpretation and develop-ment of the organic philosophy unfold, I shall have to address each received distortion at the moment most appropriate for its partial or complete refutation. My immediate concern, in keeping with the present task of explicating the relativity principle, is with the received confusions regarding the doctrine of causal objectification; for those confusions in-volve either identifying the repetition of conformation with the repetition of causal objectification, or, more commonly, ignoring that the causal objectification of an actuality is its repetition in a later actuality.

The major confusions regarding causal objectification are clearly and explicitly exemplified in Christian's influential interpretation of White-head's metaphysical system. According to Christian, the analysis of a new simple physical feeling reveals a novel subject taking into account an earlier occasion by repeating within the immediacy of its own experience some quality exhibited by the definiteness of the earlier occasion.[9] This qualitative repetition is, in Christian's account, the *only* repetition in-volved in, or presupposed by, the feeling under analysis.[10] Moreover, for Christian the repetition of the quality is brought about by an autonomous decision of the novel subject.[11] With this autonomously decided repeti-tion, Christian claims, the new subject at once conforms its definiteness to the definiteness of the earlier occasion *and* objectifies the earlier occa-sion.[12] The activity of conformation and the activity of objectification are one and the same.

From my point of view, of course, Christian's interpretation of this aspect of Whitehead's metaphysics is wrong on at least three counts: first, because he holds that "the *immediate* activity involved in objectification is the activity of the subject";[13] second, because he claims that "what effects the objectification is the subject's feeling of the object";[14] and third, because he maintains that "the notion of conformity of subjective form is the core of Whitehead's theory of causal objectification, and hence the crucial feature of his doctrine of social immanence."[15] Christian's first two claims ignore the fact that "objectifications constitute the objective conditions *from* which an actual occasion . . . *initiates* its successive phases of feeling" (PR 489; italics mine). In other words, they ignore the fact that the objectifications precede even the first phase of subjective feelings, and thus they precede also any activity that could be conceivably attributed to the subject. Similarly, the third claim takes no account of the fact that causal objectification precedes, and hence differs from, conformation. Indeed, this last claim flies in the face of Whitehead's explicit contention that "the past consists of the community of settled acts which, through their objectifications in the present act, establish the conditions to which that act must conform" (S 36).

One reason for Christian's confusion is his failure to recognize that in the organic philosophy there are two basic kinds of repetition.[16] There is the repetition of one actuality in another; this kind of repetition *is* the crucial feature of Whitehead's doctrine of immanence. This repetition of particulars is the true core of the theory of causal objectification. Then, too, there is the repetition of the definiteness of subjective form by which a new occasion is conformed to the objectification of an earlier occasion; this is the kind of repetition by reason of which the subjective form of a simple physical feeling is said to re-enact the definiteness of the feeling's objective datum. This repetition of universals is the core of the doctrine of conformation. The point is that causal objectification and conformation are two distinct doctrines corresponding to two different kinds of repetition.

Another reason for the confusion of causal objectification with conformation is the ambiguous meanings of the terms 'objectification' and 'datum'. For 'objectification', in addition to the meaning associated with the causal, presentational, and anticipatory modes of objectification, has a more general meaning. In this more general meaning the term refers to both the activity and the result of any process-subphase, insofar as the result is one object, or a datum, for a subsequent process-subphase. Obviously, the term 'datum' must share in the ambiguity of the term 'objectification'. Now, given the more general meanings of these ambiguous terms, it follows that each intermediate creative phase, insofar as it adds its results to those of the immediately antecedent phase, creates a new objective datum for the immediately subsequent phase. Accordingly, in this general sense, every phase of an occasion's becoming may be construed as a process of objectification, since what issues from its activity is an object, or a datum, for the subsequent phases or for the subsequent occasions. In this sense, then, the result of the conformal phase constitutes a complex objective datum for the phase of conceptual feelings. Hence, conformation does effect a kind of objectification, even though it does not effect the causal objectification of attained actualities.

But the general senses of 'objectification' and 'datum' must not be confused with the special senses in which those terms are associated with the efficient process whereby the many past occasions become one complex objective datum for the initial feelings of a new subject. This complex objective datum is made up of the causal objectifications of the past occasions. As Whitehead says,

> When it is desired to emphasize this interpretation of the datum, the phrase 'objective content' will be used synonymously with the term 'datum'. [Thus] the phrase 'objective content' is meant to emphasize the doctrine of 'objectification' of actual entities. (PR 230)

The datum provided by the settled past, Whitehead also says, "is the objective content of experience" (PR 227). Given this meaning of 'objective content', the difference between conformation and causal objectification is made abundantly clear by Whitehead when he says that "the conformal stage merely transforms the objective content into subjective feelings" (PR 250). Surely, the stage that *transforms* the objective content into subjective feelings cannot be the same stage that *creates* the objective content. Hence, the ambiguities of Whitehead's terminology aside, it is clear that the process of conformation presupposes, and is not the same as, the antecedent process of causal objectification.

Perhaps anticipating that his own faults of exposition would mislead his readers to exaggerate the scope of final causation, Whitehead made it abundantly clear also that the autonomy of the concrescent subject has no bearing on the causal objectifications composing the objective content of its experience:

> Again the selection involved in the phrase 'selective concrescence' is *not* a selection among the components of the objective content; for, by hypothesis, *the objective content is a datum.* The compatibilities and incompatibilities which impose the perspective, transforming the actual world into the datum, are inherent in the nature of things. Thus the selection is a *selection of relevant eternal objects* whereby what is a datum from without is transformed into its complete determination as a fact within. The problem which the concrescence solves is, *how* the many components of the objective content are to be *unified* in one felt content with its complex subjective form. (PR 233; italics mine)

In other words, the subject merely selects, by the autonomous valuations of its conceptual reversions, which relevant eternal objects are to be physically ingressed so as to produce an aesthetic unification of the many components of the objective content; for those components, it should be remembered, are not unified by the initial conformal feelings.

Moreover, the subject's autonomous selectivity presupposes its subjective aim (PR 374). There is no autonomous subject until there is a feeling of initial subjective aim. This is why Whitehead says that "the mental pole introduces the subject as a determinant of its own concrescence" (PR 380). Therefore, the subject's selective autonomy is necessarily subsequent to the phase of conceptual reproduction whereby the subject is endowed with its initial subjective aim. But the phase of conceptual reproduction itself presupposes, and thus is subsequent to, the phase of initial conformal feelings, *i.e.*, the phase of simple physical feelings constituting what Whitehead terms the 'physical pole' of the occasion (PR 366). Finally, the phase of conformal physical feelings itself presupposes, and thus is subsequent to, the dative phase or objective content. It follows that the autonomous selective activity of the subject presupposes, and is subsequent to, the first three phases of the occasion's existence. Accordingly, the three initial phases of an occasion's becoming are entirely outside the scope of the occasion's own final causation, and constitute the complex datum for the selective and integrative activity of the autonomous subject.

It should be noticed that the supersessional order of the two poles of an actual occasion—first the physical, then the mental—is an explicit tenet of Whitehead's metaphysics. "The mental pole starts with the conceptual registration of the physical pole" (PR 379). Indeed, the order of an actuality's two poles is a sufficient criterion for differentiating the temporal actualities from the one Divine Actuality:

> An actual entity in the temporal world is to be conceived as originated by physical experience with its process of completion motivated by consequent, conceptual experience initially derived from God. God is to be conceived as originated by conceptual experience with his process of completion motivated by consequent, physical experience, initially derived from the temporal world. (PR 524; see also 528)

There can be no doubt, therefore, that a temporal occasion's mental pole presupposes the existence of, and hence is supersessionally subsequent to, its physical pole. Moreover, since the autonomous activity of a temporal subject begins with the second phase of the mental pole, and since the physical pole is made up of the objective content and the conformal subjective forms, there can be no doubt either that the production of causal objectifications, and of conformal physical feelings, supersessionally precedes, and hence falls outside the scope of, the subject's immediate activity of self-formation.

What does fall under the scope of immediate self-formation is the origination of novel subjective forms by which the autonomous subject integrates its many initial physical feelings and its many initial conceptual feelings (PR 165, 359). The autonomous subject "admits or rejects, eternal objects which by their absorption into the subjective forms of the many feelings effect this integration" (PR 233–34). The integration weaves together, into a unity of experience, the two poles of the occasion. In this regard, it is important not to confuse the two poles with the earlier and later halves of the occasion's becoming. The two poles are the earliest stages of an occasion's existence; they are superseded by a third stage wherein the two poles grow together, or concresce, through the aesthetic integration of the physical with the mental. Thus, contrary to what Christian claims, a subject's immediate activity of self-realization is limited to this stage of integration and to a phase of reverted conceptual feelings preceding, and guiding, the integration. This complex aspect of the organic philosophy is aptly summarized by Whitehead as follows:

> Each actuality is essentially bipolar, physical and mental, and the physical inheritance is essentially accompanied by a conceptual reaction partly conformed to it, and partly introductory of a relevant novel contrast, but always introducing emphasis, valuation, and purpose. The integration of the physical and mental side into a unity of experience is a self-formation which is a process of concrescence, and which by the principle of objective immortality characterizes the creativity which transcends it. (PR 165/CPR 108)

10. Causal objectification as the reproduction of particulars

The main reason why Whitehead's theory of causal objectification has been so thoroughly misrepresented by Christian and, in one way or another, by most other interpreters is that, as children of philosophical tradition, they approached this theory convinced that particulars are precisely the sort of entities that cannot be repeated. As a result, they refused to take Whitehead literally whenever he said that earlier actualities are reproduced in later ones. Then, with considerable ingenuity they set about to interpret causal objectification in a way that would avoid positing the repeatability of actualities. Unfortunately, by so doing, they distorted not only the theory of causal objectification but also the entire metaphysical system of the organic philosophy. For they emptied the relativity principle of its metaphysical import the moment they disavowed the repetition of actual entities. Moreover, not having recognized the full import of the relativity principle, they could not hope to obtain an adequate elucidation of the solidarity of discrete individuals.

Let me now explain the bearing of the theory of causal objectification on the doctrine of solidarity. According to the thesis of solidarity, a completed occasion must both transcend, and be immanent in, all occasions later than itself. This is possible, I maintain, because the earlier occasion achieves immanence in the later one by being reproduced in it. The earlier occasion remains, *qua* superject, *outside* the later occasion; but the earlier occasion is also, *qua* its own reproduced self, *inside* the later occasion. The one occasion is both transcendent and immanent relative to the other. But there is a numerical difference between the earlier occasion as transcendent and that same occasion as immanent. The problem, of course, is to justify the identification of the completed occasion as such with its reproduction in another occasion. The discussion of *why* a superject and each of its causal objectifications are taken to be the 'same' entity must be postponed until the theory of the extensive continuum has been examined. However, *that* there is a numerical difference between a superject and each of its causal objectifications can and must be argued at this time.

In support of my interpretation of causal objectification as the reproduction of one actuality in another, I now point out that Whitehead speaks of the *many* objectifications of *one* settled actuality as being *beyond* that actuality. Thus, for him, as we saw earlier, an attained actuality is "a creative determination, by which the objectifications of the entity beyond itself are settled" (PR 130; also PR 337). The important question now is: In what sense are the objectifications of a settled actuality *beyond* itself? And the only intelligible answer, I contend, requires that there be a numerical difference between an attained actuality and each of its objectifications.

The meaning of 'beyond', in this context, is related to the extensive character of actual occasions. For, as I hope to demonstrate later, every actual occasion occupies or embodies a unique region of the extensive continuum, and there is no overlapping of such regions. In other words, the extensive regions occupied by actual occasions, each its own, are mutually transcendent. If this is true, and if by the many objectifications of a settled occasion is meant its reproductions *within* the extensive regions of later occasions, then Whitehead can legitimately claim that in its objectifications the settled occasion literally "transcends itself" (PR 347; see also AI 256). For the objectifications of the completed occasion *are literally beyond its own extensive region*. Thus, in each of its objectifications the completed occasion is transcending itself, while also being immanent in another occasion.

In this connection, I must now briefly consider two popular, but surely mistaken, interpretations of the doctrine of causal objectification. On one of these interpretations, the causal objectification of one occasion in another is taken to mean that an eternal object characterizing the earlier occasion is repeated in the later occasion.[17] This interpretation must be rejected because if it were true we would not be able to interpret causal objectification as the self-transcendence of an actual occasion. On this interpretation, we would simply have one instance of an eternal object transcending another instance of that same eternal object. But that universals should have mutually transcendent instantiations is hardly a new, much less a revolutionary, doctrine. Whitehead's true doctrine, however, is quite new and revolutionary; for it claims that concrete particulars, when completed, are reproduced within other concrete particulars, and thus achieve self-transcendence.

On the second popular interpretation of causal objectification, it is held that earlier occasions are included literally, and not merely as reproduced, in later occasions.[18] By virtue of this inclusion, the earlier occasion is both an object for, and a cause of, the later occasion's process of concrescence. Though closer to Whitehead's meaning, this interpretation of causal objectification must also be rejected because, if it were true, it would make no sense to speak of an actual occasion as transcending itself in each of its objectifications. For example, let us say that actual occasion A is causally objectified in actual occasion B. If this means that A is literally included (*sans* repetition) in B, then: first, it would be true that superject A is immanent in B; and, second, it would also be true that B transcends A, in the sense that B includes, but is more than A; but, third, it would *not* be true that A transcends itself. The inclusion of superject A in B does not make superject A self-transcendent.

Accordingly, on either of the interpretations of causal objectification just considered, the notion of a completed occasion transcending itself would be quite meaningless. If, on the other hand, we interpret superject A and the objectification of A in B as being numerically distinct, however identical in other respects, we can then provide the requisite meaning of 'self-transcendence'. For the extensive regions embodied by A and B do not overlap; whereas the reproduction of *A* in *B* embodies a subregion of *B*'s extensive region. Thus, the objectification of *A* in *B* is quite literally beyond *A*. Consequently, to the extent that *A* and its objectification in *B* are, in some non-numerical sense, the 'same' entity, *A* may truly be said to be self-transcendent.

The numerical distinction between a superject and each of its causal objectifications fits well with the characterization that Whitehead gives of an object as being both immanent and transcendent relative to the occasion for which it is an object. For the distinction between an object as a capacity for determination and an object as a realized determinant corresponds, I maintain, to the distinction between a completed occasion as superject and a completed occasion as causally objectified in a later occasion. In this regard, my contention is that the objective reality of a completed occasion is twofold. In itself, as superject, the completed occasion is a capacity, or potential, for the determination of occasions later than itself. As superject, it will be involved in the macroscopic processes whereby those later occasions are begotten; nevertheless, as superject, it will remain outside the extensive standpoints of those later occasions. As causally objectified or reproduced, however, the completed occasion will be involved in the microscopic process, or concrescent immediacy, of every occasion later than itself, and it will also be immanent in the extensive standpoint of each such occasion. In this manner, a completed occasion is, in one sense, a transcendent capacity for the determination of all later occasions, and is also, in another sense, an immanent determinant of each of those later occasions.

Let us reconsider our earlier example involving the causal objectification of *A* in *B*. On the doctrine of the twofold objective reality of *A*, *A qua* superject is a datum for the process of transition whereby *B* emerges as in its very first phase of existence. This process of transition at once begets the novel occasion *B* and reproduces in it the earlier occasion *A*.[19] As its original self, *A* continues to transcend *B*; but as its reproduced self, *A* is immanent in *B*, and is thus a realized determinant of *B*. Moreover, as reproduced or causally objectified, *A* is an object for the process of concrescence whereby *B* fashions its own ultimate definiteness; for the product of transition is the datum for concrescence. Consequently, *A* plays two objective roles: one for the transition that begets *B*; the other for *B*'s own concrescence. In both roles it is relevant to something not itself.

The numerical distinction between a superject and each of its causal objectifications is also evident in Whitehead's characterization of actuality as being both cumulative and reproductive. For, according to the organic philosophy, the actual universe is continually expanding by the addition of new actualities, each actuality transcending all others, yet also uniting within itself the reproduced selves of all other actualities (PR 438). In other words, the universe's creative advance leaves in its wake, as it were, an ever-growing multiplicity of attained actualities. This is the cumulative character of actuality. But the universe is not only a multiplicity of discrete actualities; it is also the solidarity of all actualities: each in all, and all in each (PR 254, 529). Thus, there is a solidarity of actualities because all the attained actualities that have accumulated in the wake of the universe's creative advance are reproduced within each new actuality in attainment at the utmost verge of the creative advance. This, I maintain, is what Whitehead means when, using 'time' figuratively in place of the more systematic notion of actuality's 'creative advance', he says that "time is cumulative as well as reproductive, and the cumulation of the many is not their reproduction as many" (PR 365).

In respect to the creative advance of the universe, then, or in respect to time in its metaphysical sense, superjects as such constitute the cumulative 'many', whereas the causal objectifications or reproductions of those superjects—their objective or transcendent functionings—in later occasions constitute the 'many' as reproduced. The cumulated many and the reproduced many are numerically distinct. But notice that, since the many as accumulated and the many as reproduced are, in some non-numerical sense, the 'same' entities, it is just as correct to say that the accumulated actualities lie within a novel occasion as it is to say that they lie outside it. Thus, there are two different, but intimately related, senses of 'cumulative character'. In the second sense, the causal objectification within an occasion of its antecedent world may be construed as the cumulative character of time, or, in more systematic terms, of the creative advance of actuality (PR 363). "The irreversibility of time depends on this character" (PR 363).

The double meaning of 'cumulative' is another instance of the systematic ambiguity which attaches, in the organic philosophy, to all terms denoting repeatable entities. Here it is worth noting again that what the universe is by way of attained actuality, relative to a new occasion, is constituted by all the superjects already accumulated, relative to the initiation of the new occasion's becoming. The universe thus constituted is termed the actual world of the occasion in question (PR 34, 101). But, as we saw earlier, the phrase 'the actual world of an actual entity' is also systematically ambiguous: it may refer to the accumulated actualities as their own original selves; or it may refer to the reproduction of those actualities within the actuality relative to which that settlement of actualities is defined. This double meaning of 'actual world' is systematic, we said earlier, because it follows from the fact that a superject and each of its causal objectifications, though numerically distinct, are yet taken to be the *same* entity. Speaking with broader generality, however, the double meaning is systematic because it follows from the principle of relativity. The double meaning merely mirrors the dual reality which is exhibited by all entities of all types.

Our concern now is with the twofold reality of attained actualities: their cumulative reality and their reproduced reality. Their cumulative reality, it must be noted, provides a conclusive argument against the view that a completed occasion ceases to exist in itself as soon as it is reproduced in the occasion immediately succeeding it. For, as we have just seen, the notion of cumulation, in its primary sense, refers to completed occasions as such, and not to their reproductions in other occasions, though, apart from their being reproduced, the accumulated actualities would be indistinguishable from non-entity. Hence, if the view in question were true, it would be impossible to contrast the many actualities as accumulated with the many actualities as reproduced. The unavoidable conclusion, therefore, is that there could not be an accumulation of attained actualities if each attained actuality ceased to exist as soon as it was causally objectified.

On the view under attack, a completed occasion, say D, in the remote past of an emerging occasion, say A, is available for objectification in A, only to the extent that some character of D, *via* a chain of immediate objectifications, is to be found in B, where B is an occasion immediately antecedent to A. To interpret Whitehead in this manner, however, is to openly disregard the relevant texts. For Whitehead explicitly asserts the opposite view in more than one passage of PR (*e.g.*, 345–46, 435, 438, 468–69). What Whitehead maintains—and I am merely paraphrasing him (PR 345–46, 435)—is that D is available for objectification in A both *directly* as crude initial datum, and *indirectly* as objectified in B or, for that matter, in any occasion later than D but earlier than A. Now, D must be objectified in A in at least one of these ways, but it may be objectified in several, or in all, of these ways. The manifold objectification of D in A, if it occurs, gives rise to a manifold of prehensions, each such prehension having one of the objectifications of D as its objective datum. A's several prehensions of D would occur in the early phases of A's becoming, beginning with the phase of conformal feelings. However, according to the second Categoreal Obligation, "there can be no duplication of any element in the objective datum of the 'satisfaction' of an actual entity, *so far as concerns the function of that element in the 'satisfaction'"* (PR 39; italics mine). This means that the many prehensions of *D* by *A* must be integrated into one complex prehension of *D* before the satisfaction of *A* is achieved. Thus, in the final integral experience of *A*, *D* is felt as one integral entity with one complex, but self-consistent, functioning in *A*, and in the world of *A* (PR 89).

How *A* integrates the many objectifications of *D* is but one aspect of how *A* integrates its actual world. But, again, it must be emphasized that what *A* integrates within the final unity of its experience is its actual world as reproduced within *A*'s own extensive standpoint, and is not its actual world as it exists beyond that standpoint. This must be emphasized because, unless we accept that Whitehead attaches a twofold reality to all completed actualities and, more generally, to all entities of all types, we will not be able to obtain a satisfactory understanding of the principles of ontology and creativity. Moreover, unless these two fundamental principles are correctly understood, we will be unable to solve the paradox of solidarity. I now proceed to examine these two principles in the light of my interpretation of the relativity principle as positing the repeatability of all entities, including actual entities.

THREE

The Principles of Ontology and Creativity

Because the principles of ontology and creativity are intimately related, an elucidation of one presupposes an elucidation of the other. Taking the ontological principle first, I will explain the two kinds of causes—efficient and final—which it posits. Then I will examine the relationship between the organic doctrines of cause, causation, and creativity, thus gradually shifting the discussion to the creativity principle or Category of the Ultimate. I will then distinguish from one another the processes of transition and concrescence, which are, respectively, the processes of efficient and final causation involved in the becoming of every actual occasion. In this manner, I will focus my attention once more on the ontological principle, particularly in regard to the notions of transcendent and immanent decisions. The interpretation of the processes of efficient transition and teleological concrescence will clearly exhibit the mutual relevance of the ontological and creativity principles and will demonstrate the bearing of these two principles, together with the relativity principle, on the solidarity of actual entities.

1. The principle of efficient, and final, causation

According to Whitehead, the ontological principle "constitutes the first step in the description of the universe as a solidarity of many actual entities" (PR 65). But, as we shall soon see, even this first step cannot be taken without the support provided by the principle of relativity. The essential bearing in this regard of the relativity principle on the ontological principle should not come as a surprise; for we have seen that the objective functioning of all entities of all sorts, entailed by the relativity principle, is the "metaphysical character which constitutes the solidarity of the universe" (PR 336). We have seen, in addition, that both these principles "blur the sharp distinction between what is universal and what is particular" (PR 76). There is every reason to expect, therefore, that the relativity principle should help illuminate the relevance of the ontological principle to the solidarity of actual entities.

In the categoreal scheme, the ontological principle is the eighteenth Category of Explanation and reads as follows:

> (xviii) That every condition to which the process of becoming conforms in any particular instance, has its reason *either* in the character of some actual entity in the actual world of that concrescence, *or* in the character of the subject which is in process of concrescence. This category of explanation is termed the 'ontological principle'. It could also be termed the 'principle of efficient, and final, causation'. This ontological principle means that actual entities are the only *reasons;* so that to search for a *reason* is to search for one or more actual entities. It follows that any condition to be satisfied by one actual entity in its process expresses a fact either about the 'real internal constitutions' of some other actual entities, or about the 'subjective aim' conditioning that process. (PR 36–37)

Of immediate interest is the fact that the eighteenth Category of Explanation can also be termed the *principle of efficient, and final, causation;* for elsewhere Whitehead tells us that the "'objectifications' of the actual entities in the actual world, relative to a definite actual entity, constitute the efficient causes out of which *that* actual entity arises; the 'subjective aim' at 'satisfaction' constitutes the final cause, or lure, whereby there is determinate concrescence" (PR 134). Clearly, then, the ontological principle is meant to establish the kinds of particular causes—or, equivalently, of particular reasons or conditions—that can be given as explanatory of how and why a particular actual entity came to have the determinate characters it has. All such causes, reasons, or conditions are to be sought either in the determinate characters of past actual entities, to the extent they had objective functioning within the actual entity in question, or in the particular actual entity itself, to the extent it was a self-functioning entity. Thus, actual entities are the only reasons, the only causes.

Notice that this straightforward interpretation of the ontological principle is not hindered by the mistaken belief that to exist as actual is to exist as a self-realizing process. For if that belief were correct—were it true that an occasion which is no longer self-realizing cannot be actual—the in-

terpretation of the ontological principle would become hopelessly prob-
lematical. My point is this: if past occasions are held to be no longer in
existence, and if, as Whitehead holds, contemporary occasions do not
interact, then every actual occasion must be held to be exclusively self-
caused. The teleological process of self-realization alone must explain why
an actual occasion is what it is and where it is; for the determinateness of
that occasion—its definiteness and its position—cannot be explained by
appealing to any actual occasion other than itself. Thus, if it is held that
there are no occasions actually existing other than those which are now in
process of concrescence, one half of the ontological principle is rendered
superfluous: the half which holds that only actual occasions can function
as efficient causes. For, on that view, there are no occasions actually
existing that could so function.[1]

The true organic doctrine, however, is that an actual occasion is as
much the result of efficient causation as of final causation. Now, since
only actual occasions and God can be causes or reasons, efficient causation
presupposes that completed, or past, occasions are in existence, that they
are properly termed 'actual', and that they function in later occasions by
being reproduced, or objectified, in them. To be sure, more than this is
involved in the organic notion of efficient causation; but that this much is
involved Whitehead leaves no doubt:

> The various particular occasions of the past are in existence, and are
> severally functioning as objects for prehension in the present. This
> individual objective existence of the actual occasions of the past, each
> functioning in each present occasion, constitutes the causal relation-
> ship which is efficient causation. (AI 250–51)

The objective functionings of the past occasions, I should emphasize
again, are their abstractive reproductions *within* the new occasion. Thus,
the objectifications of the past occasions are constituents of the new
occasion; to that extent, therefore, the new occasion is their effect. "The
novel actual entity, which is the effect, is the reproduction of the many
actual entities of the past" (PR 364). This is one reason, we have seen
another, why this particular mode of objectification is termed 'causal
objectification'.

The ontological principle voices, in the first half of its formulation, a
doctrine of efficient causation and also, in the second half, a doctrine of
final causation. Its doctrine of efficient causation presupposes, it should
now be obvious, that completed occasions are actual and that they accumulate in the wake of the universe's creative advance. But it presup-

poses, in addition, that the accumulated actualities are reproduced in each new unit of creative advance. Any other interpretation of the objectification of the past, I have already contended, necessarily fails to do justice to the self-transcendence exhibited by past actualities in their realized objective functionings. Let me now present additional arguments for this contention.

2. Causal objectifications as efficient causes

In what sense are the past occasions efficient causes of the new, particular occasion? The answer to this question, even without the considerations already advanced in this essay, requires that the past occasions be, in some sense, immanent in the novel occasion. For, no matter what is meant by an objectified actual occasion, it is almost universally agreed that the objectified past occasions are data for the feelings originated by the new concrescence or subject. But for Whitehead these data are not external to the subject: "They constitute that display of the universe which is inherent in the entity. Thus the data . . . are themselves components conditioning the character of the . . . subject" (PR 309). Surely this immanence of the data is precisely what we should expect given Whitehead's commitment to the doctrine that a subject's experience is the inclusive whole required by the connectedness, or solidarity, of the many in one. And surely, too, the requisite immanence of the data in the subject is one reason why Whitehead says that the ontological principle amounts to the assumption that each actual entity has to be the locus for its actual world or universe (PR 123).

Efficient causation, it then follows, "is nothing else than one outcome of the principle that every actual entity has to house its actual world" (PR 124). Why each actuality must house its actual world will be explained, in later chapters, in terms of the metaphysical properties of extension. What must be emphasized now is that a novel occasion is the product of its efficacious actual world because it includes within itself the objectification of that world. For the same reason, each concrete component of the occasion's transcendent actual world—*i.e.*, the accumulated attained actualities, and God in respect to those aspects of himself that are completely determinate relative to the origination of the new occasion—is an efficient cause of the occasion in question. But there are additional reasons why the concrete components of the transcendent actual world are efficient causes of the new occasion. For the nascent subject has to be conformed to each individual datum provided by the efficacy of the transcendent world. Thus, the initial definiteness of the subject's subjective form is what it is because the immanent data are what they are. The conformal subjective forms of the simple physical feelings, let us remember, are dictated by the immanent data. Moreover, the subject's initial conceptual reproductions, including the initial subjective aim, are conformally derived from the simple physical feelings. The conformation to the immanent data is thus mental as well as physical. But the immanent data are what they are because the transcendent world, and each of its concrete components, is what it is. Accordingly, the causal efficacy of an occasion's transcendent actual world, and of each concrete component therein, is to be discerned in the production of the occasion's three earliest phases, or, equivalently, in the production of its objective content and of its initial conformal feelings, both physical and mental.

Here it is important to remember that 'efficient cause' is a systematically ambiguous term. For, since an attained actuality and its causal objectification in a later actuality are, in a non-numerical sense, the *same* entity, it follows that both the original and the reproduction can be legitimately considered an efficient cause of the later actuality. The attained actuality is the efficient cause of its objectified self, and its objectified self is the efficient cause of the new actuality's conformal stage. In other words, the objectifications in the objective content of the new actuality are the immanent data dictating both the subjective forms of its simple physical feelings, and the data of its conceptual reproductions. Hence, in its conformal stage, the subject may be legitimately construed as the effect of the objectifications of the actual entities in its transcendent actual world. This is why Whitehead says, in the passage quoted earlier, that the *objectifications* of the actualities in an actual entity's correlative actual world "constitute the efficient causes out of which *that* actual entity arises" (PR 134). With this meaning of 'efficient cause', however, it would be more accurate to describe efficient causation as one outcome of the principle that every actual entity has to house its actual world *and conform to it.*

In the becoming of an actual occasion, the influence of its given objectifications goes beyond their determination of the conformal stage. For the novel subjective forms realized by the self-determining subject in the subsequent integrative phases must be compatible for synthesis with the conformal subjective forms of the simple physical feelings. Thus, even the novel subjective forms are *conditioned*, though not determined, by the given objectifications. If this final influence is subsumed under a broadly conceived notion of efficient causation, then, as Whitehead says, "we must admit that, in the most general sense, the objectifications express the causality by which the external world fashions the actual occasion in question" (PR 489). Of course, this final influence is outside the realm of efficient causation, strictly conceived. But the point is that the world external to the occasion determines its conformal phases and conditions its integrative phases of novel immediacy only by reason of its reproductive immanence within the occasion. The actual world is causally efficacious only by means of its objectification within the occasion. This is precisely why Whitehead construes efficient causation as an outcome of the principle that every actual entity has to be a locus for its universe. The first half of the ontological principle, we may therefore conclude, asserts the immanence of the universe in each of its component actualities, and, to that extent, constitutes a first step in the description of the universe as a solidarity of the whole in each of its actual parts.

The sense in which an occasion's actual universe is immanent in the occasion is a major bone of contention among the interpreters of Whitehead's thought. My own position, of course, is that the actual universe is immanent only as reproduced or causally objectified; the actual universe as its own original self remains external to the occasion. My position, however, is at odds with all the received interpretations. In this regard, differences of detail aside, the major interpreters of Whitehead are divided into two groups. One group, which includes Hartshorne, asserts the literal immanence of the universe (as such) in each occasion.[2] The other group, which includes Christian, Johnson, Leclerc, Schmidt, and Sherburne, apparently denies the immanence of earlier occasions in later ones, holding instead that there is immanence only in the sense that an eternal object characterizing the subjective form of an earlier occasion is repeated in a later occasion so as to characterize the latter's subjective form also.[3] Nevertheless, the difference between the interpretations propounded by the two groups is, in respect to my purposes here, merely verbal. For those who interpret immanence in terms of the reproduction of eternal objects, or of subjective forms, also hold that the earlier occasions are data, in one way or another, for the conformal experience of later occasions. But to the extent that such data are experienced or prehended by later occasions, they are already immanent in them, and they are so even before there is any conformal reproduction of subjective forms. If this fact has escaped the interpreters in the second group, it is because they have forgotten that experience is not a relation of an occasion to something external to it, but is itself the 'inclusive whole' required for the connectedness of 'many in one.'

Only two possibilities, then, are left: either the immanent datum for a subject's experience is the universe in itself, or it is the universe as repeated. But if we choose the former alternative, the avowed pluralism of the organic philosophy collapses into an extreme monism. The experiencing subject would be the universe—literally! And this conclusion cannot be avoided by claiming that the experiencing subject would not include other subjects contemporary with it; for Whitehead explicitly asserts that any two mutually contemporary occasions are also (in a sense not involving causal objectification) mutually immanent (AI 278, 254; PR 91; SMW 102). Moreover, even if the mutual immanence of contemporary occasions were denied, it would still be the case that the literal immanence in occasions of their respective actual worlds would abolish their discreteness; even mutually contemporary occasions would overlap because they have a common past, *i.e.*, because their respective actual worlds also overlap.

Accordingly, either the first half of the ontological principle turns the organic philosophy into a monistic system, through and through, or one occasion is included within another *only as repeated*. Which of these alternatives we ought to opt for, and what bearing the principle of relativity (and with it the notion of repetition) has on the ontological principle, Whitehead himself tells us in the following passage:

> It follows from the ontological principle . . . that the notion of a 'common world' must find its exemplification in the constitution of each actual entity, taken by itself for analysis. For an actual entity cannot be a member of a 'common world', except in the sense that the 'common world' is a constituent of its own constitution. It follows that every item of the universe, including all the other actual entities, are constituents in the constitution of any one actual entity. This conclusion has already been employed under the title of the 'principle of relativity'. This principle of relativity is the axiom by which the ontological principle is rescued from issuing in an extreme monism. Hume adumbrates this principle in his notion of 'repetition'.
>
> Some principle is now required to rescue actual entities from being undifferentiated repetitions, each of the other, with mere numerical diversity. (PR 224)[4]

What Whitehead is saying, in other words, is that each actual entity exemplifies the 'common world' because the world as a whole is *repeated* in every actual entity. Thus, for any occasion there are two 'worlds': the 'world' including the occasion, and the 'world' included in the occasion. But the latter 'world' is a repetition of the former. Accordingly, the principle of relativity, as I construe it, not only saves the ontological principle from issuing in an extreme monism, but also explains how there can be "one world without and within" (AI 293). For the world within, it is now evident, is the repetition of, and hence is numerically different from, the world without. To that extent the problem posed by the thesis of solidarity has been alleviated.

To that extent, too, the alleviation of the problem has required the blurring, by the ontological and relativity principles, of the sharp distinction between universals and particulars. The former principle blurs the distinction because its doctrine of efficient causation requires that earlier occasions be present in, and hence characterize, later occasions. The latter principle blurs the distinction because it holds that one occasion is present in another, not *simpliciter*, not in itself, but only as reproduced, only as objectified. In these ways, the two principles ascribe to actual entities functions traditionally restricted to universals.

3. *The subjective aim as final cause*

Neither the objectifications of the actual entities in an occasion's actual world nor the physical and conceptual conformation those objectifications dictate determine the final, novel, integrative character of the completed occasion. For the completed occasion is the product of final causation as well as of efficient causation. The determinate characters gained by an actual occasion during its autonomous phases of concrescence both supplement and synthesize the characters given to it by the efficacious objectification of its actual world. In other words, the determinateness of a completed occasion cannot be explained by appealing solely to the actual entities in its actual world; rather, its explanation requires also an appeal to the subjective aim which guided the concrescence of that occasion. Explanation by efficient causes is necessary, but not sufficient; it must be supplemented with explanation by final cause.

The subjective aim, we noted earlier, is the subject's conceptually prehended ideal of what it wants to be as the superject of its own process. "The ideal, itself felt, defines what 'self' shall arise from the datum; and the ideal is also an element in the self which thus arises" (PR 228). By reason of this ideal, then, the subjective concrescence is a teleological process of self-creation, or, more accurately, of self-completion. The subjective aim is thus that ideal factor whereby the occasion's aesthetic concrescence is a determinate process, the self-realizing subject, issuing in a determinate product, the self-realized superject (PR 130). The subjective aim, in brief, is the factor in virtue of which an attained actuality is partly the outcome of final causation.

It is important to realize, however, that an occasion's subjective concrescence is not only a teleological process but also a self-determining process. The subjective aim is not a fixed, determinate ideal which the occasion must inevitably actualize, willingly or unwillingly. To be sure, the subjective aim does function as a lure towards the realization of a subjective definiteness capable of providing intensity of feeling in the immediate subject and in the subject's relevant future (PR 41). But the subjective aim, thus luring the subject, exhibits the vagueness and lack of specificity that necessarily separate the ideal from the actual. Its actualization requires a succession of subjective decisions which its own vagueness and generality make possible but which it in no way dictates. In other words, it is necessary that the subject make some decisions regarding the further definition and specification of its subjective aim; but no particular decision is necessitated or compelled by the subjective aim itself. Thus, all decisions effecting the gradual definition, specification, and realization of the subjective aim are made *freely* by the subject. The decisions are not inherent, much less preprogrammed, in the initial subjective aim inherited from the primordial nature of God. They issue from a subjective autonomy which is absolute and ultimate, however much it may be conditioned by the efficacy of actuality and the lure of ideality.

Indeed, without the subject's autonomous decisions, the initial subjective aim could not guide the origination of novel subjective forms by which the integration and reintegration of feelings is accomplished. For the initial subjective aim, as immediately inherited from God, is an appetition for the realization of any one of a number of complex patterns of definiteness which are individually compatible for synthesis with the occasion's inherited definiteness, but which are incompatible with one another respecting their joint realization in that ocasion. Moreover, each realizable pattern, as I will show in the next chapter, is a complex eternal object whose realization requires the realization of simpler patterns and, ultimately, of simple eternal objects. But the initial subjective aim does not specify with what particular components the broader complex pattern is to be realized, though it does provide a range of alternative components. Thus, the initial subjective aim is much too general and vague to effectively guide the integrative phases of the occasion's becoming. Its effective functioning as a lure presupposes the autonomous subject whose free decisions finally specify what pattern is to be realized, with what components, and with what intensity. These free decisions transform the initial subjective aim into a progressively more specific aim which, at each stage of its successive specification, effectively guides the creations and integrations produced in the particular phase for which it is evolved (PR 342).

This is why Whitehead says that the subject "derives from God its basic conceptual aim, relevant to its actual world, yet with indeterminations awaiting its own decisions. This subjective aim, in its successive modifications, remains the unifying factor governing the successive phases of interplay between physical and conceptual feelings" (PR 343).

Thus, the initial stage of the subjective aim is indeed an endowment received from God, and it does serve, in its successive modifications, as the *télos* guiding the concrescence toward its satisfaction; but this double fact does not in any way derogate from the autonomy or freedom of the subject in concrescence. The subject is created by a process of efficient causation over which it can have no control. This efficient causation, which is what Whitehead means by the macroscopic process of transition, does give to the subject its objective content, its simple physical feelings, its initial subjective aim, and its other conceptual reproductions. However, once created in this bipolar fashion, the subject is the autonomous master of its own concrescence (PR 374). Its immanent freedom of self-determination is absolute, not to be challenged, compelled, or constrained by anything external to it, whether actual or ideal. Of course, it cannot avoid the objective content and primary feelings it has received from its actual world; but how it absorbs these received elements into its own final unity of private feeling is entirely the result of its own autonomous self-determination, albeit under inescapable metaphysical conditions.

Two qualifications of the absoluteness of subjective autonomy must be made explicit. First, if by freedom is meant freedom from imposed empirical circumstances, then the subject is not absolutely free. For, in respect to this sense of the term, "there is no such fact as absolute freedom; every actual entity possesses only such freedom as is inherent in the primary phase 'given' by its standpoint of relativity to its actual universe" (PR 202/CPR 133). This is why it can avoid neither its objective content nor its primary feelings. Second, if by freedom is meant freedom from metaphysical constraints, then again the subject is not absolutely free. For the concrescence of every actual entity is in the grip of that ultimate necessity which is the purpose of metaphysics to capture and express. According to Whitehead, the nine Categoreal Obligations—or categoreal conditions, as they are referred to in most of the text of PR—express the metaphysical demands governing, and thus exemplified in, every concrescence (PR 31, 335, 346). It follows that the subject's freedom is limited by, and thus relative to, the metaphysical demands, or Categoreal Obligations, which it must perforce meet.

But there still remains a legitimate and important sense in which the subject's freedom is absolute. For the immanent freedom whereby each concrescence is essentially a process of autonomous self-determination is itself a metaphysical necessity, as expressed in the ninth Categoreal Obligation, the *Category of Freedom and Determination:* "The concrescence of each individual actual entity is internally determined and is externally free" (PR 41; also PR 74). Thus the subject's freedom is rooted in the ultimate character of the universe. It is an immediacy of self-realization devoid of extrinsic determination. The immediacy is concerned with, or referent to, received feelings which are externally determined; but the immediacy is only conditioned by its received elements. Moreover, the subject's freedom is not given to it by something, or someone, that could conceivably withhold it or take it back. Finally, it is a freedom which the subject can neither escape nor renounce. The subject *must* exercise its freedom in the activity of synthesizing its received elements. It must do so because its creative freedom is essentially accompanied by an urge towards the realization of aesthetic synthesis. The freedom and the urge are aspects each of the other because they are both rooted in, and are manifestations of, the same ultimate principle—the eternal creativity of the universe. Thus, the subject's creative freedom is an individualization of "a creativity with infinite freedom" (RM 117); and the subject's urge towards aesthetic synthesis is an individualized manifestation of the "ultimate principle by which the many, which are the universe disjunctively, become the one actual occasion, which is the universe conjunctively" (PR 31).

The subject's freedom, we may conclude, is, first, metaphysically necessary; second, devoid of any external determination; third, irrevocable; and fourth, unavoidable. To that extent, subjective freedom is absolute and must be exercised. But this is not to deny that the subject's freedom is conditioned both empirically and metaphysically. The subject must exercise its freedom; but it can exercise it only amid the given circumstances of its birth and only in accord with metaphysical conditions that are as ultimate as its own freedom, and of a piece with that freedom (PR 390).

4. Causation, autonomy, and the arbitrariness of history

The concrescence of an actual entity, it should now be evident, may be construed indifferently as a process of teleological self-determination or as a process of self-determining teleology. The true organic doctrine is that final causation and self-causation involve one another and presuppose the efficient causation whereby the autonomous subject is begotten. Accordingly, the complete determinateness of an attained actuality requires explanation by efficient causes, explanation by final cause, and explanation by autonomous self-determination. Of course, the last two explanations are interconnected by the common relevance of the subjective aim. But the fact remains that explanation by efficient cause, and explanation by final cause, are not jointly sufficient to explain the final concrete character of a satisfied actuality. For each actual entity is—in part only, but essentially so—its own reason for being what it is.

The subject's autonomy is the reason why Whitehead says that the occasion's subjective aim is at once an example and a limitation of the ontological principle.

> It is an example, in that the principle is here applied to the immediacy of concrescent fact. The subject completes itself during the process of concrescence by a self-criticism of its own incomplete phases. In another sense the subjective aim limits the ontological principle by its own autonomy. (PR 373)

The autonomy of the subjective aim is simply the autonomy of the subject which modifies and specifies the initial subjective aim and thus appropriates it as "its living aim at its own self-constitution" (PR 373). Subjective autonomy is also the reason why Whitehead says that the peculiar history of the universe illustrates the joint relevance of the ontological principle and the ninth Categoreal Obligation. In this last regard, Whitehead's point is a complex one; but its relevance to the organic philosophy's understanding of freedom and causation requires that I examine it briefly.

The course of universal history exhibits most clearly the functionings of efficient causes, and thus it "can be rationalized by the consideration of the determination of successors by antecedents" (PR 74). But any attempt to *understand* universal history, as opposed to rationalizing it, requires an appeal to final causes. However, if final causes are taken to compel history towards some pre-ordained *télos*, then we have merely substituted rationalization through final causes for rationalization through efficient causes. Nor is it enough to juxtapose the two kinds of causes and thereby rationalize each moment of history in terms of a push from the actual past and a pull from the ideal future. Rather, understanding the evolution of history requires that we take seriously the ninth Categoreal Obligation. We are then able to understand universal history in its true character of exhibiting, in each of its constituent moments, an internal determination which is not reducible to any mechanical operation of efficient or final cause. Every moment assumes the evolution of history up to that moment; but the accumulated history, though productive of the nascent moment, merely conditions its internal determination. Also, the moment's own achievement is the realization of what was previously a mere possibility; but the possibility thus realized is only one of many that were equally compatible with the course of history up to that moment. Accordingly, history exhibits an inescapable moment to moment arbitrariness that forbids its ever being understood as a mere unfolding, whether by efficient push or final pull, of a predetermined course of moments or events.

The moment to moment arbitrariness is simply the reflection on history of the "ultimate freedom of things, lying beyond all determinations" (PR 75). In each instance the arbitrariness is the reflection of an actual occasion's individual autonomy. But history reflects also an even wider, more absolute arbitrariness. In respect to this more general arbitrariness, the evolution of history is incapable even of rationalization

> because it exhibits a selected flux of participating forms. No reason, internal to history can be assigned why that flux of forms, rather than another flux, should have been illustrated. It is true that any flux must exhibit the character of internal determination. So much follows from the ontological principle. But every instance of internal determination assumes *that* flux up to *that* point. There is no reason why there could be no alternative flux exhibiting that principle of internal determination. The actual flux presents itself with the character of being merely 'given'. (PR 74)

We have in this statement a veiled appeal to the unavoidable relevance to history of God's primordial nature, and an even more veiled allusion to the absolute irrelevance, to God's primordial nature, of the actual course of history. For "the given course of history presupposes his primordial nature, but his primordial nature does not presuppose it" (PR 70).

Here I must foreshadow the more complete characterization of God's primordial nature to be given in the next chapter. The primordial nature is the aboriginal superject resulting from the aboriginal individualization of the eternal creativity. Relative to this primordial creative act, there is no actual world (PR 134). Its only data are the eternal objects. The primordial act orders and evaluates the eternal objects into schemes of relevance which, themselves evaluated and ordered, constitute an ideal creative order for the physical ingression of eternal objects or forms (PR 46–48).

Each scheme of relevance is a complex conceptual feeling integrating other conceptual feelings. The ultimate data, which are the eternal objects, are not integrated; what are integrated are the subjective forms of the feelings. These subjective forms are the valuational appetitions whereby the schemes of relevance and the ideal creative orders are constituted. The final all-encompassing conceptual feeling resulting from the synthesis of all other primordial feelings is an aboriginal satisfaction of infinite conceptual realization. The subjective form of this satisfaction is the primordial definiteness of God, which constitutes, together with its data, the primordial nature of God. This aboriginal superject of creativity, by reason of its objective immortality, necessarily conditions all other individualizations of creativity—the individual temporal occasions and the individual stages of God's consequent nature (PR 378).

The subjective form of the primordial nature exhibits an infinite appetition for the physical realization of eternal objects in accord with the ideal creative order expressed by the ordered schemes of relevance. In other words, the primordial appetition is that any set of eternal objects already ingressed in the temporal world shall constitute a lure for the ingression of other eternal objects which are as yet unrealized in the temporal world, but which, in the primordial nature, are proximately relevant to those which are already temporally ingressed (PR 134). Here 'proximately relevant' means 'proximate in some scheme of relevance involving both the eternal objects already temporally ingressed and those awaiting temporal ingression'. Thus, the 'proximity' is ultimately to be found in the component conceptual feelings of God's primordial nature.

Of immediate interest now is that the component feelings of the primordial nature include the *divine counterparts* of the initial subjective aims of the temporal occasions constituting the concrete moments of universal history. For, as we have noted already, the primordial nature is objectified in an occasion under the perspective of one of its component conceptual feelings, and the occasion's initial subjective aim is itself a conceptual feeling reproducing for its subject the data and valuation of the feeling by which the primordial nature has been objectified. The initial subjective aim and its primordial counterpart are two distinct feelings, and belong to two different subjects, the one temporal, the other divine. Nonetheless, the two feelings exhibit a non-numerical identity in regard to the eternal objects constituting their respective data, and in regard to the valuations constituting their respective subjective forms. To that extent, an occasion's initial subjective aim is a primordial conceptual feeling inherited from God.

It could be said also, with equal truth, that the initial subjective aims of actual occasions are the temporal counterparts of primordial conceptual feelings. Since these initial subjective aims, as modified by their subjects, function as the final causes of the concrete moments of temporal history, it follows that the ideal of creative order inherent in God's primordial nature is reflected on the universe's history as a peculiar flux of realized forms. But the important thing to notice, in this regard, is that the ideal creative order, thus manifesting itself in temporal history, is an autonomous, unconditioned, divine creation. For the concrescence of the primordial nature, like any other concrescence, is internally determined and externally free. This much follows from the Category of Freedom and Determination. In addition, the primordial concrescence is unconditioned because, being the absolutely first concrescence, there are no antecedent attained actualities to condition it through their causal efficacy. Therefore, aside from God's own primordial autonomy, no reason can be given for the ideal creative order being what it is (SMW 249–50). God's primordial nature *could have been different*. Even more to the point, had God's primordial nature been different, the course of universal history would have exhibited a different, but no less peculiar, no less arbitrary, flux of realized forms.

By reason of God's primordial nature, we may conclude, the actual course of history exhibits not only the determinations of logic, efficient causation, and autonomous final causation that are manifest in the particularity of each concrete moment but also a given limitation of possibilities that is antecedent to the whole course of history and is presupposed by each of history's concrete moments (SMW 247–51). The relevance of the primordial nature to history is, in other words, the reason for the general arbitrariness inherent in the peculiar flux of forms which history does in fact exhibit. Therefore, the arbitrariness of history, both in its general and in its particular aspects, is ultimately grounded in the self-creative autonomy, or internal determination, which is a metaphysical feature of every concrescence, be it divine or temporal.

The primordial autonomy, we must remember, does condition each temporal autonomy (PR 165). Also, the impact of the autonomy of low-grade occasions on history may be individually negligible in comparison with the massive impact of efficient causation (PR 75). Nonetheless, however negligible the achievement of a temporal occasion may be, it represents an autonomous decision which, for better or for worse, affects the course of history, even if barely so. Obviously the decisions of more complex occasions, such as those constituting the stream of experience of a human being, will have a significantly greater impact on the course of events. In any case, the final accumulation of all such decisions—the decision of God's nature and the decisions of all occasions—constitutes that special element in the flux of forms in history, which is 'given' and incapable of rationalization beyond the fact that within it every component which is determinable is internally determined. (PR 75)

To sum up: The general arbitrariness of the course of history is due to the autonomy of the primordial concrescence, and the more particularized arbitrariness of each concrete moment of history is due to the autonomy at the heart of that moment's concrescence. But the general arbitrariness conditions each particularized arbitrariness by reason of the fact that the primordial nature of God provides each temporal concrescence with its initial subjective aim. This is simply another way of saying that the autonomy of each temporal concrescence is conditioned by the superject of the primordial autonomy. Thus, the arbitrariness inherent in each concrete moment of temporal history is a further specification, amid received conditions, of the more general arbitrariness at the base of that history.

5.   *The free initiation and free conclusion of each concrescence*

The relation of each temporal autonomy to the primordial autonomy, whereby the former is conditioned by the latter, leads Whitehead to say, somewhat misleadingly, that "each [temporal] concrescence is to be referred to a definite free initiation and a definite free conclusion" (PR 75). This statement does *not* mean that the becoming of an actual occasion is from its outset an autonomous process of self-realization. For, as we noted earlier, an occasion's autonomous self-realization does not begin until the phase of conceptual reversions and presupposes that the occasion has already inherited from God an initial subjective aim—an aim which the occasion in no way chooses, though the occasion does freely modify the aim once it has inherited it. Thus, to understand what Whitehead's statement does mean, the first thing to notice is that an occasion's first three phases of becoming, the phases preceding the phase of conceptual reversion, are not part of the process of concrescence proper. They belong to the supersessionally earlier process of transition by which God and the antecedent occasions beget the novel subject, with its received subjective aim, its other feelings of conceptual reproductions, its simple physical feelings, and its objective content (PR 374).

The second thing to notice, in order to understand Whitehead's statement, is that the initial subjective aim from which the process of concrescence truly begins is ultimately derived from its exact counterpart in the

primordial nature of God. This means that the conceptual feeling accounting for the initiation of the temporal concrescence may be traced to the
autonomy of the primordial concrescence. This is precisely the sense in
which the temporal concrescence has a free (divine) initiation. "In this
sense God is the principle of concretion; namely, he is that actual entity
from which each temporal concrescence receives that initial aim from
which its self-causation starts" (PR 374). The third and final thing to
notice, in this regard, is that the initial subjective aim, because of its
generality, cannot guide the temporal concrescence to its satisfaction
unless it is autonomously modified by the subject to which it belongs.
This means that what is started by God's autonomy must be completed by
the autonomy of the temporal concrescence. "Thus the initial stage of the
aim is rooted in the nature of God, and its 'completion' depends on the
self-causation of the subject-superject" (PR 373).

Accordingly, in order to understand the free initiation and free conclusion of a temporal occasion, we must appeal to the internal determination,
or freedom, of two different actualities or facts. The first fact, which is the
primordial nature of God, accounts for the free initiation of the subjective
aim of the temporal occasion. The second fact, which is the temporal
occasion itself *qua* autonomous subject-superject, accounts for the free
completion of the subjective aim in respect to its specification and physical
realization. The first fact is relevant to all occasions. The second fact is the
enjoyment of its own unique and autonomous self-relevance. The necessary appeal to these two facts is what Whitehead had in mind when he
wrote the statement in question. If the preceding considerations are kept
in mind, the meaning of the statement is transparently obvious when read
in its proper context:

> The doctrine [of self-creation] is, that each concrescence is to be
> referred to a definite free initiation and a definite free conclusion. The
> initial fact is macrocosmic, in the sense of having equal relevance to all
> occasions; the final fact is microcosmic, in the sense of being peculiar
> to that occasion. Neither fact is capable of rationalization, in the sense
> of tracing the antecedents which determine it. The initial fact is the
> primordial appetition, and the final fact is the decision of emphasis,
> finally creative of the 'satisfaction'. (PR 75–76)

6.   The primordial counterpart of the initial subjective aim

I have labored the explication of the sense in which each temporal concrescence is to be referred to a definite free initiation because I want to
eliminate any vestige of textual support for the claim, commonplace in the

received interpretations of Whitehead, that an actual occasion's becoming is from its outset an autonomous process of self-causation. This claim rests largely on the mistaken assumption that an occasion's entire becoming is to be equated with its process of concrescence—an assumption which either misconstrues, or neglects altogether, the role that the process of transition plays in an occasion's becoming. I shall deal with this erroneous assumption later in this chapter. Of more immediate interest is the fact that the mistaken equation of an occasion's becoming with its concrescence is aided and abetted by Whitehead's failure, through sheer expository carelessness, to clearly distinguish from each other the initial subjective aim of an occasion and the primordial conceptual feeling from which that aim is ultimately derived. For a contributing factor to the received confusions on this matter is the occasional confounding, in Whitehead's exposition, of the role which the initial subjective aim plays in an occasion's concrescence with the role which the primordial counterpart of *that* aim plays in the process of transition begetting *that* occasion.

First let us be clear as to the sphere of influence of the initial subjective aim, in respect to the determination of the occasion to which it belongs. The initial subjective aim, through its successive modifications resulting from the occasion's own autonomy, can influence only the origination of conceptual reversions and the origination of novel subjective forms effecting the integration of feelings in the remaining supplemental phases. The initial subjective aim *cannot* in any way influence the begetting of the dative phase and the conformal phase because these two phases are supersessionally earlier than the phase of conceptual reproduction wherein the initial subjective aim is itself begotten. Nor can the initial subjective aim influence the generation of the other conceptual reproductions which, together with it, constitute the first phase of the mental pole. Thus, the becoming of the occasion's physical pole and the becoming of the first half of its mental pole are alike outside the sphere of influence of the occasion's initial subjective aim.

Of course, what is outside the initial subjective aim's sphere of influence is the *begetting* of the occasion's three earliest phases of existence. After all three phases are begotten, and thus after the initial subjective aim has itself been begotten, these phases are subject to modifications that most definitely result from, and are steps toward the realization of, the occasion's freely modified subjective aim. For example, the subjective forms of the original conformal feelings are altered through intensification or attenuation and through supplementation and integration. But the autonomous teleological activity of alteration presupposes the existence of, and thus is supersessionally subsequent to, that which it is in the process of altering. The point is that the initial subjective aim influences the alteration, but not the begetting, of the occasion's three earliest phases.

Nevertheless, the becoming of the occasion's first three phases of existence, although it cannot be influenced by the occasion's initial subjective aim, *is* influenced by the primordial counterpart of that initial subjective aim. The thing to remember in this regard is that God's primordial nature is a concrete component of the actual world correlative with the actual occasion in question. As part of the occasion's actual world, the primordial nature functions as an efficient cause of the occasion. But the primordial nature is no ordinary cause of the occasion. By its aboriginal relevance to all possible physical realization, it conditions: (i) the individual objectification in the novel occasion of every actuality in the occasion's actual world; (ii) the conformation which the immanent objectifications impose on the subjective forms of the novel occasion's initial physical feelings; and (iii) the initial subjective forms, or valuations, of the conceptual feelings that are reproductively derived from the nascent occasion's initial physical feelings. "Thus the transition of the creativity from an actual world to the correlate novel concrescence is conditioned by the relevance of God's all-embracing conceptual valuations to the particular possibilities of transmission from the actual world, and by its relevance to the various possibilities of initial subjective form available for the initial feelings" (PR 374).

The relevance of the primordial nature to the possibilities of transmission from the actual world to the novel occasion exerts a coordinating influence on the causal objectification in that occasion of the concrete components of that actual world. The primordial nature is *not* the reason for the causal objectification of the concrete components. Every concrete component, or superject, is its own reason for its objectification in the new occasion. Indeed, every superject contains within itself a determination as to *how* it is to be objectified in actualities later than itself (PR 422). But the individual determinations, inherent in the different superjects, stand in need of coordination because the many objectifications in the new occasion's dative phase must give rise to conformal physical feelings that are compatible for felt synthesis in the final unity of the occasion's satisfaction. This compatibility for synthesis is a metaphysical necessity. "The limitation, whereby the actual entities felt are severally reduced to the perspective of one of their own feelings, is imposed by the categoreal condition of subjective unity, requiring a harmonious compatibility in the feelings of each incomplete phase" (PR 362).

In other words, the objectification of the occasion's actual world, since it is the first step in the production of the occasion's primary feelings, is effected under the limitation imposed by the category of Subjective Unity, or first Categoreal Obligation (PR 364). Moreover, the origination of the initial phase of physical feelings is effected under the same limitation (PR 378). The problem for the interpretation of this limitation is that the first Categoreal Obligation appeals to the unity of a subject which does not actually exist until the initial physical feelings have been originated. Here is how Whitehead formulates this category: "The many feelings which belong to an incomplete phase in the process of an actual entity, though unintegrated by reason of the incompleteness of the phase, are compatible for integration by reason of the unity of their subject" (PR 39; also 341). Whitehead then explains that

> this category is one expression of the general principle that the one subject is the final end which conditions each component feeling. Thus the superject is already present as a condition, determining how each feeling conducts its own process. Although in any incomplete phase there are many unsynthesized feelings, yet each of these feelings is conditioned by the other feelings. The process of each feeling is such as to render that feeling integrable with the other feelings. (PR 341)

But Whitehead's explanation raises the interpretative issue of how the superject can be present as a condition determining the objectification of the actual world, or as a condition determining the origination of the primary physical and conceptual feelings.

To be sure, the superject is present as an ideal and not as an attained actuality. The problem is that the superject can be ideally present only insofar as it is the objective datum of a conceptual feeling. This is not a problem in respect to those phases of an occasion's becoming which are supersessionally subsequent to the origination of the occasion's conceptual feeling of initial subjective aim, for the objective datum of that feeling is the ideal superject as in its initial stage of conceptual specification. But it is a problem in respect to the becoming of the occasion's dative phase, conformal phase, and phase of conceptual reproduction, because the occasion's initial subjective aim is originated in the last of these three phases, and thus they can be conditioned neither by the subjective aim nor by its objective datum. How, then, are these three phases conditioned by the ideal presence of the superject? The answer, I have already intimated, is that the ideal superject is present to condition these phases by reason of its being the objective datum of that divine conceptual feeling which is the primordial counterpart of the initial subjective aim. I must now take a closer look at the objective functioning, first as transcendent capacity, then as immanent determinant, of this divine feeling.

In the transition from actual world to novel occasion, there are indeterminations concerning how the settled actualities are to be jointly objectified in the new occasion so as to fulfill the first Categoreal Obligation. These indeterminations cannot be solved by the agency of the new occasion, precisely because the new occasion does not begin to exist until the settled actualities are objectified to form its dative phase. Nor can the temporal attained actualities solve these indeterminations; for their constitutive determinations regarding how they are to be individually objectified were not generated in concert and thus are not harmonized with one another. Only God can solve the indeterminations concerning the objectification of the actual world in the new occasion.

God can exercise this coordinating function because his primordial nature is made up of an infinity of conceptual feelings which are individually relevant to all realizable basic conditions (PR 134). Since the actual world in question involves the physical realization of a specific basic condition—i.e., of a specific set of eternal objects—there is in the primordial nature a complex conceptual feeling representing a primordial determination, or decision, as to how *that* actual world is to be objectified in, and for, its correlative novel occasion. By reason of this complex conceptual feeling, the primordial nature of God is a specific transcendent capacity for the determination of the occasion which is to arise from that actual world. The specific relevance of this divine transcendent capacity is the *actual reason* explaining the *harmonization* of the causal objectifications of all the settled actualities in the occasion's actual world. Because of it "objectification is an operation of mutually adjusted abstraction, or elimination, whereby the many occasions of the actual world become one complex datum" (PR 321).

The complex divine feeling, in virtue of which the primordial nature is specifically relevant to the transition from actual world to new occasion, includes the primordial counterpart of the occasion's initial subjective aim but is not reducible to it. Rather, the complex divine feeling is the conceptual integration of the primordial counterpart with other primordial conceptual feelings. The primordial counterpart is the divine ideal, vague and general, of the individual outcome to be derived from the specific basic condition which the actual world happens to exhibit. But the primordial counterpart presupposes, is presupposed by, and is integrated with, other divine conceptual feelings relevant to how the actual world is to be objectified in, and conformed by, the new occasion so as to constitute the real immanent basis for the physical realization of the primordial counterpart. Thus, the primordial counterpart of the occasion's initial subjective aim is only a component feeling of the complex divine feeling coordinating the origination of the new occasion's dative and conformal phases (PR 374).

Notice that the complex divine feeling must include a simpler feeling representing a decision as to how the primordial nature is itself to be objectified in, and conformed to by, the nascent occasion, for the primordial nature is included in the occasion's actual world. In respect to his primordial nature, therefore, God is causally objectified as the subject of a complex conceptual feeling which is immediately relevant to the objectified temporal world given for the nascent occasion's first phase of physical feelings (PR 343). The feeling by which God is thus objectified is the primordial counterpart of the occasion's initial subjective aim. In other words, the objectified primordial counterpart is the mode in which God's primordial nature has become an immanent realized determinant of the new occasion. As an immanent determinant, it dictates both the conformation of the new subject to the divine objectification and the coordination of the subject's conformation to the temporal occasions objectified for it. In turn, the subject's hybrid physical feeling of God both dictates its own sympathetic conceptual reproduction and coordinates the derivation, from the conformal physical feelings, of the other feelings of conceptual reproduction constituting the first phase of the occasion's mental pole.

It is now evident that the primordial counterpart of the occasion's initial subjective aim is at work in the creation of the occasion's three phases of existence that supersessionally precede the creation of that initial subjective aim. Moreover, since the objective datum of the primordial counterpart is the ideal superject to be derived from the occasion's actual world, it follows that the superject is indeed ideally present as a condition insuring that the occasion's simple physical feelings, and its primary mental feelings, are all compatible for felt synthesis in the final satisfaction. It is evident, also, that the Category of Subjective Unity does in fact condition every phase of an occasion's becoming, even though there is no real subject until the second phase of that becoming, no initial subjective aim until the third phase, and no autonomous subject until the fourth phase.

In the three earliest phases of the occasion's becoming, which jointly constitute the macroscopic process of transition, the Category of Subjective Unity is operative through that feeling in God's primordial nature from which the occasion's initial subjective aim will be ultimately derived. In this respect, then, God's primordial nature "solves all indeterminations of transition" (PR 315). In the remaining phases of the occasion's becoming, which jointly constitute its microscopic process of concrescence, the Category of Subjective Unity is operative through the occasion's initial subjective aim, in its successive autonomous modifications. Thus, in respect to the production of feelings compatible for aesthetic synthesis, the ultimate factor coordinating the process of transition is a conceptual feeling belonging to God's primordial nature, whereas the ultimate factor coordinating the process of concrescence is a conceptual feeling belonging to the novel subject. However, since the latter feeling is conformally derived from the former, it follows that God's primordial nature "is a character of permanent rightness, whose inherence in the nature of things modifies both efficient and final cause, so that the one conforms to harmonious conditions, and the other contrasts itself with an harmonious ideal" (RM 61).

7. Causes, causation, and creativity

The final cause of an actual occasion is its autonomously modified subjective aim. The complete efficient cause of an actual occasion is its correlative actual world, but only insofar as that world is made up of the primordial superject and the other accumulated superjects of creativity. Thus, in the final analysis the causes of an actual occasion are its own subjective aim and the objectifications of the settled actualities in its actual world. A completed actuality is what it is because its causes are what they are—that is the import of the ontological principle, the principle of efficient and final causation. But the full import of this principle requires not only an appeal to the relativity principle, which we have already made, but also an appeal to the principle of creativity, which we must now begin to make.

To say that objectified occasions function as efficient causes, and that subjective aims function as final causes, is not to exhaust the analysis of the organic doctrine of causation. For it must be remembered that completed actualities are in themselves inactive, and that the same is true of the ideals of final self-definiteness at which the different subjects aim. Yet causation, whether efficient or final, is a dynamic and productive affair. To bridge the gap between static cause and dynamic causation, it is necessary to appeal to the principle of creativity. There are no causal processes in isolation from the eternal creativity of the universe. Nevertheless, for Whitehead, the eternal creativity is not itself the cause of anything.

In this connection, Whitehead's use of the terms 'cause' and 'causation' may appear at first to be needlessly paradoxical. Yet his usage is, I think, entirely justified. For Whitehead is construing the search for 'causes', whether the inquiry be scientific or metaphysical, as a search for 'reasons'. This much is evident in the way in which he uses 'cause' and 'reason' as interchangeable terms.[5] Moreover, what the causes, or reasons, have to explain in any given inquiry, are the *particular* characters of a *particular* event, the characters which differentiate that event from all other events— the characters, if you wish, that make it *that* event rather than another. But since the eternal creativity is involved in the becoming of *all* events, it cannot function as a reason for the *unique* particularity of a given event.

In other words, that occasions become at all is explained by, or requires a reference to, the creative factor of the universe. But this creative factor cannot by itself explain why a given occasion became as it did, or why it has the determinate characters which it does have. Consequently, the reasons, or causes, of a particular occasion are to be found, not in the creativity, but in the completed actualities in that occasion's past, and in the subjective aim which animated the self-completion of that occasion.

Nevertheless, the fact remains that, without the creativity, neither past occasions nor ideal aims can function as causes. The actualities in an occasion's past and the subjective aim of that occasion are the passive determinants of its final make-up; the creativity, on the other hand, is the active vehicle whereby these passive determinants gain their effectiveness. The becoming of the occasion is both a manifestation and an individualization of the underlying eternal creativity; but, in this becoming, past actualities function as efficient causes because, through their objectifications and through the conformation their objectifications dictate, they give the newborn occasion its initial character. Also, in this becoming, the subjective aim functions as a final cause because, as inherited and autonomously modified, it dictates how the subject reacts to and makes use of the datum from the past—it dictates, in short, what self shall arise from the datum. The characters given to the occasion by the objectification of, and conformation to, past actualities and the characters which the occasion bestows on itself constitute the whole of the occasion's final character. They constitute, in brief, what that occasion is. Thus, what the occasion is *is* due to the actualities in its past and to its own subjective aim. Nevertheless, that the occasion came to be, that the past actualities are objectified in it, and that it acquired a complex subjective form consonant with its subjective aim are all due to the creativity manifesting itself either transcendentally, as in transition, or immanently, as in concrescence.

Our conclusion may be put as follows: though the actualities in an occasion's past, and the occasion's own subjective aim, are the specific causes of the final determinateness of that occasion, they do not account for the fact that there was a process of causation productive of that occasion. Causation, then, is a dynamic process presupposing the creativity of which each occasion, in its becoming, is a particular manifestation and individualization. However, because it abstracts cause and causation from one another, this conclusion distorts to some extent the nature of the creative process by which an actual occasion comes to be. The ultimate fact in this respect is the indissoluble relation between the creative process and the causes which determine *what* is created. For no explanation can be provided for the fact that a completed occasion, by its mere existence, provokes its reproduction in every subsequent occasion. Nor is there an explanation for the allied fact that an occasion, once it exists with its immanent datum of objectified occasions, and with its initial conformal feelings (both physical and mental), proceeds to fashion its own subjective character in accord with its autonomously modified subjective aim. In other words, the two species of causation—efficient and final—involved in the becoming of every actual occasion are ultimate facts.

The metaphysical ultimacy of the two interrelated processes of causation—or, equivalently, the ultimacy of the interrelated creative processes of transition and concrescence—is what the principle of creativity, insofar as it is identified with the Category of the Ultimate, cryptically asserts: that the many (as reproduced by the process of transition) become one (as synthesized by the process of concrescence) and are increased by one (as accumulated superjects). It is now time to examine the Category of the Ultimate in some depth.

8. The Category of the Ultimate

According to Whitehead, the notions of *creativity*, *many*, and *one* are essential components of the Category of the Ultimate. When used in the senses pertinent to this Category, the terms 'one', 'many', and 'creativity', stand respectively for the singularity of an entity, for a disjunctive diversity of singular entities, and for "that ultimate principle by which the many, which are the universe disjunctively, become the one actual occa-

sion, which is the universe conjunctively" (PR 31). The basic metaphysical notion captured by this Category is then formulated as follows:

> 'Creativity' is the principle of *novelty*. An actual occasion is a novel
> entity diverse from any entity in the 'many' which it unifies. Thus
> 'creativity' introduces novelty into the content of the many, which are
> the universe disjunctively. The 'creative advance' is the application of
> this ultimate principle of creativity to each novel situation which it
> originates.
> 'Together' is a generic term covering the various special ways in
> which various sorts of entities are 'together' in any one actual occa-
> sion. Thus 'together' presupposes the notions 'creativity,' 'many,'
> 'one', 'identity' and 'diversity'. The ultimate metaphysical principle is
> the advance from disjunction to conjunction, creating a novel entity
> other than the entities given in disjunction. The novel entity is at once
> the togetherness of the 'many' which it finds, and also it is one among
> the disjunctive 'many' which it leaves; it is a novel entity, disjunc-
> tively among the many entities which it synthesizes. The many
> become one, and are increased by one. In their natures, entities are
> disjunctively 'many' in process of passage into conjunctive unity.
> This Category of the Ultimate replaces Aristotle's category of 'pri-
> mary substance'. (PR 31–32)

In its most succinct formulation, then, the Category of the Ultimate
tells us that by reason of creativity the many entities of the universe are
always becoming one and are also being increased by one. But since God
is the eternal actual entity in whose primordial nature are included all the
eternal objects, and since all entities of all other types are either constituents of, or constituted by, actual entities, we may safely assume that the
'many entities' referred to by the Category of the Ultimate are actual
entities. Accordingly, what this ultimate principle is telling us, in effect, is
that the many actual entities become one and are increased by one. But
with this we are brought face to face with either a contradiction or the
familiar paradox of solidarity.

Without the twofold reality which the principle of relativity attaches to
all completed actualities (and, more generally, to every entity of every
type) the most general and fundamental principle of Whitehead's metaphysics—the Category of the Ultimate—would be an outright contradiction. The contradiction is not immediately obvious in Whitehead's characterization of creativity as "that ultimate principle by which the many,
which are the universe disjunctively, become the one actual occasion,
which is the universe conjunctively" (PR 31). But as Whitehead elaborates
on this principle, what he says, if taken literally, is hopelessly self-

contradictory. For the novel occasion created by the advance from disjunction to conjunction, Whitehead tells us, "is at once the togetherness of the 'many' which it finds, and also it is one among the disjunctive 'many' which it leaves; it is a novel entity, disjunctively among the many entities which it synthesizes. The many become one, and are increased by one" (PR 32). This means, in effect, that each novel occasion "is one among others, and including the others which it is among" (AI 231). But how can the new occasion be one *among* the many other occasions and also *contain within* itself those same other occasions?

The problem raised by any literal reading of the Caegory of the Ultimate may be put this way: how can an actual occasion be at once the creative synthesis of, and a novel addition to, the many occasions of its correlative universe? The new occasion, through its subjective reactions, does add novelty to what it finds. But this is not the sense in which the novel entity is an addition to the disjunctive many which it finds, for the new occasion synthesizes within itself both what it finds and what it adds. Moreover, if the many entities which the novel occasion finds are united *within* that novel occasion, if they are together *in* it, then that novel occasion cannot be also *alongside*, as it were, the entities it found. The new occasion exists as their synthesis; it includes them; it cannot exist also side by side with them; for that would require that the many entities be both inside and outside the new occasion—a logical impossibility. Accordingly, the novel occasion cannot both synthesize and add itself to the many completed occasions it finds as already existing in its universe. It cannot both reduce a multiplicity to one and increase it by one. Hence, the Category of the Ultimate, or principle of creativity, is self-contradictory—unless, of course, it be interpreted in light of the twofold reality of completed occasions that is implied by the principle of relativity. In that light, what first appeared as a logical impossibility now becomes the familiar paradox of the solidarity of occasions.

If the twofold reality of entities is accepted, if each entity is real as a transcendent potential and real as an immanent determinant, then the paradox associated with the Category of the Ultimate is alleviated; but it is not erradicated, since there emerges a new paradox: In what sense are the numerically distinct transcendent potential and immanent determinant the same entity? Indeed, the acceptance of the systematic ambiguity attaching to the notion of an entity merely replaces one paradox with another, but, for our present purposes, we may assume the eventual resolution of this second paradox and proceed to examine how the first paradox is eliminated.

Here we must remember Whitehead's assertion that the "cumulation of the many is not their reproduction as many" (PR 365). For the original paradox is dispelled as soon as we equate 'disjunctive many' with 'cumulated many', and 'conjunctive many' with 'reproduced many'. The actual occasions forming the disjunctive many are the self-same actual occasions forming the conjunctive many, but there is a *numerical* difference between each actual occasion in the disjunctive many and its counterpart, or objectification, in the conjunctive many. We have to distinguish, therefore, between the growing accumulation of completed actualities *qua* their original selves, or superjects, and those same actualities *qua* their reproduced selves, or objectifications.

In respect to the creative advance of the universe, then, superjects constitute the cumulative or *disjunctive* many, whereas the causal objectifications of those superjects in later occasions constitute the reproduced or *conjunctive* many. The many entities, in either case, constitute the universe correlative to a new occasion. Hence, the universe as including the new occasion is a disjunctive diversity which yet functions as a conjunctive diversity within the new occasion. For the disjunctive universe has a capacity for functioning as a determinant of the new occasion, but it exercises that capacity by being reproduced within the new occasion. In this manner, the correlative universe of an actual occasion is both beyond and within that occasion, and the immanent universe has as many actual components as the transcendent universe. But it is the components of the immanent universe that are integrated by the occasion *qua* concrescent subject into subordinate elements of its final unity (PR 233). In the final satisfaction, therefore, the many (as their reproduced selves) have become one within the novel addition to the many (as their original selves). We thus arrive at the only logically consistent sense in which a novel occasion can be "disjunctively among the many entities which it synthesizes." For what Whitehead means is that the novel occasion is disjunctively among the many entities *whose reproductions* it includes and synthesizes.

The Category of the Ultimate, then, construes the universe as an evergrowing community of actual occasions. Every new settlement of that community, every new disjunctive multiplicity of attained actualities, gives rise, through the transcendent process of *transition*, to a new occasion in which that particular settlement is reproduced, and the settlement as reproduced is then synthesized into a final unity of experience by the immanent process of *concrescence*. But the original settlement is thereby added to; there is now a new settlement which includes the new occasion and all the occasions of the old settlement (PR 364). There is thus a new disjunctive multiplicity from which yet another new occasion takes rise. In other words, each new attained actuality defines a new actual world, a new creative situation, from which an even newer actuality emerges. The universe's creative advance "is the application of this ultimate principle of creativity to each novel situation which it originates" (PR 32). But the creative advance involves both the accumulation and the reproduction of actualities. The universe, then, "expands through recurrent unifications of itself, each, by the addition of itself, automatically recreating the multiplicity anew" (PR 438; see also PR 89).

As reproduced, then, and only as reproduced, the universe's many accumulated actualities become one within the new actuality housing their reproductions; and, when the new actuality is completed, its superjective existence increases by one the number of the accumulated many. That, in a nutshell, is the only logically consistent interpretation to which the Category of the Ultimate is amenable. This interpretation of the most fundamental organic principle, the principle presupposed by all the other organic categories, emphasizes the fact that the oneness of the universe, according to Whitehead, repeats itself, without loss of self-identity, in each of its component creatures. But this repetition of the universe necessarily involves the repetition of each of its actual components. Hence, the universe and every item in it are constantly becoming many. The impact of the Category of the Ultimate is thus twofold: "On the one side, the one becomes many; and on the other side, the many become one" (PR 254).

9. Solidarity, the Ultimate, and the Categoreal Scheme

Obviously, the paradox of the Category of the Ultimate is of a piece with the paradox of the thesis of solidarity. Indeed, the Category of the Ultimate is really the thesis of solidarity in disguise. It is that thesis cryptically reformulated to emphasize the dynamic character of the universe; for the universe as a solidarity of actualities is not a static fact, given once and for all; rather, it is an ongoing achievement. Accordingly, the Category of the Ultimate gives expression to this ultimate fact about the universe: that it is creative and that by virtue of its creativeness its many entities are ever becoming one and are thus being increased by one. There is no explaining this fact.[6] "Each creative act is the universe incarnating itself as one, and there is nothing above it by way of final condition" (PR 375).

However, though the fact of creative advance cannot be explained by reference to anything more ultimate than itself, it can and must be elucidated. To elucidate it is to ascertain what the basic units of creative advance are, how they relate to one another, what generic features they have, and what other metaphysical principles they presuppose. Equivalently, to elucidate it is to come up with categories capable of clarifying the paradox of the connectedness of entities—the many entities, the one universe without and within. Thus, the sorts of entities involved in the creative advance, the what and how of each process of synthesis, and the other metaphysical constraints governing each such process, are respectively rendered explicit in the Categories of Existence, of Explanation, and of Obligation. In this regard, therefore, the other categories of the organic philosophy represent an attempt to make explicit what is implicitly asserted in the Category of the Ultimate.

By way of illustration, let us examine how the principle of process, the principle of relativity, and the ontological principle make clear or explicit much of what is vague or implicit in the principle of creativity. The Category of the Ultimate asserts that the creative advance "is the universe always becoming one in a particular unity of self-experience, and thereby adding to the multiplicity which is the universe as many" (PR 89). In that regard, the principle of process formulates the relationship between a unit of creative advance considered as a synthesizing process and that same unit considered as added product (PR 34, 360). It emphasizes that the unit-process and the unit-product are the same entity in two successive modes of existence: first, as a self-realizing subject and, next, as a self-realized superject. The principle of relativity, in turn, establishes the metaphysical character which each unit-product shares with all entities of all types—namely, that they are, each and all, capacities for the determination of unit-processes, exercising their respective capacities by being reproduced within each unit-process that finds them already in existence. Finally, the ontological principle establishes the sorts of particular reasons, or of particular causes, that can be given as explanatory of how and why a particular unit-product of the creative advance came to have the determinate characters that it has. All such reasons or causes, this principle asserts, are to be sought either in that unit itself, to the extent that it was a self-functioning (or self-realizing) entity, or in the character of other unit-products, to the extent that they had objective functioning within (or were reproduced in) the unit in question (PR 36, 134).[7]

Notice that in the elucidation of the Category of the Ultimate the ontological principle is more fundamental than the principle of process.

For the former principle establishes that each unit-product is the outcome of two different species of creative process: one of efficient, the other of final, causation (PR 228, 320); whereas the latter principle merely emphasizes that the teleological process is immanent to the entity, *i.e.*, that final causation *is* the partly determinate entity as in the process of becoming completely determinate through the realization of its subjective aim (PR 135, 423, 130, 373, 390, 524). The ontological principle, however, is less fundamental (because more specialized) than the principle of relativity. For the efficient process of transition involves the objectification of past actualities, and the teleological process of concrescence involves the ingression of eternal objects. Hence, both processes involve the repetition of entities, and thus both presuppose the repeatability of all entities— presuppose, that is, the principle of relativity. Accordingly, when Whitehead says that the relativity principle is the basic doctrine on which his metaphysical system is founded, I take him to mean that it is the most basic principle for the elucidation of the Category of the Ultimate or, equivalently, of the thesis of solidarity.

But, as is the case with all the other (nonultimate) categories, the relativity principle not only elucidates but also presupposes the Category of the Ultimate. It presupposes it because the repeatability of entities presupposes the creativity whereby there is repetition. Thus, the principle of creativity is ultimate in one sense, and the principle of relativity is basic in another; thus, too, what is indefinable in one notion is presupposed by, or is relevant to, what is indefinable in the other. This mutual relevance, or coherence, of the two principles is particularly evident when Whitehead says: "The oneness of the universe, and the oneness of each element in the universe, repeat themselves to the crack of doom in the creative advance from creature to creature, each creature including in itself the whole of history and exemplifying the self-identity of things and their mutual diversities" (PR 347–48). Unless this statement be taken seriously—and it is not so taken, I submit, in the received interpretations—much of the coherence and logical consistency of Whitehead's metaphysical system will be either lost or distorted, and worse yet, many of the system's intended applications will be overlooked.

10. Transition and the principles of ontology and creativity

The disastrous consequences of failing to take seriously the repetition of the universe within each of its actual components are nowhere more evident than in the received confusions concerning the role played by the process of transition in the becoming of every actual occasion. This is not surprising, for transition is the creative process whereby there is both the repetition of particulars associated with causal objectification and the repetition of universals associated with conformal physical feelings and conformal conceptual reproductions. Clearly, if one fails to recognize that the organic philosophy posits a doctrine of repeatable particulars, one robs the transitional process of its basic metaphysical office. One then finds it relatively easy to attribute the origination of conformal feelings to the autonomous activity of the concrescent subject. Of course, with this misguided extension of the scope of autonomous self-causation there is no room left in the organic philosophy for a legitimate theory of efficient causation—a loss overlooked by most Whiteheadian interpreters.

The received misinterpretations of transition are practically necessitated by the received misunderstandings of the organic principles of process, relativity, ontology, and creativity. For all five misapprehensions stem from the failure to recognize that actual entities are repeatable particulars; thus, the misapprehensions tend to reinforce each other. In what remains of the present chapter, therefore, my interpretation of all four basic organic principles will be used to distinguish the process of transition from the process of concrescence. But the principles of ontology and creativity will have a particularly marked relevance to this task because the processes of transition and concrescence *are* the processes of efficient and final causation and thus constitute the two major stages of the creative process whereby the many become one and are increased by one. In this respect, then, the considerations that follow further our interpretation of the principles of ontology and creativity by showing their mutual relevance in their illumination of the organic doctrines of efficient and final causation.

11. *Transition distinguished from concrescence*

Transition and concrescence, according to Whitehead, are two distinct species of creative process equally involved in the becoming of every actual occasion. That much, at least, is clearly and explicitly stated in "Process," the tenth chapter of Part II of PR. In fact, even the most cursory examination of "Process" would reveal that Whitehead is there preoccupied with carefully characterizing and contrasting two species of creative process: the macroscopic process of transition, which is the vehicle of the efficient cause or actual past, and the microscopic process of concrescence, which is the vehicle of the final cause or subjective aim (PR 320, 327). Both species of process are involved in the becoming of every actual occasion, but they make contrasting contributions to the final determinate make-up of each actual occasion: transition is the creative process providing the conditions really governing the attainment of an actual occasion (PR 322, 327), whereas concrescence is the creative process providing the ends actually attained by an actual occasion (PR 327).

The contrasting roles of transition and concrescence are thus so clearly and explicitly formulated by Whitehead that it is truly puzzling to note how the lion's share of Whiteheadian scholarship, in respect to the becoming of occasions, has been devoted to the analysis and elucidation of concrescence while no more than a passing glance has been given to transition.[8] It is even more puzzling to note, however, that what little attention has been given to transition has resulted in interpretations of it which refuse to take Whitehead at his word. For despite Whitehead's straightforward characterization of transition as a creative process involved in the becoming of every actual occasion, and despite the great care he took to contrast transition and concrescence, the tendency among Whiteheadian scholars has been either to construe transition as a mere succession of concrescences and not as a genuine creative process, or to take transition and concrescence to be one self-same process viewed from two different perspectives.[9]

A typical statement of the first of these misinterpretations is provided by Ivor Leclerc in his influential *Whitehead's Metaphysics*.[10] By equating the *whole* of an occasion's becoming with its concrescence or process of self-realization (an equation which is surely mistaken, as I hope to show here), Leclerc eliminates any possibility of construing transition as a genuine creative process.[11] For if the occasion is entirely self-realized or self-caused, and if—as it is generally agreed—the process of self-realization *is* the process of concrescence, then the process of transition, whatever else it may be, cannot be genuinely creative or productive of the occasion.[12] According to Leclerc, therefore, transition is not a creative process at all; rather, it is a process only "in the derivative sense of the supersession of the epochal acts of becoming."[13] What Leclerc would have us believe, then, is that by 'the process of transition' nothing more is meant than 'a succession of processes of concrescence'.

The second misinterpretation is primarily associated with Donald Sherburne, who first introduced it in his well-known *A Whiteheadian Aesthetic*.[14] Sherburne also equates the whole of an occasion's becoming with its process of self-realization. But he manages to construe transition as a creative process by the simple expedient of taking transition and concrescence to be the self-same process of self-realization viewed from two different angles. As Sherburne understands it, there is only one creative process involved in the becoming of an occasion, but Whitehead alternates between calling it 'transition' and calling it 'concrescence' according to which of two major aspects of that process he wishes to emphasize. 'Transition' refers to the production of novelty, the novelty of the occasion that has come into being. 'Concrescence' refers to the production of togetherness, the togetherness of the past occasions within the experience of the new occasion. But the production of togetherness and the coming into being of the new occasion happen simultaneously. The becoming of the novel occasion *is* the production of togetherness. Hence, transition and concrescence, as Sherburne understands them, are one and the same process.

In opposition to Leclerc and Sherburne, and in accord with my interpretation of the principles of process, relativity, ontology, and creativity, I shall argue here that the process of concrescence cannot be equated with the whole of an occasion's becoming, and that the process of transition is the earliest major stage in the becoming of an occasion. I argue, moreover, that transition is a creative process begetting a novel but incomplete occasion, and that the realities at work in this begetting of an occasion's earliest stage of existence are the already completed actualities and the underlying eternal creativity of the universe. Thus, a major part of my interpretation is that a new occasion, in respect to the three earliest phases of its becoming and existence, the phases constituting the stage of transition, cannot be construed in any way as creating itself. It is created, or brought into existence, by its correlative universe. Its self-realization, by which no more is meant than its self-completion, is the province of the next major stage of its becoming and existence, the stage of concrescence, a stage made up of the phases of conceptual reversion and aesthetic integration.

More specifically, I shall argue here that the creativity involved in the becoming of an actual occasion manifests itself in two supersessionally successive processes. The earlier process, which has the many settled actualities of the universe as its initial data, at once begets the occasion relative to which that settlement is defined and also abstractly objectifies, or reproduces, that settlement within that occasion. The earlier process, in addition, begets the initial subjectivity of the occasion and conforms it to the settlement as objectified for it. This earlier process is the efficient, transcendent, macroscopic process of transition. The later process, which has the product of transition as its complex datum, starts from that datum, reacts to it, and ultimately fuses both the datum and the reactions in the final integral unity of feeling which is the satisfaction. This later process is the teleological, immanent, microscopic process of concrescence.

Whitehead leaves no doubt that the immanent objectifications of the settled actualities are *not* produced by the process of concrescence, but constitute a *given* for it:

> The discussion of how the actual particular occasions become original elements for a new creation is termed the theory of objectification. The objectified particular occasions together have the unity of a datum for the creative concrescence. (PR 320–21)

The datum, then, is already in existence when the concrescence begins (PR 356, 489; AI 229). But what creates the datum? Whitehead's answer to this question is clear and explicit:

> The creativity in virtue of which any relative complete actual world is, by the nature of things, the datum for a new concrescence, is termed 'transition'. Thus, by reason of transition, 'the actual world' is always a relative term, and refers to that basis of presupposed actual occasions which is a datum for the novel concrescence. (PR 322)

The concrescence, it should now be obvious, begins from the datum which the transition provides for it. This is why Whitehead says, again and again (but to the utter puzzlement of his major interpreters[15]), that the past occasions are objectified *for* the concrescence (*e.g.*, PR 38, 66, 82, 208, 321).

One function of the process of transition, therefore, is to objectify in and for every novel occasion all the completed occasions already in existence. We thus arrive at the concept of the actual world of any actual entity as a nexus of completed or settled actualities "whose objectification constitutes the complete unity of the objective datum for the physical feeling of that actual entity" (PR 351; see also 320–21 and 101). But inasmuch as the datum for feeling must itself be immanent in, and constitutive of, the novel entity, this means that the first product of transition is not only the objective datum for concrescence but is also the entity itself as in its earliest, or dative, phase of existence (PR 101, 234, 309–10; AI 299). This dative phase, this already existing but incomplete occasion, is the *objective content* of the novel entity (PR 101, 230–37). It is what the concrescent subject will experience as objectively given.

Another function of the process of transition is to beget the occasion's subjective immediacy while conforming it, both physically and mentally, to the definiteness of the actualities in the objective content. There are thus two major aspects to the transitional process. On the one hand, transition creates the initial objective pole of the new occasion. This objective pole is composed primarily, but not exclusively (as we shall see in later chapters), of the objectifications of the attained actualities of its actual world. On the other hand, transition creates the initial subjective pole of the new occasion, with its initial definiteness of physical enjoyment, conformally derived from the objective pole, and with its initial definiteness of conceptual appetition, conformally derived from the physical enjoyment.

In regard to the first aspect of transition, the occasion is created as the *recipient* of the objectification of its actual world. In regards to the second aspect, the occasion's subjective immediacy is created as the *patient* of an imposed conformation to its received objective content. In other words, its initial subjective forms of emotions and valuations are not of its own choosing. It is born with them; they constitute the second-hand character which the subject inherits from its given world. Thus the new subject is born as the *recipient* of its objectified actual world and as the *patient* of its conformal primary feelings.

After it is born—in the sense of 'after' appropriate to the nature of intrinsic supersession—the subject is an *agent* deciding what it is to be and how it is to affect the relevant future (PR 130, 374). This subjective agency is precisely the aspect of an actual occasion that is *not* produced by the process of transition. For, in this context, 'agency' means autonomous, teleological self-causation—means, in short, concrescence. Accordingly, transition is the process whereby the subject has its double character of recipient and patient, whereas concrescence is the process whereby the subject has its character of agent. However, since intrinsic supersession is a cumulative process, it follows that the concrescent subject "never loses its triple character of recipient, patient, and agent" (PR 481).

These three characters are cryptically expressed by Whitehead in the following account of the two contrasting kinds of process, or of flux, involved in the becoming of every actual occasion:

> One kind is the *concrescence* which, in Locke's language, is 'the real internal constitution of a particular existent'. The other kind is the *transition* from particular existent to particular existent. This transition, again in Locke's language, is the 'perpetual perishing' which is one aspect of the notion of time; and in another aspect the transition is the origination of the present in conformity with the 'power' of the past. (PR 320/CPR 210)

Unfortunately, Whitehead's use of Lockean phrases—'real internal constitution', 'perpetual perishing', and 'power'—to convey these basic organic doctrines is more misleading than helpful. By the 'internal constitution' of an existent, Locke meant only the internal make-up of a substance. Moreover, in Locke's view, the internal constitution of substances, other than our own individual minds, is unknowable by us. Indeed, he seems to have chosen the terms 'internal' and 'constitution' to convey, respectively, the hiddenness or interiority of substances, and the fact that what is hidden is the substance's very essence. Also, the term 'constitution' was not intended by Locke to connote any notion of self-formative, or self-creative, activity.[16]

Whitehead, on the other hand, uses this Lockean phrase to signify the intrinsic creation, or autonomous self-realization, of an actual entity, though he uses it also to signify the make-up of a completed actuality insofar as that make-up is the result of autonomous self-causation. The radical departure from Locke's meaning is again evident in the fact that the internal make-up of a completed actuality is revealed to later occasions by reason of its abstractive objectification in them. Objectification "is self-revelation" (PR 347). Thus, there are few similarities between what Locke and Whitehead meant each by the internal constitution of an existent. In any case, what Whitehead signifies by Locke's phrase is the process of self-realization whereby the actual occasion is a partial determinant of itself and of the future beyond itself (PR 130). Accordingly, the process of concrescence exhibits the occasion's subjective agency in respect both to its own satisfaction and to its own transcendent causal objectifications.

Whitehead's use of the phrase 'perpetually perishing' is even more misleading. In the first place, Locke does not use the phrase in connection with the idea of time. For him, time is an idea derived from duration, which is an idea derived from succession, which is an idea derived from the experienced stream of ideas. It is in Locke's attempt to explain what is to be understood by 'duration' that the phrase under consideration occurs. According to Locke, duration "is another sort of distance, or length, the idea whereof we get not from the permanent parts of space, but from the fleeting and perpetually perishing parts of succession."[17] In the second place, leaving aside the mind's power to retain or revive ideas, the crucial feature of Locke's doctrine is the evanescent character of the parts of succession. There is no accumulation of the parts of succession; each part vanishes the moment it ceases to be present.

Whitehead's most general use of 'perpetually perishing' is to signify the supersessional process of creative advance, a process which, in one sense, is inherent in every actuality, and which, in another sense, has every

actuality inherent in it (IS 240). Here we must remember that supersession is a threefold process. Each actuality supersedes other actualities, is
internally a process of supersession, and is superseded by other actualities
(IS 241). Supersession as inherent in an actuality is nothing other than the
latter's process of concrescence. But the settled actualities in the nascent
creature's actual world are inherent in the supersessional process whereby
there is a transition from that actual world to the given, pre-concrescence,
phases of that creature. Similarly, the completed creature is inherent in
every supersessional process whereby there is a transition from an actual
world of which that creature is a settled component to the given phases of
another new creature. Thus, transition to, and from, a new creature, are
the other two aspects of supersession.

But the point to emphasize now is that transition *to* a new actuality, and
transition *from* a new actuality, are as much parts of the actuality's real
essence as is its concrescence (PR 327; IS 241–43). Why this is so cannot
be adequately explained until I have developed Whitehead's theory of
metaphysical extension. Suffice it to say for now that the transition to the
new creature is physically anticipated by some actualities in its past, and
that the new creature physically anticipates the transition from itself to
some actualities in its future. Thus, physical anticipation, which involves
the objectification of the future in the present,

> illustrates the truth that the creativity, whereby there is supersession,
> cannot be disjoined from the creature which is superseded. The
> character of the creativity is found in the analysis of the creature. The
> creativity *for* the creature has become the creativity *with* the creature;
> and the creature is thereby superseded. (IS 243)

Also, the creativity *for* the creature is the creativity *with* the completed
earlier creatures. Accordingly, the real essence of an actual occasion
cannot be divorced from the threefold character of supersession.

With this in mind, and given the cumulative character of the product-
phases of supersession, Whitehead's equation of supersession with perpetual perishing is as careless as it is misleading. Here is what Whitehead
says:

> Thus in the place of Descartes's substance with "endurance" as one of
> its principal attributes, we must put the notion of an "occasion" with
> "supersession" as part of its real essence. By Locke, the phrase
> "perpetually perishing" is used in the same sense as "supersession"
> here. (IS 240)

Of course, Locke never used, nor could he even have dreamt of using, the phrase in question to signify what Whitehead means by supersession. In Locke's theory the parts of succession are externally related to one another; in Whitehead's theory the parts of concrete time are internally related to one another. Similarly, for Locke the parts of succession vanish completely and in no way accumulate; for Whitehead the parts of concrete time perish subjectively, but are immortal objectively, and thereby constitute the cumulative character of actuality's creative advance. In other words, though the process-subphases of supersession are as fleeting for Whitehead as the parts of succession are for Locke, the fact remains that the product-subphases of supersession accumulate to form satisfied occasions, and that the satisfied occasions accumulate to form the ever-expanding actual universe. Thus, Whitehead's use of 'perpetually perishing' is misleading precisely because Locke's phrase cannot capture—indeed, it is antithetical to—the notion of time's cumulative character. It can do justice neither to the accumulation of phase-products, nor to the accumulation of attained actualities.

Whitehead's use of Locke's phrase, in the passage under consideration, is particularly misleading because it is not being used to signify the threefold process of supersession but only that aspect of supersession which falls under the heading of *transition to* a new occasion. Fortunately, in the passage Whitehead links transition to two aspects of time: perpetual perishing and conformity to the power of the past. This is fortunate because the reference to the second aspect of time helps to illuminate Whitehead's meaning, even though the notion of power is also borrowed from Locke and liberally modified. The illumination does not result from any identity of meaning between 'power' as used by Locke and 'power' as used by Whitehead. In fact, for the former the term meant the ability to produce, or the ability to receive, change; whereas for the latter, since actual occasions become and perish but do *not* change (a paradox which I will explain in later chapters), the term means an occasion's capacity to give, or to receive, determination, including the capacity to determine itself.[18] The illumination results, instead, from passages where Whitehead makes clear what he means by the power of past actualities.

Under this illumination, time's aspect of perpetual perishing is best construed as the *perpetual objectification* of completed actualities, which is the reason for the immanence of the immortal past in every new occasion. Time's aspect of conformity to the past is then straightforwardly understood as the generation of the *reproductive subjective forms* whereby an occasion's conformal physical feelings are constituted. Thus, in the passage in question, Whitehead is ascribing to transition the functions of objectifying the past actualities in and for the new occasion and of conforming the occasion's initial subjectivity to the objectified past. Thus, too, transition accounts for those aspects of an occasion whereby it may be understood as receptive and as patient.

That the passage is correctly interpreted in this manner is a contention amply supported by an examination of relevant notions and texts. Four major considerations are particularly pertinent. First, the organic notion of supersession is broader than the organic notion of concrete time, for the latter notion concerns primarily the physical pole of the occasion, yet the mental pole is held to supersede the physical pole (PR 378–79; IS 241). Hence, "the linkage between the physical and the mental pole of an occasion illustrates the truth that the category of supersession transcends time, since this linkage is both extratemporal and yet is an instance of supersession" (IS 241). Therefore, time's aspect of perpetual perishing cannot be equated, *in the passage in question*, with the entire supersessional process associated with a particular actual occasion.

Second, the occasion's physical pole, we have seen already, is composed of the dative and conformal phases insofar as the former phase is absorbed by the latter. Accordingly, the analysis of the physical pole yields the occasion's simple physical feelings and yields no other feelings belonging to the occasion. But

> simple physical feelings embody the reproductive [*i.e.*, conformal] character of nature, and also the objective immortality [*i.e.*, objectification] of the past. In virtue of these feelings time is the conformation of the immediate present to the past. Such feelings are 'conformal' feelings. (PR 364)

Given that it is only through their objectifications in a new act that the settled acts of the past "establish the conditions to which that act must conform" (S 36), it follows that what a simple physical feeling embodies are a conformal subjective form and the causal objectification which imposed the conformation. These two components of conformal feelings, it must now be argued, are the same two aspects of time associated with, and generated by, the process of transition.

Third, to say that time is the conformation of the immediate present to the past is to say that time is the *felt* conformation of subjective immediacy to the causal objectifications given *for* that immediacy. This is part of the reason why Whitehead says that "the immediate present has to conform to what the past is for it, and the mere lapse of time is an abstraction from the more concrete relatedness of 'conformation'" (S 36). In this regard, the point I am stressing is that Whitehead is here construing time as a relation between two supersessionally related components of an actual occasion—the objective content and the initial conformal immediacy. This, however, is not the only metaphysical meaning that the term 'time' has in the organic philosophy; for insofar as 'time' denotes a relationship between actual entities, it necessarily shares in the systematic ambiguity of 'actual entity'. The point, then, is that metaphysical time has a twofold reality in the organic philosophy. On the one hand, it is the macrocosmic creative advance whereby there is a supersession of mutually transcendent actual occasions. On the other, it is the microcosmic creative advance from objective content to conformal feelings. For just as occasion A is super-seded by occasion B, so too the objectification of A in B is superseded by the conformation of B's subjectivity to the objectification of A. Thus there is a macrocosmic advance marked by the absolutely initial birth, or dative phase, of a new occasion, and there is a microcosmic advance marked by the birth of the new occasion's conformal subjectivity. The former advance is inter-occasional; the latter is intra-occasional. But the microcosmic advance is the immanent mirroring within an actual occasion of the macrocosmic advance from its own actual world to its own dative phase. For this reason, microcosmic time carries the imprint of, and gives witness to, macrocosmic time.

But since both aspects of time—the perpetual objectification of the past and the conformation of the immediate present to the objectified past—are generated by the macroscopic process of transition, it follows that the transitional process produces both kinds of creative advance: the macrocosmic passage from transcendent actual world to immanent objective content, and the microcosmic passage from objective content to conformal feelings. This means, therefore, that transition begets the first two phases of an occasion's existence—its dative phase and its conformal phase. It produces both the objective datum and the conformal subjective form of every simple physical feeling. Thus, in virtue of its two-phase generation of simple conformal feelings, transition exhibits on the one hand the macrocosmic aspect of time, which is the perpetual perishing of the past, and on the other hand the microcosmic aspect of time, which is the conformation of the immediate present to the power of the past (PR 320, 364; S 35–37; IS 243–44).

Fourth, my interpretation of transition is now easily corroborated by Whitehead's illuminating remarks concerning the notion of power. Whitehead explicitly says that Locke's doctrine of power is reproduced in the organic doctrine of objectification (PR 91). In respect to the objectification of past actualities this means that "the philosophy of organism holds that in order to understand 'power,' we must have a correct notion of how each individual actual entity contributes to the datum *from which* its successors arise and *to which* they must conform" (PR 88). But the datum from which an actual entity arises, and to which it must conform, is the immanent datum, or objective content, which is the occasion's dative, and first, phase of existence. In other words, a completed actuality contributes to the datum of a later occasion by being causally objectified in it (PR 117–18, 127).

> In 'causal objectification' what is felt *subjectively* by the objectified actual entity is transmitted *objectively* to the concrescent actualities which supersede it. In Locke's phraseology the objectified actual entity is then exerting 'power'. (PR 91)

Given that the objectified actuality dictates how it is to be conformed to by the initial subjectivity of the later actuality (AI 327), we must conclude that "the 'power' of one actual entity on the other is simply how the former is objectified in the constitution of the other" (PR 91).

The link between the two aspects of time—perpetual perishing of, and conformity to, the past—and the first two phases of transition is now conclusively established. The first aspect of time is due to the first phase of the macroscopic transition—the phase whereby the actual world becomes an immanent datum for a new occasion (PR 322). This is the process-subphase by which the objective content of a new occasion is originated. The second aspect of time is due to the second phase of the macroscopic transition—the phase whereby the subjective immediacy of the new occasion is originated in conformity with the objectification, or power, of the past (PR 320). This is the process-subphase by which the simple physical feelings are begotten (PR 364).

There is yet a third phase of transition, though the passage we have been examining does not allude to it. I mean, of course, the phase of conceptual reproduction. Whitehead never explicitly subsumes this phase under the process of transition. But there is no possibility of consistently attributing the production of this phase to the microscopic process of concrescence. In the first place, the concrescence of an actual occasion is clearly characterized by Whitehead as a process of self-formation integrating the occasion's physical and mental poles into a unity of experience

(PR 165). Thus, the process of concrescence presupposes the prior existence of at least one phase of the mental pole, as well as the existence of the entire physical pole (PR 374). Since the feelings of conceptual reproduction constitute the first phase of the mental pole (PR 380–81), this means that the process of concrescence must start *after* the conceptual reproductions have been begotten.

In the second place, the concrescence of an actual occasion is explicitly held by Whitehead to be a process of self-realization guided by a subjective aim initially derived from God (PR 164, 343). But the initial subjective aim is a simple conceptual feeling whose data and subjective form are reproductively derived from the occasion's hybrid physical feeling of God (PR 343–44). In other words, the initial subjective aim is itself a feeling of conceptual reproduction generated by the occasion's third phase of becoming. Hence, there can be no process of concrescence until after the phase of conceptual reproduction has produced for the occasion its initial subjective aim. This is why Whitehead says that the concrescence starts *from* (and not *with*) the occasion's reception of its initial subjective aim (PR 374).

In the third place, the concrescence of an actual occasion is explicitly described by Whitehead as being an autonomous teleological process. But the occasion's first exhibition of autonomy is the modification of the initial subjective aim that takes place in the phase of conceptual reversion (PR 390, 374–75, 343). Since this phase is supersessionally subsequent to the phase of conceptual reproduction (PR 380–81), it follows that the process of concrescence begins with the generation of conceptual reversions, and after the generation of conceptual reproductions. Put another way, the concrescence of an actual occasion begins with the second phase of its mental pole; for although the first mental phase introduces purpose into the occasion, it is only the second mental phase that exhibits autonomy and thus "introduces the subject as a determinant of its own concrescence" (PR 380).

The preceding arguments prove conclusively that the phase of conceptual reproduction, since it cannot be attributed to the autonomous concrescence, belongs to or is generated by the macroscopic process of transition. But they also prove that the phases of causal objectification and physical conformation cannot be attributed to the process of concrescence; for, as constituents of the occasion's physical pole, these two phases must be in existence already when the first phase of the mental pole is originated. *A fortiori* their existence is supersessionally earlier than the second phase of the mental pole with which the concrescence begins. Transition, we may confidently conclude, is the creative process by which the first three phases of an occasion's existence are begotten.

The reproductive conceptual feelings of the third phase, it should be noted, are the primary mental feelings of an actual occasion, whereas the reverted conceptual feelings of the fourth phase are its secondary mental feelings (PR 425). Like the occasion's primary physical feelings, the primary mental feelings are conformal in nature (PR 165, 377). Taken together, therefore, the primary mental and physical feelings exhibit the occasion as patient of its subjective conformation to the world given for it. The occasion's objective content, on the other hand, exhibits it as recipient of its actual world. But the distinction between the occasion as patient and the occasion as recipient should not be allowed to obscure the fact that the occasion's three earliest phases constitute a given from the point of view of the occasion's autonomous concrescence. The three phases generated by the process of transition thus form a complex datum for the process of concrescence. In this respect, the autonomous concrescent subject is born as the recipient of a threefold determination produced by the transitional process. This threefold determination conditions all attainments possible for the concrescent subject, but the subject itself determines the goals it actually attains. This is why Whitehead says of transition and concrescence that "the former process provides the conditions which really govern attainment; whereas the latter process provides the ends actually attained" (PR 327).

The process of transition, we may conclude, is supersessionally earlier than, and provides a threefold datum for, the process of concrescence. It begets the novel occasion, objectifies in it its correlative actual world, and generates its initial subjectivity in physical and mental conformity to the objectified world. The concrescence, on the other hand, is the process of autonomous self-realization whereby the already existing occasion—starting from, and including within itself, the product of transition—completes itself through the acquisition of novel subjective forms, and through the integration and reintegration of its feelings (PR 249, 373, 232–35). Since the threefold datum is repetitive through and through, and since all novel immediacy is generated by the concrescence, my interpretation of transition and concrescence is in accord with what Whitehead's presystematic analysis of memory suggests—that every becoming involves repetition transformed into novel immediacy. In other words, my interpretation emphasizes that the becoming of every occasion is analyzable into two successive stages: first, there is the becoming of the threefold datum; afterwards, there is the becoming of the self from that datum (PR 228).

In light of this emphasis, it should be evident that Sherburne and Leclerc are wrong in equating the whole of an occasion's becoming with its process of concrescence; for the complex datum has already become when the concrescence begins (PR 355–56). Moreover, since the process of transition both precedes, and provides the datum for, the process of concrescence, it should be evident also that Sherburne is mistaken in construing transition and concrescence as happening simultaneously, or as being one and the same process. Finally, since the process of transition at once begets a novel but incomplete occasion, and provides it with a threefold determination, it should be no less evident that Leclerc is wrong in construing transition as a mere succession of concrescences.

12. Threefold causation, decision, and the ontological principle

Of a piece with the mistake of equating the whole of the occasion's becoming with its process of concrescence is the mistake of taking the occasion to be in all respects self-caused. For an actual occasion is as much the result of efficient causes as it is the result of self-causation (PR 134). But to be the result of efficient causes is to be caused by others. An actual occasion, then, is other-caused as well as self-caused. In addition, an actual occasion is other-causing. It is other-causing insofar as it is objectified in the occasions in its future, just as it is other-caused insofar as past occasions are objectified in it.

By reason of its being other-caused, self-caused, and other-causing, an actual occasion is said to have

> a three-fold character: (i) it has the character 'given' for it by the past; (ii) it has the subjective character aimed at in its process of concrescence; (iii) it has the superjective character, which is the pragmatic value of its specific satisfaction qualifying the transcendent creativity. (PR 134)

Only in respect to the second of these characters, Whitehead explicitly tells us, can the occasion be conceived as *causa sui* (PR 135). In regard to its other two characters, the occasion is dependent on processes of efficient causation. But to say this is to say that the first and third characters of the occasion are due to processes of transition; for transition, it must be emphasized again, is to efficient other-causation what concrescence is to teleological self-causation. This much Whitehead makes absolutely clear in passages such as the following:

> According to this account, efficient causation expresses the transition from actual entity to actual entity; and final causation expresses the internal process whereby the actual entity becomes itself. . . . An actual entity is at once the product of the efficient past, and is also, in Spinoza's phrase, *causa sui*. (PR 228)

> Concrescence moves toward its final cause, which is its subjective aim; transition is the vehicle of the efficient cause, which is the immortal past. (PR 320)

> The 'objectifications' of the actual entities in the actual world, relative to a definite actual entity, constitute the efficient causes out of which *that* actual entity arises; the 'subjective aim' at 'satisfaction' constitutes the final cause, or lure, whereby there is determinate concrescence. (PR 134)

Clearly, then, the occasion's first and third character are due to the process of transition. But we must be careful to distinguish between transition *to* the occasion, which creates the occasion's threefold datum, and transition *from* the occasion, which objectifies the completed occasion in all later occasions.

Between being other-caused and being other-causing, every actual occasion is also self-causing. But by the self-causation of an actual occasion Whitehead cannot mean that the occasion brings itself into existence. For to say that something is absolutely self-caused, or self-created, is to say that that which is non-existent somehow brings itself into existence. Thus, taken in a literal and absolute sense, self-causation is an unintelligible, self-contradictory notion. But even if absolute self-creation were an intelligible notion, it would still not be what Whitehead meant by an occasion being *causa sui;* for, as we have just seen, he held the actual occasion to be the result of efficient causation as well as of self-causation. Moreover, he took the result of efficient causation to be the given, or primary, stage of the occasion's existence, the stage *from which* self-causation starts. Thus, '*causa sui*' cannot mean 'absolute cause of its own existence'.

If not absolute self-creation, what does self-causation mean for Whitehead? His own answer is most instructive: "To be *causa sui* means that the process of concrescence is its own reason for the decision in respect to the qualitative clothing of feelings" (PR 135). To understand Whitehead's answer, however, we must realize that, as used in this passage, 'decision' is a technical term.

Insofar as Whitehead uses it as a technical term, 'decision' does not generally mean a 'conscious choice' or a 'conscious judgment', though in respect to some high-grade occasions it may mean that; instead, the term is taken in its "root sense of a 'cutting off'" (PR 68). What is 'cut off' is always some possibility or potentiality for the determinateness of an actual entity. Actual entities, God excepted, are finite things, and finitude involves exclusion; thus, 'decision' means a cutting off, or exclusion, of the potentiality for being 'that', in order to realize the potentiality for being 'this'. "'Actuality' is the decision amid 'potentiality'" (PR 68).

Keeping in mind the technical meaning of 'decision', what Whitehead means by the self-causation of an occasion becomes apparent as we unpack the implications of the following characterization of the ontological principle: "The ontological principle asserts the relativity of decision; whereby every decision expresses the relation of the actual thing, *for which* a decision is made, to an actual thing *by which* that decision is made" (PR 68). The principle thus formulated, it should be remembered, is also termed by Whitehead the principle of efficient and final causation (PR 36–37). In light of this formulation of the principle, it will be seen that the attained actualities relative to the origination of a new occasion 'decide' the datum for the novel occasion *qua* concrescence (PR 227). In the same light, it will be seen that the new concrescence 'decides' the subjective forms with which it finally clothes its feelings of each objectification in the datum (PR 135, 248–9). Let us first examine the decision providing the objective datum or content.

According to Whitehead, the datum is the decision transmitted *from* the settled past *to* the novel occasion; equivalently, the datum is the decision, or determination, the novel occasion receives *from* its actual world (PR 227). The datum, or each objectification in the datum, is a decision received because it is an immanent constituent of the new occasion and is thus a determinant of that occasion; it contributes to the occasion being 'this' rather than 'that'. But each objectification in the datum is a decision received for a second, even more important, reason: causal objectification abstracts from the full content of the definiteness of the occasion being objectified; hence, the causal objectification of an actual occasion expresses a decision as to which element of the definiteness of the occasion is to be reproduced. But this decision cannot be attributed to the novel occasion in which the settled actuality is being objectified; for, by definition, the objectification in question is a datum *for* the novel occasion. Nor can this decision be attributed to the creativity of transition; for, according to the ontological principle, all decisions are to be attributed to actual entities. Consequently, the decision in question must be attributed to the settled actuality being objectified.

Whitehead's doctrine of physical purposes is intended to explain how the constitution of an attained actuality represents a decision as to *how* it is to be objectified in and for later occasions. We need not enter here into the details of this doctrine, but a rapid sketch of it is pertinent to the task at hand. A physical purpose is a comparative feeling integrating a simple physical feeling with the conceptual feeling derived from it; its subjective form is either an *adversion* or an *aversion*, that is to say, it is either a positive or a negative valuation of its complex datum (PR 406). Adversions and aversions are types of decision (PR 388). In the synthesis of a physical feeling with its conceptual derivative, the

> valuation accorded to the physical feeling endows the transcendent creativity with the character of adversion, or aversion. The character of adversion secures the reproduction of the physical feeling, as one element in the objectification of the subject beyond itself. (PR 422/ CPR 276)

When, on the other hand, the subjective form of the physical purpose is one of aversion,

> the transcendent creativity assumes the character that it inhibits, or attenuates, the objectification of that subject in the guise of that feeling. Thus aversion tends to eliminate one possibility by which the subject may itself be objectified in the future. (PR 422)

The transcendent creativity to which Whitehead refers in these passages, it must be emphasized, is the creativity of the universe as it is manifested in processes of macroscopic transition.[19] It is the creativity whereby there is a transition from subjective concrescence to subjective concrescence (PR 428). This creativity begets the threefold datum of each occasion, but transcends the immanent creativity of each of its creatures.[20] Thus, the phrase 'transcendent creativity' is meant to signify the creativity of transition as transcending the immanent creativity displayed by every occasion *qua* concrescence. This sense of transcendence, therefore, should not be confused with the sense in which the immanent creativity of any one subject may be said to transcend the immanent creativity of all other subjects.

Accordingly, physical purposes are those elements in the constitution of an actual occasion that *decide* how the transcendent creativity of transition is to objectify that occasion into an objective datum for later occasions. Each occasion, then, decides how it is to be objectified in later occasions.

Inasmuch as such a decision refers to what is essentially beyond the occasion making it, Whitehead terms it a 'transcendent decision' (PR 248–49). The transcendent decision is made by the occasion *while* in concrescence; but it does not become effective until the occasion, being completely become, is objectified. Hence, the effectiveness of an occasion's physical purposes depends on the transcendent creativity which takes the completed occasion into account, and which serves as the *vehicle* for that occasion's transcendent decisions—the vehicle both because it objectifies, or reproduces, that occasion in accord with the occasion's own physical purposes, and because it thus "carries" that completed occasion into the make-up of another occasion.[21] This is why, according to Whitehead, "transition is the vehicle of the efficient cause, which is the immortal past" (PR 320).

In this respect, the joint functioning of the physical purposes and of the transcendent creativity provides a link between final causation and efficient causation. Thus, for Whitehead,

> the physical purposes of a subject by their valuations determine the relative efficiency of the various feelings to enter into the objectifica- tions of that subject in the creative advance beyond itself. In this function, the mental operations determine their subject in its charac- ter of efficient cause. Thus the mental pole is the link whereby the creativity is endowed with the double character of final causation, and efficient causation. (PR 423)

In other words, the physical purposes of an occasion are the results of the occasion's teleological self-causation. But when the occasion is completed its physical purposes determine how the occasion is objectified in occa- sions beyond itself (PR 69). Thus, what is originated through final causa- tion becomes the determining factor of efficient causation, and mediating between final causation and efficient causation is the transcendent creativ- ity of transition, the creativity which envisages all settled situations, and which, in relation to each novel occasion that it creates, functions as the vehicle of all efficient causes (PR 320).

As used by Whitehead, the term 'transcendent decision' is systemati- cally ambiguous: it can mean, as we have just shown, the physical pur- poses by which an occasion determines how it is to be objectified by every process of transition that will find that occasion existing as a superject; it can mean, in addition, the actual objectifications of the occasion in ques- tion (PR 227). In yet another sense, the 'transcendent decision' is itself the novel creature as in its first, or dative, phase of existence, the phase which is the objective content for the creature's concrescence. Thus construed, the decision is nothing else than the objectification of the settled past in and for the novel creature—the objectification being one and the same with the novel creature's initial, or aboriginal, or dative, character (PR 134–35, 336, 423, 439; AI 269). This decision, or dative phase, is created or produced by the process of transition. But in the first, more basic, sense of 'decision', this decision is made *for* the novel actuality *by* the actualities in its past. The process of transition merely makes this decision effective. Accordingly, though the transcendent decisions of earlier occasions become effective only through the mediation of the macroscopic process of transition, it remains true that they are decisions made *by earlier* actual things *for later* actual things. Hence, transcendent decisions have the character which the ontological principle requires of all decisions.

Transcendent decisions, however, are not the only species of decision implied by the ontological principle. Just as there are two species of creative process involved in the becoming of every occasion, so, too, there are two species of decision involved in the determination of each occasion. The parallel is not accidental: if transition is the process whereby the datum *for* the occasion is effectively decided *by* the settled world of past actualities, concrescence is the process whereby the occasion decides its own definiteness. Put another way, *qua* concrescence, an occasion is both the actual thing *for which*, and the actual thing *by which*, a decision is made. The decision, of course, is concerned with the *how* of the subject's reaction to the datum; the subject decides with what subjective forms it will finally clothe its feelings of the components of the datum; it also decides how its earlier feelings are to be integrated by later ones. Each decision represents a cutting off of some possibility for the definiteness of that occasion; for if the subjective forms realized be 'these', they cannot also be 'those'. Thus, each subjective reaction, each subjective integration, excludes some possibility of realization from being in fact realized. But the point to notice is that the subject is both the agent and the patient of its originative decisions. The subjective forms which the subject realizes are determinants of its own emerging definiteness. This is why, for Whitehead, the process of concrescence is the subject "determining what it is itself integrally to be, in its own character of the superject of its own process" (PR 369).

The decision involved in the concrescence is, therefore, reflexive or, to use Whitehead's term, 'immanent' (PR 248–49). Accordingly, immanent decision is to teleological self-causation what transcendent decision is to efficient other-causation. Both types of decisions, or of causal processes, are involved in the becoming of an occasion, both are productive of the occasion's determinate character. "In 'transcendent decision' there is transition from the past to the immediacy of the present; and in 'immanent decision' there is the process of acquisition of subjective form and the integration of feeling" (PR 248–49). But since the product of transcendent decision is the datum for the concrescence, and since this datum is the occasion itself as in its earliest stage of existence, it follows that the results of immanent decision are to be construed as *completing* the occasion, and not as absolutely originating it.

The organic meaning of *causa sui* should now be evident: by the self-causation of an occasion Whitehead understands its *self-completion*. For the primitive character of the occasion, the only character it has in its third phase of existence, is not of its own making, but is given to it by the actual past. Thus, the self-realized character of the occasion must be understood as supplementing and integrating this original character. "In this way the decision derived from the actual world, which is the efficient cause, is *completed* by the decision embodied in the subjective aim which is the final cause" (PR 423; italics mine). The outcome of transcendent decision, therefore, is an incomplete occasion, an occasion whose character is only partially determinate; the outcome of immanent decision, on the other hand, is the completely determinate occasion. The process of concrescence, or of immanent decision, is thus to be construed as a succession of creative phases whereby the occasion passes from an initial stage of partial determinateness to a final stage of complete determinateness (PR 132, 373, 524). For Whitehead, then,

> the immanent decision, whereby there is a supervening of stages in an actual entity, is always the determinant of a process of integration whereby *completion* is arrived at—at least, such 'formal' completion as is proper to a single entity. (PR 248; italics mine).

An actual occasion, it is now obvious, should not be construed as bringing itself into existence. Instead, we must conceive of it as being brought into existence by its correlative universe of settled actualities. But once it is in existence, the occasion does create itself in the limited sense of completing itself. In this sense, *the creature is created creator of itself*. The former creation is due to the process of transition; the latter, to the process of concrescence. "The subject completes itself during the process of concrescence by a self-criticism of its own incomplete phases" (PR 373).

13. Decision, objectification, and actuality

The examination of the technical meaning of 'decision' has led us to a correct understanding of the organic notion of self-causation. But we may also avail ourselves of the technical meaning of this term to further substantiate the numerical distinction that exists between a superject and each of its many objectifications.

To this end, let us first notice that a completed actuality, in virtue of the transition *from* it, originates decisions for the occasions which supersede it. Thus, to quote Whitehead, "an actual entity arises from decisions *for* it, and by its very existence provides decisions *for* other actual entities which supersede it" (PR 68). Here, however, we have to differentiate the satisfaction, which by virtue of its existence provides decisions for later occasions, from the causal objectifications of the satisfaction, which *are* the decisions in and for the later occasions. For the satisfaction is the terminal character of the occasion as in its own extensive standpoint; on the other hand, each causal objectification of the satisfaction is that same terminal character as abstractly reproduced in the extensive standpoint of some later occasion.

But if we thus distinguish the satisfaction of an occasion from its manifold objectification, we should expect Whitehead to speak of the fourfold character of an occasion, and not, as in the passage discussed earlier, of its threefold character. Fortunately, this is precisely what Whitehead does in the following passage:

> The four stages constitutive of an actual entity . . . can be named datum, process [of concrescence], satisfaction, decision. The two terminal stages [*i.e.*, the datum and the decision] have to do with 'becoming' in the sense of transition from the settled actual world to the new actual entity relatively to which that settlement is defined. [The] datum is 'decided' by the settled world. It is 'prehended' by the new superseding entity. The datum is the objective content of experience. The decision, providing the datum, is a transference of self-limited appetition; the settled world provides the 'real potentiality' that its many actualities be felt compatibly; and the new concrescence starts from this datum. . . . The final stage, the 'decision', is how the actual entity, having attained its individual 'satisfaction', thereby adds a determinate condition to the settlement for the future beyond itself. Thus, the 'datum' is the 'decision received', and the 'decision' is the 'decision transmitted'. Between these two decisions, received and transmitted, there lie the two stages, 'process' [*i.e.*, concrescence], and 'satisfaction'. (PR 227)

To reconcile these four stages of the occasion—its dative phase (datum), its concrescence (process), its satisfaction and its causal objectifications (decisions for the later occasions)—with the three characters mentioned earlier—dative, subjective, and superjective—we have only to notice that the superject or completed occasion has a twofold reality: on the one hand, there is the reality of the satisfaction in itself; on the other hand, there is the reality of the satisfaction as reproduced in and for later occasions. Thus, the satisfaction and the decision transmitted are *two and the same entity*.

We may also avail ourselves of the technical meaning of 'decision' to emphasize the double meaning which 'actuality' has for Whitehead, and thus to emphasize that there is an important difference between an occasion *qua* its first three phases of existence, and that same occasion *qua* any other phase of its existence. The two meanings of 'actuality' respectively correspond to the *becoming* that is the subject, and to the *being* that is the superject.[22] Both meanings are derivative from the notion of self-determination, or self-realization (PR 38). The one is associated with the creative process of self-causation; the other, with the created product of self-causation. Thus, there is the actuality predicated of subjects because they are self-*realizing* entities; and there is the actuality predicated of superjects because they are self-*realized* entities (PR 340). A subject is an actuality in attainment; a superject is an attained actuality (PR 326–27).

The double meaning of 'actuality' must be linked to the double meaning of 'decision'. For, according to Whitehead, "'decision' cannot be construed as a casual adjunct of an actual entity. It constitutes the very meaning of actuality" (PR 68). But there are two species of decision: transcendent and immanent. Hence, these two species must be associated, respectively, with the two meanings of actuality: the attained actuality of the superject, and the actuality in attainment of the subject. The self-realized superjects are actual because they *determine* the macroscopic processes effecting transcendent decisions; and the self-realizing subjects are actual because they *are* microscopic processes effecting immanent decisions (PR 68–69).

This analysis of the link between the double meanings of 'actuality' and 'decision' shows that there are three phases in an occasion's existence when it is not, technically speaking, actual. For the first three phases of the occasion's existence are the products of the macroscopic transition; they are other-caused rather than self-caused; hence, these phases cannot be construed as actual, since they are neither self-realizing nor self-realized. However, to deny the actuality of these phases is not to deny their real existence. This should be obvious because the organic Categories of Existence include seven categories of non-actual, but very real, entities (PR 32–33; see also the fourth Category of Explanation). These other entities are not actual either because they are in all respects eternal (eternal objects), or because they are in all respects other-realized (subjective forms, prehensions, nexūs, contrasts, propositions, and multiplicities[23]). Occasions, on the other hand, are actual because they are partially self-realized. But they are not *completely* self-realized. They are other-caused and other-causing, as well as self-caused.

My point is that in the organic philosophy a real entity need not be actual, though every actual entity must be real also. Accordingly, an occasion, in any of its phases of existence other than the first three, is both real and actual. But in its first three phases of existence the occasion is *merely* real. This means, therefore, that the process of transition is creative of the merely real occasion; whereas the process of concrescence is the means by which the merely real occasion becomes an attained actuality. Moreover, since the concrescence arises from its given phases (S 21, 86–87), the merely real occasion, and not just the dative phase, is the *real potentiality* (or equivalently, the *natural potentiality*) for the actual occasion (PR 227–29, 470; S 36, 50). But the actuality not only arises from, but also *includes*, the real potentiality. Thus, the three given phases remain a feature of the actual occasion throughout its history of self-formation (PR 470); and thus, too, the completed occasion is not only *causa sui*, but is also the product of the efficient past (PR 228).

This clarification of what Whitehead means by 'real' and 'actual' is confirmed by, and amounts to an explication of, one of the more important and illuminating characterizations of transition and concrescence offered by Whitehead:

> To sum up: There are two species of process, macroscopic process, and microscopic process. The macroscopic process is the transition from attained actuality to actuality in attainment; while the microscopic process is the conversion of conditions which are *merely real* into determinate actuality. The former process effects the transition from the '*actual*' to the '*merely real*'; and the latter process effects the growth from the *real* to the *actual*. The former process is efficient; the latter process is teleological. . . . The actualities are constituted [*i.e.*, created] by their *real* genetic phases. The present is the immediacy of teleological process whereby *reality* becomes *actual*. The former process provides the conditions which really govern attainment; whereas the latter process provides the ends actually attained. (PR 325–27; italics mine)

Understood in terms of the preceding considerations, the passage just quoted is unsurpassable for its clear statement of the contrast between transition and concrescence. It establishes that transition is a species of creative process distinct from concrescence and that both species of process are involved in the becoming of every actual occasion.

14. Summary

I must now summarize my understanding of the principles of ontology and creativity in respect to their bearing on the becoming, the being, and the solidarity of actual entities. But any appeal to these principles in connection with the elucidation of the solidarity thesis, no matter how succinct, involves an appeal to the principle of relativity. Thus, my concern here is with the relevance of the three basic organic principles to the fundamental organic thesis. Some notions which fill out my interpretation of these three principles, but which have yet to be closely examined, will be adumbrated in this summation.

In the becoming of every actual occasion, the creativity of the universe manifests itself in two distinct but intimately related processes. The first manifestation exhibits the creative universe as in the very process of individualizing itself in a new occasion under conditions imposed by the already completed actualities. The second manifestation exhibits the creative universe as already individualized and thereby exhibits the creativity itself as also individualized. The first manifestation constitutes the process of transition; the second, the process of concrescence. Thus, the creativity of transition is an individualiz*ing* activity, whereas the creativity of concrescence is an individualiz*ed* activity. What the individualizing activity of transition produces is a new incarnation of the universe and therein a new opportunity for novel achievement. What the individualized activity of concrescence achieves is the value of the new occasion for itself and for the future beyond itself.

The creativity of transition transcends, or does not belong to, the autonomous subjectivity of the new occasion. The creativity of concrescence, on the other hand, is immanent in, or belongs to, the new autonomous subject. But the creativity immanent in the new concrescent subject results from the particular manner in which the creativity of the universe, through its transcendent manifestation, "is individualized by the imposed conditions" (SMW 247). The imposed conditions, of course, are none other than the antecedent creatures of the creativity (S 39; PR 30, 101,

344). For it is the function of every attained actuality to condition, and thereby to characterize, the creativity (PR 344).

Neither manifestation of the universe's eternal creativeness ever escapes the influence of the settled actualities accumulated in the wake of the creative advance. The individualizing manifestation is determined, without remainder, by the transcendent decisions embodied in the terminal structures of the accumulated actualities; and the individualized manifestation, though self-determining, remains conditioned by the objectifications of the settled actualities and by the conformal feelings those objectifications imposed on the new occasion. Since the conformal physical feelings are generated by the individualizing manifestation, they constitute "the machinery by reason of which the creativity transcends the world already actual, and yet remains conditioned by the actual world in its new impersonation" (PR 362).

In the becoming of each actual occasion, then, the eternal creativity of the universe manifests itself in two supersessionally successive processes: the efficient macroscopic transition, and the teleological microscopic concrescence. The reasons or causes of the first process are the attained actualities of the settled world; the reason or cause of the second process is the autonomously modified subjective aim. The former process, as determined by the transcendent decisions embodied in the accumulated superjects, begets the novel occasion, objectifies in it its correlative actual world, physically conforms its initial subjectivity to the objectified actualities, and derives its reproductive conceptual feelings, including its initial subjective aim, from its conformal physical feelings. The latter process, as determined by its own immanent decisions, generates reverted conceptual feelings, modifies the subjective forms, or valuations, of its conceptual reproductions, and, through its autonomous generation of novel subjective forms, integrates its physical and conceptual feelings into the final aesthetic unity of its satisfaction.

The efficient and teleological manifestations of the universe's creativity constitute, for each pair of related manifestations, an exhaustive analysis of the becoming of an actual occasion. The crucial feature of the first manifestation is its reproduction of a disjunctive diversity of attained actualities so as to form the dative phase of a new occasion. The crucial feature of the second manifestation is the autonomous, novel, felt synthesis of the reproduced actualities by reason of which they become a conjunctive diversity. Thus, each related pair of efficient transition and teleological concrescence represents an exhaustive analysis of the two-stage supersessional process by which the many actualities of the universe become one and are increased by one.

In this manner, my interpretation of transition and concrescence exhibits the mutual relevance of the principles of creativity and ontology. It exhibits, in addition, the inherent presupposition, by these principles, of the repeatability of actual entities entailed by the relativity principle. The illumination that these three principles shed on one another is only a particular instance of the conceptual coherence exhibited by the metaphysical categories of the organic philosophy. But the mutual illumination of the principles of relativity, ontology, and creativity is especially relevant to the elucidation of the thesis of solidarity. Each of these three most fundamental principles greatly advances our understanding of the solidarity of actualities; but, even after each principle has contributed its explanation or clarification of solidarity, the paradoxical air of Whitehead's basic metaphysical thesis is not entirely dispelled.

In this regard, the principle of creativity cryptically states the thesis of solidarity while emphasizing the creative advance of the universe. It asserts that the many completed actualities of the universe are ever being synthesized into a new actuality that, by the addition of its completed self, also increases their number. Somehow, the novel actuality is disjunctively among the many actualities which are conjunctively within itself. The original many are thus asserted to be both without and within the novel one. We have here the aspect of the mutual immanence of discrete actualities that has to do with the dual relation—transcendent and immanent—of the earlier to the later. The other aspects of solidarity—the dual relation of the later to the earlier, and of contemporaries to each other—are not alluded to by the principle of creativity. In other words, the creativity principle is concerned only with the aspect of solidarity that is most relevant to the creative advance of actuality. Nonetheless, the principle explicitly asserts the basic paradoxical character of the solidarity of actualities: that the original many and the novel one constitute at once a disjunctive diversity and a conjunctive diversity.

Whereas the creativity principle, or Category of the Ultimate, merely provides an alternative formulation of one aspect of the solidarity thesis, the principles of relativity and ontology do provide that thesis with important, albeit partial, illumination. By blurring the distinction between what is particular and what is universal, these two principles allow us to construe the immanence of earlier actualities in later ones in terms of the reproduction of the former in the latter. The earlier actualities, as their *original* selves, transcend the later actualities. Therefore, the earlier actualities form a *disjunctive* diversity with any one later actuality. But those same earlier actualities, as their *reproduced* selves, are also immanent in the same later actualities. Hence, insofar as they are felt by the new actuality, the earlier actualities form a *conjunctive* diversity with, and within, any one later actuality.

By thus giving consistent meanings to the notions of disjunctive and conjunctive diversity, the principles of relativity and ontology contribute significantly to the elucidation of the solidarity thesis. But the elucidation they provide, though significant, is by no means entirely adequate; for it suffers from two major shortcomings. First, it does not by itself explain the sense in which actualities later than, or contemporary with, a given actuality are at once without and within that actuality. Second, it alleviates the problem of solidarity only at the cost of introducing the equally perplexing problem of the repeatability of particulars; for how, or in what sense, can a completed actuality be the same particular as its reproductions, or objectifications, in subsequent actualities? Until these shortcomings are remedied, the elucidation of the solidarity of actual entities cannot be deemed adequate.

FOUR

Creativity, Eternal Objects, and God

The complete determinateness of an actual occasion requires for its understanding a reference to other actual occasions, particularly to those that
were already in superjective existence when the occasion in question
began its becoming. This is one outcome of the solidarity of occasions.
But the understanding of the solidarity of actual occasions, and hence of
any individual occasion, requires a reference to factors of the universe
which, though real, are either non-actual or non-temporal. The factors in
question are: God, eternal objects, creativity, and extension. Of these,
God is an actual but non-temporal reality; whereas the eternal objects, the
creativity, and the extensive continuum are realities that are neither actual
nor temporal. Whatever else they may be, therefore, all of the factors in
question are real and non-temporal; moreover, they play each a crucial
role in the becoming of *every* actual occasion.

The four factors are construed as non-temporal or, equivalently, as
eternal, because they are each ontologically prior to, and presupposed by,
the temporal world. These factors, God excepted, are construed as non-
actual because they are not self-realizing. Whitehead explicitly refers to
three of them—creativity, eternal objects, and God—as the formative
elements of the temporal world (RM 89–91). But it is a basic contention of
this essay that the organic philosophy posits the reality of an eternal
continuum of extension which is a fourth formative element of the temporal world. This contention will receive ample support in the next two
chapters. The point I wish to emphasize now is that we cannot hope to
elucidate the solidarity of entities that are actual and temporal without
first achieving an adequate understanding of the realities that are either
non-actual or non-temporal. Accordingly, the next order of business is to

examine the theories of creativity, eternal objects, God, and extension insofar as they are relevant to the thesis of solidarity.

The examination of the theory of extension will be carried out in the next chapter. In the present chapter I will discuss the theories of creativity, eternal objects, and God. The discussion of creativity will be relatively brief, since I have already discussed this factor at length in connection with the organic doctrines of transition, concrescence, and the Category of the Ultimate. My main goal will be to establish that the reality of creativity is not exhausted by its transitional and concrescent manifestations. But in so doing I shall focus on certain characterizations of creativity that will prove to be remarkably similar to some of the characterizations of the extensive continuum or Receptacle. In this way, I shall be setting the stage for an interpretative thesis to be advanced in the next two chapters—namely, that creativity and extension are two essential aspects of one ultimate reality, a reality grounding the potentiality for the becoming, the being, and the solidarity of actual entities.

Aside from an initial section on creativity, the bulk of the present chapter is devoted to the theories of eternal objects and God. My primary concern is with those aspects of these two theories that will have a significant bearing on the elucidation of solidarity. Therefore, there will be no attempt to make the treatment of eternal objects and God exhaustive. But I want to show here, in addition, that the concept of connectedness as mutual involvement applies also to eternal objects *per se*. Some of the considerations, however, will go beyond both of these goals in order to achieve a firmer grasp of the fundamentals of Whitehead's philosophy.

1.   Creativity: its reality as a potentiality for the becoming of actualities

The thesis of solidarity is not adequately understood if it is taken to mean simply that the final, discrete constituents of the universe are internally related to one another. Such an understanding of it leaves out the fact that the relata of solidarity are not timeless entities, but are, instead, temporally emergent actualities. "A mere system of mutually prehensive occasions is compatible with the concept of a static timeless world" (IS 242). But the universe is dynamically temporal—*i.e.*, it is supersessional in the extrinsic, or macroscopic, sense. The universe involves an essential passage into novelty. Its solidarity, therefore, is an evolving solidarity, not an affair which is achieved once and for all. But this means

that the solidarity or mutual immanence of occasions cannot be exclusively a function of extension, nor of extension and eternal objects, but
must also be a function of the creativity whereby occasions come to be.
Accordingly, the nature of creativity must be such that its joint functioning with extension and eternal objects accounts for the becoming of
interconnected occasions.

Creativity, we saw in the previous chapter, manifests itself both transcendentally and immanently—*i.e.*, both in macroscopic processes of
transition and in microscopic processes of concrescence. But the reality of
creativity, or of that which manifests itself in the creative processes by
which occasions become, must transcend its past and present manifestations. This conclusion is forced on the organic philosophy by its doctrine
of anticipation. For anticipatory feelings must be construed as giving
witness to an eternal potentiality for the becomingness of future occasions
(IS 243–44; AI 247–51; PR 41, 101). No determinate future of specified
occasions is necessary; but it is necessary that there be a future of occasions superseding the anticipating occasion (PR 327–28). Thus, so long as
it maintains that it is necessary that there be a future of actualities, and
that this necessity is somehow revealed to anticipating occasions, the
organic philosophy must also maintain that the reality of creativity is not
exhausted by its past and present manifestations. It must maintain, in
short, that there exists in the universe a reality expressing a potentiality
for creative processes: this reality is creativity.[1]

To say that the creativity transcends its manifestations is not to say that
it can be intelligibly disassociated from its manifestations, past, present,
and future. There is no meaning to the organic notion of creativity in
isolation from the corresponding organic notion of actualities (PR 344).
When we have said that the creativity is a potentiality for the becoming of
actualities, and that it is involved in the becoming of every actuality, we
have already said, at least implicitly, all that can be said about it. But what
I am trying to emphasize now is the reality of the creativity in its status of
a mere potentiality for the becoming of actualities, as opposed to its reality
in its status of being involved in the actual becoming of this or that
actuality. Thus considered, the creativity emerges as a reality which is
both non-actual and non-temporal, or, to put it positively, as something
which is merely real and eternal (RM 89–93).

In other words, the creativity is a reality necessarily involved in the
becoming of every actuality, but which does not itself become. It must be
construed as eternal because the general potentiality for creation cannot be
said to be itself created, for that would initiate an endless regression to

higher-type creativities by which lower-type ones would be created. According to Whitehead, therefore, the creativity is to be construed as an eternal substratum of metaphysical energy that is ever individualizing itself into a plurality of interconnected actualities (SMW 99, 148–49, 212, 247–48). It is a general potentiality for creativeness which, in each of its individualized embodiments, is conditioned by the results of its earlier individualizations (PR 101). Thus, each actuality or "individual activity is nothing but the mode in which the general activity is individualized by the imposed conditions" (SMW 247).

The conditions imposed on each novel individualization of the substrate activity may be classified into three classes: the first class is made up of entities that are each both temporal and actual—*i.e.*, the occasions causally objectified for the novel individualization; the second class comprises the multiplicity of entities that are neither temporal nor actual—*i.e.*, the multiplicity of eternal objects, or of potentialities for the determination of the definiteness of actualities; the third class has but one member, God, the one and only non-temporal actuality, whose primordial nature structures the multiplicity of eternal objects into a graded realm of achievable values, with each possible value discriminable in regard to its proximate relevance to any specific, actualized conditions (SMW 149, 248–49). These three classes of conditions, imposed on every individualized embodiment of the creative substratum, constitute the reason why that substratum may be said to have, according to Whitehead, three essential attributes: first, its individualization into a solidarity of actualities, each actuality conditioning the others; second, the multiplicity of eternal objects whereby the achievability of novel definiteness is inherent in each individualized embodiment; and third, God, without whose functioning, the achievable novelties, relative to the actual conditions imposed on a particular creative embodiment, would be indistinguishable from non-entity (SMW 248–50, 148–52).

It is by reason of these three attributes that each actual occasion is an individualized embodiment of the creativity which, under conditions imposed by the objectification of past occasions, and guided by a relevant subjective aim initially derived from God, achieves a synthesis of character partly derived from the antecedent facts and partly from the multiplicity of ideal forms. The completed synthesis is itself a new fact imposing itself as a condition for all future embodiments of the creativity: "The definiteness of [the] fact is due to its forms; but the individual fact is a creature, and creativity is the ultimate behind all forms, inexplicable by forms, and conditioned by its creatures" (PR 30).

To say that the multiplicity of eternal objects is an attribute of the creativity is not to say, it should be noted, that any determinate character, or definiteness of form, attaches to the creativity itself, divorced from its individualized embodiments. All that is meant is that in the nature of the creativity there stands an 'envisagement' (the term is Whitehead's) of the multiplicity of eternal objects (SMW 148–49). Thus, the creativity is a potentiality for the becoming of determinate occasions, but is itself indeterminate or formless. In itself, then, the creativity is without a character of its own (PR 47). It is an ultimate reality incapable of characterization in disassociation from its involvement in the becoming of its creatures.

Of this aspect of his philosophy, Whitehead says:

> In all philosophic theory there is an ultimate which is actual in virtue of its accidents. It is only then capable of characterization through its accidental embodiments, and apart from these accidents is devoid of actuality. In the philosophy of organism this ultimate is termed 'creativity'; and God is its primordial non-temporal accident. (PR 10–11)

The 'accidents' in virtue of which the creativity can be characterized are none other than the actual entities themselves.[2] But the complete truth, in this regard, is that the creativity and the actual entities, God included, can be characterized only in terms of each other. This is why, in the Harvard lectures quoted earlier (*supra* p. 2), Whitehead stated that "the character of creativity is derived from its creatures, and expressed by its own creatures." This is also why, in PR, Whitehead wrote:

> The true metaphysical position is that God is the aboriginal instance of this creativity, and is therefore the aboriginal condition which qualifies its action. It is the function of actuality to characterize the creativity, and God is the eternal primordial character. But of course, there is no meaning to 'creativity' apart from its 'creatures', and no meaning to 'God' apart from the creativity and the 'temporal creatures', and no meaning to the temporal creatures apart from 'creativity' and 'God'. (PR 344)

The characterization of the creativity by the actualities has a twofold basis. First, each actual entity, considered as a concrescent process or subject, "is the individualized embodiment of the underlying energy of realization" (SMW 148). Second, each actual entity, considered as a product or superject, "is an individual matter of fact issuing from an individualization of the substrate activity. But individualization does not mean substantial independence" (SMW 99). The lack of independence from the substrate activity means both that the subject is conditioned by the macroscopic transition which begets its given phases and that the superject is an immortal entity "which has emerged as a real matter of fact to be taken account of by other things" (SMW 148).

The other things, of course, are the subsequent actualities. But the taking account of actualities already attained by subsequent actualities in attainment presupposes the abstractive reproduction, or causal objectification, of the attained actualities in the actualities in attainment. Thus, it is a fundamental principle of Whitehead's philosophy that

> the actual world, in so far as it is a community of entities which are settled, actual, and already become, conditions and limits the potentiality for creativeness beyond itself. This 'given' world provides determinate data in the form of those objectifications of themselves which the characters of its actual entities can provide. (PR 101)

But this means that, by virtue of its causal objectification in all subsequent actualities, each already existing superject is, to use Whitehead's phrase, "universalized into a character of creativity" (PR 249). Thus, causal objectification effects the universalization of particulars. It is only as thus universalized that determinate particulars can qualify other particulars. This universalization of particulars is the reason why actual entities also fall under the scope of the principle of relativity.

The organic doctrine under surveyance comes to this: every attained actuality characterizes the creativity by infusing its own particularity into all individualized embodiments of the creativity that are subsequent to its own existence (PR 324; S 47). But, since the number of attained actualities shifts with the completion of each new creature, the character which the creativity, in each of its embodiments, derives from the objectifications of the settled actualities also shifts. "This function of creatures, that they constitute the shifting character of creativity, is here termed the 'objective immortality' of actual entities" (PR 47).

According to Whitehead, his organic notion of creativity constitutes a novel rendering of the Aristotelian 'matter' (PR 46). But Whitehead adds that the organic notion of creativity, unlike the Aristotelian notion of matter,

> is divested of the notion of passive receptivity, either of 'form', or of external relations; it is the pure notion of the activity conditioned by

the objective immortality of the actual world—a world which is never the same twice, though always with the stable element of divine ordering. Creativity is without a character of its own in exactly the same sense in which the Aristotelian 'matter' is without a character of its own. It is that ultimate notion of the highest generality at the base of actuality. It cannot be characterized, because all characters are more special than itself. But creativity is always found under conditions, and described as conditioned. (PR 46–47)

For Whitehead, there are also some important analogies between his notion of creativity and Spinoza's notion of an infinite substance. Thus, he compares his actual entities to Spinoza's modes and asserts that Spinoza's infinite substance becomes, for him, "the one underlying activity of realization individualizing itself in an interlocked plurality of modes" (SMW 99). This analogy is not to be pushed too far, however; for Whitehead makes it clear that, though the creativity is the ultimate of the organic philosophy, it is not to be allowed "a final 'eminent' reality, beyond that ascribed to any of its accidents" (PR 11). In fact, the philosophy of organism inverts Spinoza's point of view by making the modes superior to the substance (PR 125).

The interlocking of modes or of actual entities refers, it should be noted, to their objective presence in one another. In this respect, physical anticipation reveals not only that there is a creative potential for future actualities but also that any future actuality must include within itself the causal objectification of the anticipating actuality (PR 327–28; IS 243–44). In other words, anticipatory feelings reveal the metaphysical impossibility of separating the creatures from the creativity, or the creativity from the creatures. For example, let A be the creature anticipating its supersession by another creature, say B. The datum of A's anticipatory feeling cannot be B itself, though it must reveal something essential to the character of any future actuality. Whatever the datum of the feeling is, it involves a potentiality for the creation of future occasions that must include the causal objectification of A. Thus, what A feels is the potentiality for the macroscopic process that will reproduce A in its immediate supersessor, B (PR 327–28). What is thus revealed to A is that the creativity for A will cease with A's satisfaction, and that the creativity for B will reproduce A within B. Hence, in regard to the supersession of A by B, there is a transition from the creativity *for* A to the creativity *with* A and *for* B.

Accordingly, for Whitehead,

> Physical anticipation illustrates the truth that the creativity, whereby there is supersession, cannot be disjoined from the creature which is

superseded. The character of the creativity is found in the analysis of the creature. The creativity *for* the creature has become the creativity *with* the creature; and the creature is thereby superseded. (IS 243)

But physical anticipation also gives witness to the metaphysical necessity that the universe be ever involved in a creative advance beyond its attained actualities. Thus, to the extent that each actuality experiences the necessity of its own objective immortality, it also experiences the necessity of the evolving, or temporal, character of the world's solidarity (PR 327–28).

> The reason for the temporal character of the actual world can now be given by reference to the creativity and the creatures. For the creativity is not separable from its creatures. Thus the creatures remain with the creativity. Accordingly, the creativity for a creature becomes the creativity with the creature, and thereby passes into another phase of itself. It is now the creativity for a new creature. Thus there is a transition of the creative action, and this transition exhibits itself, in the physical world, in the guise of routes of temporal succession. (RM 91–92)

Because the completed creatures *remain* with the creativity, actuality is cumulative and the number of its concrete components is ever increasing, or shifting, with the emergence of each new creature. For the same reason, each individualization of the eternal creativity is characterized by a new settlement of attained actualities. In other words, each individuali*zing* manifestation of creativity is determined by a new settlement of super-jects, and each individuali*zed* manifestation is partly the effect of, and is conditioned by, the causal objectification, or reproduction, of the new settlement.

Because actuality is cumulative and reproductive, the character which the creativity owes to its creatures is ever changing. This protean character of creativity "prevents us from considering the temporal world as a definite actual creature" (RM 92). The temporal world is not actual because, considered as a whole, it is not self-realizing, even though its concrete components are (or were) self-realizing. The temporal world is not definite, or determinate, because it is never complete. It is never a determinate matter of fact, achieved once and for all. Rather, it is a dynamic affair, ever advancing beyond its attained actualities, but ever subject to the specific determinations resulting from the necessary imma-nence of earlier actualities in later ones, and from the autonomy of each concrescent actuality. Later we shall see that the creative advance of the temporal world is determined, in a more general sense of determination, by the mutual immanence, real or potential, of actual occasions. Thus, the temporal world is to be understood as an advancing assemblage of actualities, each actuality essentially related to all others.

The protean character of creativity also prevents us from construing it as an actual entity, for it lacks the determinateness exhibited by concrete fact (RM 92). But the main reason why the "ultimate creativity of the universe" (PR 344) cannot be construed as an actuality is that it is not a self-realizing reality. In the organic philosophy, let us remember, to be actual is to be, or to have been, self-realizing. This criterion of self-realization is not met by the eternal creativity of the universe conceived in itself, divorced from its individualized embodiments. For the eternal creativity, though involved in every becoming, does not itself become. Moreover, the eternal creativity, though involved in every process whereby other realities gain determinate character and structure, is itself incapable of acquiring either determinate character or determinate structure. The eternal creativity of the universe, then, cannot be self-determining, cannot be self-realizing, cannot be actual.

To be sure, every self-realizing reality does involve an individual manifestation of the eternal creativity of the universe. However, no self-realizing reality is reducible to its immanent manifestation of the eternal creativity. In other words, each individualized manifestation of the eternal creativity belongs to, and is an essential aspect of, a particular concrescent subject; but each concrescent subject is essentially more than its immanent creativity. The concrescent subject exhibits other essential aspects, by reason of which it is a determinable entity capable of immediate enjoyment, of autonomous agency, and of purposive activity. In contrast, the eternal creativity is incapable of any immediacy of enjoyment, and "is not an external agency with its own ulterior purposes" (PR 339). Its individualizing manifestations are mere vehicles for transcendent decisions, and each of its individualized manifestations is but one essential aspect of a concrescent subject, which subject is the entity that does make decisions, that does have purposes and enjoyments. Thus, the fact that each self-realizing subject involves an immanent manifestation of the eternal creativity does not provide any valid ground for construing the eternal creativity as being itself a self-realizing, or actual, reality.

Of course, we may speak of the eternal creativity as being derivatively actual insofar as its creatures are actual. This is what Whitehead has in mind when he says that the creativity is actual in virtue of its accidental embodiments (PR 10). Strictly speaking, however, the eternal creativity is never actual. Indeed, the creativity of the universe is so far from being an actual entity that it cannot even be construed as a mere (non-actual) entity (SMW 248).

Let us recall, in this regard, that the organic criterion for being an entity, or existent, is reproducibility. But there is no sense in which the ultimate creativity of the universe can be construed as reproducible. The creativity, through its manifold manifestations, is indeed the reality whereby all entities of all types are reproduced; but the creativity is not itself a reproducible reality. If it were, we would need to appeal to a higher-order creativity to explain the reproduction of the lower-order creativity. But there is no need thus to raise the specter of an infinite regress to higher-order creativities. The essential indeterminateness and indeterminableness of the eternal creativity necessarily preclude the possibility of its reproducibility. For that which is reproducible must be determinate in some respect, so that the original and its reproduction can be identically determinate in that respect. For example, every instance of a given eternal object exhibits an identically determinate essence, and any given superject and each of its causal objectifications exhibit an identically determinate position. The eternal creativity, on the other hand, being indeterminate and indeterminable, is incapable of having instantiations or reproductions of itself.

What the creativity does have are manifestations. But its manifestations are reproductions neither of it nor of each other. Each manifestation is unique because its determining conditions are unique. The determining conditions of an individualizing manifestation are the already completed actualities of the universe; the determining conditions of an individualized manifestation are the autonomous decisions of the subject to which it belongs, decisions which are enabled by the manifestation itself. Thus, each manifestation is a particular mode of the universal creativity, with a particularity not to be divorced from its particularizing conditions.

A manifestation of the creativity, it should be noted, occurs and then is no more, though it does leave behind an immortal product which shall forever give witness to that manifestation's ephemeral reality. Thus, whereas the one ultimate creativity of the universe is eternally real, its many manifestations are each only ephemerally real. It is obvious, therefore, that the eternal creativity of the universe is not to be identified with its ephemeral manifestations. Its reality transcends each and all of its ongoing manifestations.

Finally, let us emphasize that without the eternal creativity no creature could become, but so far is it from being the eminent reality of the universe that even the most inferior of its creatures is superior to it in value. For every concrescent creature is something for its own sake, and thereby is an intrinsic, self-determining value; and every concrete creature contributes its achieved value as a potential component of the achievable values in its future, and thereby has extrinsic value—great or small, waxing or waning—for future creatures. But the value of the eternal creativity is exclusively instrumental and in an absolutely invariant manner: neither great nor small, neither waxing nor waning, it is the same for every creature. It is valuable because its individualizing manifestations provide the objective and conformal conditions constituting the real potentiality for the achievement of any novel value, and because each individualized manifestation is the aspect of a creature that enables its autonomous achievement of actual value. Without the creativity, then, there is no realization of value, but its own value is merely extrinsic and in a manner not to be divorced from its manifestations.

To sum up: The creativity of the universe is not an entity, much less an *actual* entity. It is not an actuality because it is not self-realizing, and it is not an entity because it is not reproducible. Nevertheless, though neither an actuality nor an entity, the creativity of the universe is very much a reality, an eternal reality presupposed by, and manifested in, the becoming of every actual entity. It is an inexhaustible metaphysical energy at the base of all existence and revealed to, as well as manifested in, all concrescent existents. If its transcendent reality—its reality beyond any ongoing manifestation—were not revealed to its concrescent creatures, they could never anticipate a future beyond their immediate present, could never anticipate their own immortality of objective functioning, could never feel the necessity of their supersession by subsequent creatures. Thus anticipation, insofar as it is a necessary ingredient of every concrete experience, reveals the eternal creativity underlying the entire universe, actual or potential—and reveals it as transcending its ongoing manifestations.

The elucidation of the ultimate reality posited by the organic philosophy is by no means complete, but I cannot carry it any further until I have explained the other eternal factors of the universe, particularly the eternal continuum of extension. In the remaining sections of this chapter I discuss the many eternal realities which are reproducible but not self-realizing— the eternal objects—and the one eternal reality that is both reproducible and self-realizing—God.

2. *Eternal objects: their individual and relational essences*

Eternal objects are the ideas, forms, or real universals of the organic philosophy. A definite shade of red, an emotion such as anger, the number four, any geometrical figure, and any scalar form of physical energy are all eternal objects. Every eternal object has the metaphysical status of a possibility for actualization or achievement (SMW 222). By 'possibility', in this regard, we are to understand "that in which there stands achievability, abstracted from achievement" (SMW 226). Thus, an eternal object is a possibility which can be actualized in and by an actual entity but which in itself transcends any particular actual entity. For this reason, an eternal object "is comprehensible without reference to some one particular occasion of experience" (SMW 221; see also PR 70). Eternal objects, however, cannot be understood divorced from their reference to actuality in general (SMW 222; PR 174). Either they are possibilities for actualization, which any actual entity can take into account, or they are indistinguishable from non-entity.

Moreover, an eternal object cannot be understood divorced from its reference to other eternal objects (SMW 222; PR 174). To comprehend an eternal object we must be acquainted not only with its 'individual essence', which is its essence "considered in respect to its uniqueness," but also with its 'relational essence', which is its patience for entrance into relationships with other eternal objects, as well as with actual entities (SMW 222; PR 174). The relational essence of an eternal object is not unique (SMW 230). Each eternal object shares its relational essence with other eternal objects. It is in virtue of their relational essences that we can speak of the connexity of eternal objects.

The relationships in which eternal objects function as relata are themselves eternal objects (SMW 229). They are termed 'patterns' or 'complex eternal objects' (SMW 232; PR 174–75). Each pattern expresses a 'manner' in which other eternal objects may be related. The 'manner' thus expressed is the individual essence of the pattern (PR 175). Those eternal objects which can function as relata in a particular pattern are called the 'components' of that pattern (SMW 232). The components of a pattern are those, and only those, eternal objects whose relational essences include a patience for entrance into that pattern (SMW 229–32). A pattern or complex eternal object, then, is a "definite finite relationship involving the definite eternal objects of a limited set of such objects" (SMW 232).

The components of a pattern may be other patterns, but in the last analysis a pattern requires, as ultimate components, eternal objects which are not themselves patterns. "An eternal object, such as a definite shade of green, which cannot be analyzed into a relationship of components, will be called 'simple'" (SMW 232). In PR, the term 'sensum' is used technically as a synonym for 'simple eternal object' (PR 174). It is important to keep this in mind, for, when used technically by Whitehead, the term 'sensum' need not be taken in any of its ordinary philosophical or psychological meanings. Whitehead defends the above definition of sensa or simple eternal objects as follows:

> It is possible that this definition of 'sensa' excludes some cases of contrast which are ordinarily termed 'sensa' and that it includes some emotional qualities which are ordinarily excluded. Its convenience consists in the fact that it is founded on a metaphysical principle, and not on an empirical investigation of the physiology of the human body. (PR 175)

Sensa, or simple eternal objects, are the ultimate components of complex eternal objects. However, the term 'component', as used in regards to possibility, is not intended to connote real togetherness (SMW 236). A complex eternal object merely expresses the possibility of the joint realization, in some actual entity, of itself with other eternal objects termed its components. But, as possibilities, the complex eternal object and its components are isolated from one another. This is so, because a complex eternal object does not involve the *individual essence* of any other eternal object. Whitehead expresses this doctrine in the principle of the Isolation of Eternal Objects (SMW 230–31, 236). According to this principle, eternal objects are isolated from one another *in respect to their individual essences*.

However, a complex eternal object does involve other eternal objects, but only in regard to their *relational essences*. The other eternal objects thus involved, its components, are those whose relational essences include a patience for entrance into the manner of relatedness which is the individual essence of that particular complex eternal object. But the complex eternal object is unselective as to which of these other eternal objects will function as its relata. It only specifies what relational essence other eternal objects must have in order to so function. It remains completely indifferent to their individual essences. Thus eternal objects, including sensa, have an 'analytic character' in respect to their relational essence.

> The whole principle [of the analyticity of eternal objects] is that a particular determination can be made of the *how* of some definite relationship of a definite eternal object A to a definite finite number n of other eternal objects, *without* any determination of the other n objects, x_1, x_2, . . . x_n, except that they have, each of them, the requisite status to play their respective parts in that multiple relation-

ship. This principle depends on the fact that the relational essence of
an eternal object is not unique to that object. (SMW 164)

For Whitehead, the meanings of the logical variables, 'any' and 'some'
spring from this principle or, more specifically, from the non-uniqueness
of the relational essences of eternal objects (SMW 229; PR 174–75).

3. Eternal objects: abstractive hierarchies and connexity

By reason of its relational essence, an eternal object has a definite status in
respect to other eternal objects. This status is analyzable into the role the
object plays in different schemes of possibilities termed 'abstractive hierarchies'. At the base of any such hierarchy there is either a finite or an
infinite set of simple eternal objects. This is the level of zero grade
complexity. In the next level there are complex eternal objects requiring as
components some of the simple eternal objects of the base. This is the
level of first grade of complexity. At the third level there are complex
eternal objects requiring as components some of the simple eternal objects
of the first level and at least one complex eternal object of the second level.
The third level is the level of the second grade of complexity. The number
of levels in an abstractive hierarchy may be finite or infinite, depending on
whether or not it has a highest grade of complexity. The finitude or
infinitude of a hierarchy in no way depends on whether its base has a
finite, or an infinite, number of members (SMW 234–35).

Whitehead gives the following formal definition of an abstractive hierarchy:

> An 'abstractive hierarchy based upon g', where g is a group of simple
> eternal objects, is a set of eternal objects which satisfy the following
> conditions,
>   (i) the members of g belong to it, and are the only simple eternal
> objects in the hierarchy,
>   (ii) the components of any complex eternal object in the hierarchy,
> are also members of the hierarchy, and,
>   (iii) any set of eternal objects belonging to the hierarchy, whether
> all of the same grade or whether differing among themselves as to
> grade, are jointly among the components or derivative components of
> at least one eternal object which also belongs to the hierarchy.
> (SMW 234)

The third condition establishes the meaning of connexity in respect to
eternal objects. In this regard we find Whitehead saying:

The third condition to be satisfied by an abstractive hierarchy will be called the condition of connexity. Thus an abstractive hierarchy springs from its base; it includes every successive grade from its base either indefinitely onwards, or to its maximum grade; and it is 'connected' by the *reappearance* (in a higher grade) of any set of its members belonging to lower grades, in the function of a set of components or derivative components of at least one member of the hierarchy. (SMW 168; italics mine)

We thus have in this passage further proof that the notion of connectedness, whether in respect to actualities or to eternal objects, cannot be divorced from the notion of repetition or reappearance. Moreover, the analogy between the connexity of eternal objects *per se*, and the connexity or solidarity of actual occasions, should now be obvious. For, in respect to their individual essences, eternal objects transcend one another; they are mutually isolated. But, in respect to their relational essences, there is a mutual involvement of eternal objects. One important qualification, though, is that the relational essence of an eternal object involves other eternal objects, but not necessarily all other eternal objects.

An abstractive hierarchy, we have seen, may be finite or infinite. If it is finite, its highest level can have only one member, "for otherwise the condition of connexity would not be satisfied" (SMW 235). Unfortunately, that the highest level of complexity has only one member is not sufficient to satisfy the condition of connexity. Let the one most complex member of a finite hierarchy be the sole member of a set of eternal objects belonging to the hierarchy. Now, to fulfill the condition of connexity, this most complex eternal object must be among the components of at least one eternal object which also belongs to that hierarchy. But Whitehead says explicitly that this most complex eternal object "is a component of no other eternal object belonging to any grade of the hierarchy" (SMW 235). The only way to resolve this logical inconsistency is to construe the members of an abstractive hierarchy as being each a component of itself. But Whitehead's discussion of abstractive hierarchies suggests that he was aware neither of the inconsistency to which I have alluded nor of the solution which I have proposed. For example, he says "that the components of an eternal object are necessarily of a lower grade of complexity than itself" (SMW 234). But if each eternal object is a component of itself, then not all its components are of lesser complexity than itself.

Fortunately, the inconsistency in question, once noted, seems harmless enough. Let us hold, even if Whitehead did not do so explicitly, that every eternal object in an abstractive hierarchy is a component of itself. The modification of all affected definitions is then a relatively simple matter.

For example, a simple eternal object can be construed as having no components other than itself, and the most complex member of a finite hierarchy can be construed as being a component of no eternal object, in that hierarchy, other than itself. Having thus noted how all inconsistent definitions are to be modified so as to render them consistent with the formulation of the condition of connexity, I henceforth follow Whitehead's unintentional example of ignoring the trivial fact that every eternal object is a component of itself. My exposition of this aspect of Whitehead's philosophy will thereby be much simpler, though slightly less precise.

The unique member of the highest level of a finite hierarchy is termed the *vertex* of that hierarchy. The components of the vertex (other than itself, of course) may be of varying grades of complexity, but none can be as complex as itself, and at least one component must have a complexity only one grade lower than its (the vertex's) own (SMW 236). A grade of complexity immediately below that of the vertex is termed the *proximate* grade for that vertex. The next lower grade of complexity is termed the grade of *second proximation* from the vertex. We may thus proceed downward to grades of third proximation, fourth proximation, and so forth, until the base grade of simple eternal objects is reached (SMW 236).

The notion of a group of eternal objects such that each is more or less proximate to another eternal object, as within a given abstractive hierarchy, plays an important role in Whitehead's explanation of how qualitative novelty emerges in the temporal world. In this respect, it is important to notice that each complex eternal object is the vertex of at least one finite hierarchy (SMW 235). Therefore, for every complex eternal object already physically ingressed in the temporal world, there are other eternal objects that are proximate to it, in one grade or another, in at least one finite abstractive hierarchy. Some of these proximate eternal objects will have been physically realized already in the temporal world, some necessarily in the same occasion; but some of these proximate entities may have yet to be thus realized. These unrealized eternal objects are the *proximate novelties* of which Whitehead speaks in connection with the Category of Conceptual Reversion. Their proximity to a vertex already realized in a given actual occasion increases the likelihood that they will be physically realized in that occasion, or in some occasion in the immediate future. Whether these proximate novelties are realized depends, in part, on whether the abstractive hierarchy in question is made relevant to that actuality by the objective functioning of God. This much I have already at least adumbrated in the preceding chapter. I must now explain the relationship between abstractive hierarchies and the primordial nature of God.[3]

4. God: abstractive hierarchies and his primordial nature

Abstractive hierarchies are functions of the relational essences of eternal objects. Therefore, it is by reason of their relational essences that we can speak of a 'realm', or community, of eternal objects. In other words, each eternal object, in virtue of its relational essence, stands internally related to all its possible relationships to other eternal objects. These possible relationships are expressed in the indefinite number of abstractive hierarchies with which an eternal object is associated. In this manner sets of eternal objects may be grouped into different schemes of relationships, "and all eternal objects stand in all such relationships, so far as the [relational essence] of each permits" (SMW 230). Accordingly, for Whitehead, "The realm of eternal objects is properly described as a 'realm', because each eternal object has its status in the general systematic complex of mutual relatedness" (SMW 224).

In regard to their individual essences, however, eternal objects are isolated from one another, and thus constitute a mere multiplicity and not a structured realm. For this reason, Whitehead emphasizes that,

> in dealing with hierarchies we are entirely within the realm of possibility. Accordingly the eternal objects are devoid of real togetherness: they remain within their 'isolation'. (SMW 236)

But there is a problem here. An eternal object is not detachable from its relational essence. If eternal objects are isolated from one another in respect to their individual essences, they must be equally isolated from one another in respect to their relational essences. Yet the notion of an abstractive hierarchy implies that, in regard to their relational essences, there is a kind of togetherness of eternal objects. The problem, then, is: What is the ontological status of an abstractive hierarchy?

The solution to this problem requires the introduction of another eternal factor of potentiality—what Whitehead terms 'the primordial nature of God'. The non-uniqueness of the relational essences of eternal objects, we have seen, introduces the logical variables 'any' and 'some'. This allows us to construe any abstractive hierarchy as "an elaborate logical construction" (SMW 238). But an elaborate logical construction can only subsist in the conceptual experience of an actual logician. Furthermore, insofar as the realm of possibility is eternal, the abstractive hierarchies which constitute it must also be eternal. Consequently, the notion of an eternal realm of possibility or of ideality, as Whitehead often calls it, necessitates the notion of an eternal actual logician. Enter God—or at least that abstract aspect of his concrete reality which is eternal and immutable: his primordial nature.

God's primordial nature "is the unconditioned conceptual valuation of the entire multiplicity of eternal objects" (PR 46). This valuation achieves an *ideal*—as opposed to a *real*—togetherness of eternal objects (PR 64). By this is meant that God's valuation of eternal objects abstracts from their individual essences. The 'togetherness' in question involves only their relational essences. This is the togetherness of the eternal objects in a given abstractive hierarchy. The notion of 'proximate grade', or the notion of one eternal object as 'proximately relevant' to another, cannot be understood without recourse to this sense of togetherness. "Thus 'proximate relevance' means 'relevance as in the primordial mind of God'" (PR 73; see also 381–82).

Whitehead, it should be noted, does not hold that God creates the eternal objects. On the contrary, for him, God requires the eternal objects in the same degree that they require God (PR 392). God's primordial nature, then, is the conceptual structuring of eternal objects into abstractive hierarchies. But even more important, God's primordial nature is his conceptual *valuation* of all possibilities of realization (PR 46, 64). This primordial valuation establishes hierarchies of value, or of realizable values, relevant and relative to any given actualized conditions (PR 46, 64, 134, 248, 315, 522).

According to Whitehead, no reason can be given for the particular system of values thus established. But, for him, without such a standard of value there can be no creative order; and without creative order there can be no actual world, no actual occasions, and hence, given the ontological principle, no reasons of any sort (SMW 249–51; RM 104–05, 119–20). The ultimate reason is an actual act of valuation conditioning all other creative acts, but itself unconditioned and, hence, non-rational (PR 48). Thus, for Whitehead, "No reason can be given for the nature of God, because that nature is the ground of rationality" (SMW 249–50).

In respect to its explanatory import, the functioning of God's primordial nature in the world is primarily secular and not religious (PR 315–16). For Whitehead, without the objective functioning of God's primordial nature the world of temporal occasions would be devoid of creative and qualitative order (PR 48, 392). Any emergence of qualitative novelty would be accidental, and its effective endurance, from occasion to occasion, negligible.

Whitehead's point is this: assume the non-existence of God's primordial nature; then, since the datum for the concrescence of a temporal occasion is exclusively made up of other temporal occasions, it does not provide the relevant eternal objects requisite for synthesizing its component elements into the one integral experience of them. For, given the infinity of eternal objects and their mutual isolation, a successful and innovative synthesis of the data would become all but logically impossible (RM 94). The eternal objects appropriate to the synthesis would be lost amid an infinity of irrelevant possibilities and thus would be indistinguishable from non-entity (PR 46, 392). Accordingly, under the assumed conditions a success-ful synthesis is possible only through an absence of originative responses and a preponderance of negative prehensions in the successive phases of concrescence. The completed subjective experience would then be of near-zero complexity and virtually devoid of any intensity of feeling. This type of synthesis, occurring again and again over supersessional routes of occasions, would reduce the temporal world to a barren display of ineffec-tive actualities (PR 377).

In such a world, the evolution toward higher grades of experience, or toward social structures conducive to, and permissive of, such higher grades of experience, would be practically impossible (PR 377). But, in fact, the world *is* evolutionary in character and ever richer with novel achievements. Hence, in addition to extension, creativity, and the multi-plicity of eternal objects there must exist yet another eternal factor of potentiality, the primordial nature of God:

> The order of the world is no accident. There is nothing actual which could be actual without some measure of order. . . . The universe exhibits a creativity with infinite freedom, and a realm of forms with infinite possibilities; but . . . this creativity and these forms are to-gether impotent to achieve actuality apart from the completed ideal harmony, which is God. (RM 119–20; see also 104–05)

For Whitehead, then, the order of the world, including its creative advance toward novel achievements, is to be explained as follows. In any given occasion, God's primordial nature is abstractively objectified by those elements of it which, if realized as determinants of the subjective forms of that occasion's feelings, would be compatible for integration with the eternal objects functioning as determinants of the temporal occasions objectified for that occasion (PR 377). Another way of saying this is that God's primordial nature is objectified in the given occasion in terms of those abstractive hierarchies that include in their respective bases the simple eternal objects exemplified in the objectified occasions constituting the datum for the occasion in question. Accordingly, any complex eternal object belonging to those hierarchies, if selected by the occasion to function as a determinant of its subjective forms, would be compatible for synthesis with the eternal objects ingressed as determinants of the objectified data. Thus, in virtue of his primordial nature, "the objectification of God in each derivate actual entity results in a graduation of the relevance of eternal objects to the concrescent phases of that derivate occasion" (PR 46).

In this manner, the universe's qualitative and creative order is, for Whitehead, a function of the graded relevance of eternal objects obtained by every occasion from the objectification of God within its dative phase. This secular function of God is aptly summarized by Whitehead as follows:

> In what sense can unrealized abstract form be relevant? What is its basis of relevance? 'Relevance' must express some real fact of togetherness among forms. The ontological principle can be expressed as: All real togetherness is togetherness in the formal constitution of an actuality. So if there be a relevance of what in the temporal world is unrealized, the relevance must express a fact of togetherness in the formal constitution of a non-temporal actuality. But by the principle of relativity there can only be one non-derivative actuality, unbounded by its prehensions of an actual world. Such a primordial superject of creativity achieves, in its unity of satisfaction, the complete conceptual valuation of all eternal objects. This is the ultimate, basic adjustment of the togetherness of eternal objects on which creative order depends. It is the conceptual adjustment of all appetites in the form of aversions and adversions. It constitutes the meaning of relevance. Its status as an actual efficient fact is recognized by terming it the 'primordial nature of God'. (PR 48; see also 382)

As used above, the notion of appetition is important because it alerts us to the fact that God's primordial nature is not merely the conceptual valuation of all eternal objects. Rather, his primordial valuation is made up of conceptual feelings such that the subjective form of each involves an appetition toward the realization of its datum (PR 47–50). In this respect, God's primordial subjective aim is that the subjective forms of his conceptual feelings "shall be such as to constitute the eternal objects into relevant lures of feeling severally appropriate for all realizable basic conditions" (PR 134). In these lures for feeling are to be found the roots of the subjective aims of temporal occasions.

The initial stage of the subjective aim of a temporal actuality is, as we saw in the previous chapter, "an endowment which the subject inherits from the inevitable ordering of things, conceptually realized in the nature of God" (PR 373). The endowment is transmitted to the novel subject in three successive steps: first, the primordial nature is causally objectified in the occasion's dative phase in terms of a finite number of abstractive hierarchies that are immediately relevant to the temporal world given for the occasion; second, the occasion is physically conformed to the objectification of God, and thus the occasion's phase of primary physical feelings includes the novel subject's hybrid physical feeling of the objectified primordial nature; and third, in accord with the Category of Conceptual Valuation, there is derived from the hybrid feeling a conceptual feeling that reproduces for the novel subject both the data and the valuation of God's conceptual feeling of the relevant abstractive hierarchies (PR 46, 343). This conceptual feeling, with a subjective form of appetition conformal to God's own appetition, is the initial subjective aim of the autonomous subject. Thus, the three-step transmission endows the novel subject with an appetite for the realization of eternal objects that are relevant to, and synthesizable with, the eternal objects characterizing the subject's temporal datum and its conformal subjective forms. The order in heaven has been made relevant to the evolving order of the world.

It should be noted, however, that the initial subjective aim is determined, in a sense, as much by the temporal world as it is by God. For the initial aim must be relevant to the particular temporal actualities forming the particular objective datum for the novel subject. In other words, because a given temporal world is to be objectified for the new occasion in a particular way, a given aspect of God's primordial nature is to be objectified for that occasion also in a particular way. Still, the harmonization of the two objectifications—of the temporal world and of God—is ultimately explained by the relevant divine decisions constitutive of the primordial nature.

Accordingly, the entire objective datum for a concrescence, and not just God, who is one element in the datum, provides the concrescence with lures for feeling. "The 'objective lure' is that discrimination among eternal objects introduced into the universe by the real internal constitutions of the actual occasions forming the datum of the concrescence under review" (PR 281). However, it is only by reason of God's immanence as an element in the datum, that "this discrimination also involves eternal objects excluded from value in the temporal occasions of that datum, in addition to involving the eternal objects included for such occasions" (PR 281–82). These additional eternal objects are *proximate* to, and hence compatible for synthesis with, the eternal objects exemplified in the temporal occasions of the datum. Thus, novelty can enter the world only through the mediation of God's primordial nature, the source of all initial subjective aims.

The derivation from God of an occasion's initial subjective aim, we have seen already, does not derogate from the freedom of that occasion. The initial subjective aim received from God is extremely general. By reason of the abstractive hierarchies involved, it provides the novel subject with a range of possible ways of dealing with the data and a range of relevant proximate novelties, some mutually exclusive. The initial aim, then, does not prescribe any specific satisfaction to be derived from the data, though it does indicate the general character of all possible satisfactions derivable from them. For this reason, the initial aim cannot effectively guide the concrescence to its satisfaction without the autonomous subjective decisions that modify and simplify the initial aim into a progressively more specific subjective aim (PR 342–43). This is why, beyond the initial conceptual feeling derived from God, and beyond the other reproductive conceptual feelings, "the mental pole is the subject determining its own ideal of itself by reference to eternal principles of valuation autonomously modified in their application to its own physical objective datum" (PR 380).

To sum up: God's primordial nature is his eternal envisagement of an indefinite number of abstractive hierarchies. This primordial nature does not bring about a real fusion of the individual essences of eternal objects (PR 521). Such a fusion is the achievement of the temporal actualities. God merely structures the eternal objects in regard to their relational essences. But it is in virtue of this structured realm of ideal possibilities that qualitative novelty and creative order are introduced into the world of temporal actualities. This introduction of novelty and order is achieved through the derivation from God's primordial nature of the initial aim of every actual occasion. But this derivation of initial aims does not derogate from the autonomous self-creation of the temporal creatures. Rather, such a derivation testifies to the partial determination which the entire universe, inclusive of God, effects on each of its creatures. In turn, the autonomous decisions modifying the derived aim testify to the ultimate freedom exhibited by each creature as it fashions itself into what best it can and wants to be, given the circumstances of its birth.

5. God: his consequent and superjective natures

For Whitehead, God is an actual entity subject to, and exemplifying, each of the categoreal principles of the organic philosophy (PR 521).

Accordingly, God is to be understood as inescapably bound up in the web of universal solidarity. To that extent, therefore, the full character of God merits being analyzed, if only superficially, beyond the analysis of his primordial nature. The detailed elucidation of God's character is not requisite, however, since the mutual immanence that obtains between God and every temporal occasion constitutes only a special case of the solidarity by which actualities are bound each to all, and all to each.

God's involvement in the solidarity of the universe means that he is objectified for, and felt by, every temporal actuality and that every temporal actuality is objectified for, and felt by, him (PR 47, 523, 529). It also means that God has a threefold character—primordial, consequent, and superjective—which is partly identical to, and partly different from, the threefold character of a temporal actuality—dative, subjective, and superjective (PR 134–35). In this regard, there are two main differences between God and a temporal actuality: first, the order of the first two characters of God is the supersessional reverse of the corresponding first two characters of a temporal actuality; and second, God's superjective character does not require the perishing of his subjective immediacy, whereas the superjective character of a temporal actuality does require the perishing of its subjective immediacy.

In the following passage, Whitehead discusses God's threefold character, and the reason for the order of his first two characters:

> In the case of the primordial actual entity, which is God, there is no past. Thus the ideal realization of conceptual feeling takes precedence. God differs from other actual entities in the fact that Hume's principle, of the derivate character of conceptual feelings, does not hold for him. There is still, however, the same threefold character: (i) The 'primordial nature' of God is the concrescence of a unity of conceptual feelings, including among their data all eternal objects. . . . (ii) The 'consequent nature' of God is the physical prehension by God of the actualities of the evolving universe. . . . (iii) The 'superjective' nature of God is the character of the pragmatic value of his specific satisfaction qualifying the transcendent creativity in the various temporal instances. (PR 134–35)

The difference in the order of the first two characters may also be construed as a reversal, in God, of the supersessional order of the physical pole and the mental pole, as compared to their order in the temporal actualities.

In this regard let us remember, first of all, that for Whitehead each temporal actuality is essentially bipolar, physical and mental, and the physical inheritance is essentially accompanied by a conceptual reaction partly conformed to it, and partly introductory of a relevant novel contrast, but always introducing emphasis, valuation, and purpose. The integration of the physical and mental side into a unity of experience is a self-formation which is a process of concrescence, and which by the principle of objective immortality characterizes the creativity which transcends it. (PR 165/CPR 108)

This bipolar origination holds true for all actual entities, whether they be temporal or not. But in the case of God, the only non-temporal actuality, the supersessional order of the poles is reversed. Next I quote two passages where Whitehead makes this point explicit:

Any instance of experience is bipolar, whether that instance be God or an actual occasion of the world. The origination of God is from the mental pole, the origination of an actual occasion is from the physical pole. . . . (PR 54)

In each actuality there are two concrescent poles of realization—'enjoyment' and 'appetition', that is, the 'physical' and the 'conceptual'. For God the conceptual is prior to the physical, for the World the physical poles are prior to the conceptual poles. (PR 528)

This difference between God and a temporal actuality being thus established, I pass now to a consideration of their difference in respect to their superjective characters.

To be causally objectified in another actuality, a temporal actuality must be completely determinate, that is, it must be a satisfaction or superject. Its objective immortality is a function of its completion. In this regard, the superjective character of a temporal actuality refers indifferently to what the completed actuality is in itself as static outcome, or to what it is as reproduced in and for subsequent actualities. In either case, for a temporal actuality to be a superject, or for it to have superjective or objective functioning, it must be complete, and its completion is the perishing of its subjective immediacy (PR 44, 129–30, 340).

God, who is the only non-temporal actuality, also has a superjective character. By this is meant that both the primordial nature and the consequent nature of God have immortal objective functioning; that is, they are both reproduced, or objectified, in and for every actual occasion (PR 47). In that respect, then, God does not differ from any other actuality. But God is an eternal actuality, always in concrescence, always enjoying subjective immediacy. God is thus always in attainment but never attained. This is one reason why Whitehead refers to God as a non-temporal actuality; for, as an actuality that is always in attainment, God is neither in the past nor in the future of any other actuality (PR 47, 521). Thus, in a unique sense of the term, a sense not derivative from considerations of relativity physics, God is 'contemporary' with every actual occasion (PR 523). Thus, too, God's involvement in the macroscropic processes of transition must be a special case of transcendent decision, for it does not require his completion: God is the cause that is never in the past; God is also the effect that is never in the future.

God's involvement in the transcendent decisions by which the temporal actualities have each their own inescapable datum, since it does not require the perishing of his subjective immediacy, differentiates him from all other actualities and raises a pressing problem (PR 248). How are we to reconcile the objective immortality, or the superjective functioning, of God with his eternal, non-perishing, subjective immediacy? This is a vexing problem in the interpretation of Whitehead's philosophy, for it seems to reflect a major inconsistency in Whitehead's thinking. Though my task in this essay is to elucidate Whitehead's thesis of solidarity and not to save Whitehead's entire system from every appearance of inconsistency, I will suggest one way in which Whitehead may have intended this problem to be solved.

The problem, it seems to me, comes to this: What are we to understand by 'superject'? Is it the case that whatever is a superject must be devoid of subjective immediacy? Now, the fact that Whitehead refers to God's conceptual pole as the primordial superject of creativity suggests that lack of subjective immediacy is not a requisite for being a superject (PR 48). It also suggests that a superject need not be a concrete actuality, but that what is merely an abstract aspect of an actual entity may also be construed as a superject (PR 48, 50). One thing is clear, though—being a superject is a condition for being causally objectifiable in, and for, actual entities.

From these considerations, the following meaning of 'superject' suggests itself: *a superject is any complete synthesis of data*. In the organic universe, whatsoever is such a complete synthesis of data is causally objectifiable. Thus, God's primordial nature is causally objectifiable because it is a complete ideal synthesis of all the data that exist for it—the infinite multiplicity of eternal objects (PR 48, 134, 523). Thus, too, each stage in the supersessional development of God's consequent nature is causally objectifiable because it constitutes a complete physical synthesis of all the data that exist for it—the attained actualities already in existence relative to the origination of that stage of the divine development (PR 523–24). In this manner, given the above definition of 'superject', I am able to provide a satisfactory interpretation of the superjective character, or objective immortality, of both the primordial nature and the consequent nature of God.[4]

But from the completion of his primordial nature and of each stage of his consequent nature, it does not follow that God himself is ever completed, ever an attained actuality. For God's subjective aim is infinite and can never be fully actualized. This is so because God's primordial aim is an appetition for the physical realization of the ideal possibilities he conceptually prehends, and for his own consequent enjoyment of such physical realizations (PR 134). Now, every completed actual occasion is causally objectified in God and is synthesized with the primordial conceptual feeling whose realization it constitutes (PR 524, 134). To that extent, therefore, each completed occasion—through its being objectified in, and felt by, God—represents an advance in the partial actualization of God's subjective aim. But there is always in God an infinite remainder of conceptual feelings having no physical or actual counterpart. Hence God's primordial subjective aim is incapable of full actualization. Accordingly, God is eternally an actuality in attainment and is never an attained actuality. But since God's subjective aim is always in process of actualization, his subjective immediacy must also be eternal. Given my definition of 'superject', however, the eternity of God's subjective immediacy is no impediment to the objective functioning of those aspects of God in which he constitutes the complete synthesis of all the available data.

In the case of temporal actualities, the story is somewhat different yet consistent with what has been said about God. A temporal actuality has a finite subjective aim that is grounded in, and conditioned by, the very data it is to synthesize. The aim of such an actuality is to derive a maximum of intensity of experience from its aesthetic synthesis of the available data. It follows that the complete actualization of the subjective aim of a temporal actuality necessarily coincides with the complete synthesis of its data (PR 129–30). Therefore, assuming as Whitehead does that the subjective immediacy of an actuality cannot endure beyond the complete attainment of its subjective aim (PR 129–30), we must conclude that temporal actualities are superjects—that is, are causally objectifiable—when, and only when, they are utterly devoid of subjective immediacy. In this manner, my definition of 'superject' also enables me to offer a satisfactory interpretation of the superjective character, or objective functioning, of temporal actualities—a character or functioning that presupposes the perishing of their subjective immediacies (PR 44, 448).

God, then, differs from the temporal actualities in that he is objectively immortal but does not perish subjectively, whereas they must perish subjectively in order to attain their immortal objective functioning. God also differs from the temporal actualities, as we saw earlier, in respect to the supersessional order of the physical and mental poles. In other respects, however, God does not differ from the temporal actualities. They are all alike actualities exhibiting, or exemplifying, the same metaphysical traits, though they exemplify those general traits in different ways or in different degrees. For this reason, the preceding considerations of the full nature of God are sufficient for my present purposes. I now return to the consideration of the theory of eternal objects.

6. Eternal objects: novelty and contrasts, or particular modes of ingression

The sense in which an actual entity constitutes a novel achievement cannot be grasped without reference to the principle of the isolation of eternal objects. In this connection, we must note that in respect to its individual essence, an eternal object, as realized in and by an actual occasion, in no way differs from itself as eternal potentiality. Its inclusion in an occasion does not alter its individual essence. This is the organic principle of the 'Translucency of Realization', which asserts "that any eternal object is just itself in whatever mode of realization it is involved. There can be no distortion of the individual essence without thereby producing a different eternal object" (SMW 240). For that matter, there can be no distortion of the relational essence either (PR 175–76).

The upshot of the Translucency of Realization, then, is that the realized eternal object, in respect to its individual and relational essences, is merely an instance of itself. The actual entity repeats it, and if this were all the actual entity did, it would have achieved nothing new. Repetition is the antithesis of novelty.

But an actual entity does achieve something new because it jointly realizes an indefinite number of eternal objects. Thus, there is the coming to be of a *real* togetherness of individual essences—essences which as mere possibilities eternally stand in isolation from one another. Herein lies the significance of the Principle of Isolation.

> The eternal objects are isolated, because their relationships as possibilities are expressible without reference to their respective individ-

ual essences. In contrast to the realm of possibility the inclusion of
eternal objects within an actual occasion means that in respect to some
of their possible relationships there is a togetherness of their individual essences. (SMW 230)

The novel achievement of an actual occasion, however, is not exhausted
by its joint realization of a finite set of eternal objects. For an actual
occasion is a synthesis not just of eternal objects but of other actual entities
as well.

Whitehead's technical term for the 'real togetherness' of a set of eternal
objects is 'contrast' (PR 350). Some contrasts involve only eternal objects;
others involve both eternal objects and objectified actual entities (PR 349).
Whitehead says, however, that he will avoid using the term 'contrast' to
refer to objectified nexūs (PR 349). In any case, my immediate concern is
primarily with the former kind of contrasts, and with the latter kind only
when considered in abstraction from the physical data they involve.
Considered in this manner, contrasts are made up of eternal objects
exclusively; nevertheless, contrasts are not themselves eternal. Whitehead
expresses this tenet in the third Category of Explanation: "That in the
becoming of an actual entity, novel . . . contrasts, also become; but there
are no novel eternal objects" (PR 33). The eternal objects that make up the
contrast are merely repeated in and by the parent actual entity. New
instances of themselves thus come to be, but as such they are necessarily
repetitions of their own eternal instances. Something else has come to be,
however, which is not necessarily the repetition of anything else in the
universe: the actual togetherness, or contrast, of just this set of eternal
objects.

Contrasts, it should be noted, are in principle repeatable. This is why
the real essence of an actual entity, its unique determinate character, is
primarily a function of its 'position' and not of its 'definiteness' (PR 93–94,
38).[5] It is always possible that the contrast realized by an actual entity to
constitute its definiteness may have been already realized, or may be
subsequently realized, by some other actual entity. In this sense, contrasts
are real universals that come to be. They emerge into reality at some
definite moment in the history of the universe, and they may recur in
subsequent moments of that history (PR 352). Both contrasts and eternal
objects, then, are repeatable; but contrasts are created things, while
eternal objects are, as their name implies, uncreated. It may be objected,
however, that the emergence of a contrast is just the realization of an
eternal possibility. But such an objection misses the point I have been

laboring to make. By a 'possible contrast' we can only mean the possible entrance into actuality of some complex eternal object or pattern. But a pattern, we have seen, does not specify the individual essences of its components. Thus, by 'the possibility of a contrast' we can only mean something vague, general, and indeterminate, whereas by 'contrast' we mean something that is specific, particular, and determinate.

A contrast is analyzable into factors which are its constituent eternal objects, in abstraction from their joint realization. For this reason we cannot dissect the contrast without murdering it. Be that as it may, the analysis in question yields the following factors: (i) an ingressed complex eternal object or pattern; (ii) usually, but not necessarily, a finite set of ingressed simpler patterns; and (iii) a finite set of ingressed simple eternal objects or sensa. The individual essence of the most complex pattern is the 'manner' of the contrast, while the individual essences of the simpler patterns and of the sensa constitute its 'matter' (PR 175–76). This analysis is only provisional, inasmuch as some contrasts involve factors which are not eternal objects.

The distinction between patterns and sensa may be elucidated further in connection with the notion of contrast. According to Whitehead, every eternal object, whether it be a pattern or a sensum, is in one sense simple; for "neither involves other specified eternal objects in its own realization" (PR 175). Here what are not specified are the individual essences of other eternal objects. What is meant, therefore, is that the realization of an individual essence, whether of a sensum or a pattern, does not involve the realization of other *specified* individual essences.

A pattern, however, is complex in a sense in which a sensum is not. For the individual essence of a pattern is such that it cannot be realized without "the concurrent realization of a group of eternal objects capable of contrast in that pattern" (PR 176). This should be evident from the fact that a pattern can provide only the *manner* of a contrast. A group of other eternal objects is needed to supply the *matter* of that contrast. The relational essence which each member of this group must have is specified by the relational essence of the pattern in question. But the individual essence of each member of the group is not thereby specified. The realization of the pattern might have occurred by means of an entirely different group of sensa, provided that each member of such a group had the requisite relational essence. Thus, a different contrast would have come to be—different by reason of its different *matter*—though the *manner* of the contrast would have been the same.

A sensum differs from a pattern because its realization does not necessarily involve the concurrent realization of any eternal object whatsoever (PR 174). Its realization involves only itself, *i.e.*, "its intrinsic apparatus of individual and relational essence" (PR 176). A pattern, on the other hand, necessarily involves *in its realization*, not only its own apparatus of individual and relational essences, but also the individual and relational essences of the members of one or another set of eternal objects. No *particular* set is necessary; but some set or other is necessary.

In principle, then, the realization of a sensum does not involve the becoming of a contrast. In fact, however, having regards to the complete character of actual entities, precisely the opposite is the case. For, by reason of organic principles extraneous to the theory of eternal objects, it is impossible for an actual entity to realize only one sensum. This is so, because every actual entity must take into account what the universe is by way of accomplishment, as well as what it is by way of potentiality. The accomplished universe is the totality of actual entities already become, relative to the becoming of any particular actual entity. The taking into account of these antecedent actualities by the becoming occasion involves the reproduction within itself of some of the eternal objects realized by the said antecedent actualities. (But this is not all that is involved.) The taking into account of the universe's potentiality involves the realization of some eternal objects derived from the realm of ideality. As a result of this dual taking into account of the universe, every occasion involves in its becoming the realization of a plurality of eternal objects; and its synthesis of this plurality requires still another eternal object to provide the manner of the contrast thus achieved. For this reason, therefore, the realization of sensa is ideally distinguished from the becoming of contrasts, but not in fact (PR 176).[6]

It follows from this that "no individual essence is realizable apart from *some* of its potentialities of relationship" (PR 175–76; italics mine), meaning by this that some of the potential relationships of an eternal object to other eternal objects must be realized whenever *that* eternal object is realized. This is important because it permits us to understand what Whitehead meant by the 'mode of ingression' of an eternal object. 'Ingression', we have already seen, is the technical term for the functioning or inclusion of an eternal object within an occasion. But 'mode of ingression' refers to the determinate way in which any eternal object, in being realized by and within an occasion, thereby enters into a real, determinate togetherness with a determinate set of other eternal objects also realized by and within that occasion. Thus, an eternal object's mode of ingression into a particular occasion is its inclusion in that occasion as a factor in the determinate, real togetherness, or contrast, of eternal objects come to be by reason of that occasion's activity.

Two things must be borne in mind in this respect. First, the relational essence of an eternal object determines its possible modes of ingression into any actual entity, insofar as that essence determines its possible relationships with other eternal objects.[7] Second, according to the Principle of the Translucency of Realization an eternal object is just itself in each and all of its modes of ingression; in other words, its ingression, in whatever mode, does not distort its intrinsic apparatus of individual and relational essences (PR 176). With these two things in mind, we can understand how Whitehead can speak of one self-same eternal object as having different modes of ingression. For one and the same eternal object can, in different occasions, be concurrently realized with different sets of other eternal objects. In each case, a different possible relationship of that eternal object to other eternal objects has been realized. But the eternal object in question is, in all cases, an instance of itself. Thus, an ingressed eternal object "retains its potentiality of indefinite diversity of modes of ingression" (PR 226), even though, in respect to that ingression, its indetermination as to its possible togetherness with other eternal objects has been rendered determinate. "Potentiality becomes reality; and yet retains its message of alternatives which the actual entity has avoided" (PR 226). To sum up: An eternal object, considered in regard to any one particular mode of ingression, is just an instance of itself, but as *being* in *just that* determinate relationship to *just those* other determinate eternal objects, and as *not being* in *any* of its *other possible* relationships (SMW 227).

7. *Eternal objects: their general modes of functioning*

The phrase 'mode of ingression' is not used univocally by Whitehead; for, in addition to having the signification explained above, it also signifies any one of the three general ways in which eternal objects may function in any given actuality. These 'primary modes of ingression' or of functioning are, first, as an element in the determinateness of the objective datum of a physical feeling; second, as an element in the definiteness of the subjective form of a physical feeling; and third, as an element in the datum, or as being in itself the datum, of a conceptual prehension (PR 445). If an eternal object functions in either of the first two modes, it is said to have 'unrestricted' ingression into the occasion in question. If, however, it functions in the third mode, it is then said to have 'restricted' ingression into the occasion (PR 445). The notions of unrestricted and restricted ingressions, as well as the notion of a conceptual prehension, must now be reviewed.

"A conceptual prehension," writes Whitehead, "is a direct vision of some possibility . . . as to how actualities *may be definite*" (PR 50). By means of a conceptual prehension, an actual entity can evaluate the potential unrestricted ingression into itself of some relevant eternal object. In this manner, an actual entity, *qua* subject, evaluates an eternal object as a possible contributor to its own definiteness, *qua* superject. If this eternal object is not subsequently ingressed into that actuality in either of the two unrestricted modes, then it will not be an element in the definiteness of that actuality's subjective form. The eternal object in question has functioned in that actuality considered as subject; but it does not function in that same actuality considered as superject, since the *simple* analysis of that superject's subjective form will not reveal *that* eternal object as an element of its definiteness.

Nevertheless, the functioning of that eternal object in that actuality, considered as subject, may be inferred or reconstructed by a subsequent subject from the proximate relevance of that eternal object to at least one of the other eternal objects having unrestricted realization in the actuality in question. For, in virtue of the Principle of Translucent Realization, any eternal object unrestrictively ingressed into an actual entity calls attention—upon the analysis of that actuality by a subsequent actuality—to those eternal objects proximate to itself in one or more of the abstractive hierarchies. These proximate eternal objects are then prehended by the analyzing actuality as possible forms of definiteness which the analyzed actuality rejected as determinants of its own definiteness. This is the import of the organic dictum, previously quoted, that "potentiality becomes reality; and yet retains its message of alternatives which the actual entity has avoided" (PR 226). Thus, insofar as a member of an abstractive hierarchy is unrestrictedly realized by an actual entity, it carries a message concerning the other members of that hierarchy, the members whose realization that actual entity has avoided or excluded.

It should be noted, in this last regard, that what we are considering here is the definiteness of an actual entity and not its total determinateness. The rejected eternal object is ingressed datively in the actuality so far as that eternal object is an element in the objectification, for that actuality, of God's primordial nature. The analysis of an actuality's definiteness is the analysis of its subjective form. The analysis of its total determinateness is the analysis of its objective content as well as of its subjective form.

The respective meanings of restricted ingression and unrestricted subjective ingression may be made clear now. If an eternal object has restricted ingression, it functions in the actual entity *qua* subject, but not in the definiteness of the actual entity *qua* superject. If an eternal object has unrestricted subjective ingression, it functions in the actual entity considered both as subject and as superject—in respect to the former because it is evaluated and realized in some phase of the process; in respect to the latter because it remains as an everlasting feature of the everlasting product. In either of the two unrestricted modes of functioning, an eternal object is realized as an immanent determinant of the determinateness of an occasion. But in the restricted mode of functioning, an eternal object, though really ingressed in regard to the subject entertaining it, is withheld from being realized in its function of conferring definiteness. This mode, then,

> is merely the conceptual valuation of the potential ingression in one of the other two modes. It is a real ingression into actuality; but it is a restricted ingression with mere potentiality withholding the immediate realization of its function of conferring definiteness. (PR 445)

8. Eternal objects: subjective and objective species

According to Whitehead, the two unrestricted modes of ingression are not both indifferently open to each eternal object (PR 445). For this reason, eternal objects are classified, in this regard, into two species, subjective and objective. An eternal object of the 'subjective species' may ingress into an actuality in either of the two unrestricted modes, and may in fact function both ways in one and the same actuality (PR 445–47). On the other hand, an eternal object of the 'objective species' can have unrestricted ingression only as an element in the determinateness of an objective datum and "can never be an element in the definiteness of a subjective form" (PR 445–46). The sole avocation of such an eternal object "is to be an agent in objectification" (PR 445).

Among the eternal objects of the subjective species are the scalar forms, or intensities, of physical energy; emotional forms, such as aversion and adversion; pain and pleasure; some sensa, such as a definite smell; *etc.* A member of this species is primarily an element in the definiteness of the subjective form of a prehension or feeling, but it can also be the element of definiteness by which one actual entity is objectified in another actual entity. For example, let A_1 stand for the eternal object defining the subjective form of a prehension; and let A stand for the actuality to which the prehension in question belongs; finally, let A be in the actual world of an actuality in attainment, say B; we then have the following possibility:

> A_1 may be that component of A's constitution through which A is objectified for B. Thus when B feels A_1, it feels 'A with *that* feeling'. In this way, the eternal object which contributes to the definiteness of A's feeling becomes an eternal object contributing to the definiteness of A as an objective datum in B's prehension of A. The eternal object can then function both subjectively and relatively. It can be a private element in a subjective form, and also an agent in the objectification. (PR 446)

In this example, A_1 is first a private factor in the definiteness of the subjective form of a prehension belonging to A; subsequently, A_1 becomes a public factor expressing the definite way in which A is objectified in B. A_1 is now said to be public because other actual entities, say X and Y, may have A objectified for them under the aspect of A_1.

It should be noticed that A_1 may have a two-way functioning in a single actual entity B. This would obtain if A_1, in addition to being the objective datum of B's prehension of A, were also the subjective form of that prehension, or at least an element of that form. This is the type of prehension termed 'conformal feeling'.

> In the first stage of B's physical feeling, the subjective form of B's feeling is conformed to the subjective form of A's feeling. Thus this eternal object in B's experience will have a two-way mode of functioning. It will be among the determinants of A for B, and it will be among the determinants of B's way of sympathy with A. (PR 446–47)

By reason of their twofold function in conformal feelings, eternal objects of the subjective species play an essential role in the evolving solidarity of the universe.

> In the conformal feelings the *how* of feelings reproduces what is felt. Some conformation is necessary as a basis of vector transition, whereby the past is synthesized with the present. The one eternal object in its two-way function, as a determinant of the datum and as a determinant of the subjective form, is thus relational. In this sense the solidarity of the universe is based on the relational functioning of eternal objects. (PR 249)

But the sense of solidarity to which Whitehead is alluding here—that the past contributed some of its qualities to the subjective immediacy of each present—presupposes the more basic sense of solidarity—that actualities are immanent each in the others. For the past can contribute qualities to the immediacy of a present subject only if that past is causally objectified for that subject. For this reason, the eternal objects most relevant to the basic sense of solidarity turn out to be those of the objective species.

Accordingly, the eternal objects of the objective species are of special interest to us because "the solidarity of the world rests upon the incurable objectivity of this species of eternal objects" (PR 446).

> A member of this species inevitably introduces into the immediate subject other actualities. The definiteness with which it invests the external world may, or may not, conform to the real internal constitutions of the actualities objectified. But conformably, or non-conformably, such is the character of that nexus for that actual entity. . . . Eternal objects of the objective species are the mathematical Platonic forms. They concern the world as medium. (PR 446)

Whitehead could have said, just as well, that they concern the world as extended. Here under 'mathematical form' we are to include 'geometrical form', and this without imposing any restriction upon the number of dimensions that may be associated with such forms. It is by reason of these geometric forms that actual entities, both in themselves and as objectified in other actualities, are invested with a dimensional, morphological character. But the extensive character of actual entities and of their objectifications is antecedent to, and indeed presupposed by, their dimensional and morphological character. This point will become clearer when, in the next chapter, we examine the organic theory of extension. In the chapter after that, Chapter Six, we shall see that the eternal extension of the universe and the objective species of eternal objects are the ultimate metaphysical elements grounding the mutual immanence of all actualities.

For the moment, I can take advantage of the fact that eternal objects of the objective species cannot function as elements in the definiteness of subjective form to provide yet another reason why it is a mistake to equate the objectification of the past with the conformation to the past. Causal objectification necessarily involves eternal objects of the objective species, but it is impossible that conformation could involve that species of eternal objects. For the "doctrine of conformation only holds for the qualitative side of the content of the objective datum" (AI 326). Thus, the doctrine of conformation merely expresses the fact that "the qualitative content of the object prehended enters into the qualities exemplified in the subjective form of that prehension" (AI 326). But "only the qualitative components of an actuality in the datum can pass into the subjective form" (AI 327). Clearly, then, "the doctrine of conformation does not apply to mathematical pattern" (AI 326). Therefore, since conformation does not involve geometrical forms, that is, since it does not involve eternal objects of the objective species, it cannot be the same thing as causal objectification.

9.   Eternal objects: their connectedness or ideal solidarity

In the greater part of this chapter, I have been examining those aspects of the theory of eternal objects, and of the related theory of God's primordial nature, that will play significant roles in the final elucidation of the becoming, the being, and the solidarity of actual entities. But I have been examining also the extent to which the concept of connectedness, or the more general sense of solidarity, is applicable to eternal objects in themselves. For I have shown that eternal objects transcend one another in respect to their individual essences, but involve one another in respect to their relational essences.

The first half of this last statement is true without qualification, since even the individual essence of a pattern does not specify the individual essences of its required set of compossible components. But the second half is not unqualifiedly true, because the relational essences of some eternal objects are mutually exclusive. In other words, it is in the nature of things that some eternal objects cannot have joint unrestricted realization in the definiteness of the same actual entity.

This qualification aside, however, I have shown in this chapter that eternal objects, to the extent that they are objects of God's primordial conceptual valuation, form a systematic realm of mutual relatedness (SMW 224). Thus, eternal objects among themselves, divorced from any ingression into the temporal world, exemplify the connexity that pervades the universe. I have also shown here that the connexity of eternal objects is to be explained in terms of the reappearance of any set of lower members of an abstractive hierarchy in the function of being components of at least one higher member of that hierarchy. The reappearance is, in this case, merely ideal or logical; but it exhibits the fundamental role that repetition—be it physical, conceptual, or logical—plays in the all-encompassing solidarity of the universe.

10.   Solidarity and the formative elements: a revealing review

The three formative elements studied in this chapter—eternal objects, God's primordial nature, and the eternal creativity of the universe—are obviously relevant to, but cannot by themselves provide, an adequate elucidation of the thesis of solidarity. Their failure, in this respect, is easily revealed by a quick review of their relevance.

Both the subjective and the objective species of eternal objects are explicitly linked by Whitehead to the elucidation of universal solidarity (PR 249; 445–46). Members of the subjective species, through their two-way functioning in conformal feelings, explain how the definiteness of earlier subjects is precipitated into, and synthesized with, the definiteness of later subjects. They thus explain how the solidarity of the universe manifests itself in the contributions which earlier actualities make to the subjective forms of later actualities. But those contributions presuppose that the earlier actualities first contribute their objectified selves as data for the conformal feelings of the later actualities. In turn, the objectifications of past actualities presuppose the functioning of eternal objects of the objective species. Members of this species cannot function as determinants of subjective form. Their main avocation is to be agents of objectification. Thus, when unrestrictedly ingressed, the basic function of a member of this species is to introduce one actuality, or one nexus of actualities, into the constitution of another actuality (PR 445).

Clearly, eternal objects are to be construed as playing an essential role in the solidarity of actual entities. That much, Whitehead has made explicit. What he has not made explicit is *how* eternal objects are supposed to play such a role. For an eternal object ingressed into one actuality cannot by itself provide any information as to its ingression into other actualities. Remember, in this regard, the import of the principle of the Translucency of Realization: an eternal object, in each and every one of its ingressions, is just its identical self (SMW 240). Accordingly, the nature of an eternal object "does not disclose the private details of any actuality" (PR 444). An eternal object may have been ingressed into earlier occasions, but its current ingression into a given actuality can tell no tales about its past ingressions (PR 391). For that matter, its current ingression can tell no tales about its ingression into occasions contemporary with, or future to, the given actuality. How, then, can an eternal object be an ingredient of one actuality under the guise of qualifying another actuality (SMW 146)?

Put another way, how can an eternal object introduce into the make-up of one actuality the self-identity or particularity of another actuality? Has not Whitehead explicitly said that the particularity of an actual entity, or of a nexus of actual entities, involves more than a contrast of eternal objects (PR 350–51)? If the particularities of actualities and nexūs are "not expressible wholly in terms of contrasts between eternal objects" (PR 350), then how can the mere ingression of eternal objects ever convey those particularities into the constitution of another particular actuality? None of the organic doctrines and categories we have so far considered enable us to answer this question satisfactorily. Accordingly, eternal objects, although necessary to the elucidation of solidarity, are not sufficient for that task.

The primordial nature of God is essentially involved in the macroscopic processes productive of the given phases of all actual occasions. But this functioning of God is only a special case of the functioning of all accumulated superjects in the creative transition to a new subject. The ultimate fact is that each new actuality has to house every settled fact in its universe. Since God is a settled fact in respect to his primordial nature—and also, for that matter, in respect to the latest specific satisfaction of his consequent nature—each new actuality must house the objective reality of God. Thus, though God plays a crucial role in the macroscopic processes whereby the housing of the universe in each of its actualities is achieved, he is not the reason why actualities have to house each the others.

In other words, we should not expect the organic theory of God to resolve the paradox of solidarity; for the philosophy of organism construes God as an actual entity and thus as subject to all the truly ultimate metaphysical principles (PR 521). Accordingly, God is immanent in every temporal occasion, and every temporal occasion is immanent in God; moreover, God transcends, and is transcended by, every temporal occasion (PR 528). The mutual immanence of God and any temporal actuality, therefore, is only a special case of the universal solidarity by which actualities are bound each to all, and all to each (PR 529). It is a special case because the functioning of God in any actuality, or of any actuality in God, is never negligible. Thus, the functioning of God in the temporal actualities is the eminent case of the functioning of the one in the many; and thus, too, the functioning of the temporal actualities in God is the eminent case of the functioning of the many in the one.

The solidarity between the temporal world and God is special, in addition, because the temporal occasions achieve their most harmonious unification in their objective functioning in God's experience. By contrast, the unification of temporal occasions in one another always suffers from deficiencies. To be sure, temporal occasions never fail to be objectified for one another, but the contributions they make to each other's experience are often either negligible or incompatible for felt synthesis. In this sense, in the temporal world "there is deficiency in the solidarity of individuals with each other" (PR 532). It is this deficiency which God overcomes in the aesthetic harmony of his consequent experience. Thus, solidarity achieves its perfection in the divine nature (PR 532). For all its perfection, nonetheless, divine solidarity remains a special case of universal solidarity. As such, the concept of divine solidarity is just as paradoxical, and stands in as much need of elucidation, as the concept of universal solidarity. The divine species exemplifies the universal genus, but does not explain it.

We come at last to creativity, the principle of novelty. Its necessary involvement in the solidarity of actual occasions is made abundantly evident in the Category of the Ultimate. Creativity is there said to be "that ultimate principle by which the many, which are the universe disjunctively, become the one actual occasion, which is the universe conjunctively" (PR 31). But to what purpose is the creativity being invoked? Is it to ground the *mutual immanence* of occasions? Or is it to ground the *becoming* of mutually immanent occasions? That the creativity is not being invoked to ground the relationship of mutual immanence is implicit in Whitehead's claim that a "mere system of mutually prehensive occasions is compatible with the concept of a static timeless world" (IS 242). For a static timeless world is one devoid of any becoming; in such a world, all entities, and all relationships between entities, exist timelessly. The solidarity of such a world is a surd to which a principle of novelty can bear no relevance whatever. On the other hand, a world whose ultimate actualities are essentially interrelated acts of becoming—that is to say, the real world as conceived by the philosophy of organism—is a world that cannot be conceived without positing a principle of novelty. But the principle of novelty is posited to ground the becoming of the actualities and not their mere solidarity.

Of course, the whole point of the Category of the Ultimate is that the entire universe functions in and for each instance of creative advance. So, in fact, the solidarity of occasions and the becoming of occasions are ultimate features of reality that cannot be abstracted from one another. The solidarity of the universe is an ongoing achievement, ever renewing itself in each instance of creative advance; and the relata of solidarity are the instances of creative advance—the occasions which become, yet involve each other. Accordingly, there is no elucidating the universe's solidarity without appealing to the principle of creativity. But, by the same token, merely appealing to the principle of creativity cannot elucidate the solidarity of the universe.

I next examine the organic theory of eternal extensive continuity. This theory, more than any other single organic theory, provides the solution to the paradox of solidarity. Indeed, it is only in its light that the other organic theories, doctrines, and principles find their proper place in respect to the elucidation of universal solidarity.

FIVE

The Extensive Continuum

The understanding of Whitehead's philosophy advanced in this essay rests on two closely related interpretive claims. The first of these claims is that the solidarity of actual entities is the fundamental thesis of the organic philosophy. An ever expanding universe of mutually immanent, but discrete, actualities constitutes, according to this claim, the basic metaphysical thesis nerving the organic system's development and coloring each of its doctrines and theories. Admittedly, the thesis of solidarity is a baffling, antithetical paradox. Whitehead has said as much (MT 224). But the thesis' elucidation, Whitehead has said also, is the one task common to all the organic categories (AI 293). The preceding chapters have provided ample evidence of the central importance of this thesis and of the manner in which major organic categories contribute, or are intended to contribute, to its elucidation. Thus far, however, the categories and doctrines I have considered have not enabled me to provide an entirely adequate elucidation of solidarity. Their failure in this respect makes evident the relevance of the second interpretive claim underlying my understanding of Whitehead's philosophy—that the intelligibility and logical consistency of the solidarity thesis presupposes positing the existence of an eternal continuum of extension whose metaphysical function is to ground the mutual transcendence, and the mutual immanence, of any two actual entities.

Demonstrating that Whitehead does indeed posit the existence of an eternal extensive continuum is one of the crucial tasks undertaken in this and the next chapters. That such an undertaking is at all necessary signals Whitehead's neglect to make sufficiently explicit the metaphysical function his philosophy assigns to extensive continuity. As a result of precisely

this neglect, Whiteheadian scholars heretofore have been at a loss to make
genuine sense of the mutual immanence of discrete actualities; for there
can be no truly adequate understanding of solidarity without recourse to
the metaphysical theory of extension implicit in, and presupposed by,
Whitehead's systematic writings. In fact, without recourse to the metaphysical function of extension there can be no truly adequate understanding of the philosophy of organism as a systematic whole.

It may be objected, with considerable textual justification, that extension cannot have the metaphysical function here claimed for it because the
extensive continuum is merely a contingent, derivative feature of our
cosmic epoch. In addition, it may be objected that if Whitehead had
construed the extensive continuum as eternal, he would have included it
among the formative elements of the temporal world. Since his discussion
of formative elements is limited to creativity, eternal objects, and God's
primordial nature (RM 89–90), we have yet another reason to construe the
extensive continuum as contingent and derivative. Finally, it may be
objected also that if Whitehead had posited extension as a metaphysical
principle, he would have discussed it in the categoreal scheme of PR.
Since the extensive continuum is not even mentioned in the categoreal
scheme, but is in fact discussed as a derivative notion in the third chapter
of that book's first part, it follows that extension cannot be a metaphysical
principle of the organic philosophy.

These objections are not as formidable as they first appear. The first
objection assumes that 'extensive continuum' can have only one and the
same sense throughout Whitehead's writings. But, as I shall soon demonstrate, the term has in fact a variety of interrelated senses in Whitehead's
philosophy. It is only in one of those senses that the term is meant to
denote a contingent, derivative feature of our cosmic epoch. This feature
is the spatio-temporal continuum of relativity physics as understood by
the organic philosophy. Now I not only agree, but also insist, that the
spatio-temporal continuum, precisely because it is just a contingent feature of our cosmic epoch, cannot serve to ground the mutual immanence
of discrete occasions. In other words, since the solidarity of actualities is a
metaphysical feature of reality and hence obtains in all cosmic epochs, it
cannot be explained in terms of a contingent feature of a particular epoch.
Given that this is so, how are we to understand the many passages where
Whitehead explicitly links the solidarity of actual entities to the functioning of an extensive continuum? Surely, in those passages, 'extensive
continuum' cannot be intended to denote the spatio-temporal continuum.
The existence of at least one other meaning for this term is thus made
evident. The continuum which grounds the solidarity of the universe

cannot be the spatio-temporal continuum contigently characterizing our cosmic epoch. It must be instead an eternal continuum underlying all cosmic epochs, actual or potential.

The other two objections will lose most of their force as soon as I have demonstrated that the eternal continuum and the eternal creativity are two sides of the same ultimate metaphysical coin. Extension and creativity will then be understood as distinguishable, but inseparable, aspects of the one ultimate reality grounding the becoming, the being, and the interconnectedness of actual entities. I shall thus be in a position to argue that 'creativity' is the term with which Whitehead refers to an ultimate metaphysical ground that is extensive as well as creative. But if 'creativity' signifies an extenso-creative reality, the list of formative elements and the organic categoreal scheme already include the notion of extensive continuity.

The manner in which the three objections are to be countered has now been foreshadowed; their final dissolution must be deferred until I have articulated my understanding of Whitehead's theory of metaphysical extension. Articulating that understanding is the immediate task of this chapter. I shall return to the objections in the next chapter.

A sustained, explicit treatment of a theory of metaphysical extension is nowhere to be found in Whitehead's works. But hints of, or allusions to, an eternal extensive continuum are found in passages where Whitehead is dealing either with basic metaphysical doctrines, such as solidarity and objectification, or with the special features which extensive continuity displays in our cosmic epoch. My efforts in this chapter, therefore, constitute an attempt to recover, reconstruct, and develop the theory of metaphysical extension implicit in, or implied by, Whitehead's metaphysical and cosmological writings. To that end, in the sections that follow I will attempt to establish, first, of course, that Whitehead does posit the existence of a metaphysical continuum of extension; second, that this metaphysical continuum of extension differs from, and is presupposed by, the epochal continuum of spatio-temporalized extension; and third, that the separative, modal, and prehensive properties explicitly attributed, in SMW, to spatio-temporal volumes are in fact properties of metaphysical extension—the very properties in terms of which the solidarity of the universe is to be understood.

1.   The metaphysical extensive continuum or receptacle

The metaphysical extensive continuum is that eternal factor of the universe *wherein* the creative advance of actuality occurs. It is eternal because it is involved in the becoming of every actual entity, but it does not itself become. Thus, according to Whitehead, the creative advance of the universe presupposes the metaphysical continuum of extension (PR 442). All actual occasions come to be in this continuum, but they do not create the continuum. Instead, the eternal continuum 'receives' each actuality, and each actuality 'embodies' or 'occupies' a region of the continuum (PR 97–98). By reason of this embodiment, or occupation, of an extensive region, every actual occasion is truly and necessarily an extended thing (PR 107).

Thus, although actual entities are extended things, their extensiveness is not a byproduct of their becoming. It may be objected, however, that Whitehead does speak of actual entities 'realizing', as well as including, regions of extension (PR 97). This is true enough; but what the actual entities realize are *regions* of extension, and not the *extension* of their regions. This is an important, if seemingly obscure, distinction. Before I can clarify it I must discuss two basic properties of the metaphysical extensive continuum.

The properties in question are: first, that the extensive continuum is *unbounded*, by which Whitehead means not only that it is infinite (*i.e.*, without limits or boundaries), but also that, considered in itself, it is *undivided;* second, that the extensive continuum, though undivided, is, nevertheless, *indefinitely divisible* (PR 103). By reason of these two properties, we may speak of *regions* into which the extensive continuum could be divided, but into which it is not, in fact, divided. According to Whitehead, however, the notion of a region involves the notion of "a certain determinate boundedness" (PR 546, Corrigenda).

> The inside of a region . . . has a complete boundedness denied to the extensive potentiality external to it. . . . Wherever there is ambiguity as to the contrast of boundedness between inside and outside, there is no proper region. (PR 546)

A proper or real region, then, presupposes its boundary; but in the extensive continuum, considered in itself, there are no boundaries. Therefore, the regions into which the extensive continuum is divisible are not real or proper regions. They are *potential* regions. Regions that might be, but are not. Notice, however, that it is of the potential regions that we say that they might be, and not of the extension which they would divide if they obtained.

The extensive continuum, then, is a potentiality for regions of itself.

But for Whitehead these regions obtain—that is, become real—only by reason of the actual entities that come to be in the field of extension. The extensive continuum, he writes, "is in itself merely the potentiality for division; an actual entity effects this division" (PR 104). The becoming of an actual entity involves the realization of a proper region. Hence, an actual entity realizes that which was previously potential: a region of extension (PR 112). We can thus speak of an actual entity realizing a region of extension, without meaning by this that an actual entity realizes the extension of its region.

The notion that an actual entity realizes an extensive region has to be qualified in another way. An actual entity does not first exist and then realize its region. Rather, a proper region and the process by which that region is created constitute the first phase in the becoming of an actual entity. In other words, the process by which a potential region is bounded and thus made real is one and the same with the process by which an actual entity in its first phase of existence is created. There is no proper region unless there is an actuality in attainment, and there is no actuality in attainment unless there is a proper region. Or, to speak more systematically, the occasion cannot exist, not even as merely real, unless its proper region exists; and a proper region cannot exist unless its correlative occasion also exists, at least as merely real.

The proper region correlative to an actual entity remains a feature of that entity throughout the latter's history of self-formation. The proper region is thus the first feature of the actuality in attainment and is also one of the features of the attained actuality (PR 441, 98, 470). But all other features of the actuality—the products of its several phases of becoming—find their place within the actuality's own extensive region. Thus, the first character to emerge in the becoming of an actual entity is the latter's extensive region, and this region constitutes the creative domain of that actuality.

An actual entity is said to occupy, or to include, the region it realizes (PR 97). Hence, an actual entity is extensive by reason of the region it occupies, and the occupied region is real by reason of the actuality that occupies it. The occupied region is the 'extensive standpoint' of the occupying actuality (PR 546, Corrigenda).

Insofar as extensive standpoints are real or proper regions of the extensive continuum, the latter may be conceived as a potentiality for the standpoints of actual entities. But there is a difference between conceiving of the extensive continuum in this manner and conceiving of it as sheer potentiality for divisions of itself. Actual entities, we must remember, are discrete individuals. For this reason, their extensive standpoints cannot overlap. Extensive standpoints are mutually transcendent (PR 440). Hence, the conception of extension as a potentiality for standpoints is more restrictive than the conception of extension as a potentiality for divisions of itself. The one concept precludes the notion of overlapping standpoints, whereas the other does not preclude the notion of overlapping potential regions. The former concept, moreover, introduces the notion that the extensive continuum is divisible into an infinite number of non-compossible schemes of compossible extensive standpoints.

Notice, in this regard, that to consider a single potential standpoint is just to consider a single potential region. However, if we consider a plurality of extensive standpoints, the notion of non-compossibility arises. A scheme of compossible standpoints is a scheme of non-overlapping potential regions. Schemes of compossible standpoints form a subset within the set of schemes of potential divisions. Only the members of this subset are in principle realizable, though not jointly.

For example, consider the set S of potential regions A, B, C, and D. Let C completely overlap B; and let B completely overlap A; finally, let D partially overlap both B and C, but not A. Now each of these potential regions is also a potential standpoint; but only A and D form a scheme of compossible standpoints. Thus the actualization of A leaves open the possibility that D be actualized also; and *vice versa*. But the actualization of either B or C forever destroys the possibility that any other member of S be also actualized. Notice, too, that though the realization of B bestows a certain derivative actuality upon A (since A is a part, or a subregion, of B), A as such is not a proper region, since A itself is not bounded. In other words, A is part of an actual standpoint, but A is not itself an actual standpoint. This is only to say that the extension of a standpoint retains its character of indefinite divisibility.

The distinction between sets of potential regions and sets of compossible standpoints is the reason why Whitehead contrasts the 'contrary potentialities' offered by the 'mere continuum', with the 'one coherent set of real divisions' effected by 'definite atomic actualities' (PR 104). The mere continuum, that is, the continuum considered in itself, is divisible; and by reason of its divisibility, we may construe it as made up of potential regions or, as Whitehead somewhat misleadingly calls them, 'entities'

> united by the various allied relationships of whole to part, and of overlapping so as to possess common parts and of other relationships derived from these primary relationships. (PR 103)

Considered in respect to its real division, however, the extensive continuum is to be construed as forming an ever-expanding, coherent system of non-overlapping proper regions or standpoints.

This one coherent system of real division is termed, somewhat inappropriately, 'the region of actuality' (PR 104). The term is inappropriate because an aggregate of proper regions does not itself constitute the standpoint of an actual entity; the aggregate is merely a potential region. Moreover, insofar as the actual world is always expanding through the emergence of new actualities, no determinate boundary can be assigned to the region of actuality. Thus, whereas the boundaries of proper regions are immutable—actual entities become, but they do not change—the boundary of the region of actuality changes with each expansion of the actual world. The region of actuality, therefore, is not an actual, or proper, region.

To put this differently, the actual world relative to some specified actual entity—that is, the world of attained actualities relative to that entity—defines, through the aggregation of the extensive standpoints of its component actualities, a 'region' of the extensive continuum. But this region, termed the region of actuality, is not a proper region. It is only a potential region. It might have served as the standpoint of a hypothetical actual entity (PR 439); but in fact it does not serve, nor could it serve in the future, as such as standpoint.

Nevertheless, though not a proper region, the region of actuality has a derivative determinateness that prevents us from treating it as merely another potential region. Beyond it, the extensive continuum is a sheer potentiality for division but is as yet undivided. Within it, however, the continuum is really divided into a scheme of mutually external regions or standpoints (PR 104). For this reason, the region of actuality is best construed as a quasi-proper region.

2.   *Extension contrasted with actualized extension*

It should be noted that the notion of an actual world, and thereby the notion of a region of actuality, is always relative to some specified actual entity. When the specified entity is completely actual, that is, when it is a superject, it adds itself to the actual world, thus transforming its 'old' actual world into a 'new' actual world, relative to some new entity superseding the one in question. This is what is meant in the organic philosophy by the expansion of actuality, and also therefore by the expansion of the region of actuality.

This last point is important; for when Whitehead says that there is a becoming of continuity (PR 53; IS 246), we must understand him to mean, not that mere extensive continuity becomes, for the continuum of pure extension is by hypothesis eternal, but that *actualized* extensive continuity becomes. In this regard, by actualized extension, as opposed to mere extension, we are to understand any extensive region that is either (i) the standpoint of an actual entity, or (ii) a component subregion of such a standpoint, or (iii) an aggregate of such standpoints. In respect to (i) and (ii), it is obvious that the actualized extension internal to an actual entity is a bounded or finite continuum, and it is also obvious that any extensive subregion of such a finite continuum is continuous with some other subregion of it. Thus an actual standpoint is a finite continuum of actualized extension; and, consequently, the subregions of such a standpoint are directly or indirectly continuous with one another. There is no necessity, however, for an aggregate of actual standpoints to form a continuum of actualized extension—unless we introduce the additional premise that attained actualities must form a plenum, that is, that they must be continuous with one another, without leaving among themselves any 'gaps', so to speak, of *unactualized* extension.

For Whitehead, however, this additional premise cannot be construed as a metaphysical principle. Whitehead does hold that in our world or cosmic epoch there is an ongoing creation of a continuum of actualized extensive regions;[1] but he also holds that we cannot safely generalize this feature of our cosmic epoch into a necessary, or metaphysical, feature of *all* cosmic epochs.

> In the present cosmic epoch there is a creation of continuity. Perhaps such a creation is an ultimate metaphysical truth holding of all cosmic epochs; but this does not seem to be a necessary conclusion. The more likely opinion is that extensive continuity is a special condition arising from the society of creatures which constitute our immediate cosmic epoch. (PR 53)

Our cosmic epoch, we must remember, is "that widest society of actual entities whose immediate relevance to ourselves is traceable" (PR 139). The meaning of social order, we must also remember, is that the later members of a society inherit the defining traits of that society from its earlier members. With this in mind, it should be obvious that when Whitehead speaks of the becoming of continuity, what he means is that in our cosmic epoch there is a social imposition of an order, or of a set of defining characteristics, requiring that each actual entity be finally contiguous with other actual entities, so as to gradually form "an extensive plenum of actual entities" (PR 119).[2] But what is true of our cosmic epoch need not be true of the vaster nexus constituting the actual universe.

Correlative to our cosmic epoch, then, there is a quasi-proper region of extension—the aggregate of the extensive standpoints of the actualities of the epoch—which is, in effect, a plenum of actualized extension. This plenum or continuum of actualized extension is 'bordered', so to speak, by unactualized extension. But this 'border', marking the fringes of (attained) actuality, is ever shifting with the coming to be of new actualities. Our cosmic epoch gains new members, and each member adds its extensive standpoint to the expanding continuum of actualized extension. It is in this sense that there is a becoming of continuity, that is, of continuous *actualized* extension.

It must be noted, nevertheless, that the continuity of actualized extension is just the continuity of the eternal extension wherein the individual occasions have come to be. As Whitehead says,

> from the standpoint of any one actual entity the 'given' actual world is a nexus of actual entities, transforming the potentiality [*i.e.*, the potentiality for division] of the extensive scheme into a plenum of actual occasions; . . . *the plenum is continuous in respect to the potentiality from which it arises, but each actual entity is atomic.* (PR 119; italics mine)

Clearly, the continuum of extensive potentiality 'from which' the actual entities have arisen cannot be a byproduct of their becoming, since they presuppose it as that in which they become, and as that which they divide into proper regions. What indeed constitutes, in our cosmic epoch, a byproduct of their becoming is the aggregate, quasi-proper region of actualized extension that they have created, extensive quantum by extensive quantum.

Some differences between mere extension and actualized extension should now be noted. First, mere extension is divisible but undivided, determinable but undetermined,[3] whereas actualized extension is actually divided into proper regions and is also determinate, inasmuch as it is characterized by all the eternal objects that have ingressed into these proper regions. Second, mere extension is eternal, whereas actualized extension is created—though, once created, it is immortal. Third, mere extension partly expresses the potentiality for actualized extension; it does not by itself express this potentiality because it presupposes, in this regard, the cooperation of creativity and the eternal objects. Actualized extension, therefore, exhibits itself as the outcome of the joint metaphysical functioning of mere extension, creativity, and the eternal objects. Finally, mere extension is necessarily a boundless continuum; its potential regions are directly or indirectly continuous with one another. Actualized extension, on the other hand, is made up of finite, bounded extensive regions that need not be continuous with one another. That they do form a continuum in our cosmic epoch is a contingent fact. "Continuity concerns what is potential; whereas actuality is incurably atomic" (PR 195).

It was said above, in effect, that the potentiality for actual entities is to be understood in terms not only of extension but also of creativity and the eternal objects. I should now emphasize that in the philosophy of organism what is a potential for something else is not on that account mere nothingness. Mere extension is merely real, but it is real. Its possible divisions are the potential loci of actual entities. Eternal objects as such are mere potentials for the definiteness of actual entities, but they are real; they exist whether or not they have ingression into actual entities, though in abstraction from their ingression in God's primordial nature they would be so ineffective as to be indistinguishable from non-entity. Finally, creativity—the whereby of all becoming—is itself real, even aside from its present manifestations, or else all talk of future actualities is sheer nonsense. Thus, what the universe is by way of pure potentiality (MT 91) is not a function of sheer nothingness but of factors that are real and eternal. A fourth such factor is God's primordial nature. In the last analysis, however, the potentiality for an actual entity is never pure, never merely a function of eternity, for it also involves the already actual, and thus everlasting, superjects. "A new creation has to arise from the actual world as much as from pure potentiality; it arises from the total universe and not solely from its mere abstract elements" (PR 123).

3. Extension and the spatio-temporal continuum

This principle—that a new actual entity has to arise from its actual world as much as from pure potentiality—will enable me to explain how the actualized extension of our cosmic epoch comes to have features which, though pervasive, are nevertheless contingent. And this in turn will enable me to distinguish the continuum of spatio-temporalized extension from the continuum of mere extension. I will now throw some light on this issue by indicating which properties belong to extension as such, and which only to the actualized extension associated with our cosmic epoch.

The properties of the extensive continuum as such, that is, the properties of extension apart from any consideration of actuality, are very few.

> In its full generality beyond the present epoch, it does not involve
> shapes, dimensions, or measurability; these are additional determina-
> tions of real potentiality arising from our cosmic epoch. (PR 103)

Indeed, it is the arbitrary character of these determinations that warns "us
that we are in a special cosmic epoch" (PR 139).[4] For our cosmic epoch—
that is, the physical universe insofar as it communicates with us in any
degree of relevance—exhibits itself as an actual extensive continuum,
analyzable in terms of certain geometric axioms, and displaying within
itself vast electronic and protonic societies that conform, however imper-
fectly, to electromagnetic laws. But these laws are arbitrary. Moreover,

> the arbitrary factors in the order of nature are not confined to the
> electromagnetic laws. There are the four dimensions of the spatio-
> temporal continuum, the geometrical axioms, even the mere dimen-
> sional character of the continuum—apart from the particular number
> of dimensions—and the fact of measurability. (PR 140)

It is thus evident, according to Whitehead,

> that all these properties are additional to the more basic fact of
> extensiveness; also, that even extensiveness allows of grades of spe-
> cialization, arbitrarily one way or another, antecedently to the in-
> troduction of any of these additional notions. (PR 140)

The notion of grades of specialization of extensiveness refers to the fact
that actualized extension may or may not form a continuum and also to the
fact that the actualized regions of a cosmic epoch, whether they are
continuous with one another or not, may fall into one or more classes,
according to the geometrical axioms they each introduce.

Of immediate interest to us is the type of dimensionality characterizing
our cosmic epoch's continuum of actualized extension. According to
Whitehead, the "physical extensive continuum with which we are concerned in this cosmic epoch is four-dimensional" (PR 464). This fourfold
dimensionality of our epoch's physical continuum is what we know as its
spatio-temporal structure. For this reason, in saying that extension as such
need not be dimensional, let alone four-dimensional, Whitehead is saying
that physical space and physical time are *not* metaphysical features of the
universe, though they are pervasive features of our world or cosmic epoch.
I must hasten to add here that what Whitehead means by physical time is
not to be confused with real or concrete time. The latter is a metaphysical
feature of the universe, and is best understood as its creative advance—

this advance being a function of the creativity whereby there is a supersession of actual entities. Physical time, on the other hand, is only a special byproduct of the creative advance of our cosmic epoch.

Our cosmic epoch generates such a byproduct because its component actualities form a plenum and because the becoming of each component actuality involves the becoming of spatial and temporal determinations in the region which that actuality is realizing and embodying. Thus, "the extensiveness of space is really the spatialization of extension; and the extensiveness of time is really the temporalization of extension" (PR 442).[5] But extension is ontologically prior to these determinations and in no way necessitates them.

> So far as mere extensiveness is concerned, space might as well have three hundred and thirty-three dimensions, instead of the modest three dimensions of our present epoch. The three dimensions of space form an additional fact about the physical occasions. Indeed the sheer dimensionality of space, apart from the precise number of dimensions, is such an additional fact, not involved in the mere notion of extension. Also the seriality of time, unique or multiple, cannot be derived from the sole notion of extension. (PR 442)

Hence, for Whitehead,

> The immediately relevant point to notice is that time and space are characteristics of nature which presuppose the scheme of extension. But extension does not in itself determine the special facts which are true respecting physical time and physical space. (PR 443)

The fact remains, of course, that our world is spatio-temporal; but, for Whitehead, this means only that the actual entities of the contemporary actual world inherit from antecedent actualities, and transmit to subsequent ones, the defining characteristics of our cosmic epoch (MT 212), one of which characteristics is the four-dimensional structure known to us as 'space-time'. In other words, physical space and physical time are among the abstract constituents of the social order characterizing our cosmic epoch—characterizing, that is, what we familiarly term 'our world' (PR 303, 146–47). But this social order, however prevalent or pervasive, cannot be construed as a necessary feature of the universe.

> [Our] epoch may be, relatively to our powers, of immeasurable extent, temporally and spatially. But in reference to the ultimate nature of things, it is a limited nexus. Beyond that nexus, entities

with new relationships, unrealized in our experiences and unforeseen by our imagination, will make their appearance, introducing into the universe new types of order. (PR 441–42)[6]

This is only to say that our world, with its defining social order, is an emergent in the creative advance of the universe. It has superseded earlier worlds or epochs; and it will, in turn, be superseded by worlds with novel types of social order. Thus for Whitehead, "the creation of the world is the incoming of a type of order establishing a cosmic epoch. It is not the beginning of matter of fact, but the incoming of a certain type of social order" (PR 147).[7]

Whitehead holds that, in respect to this doctrine, he is following closely the Plato of the *Timaeus* (PR 147). He is also following Plato in another respect; for Whitehead's doctrine is that our world has emerged, and continues to emerge, in a real, and ontologically prior, continuum of extension—the Whiteheadian analogue to the Platonic Receptacle. Our world, therefore, is to be construed as resulting from the incoming of certain forms into the real potentiality provided by the extensive continuum or Receptacle (PR 147; AI 241–42).

Physical space and physical time are two such incoming forms (MT 100, 212; AI 241–42). They are eternal objects of the objective species which have become, through social reproduction, pervasive features of the actualities of our world. Furthermore, it is because of their pervasiveness in the relevant supersessional past that their continued reproduction in the relevant supersessional future is, for all practical purposes, guaranteed. In other words, the world as attained imposes its own pervasive forms on the world as in attainment. In this manner, spatio-temporality, though not a true metaphysical category, becomes, nonetheless, a 'categoreal' feature of the actualities of our world (SMW 252; PR 507–08; MT 211–12). It thus comes about that the actualities of our cosmic epoch are not merely extended; they are spatio-temporally extended. And this is *not* to say, I must emphasize, that they are extended *in* space-time; rather, it is to say that their extensiveness is spatio-temporally structured; for, as I have explained, extension is ontologically prior to, as well as a logical presupposition of, the spatio-temporal structure that it gains by reason of this world's component actualities.

The spatial and temporal determination of the proper regions correlative to the actualities of the world are produced in the earliest phase of each entity's respective becoming; consequently, for each actual entity, the later phases of its becoming have the spatio-temporally structured region as their datum—they arise from it, are concerned with it, and are thus ultimately limited by it. For these reasons, the relation of mere extension to spatio-temporalized extension is that of pure potentiality to limited, or conditioned, potentiality. This doctrine is made explicit in both PR and AI. In the former, Whitehead states that, "according to the philosophy of organism, the extensive space-time continuum is the fundamental aspect of the limitation laid upon abstract potentiality by the actual world" (PR 123).[8] In the latter, Whitehead holds that "the notion of Space-Time represents a compromise between Plato's basic Receptacle, imposing no forms, and the Actual World imposing its own variety of forms" (AI 241–42).

This compromise, it should be noted, is one outcome of the principle that each new actuality "has to arise from the actual world as much as from pure potentiality" (PR 123). Because of this principle, pure potentiality is an abstraction from real potentiality; for the latter is always impure, that is, always conditioned by attained actuality. The universe *qua* potential, and the universe *qua* actual, are both abstractions from the one universe, which is both actual and potential.

These last observations should be borne in mind when one interprets the following, often-quoted, passages from PR:

> This extensive continuum expresses the solidarity of all possible standpoints throughout the whole process of the world. It is not a fact prior to the world; it is the first determination of order—that is, of real potentiality—arising out of the general character of the world. . . .
> This extensive continuum is 'real' because it expresses a fact derived from the actual world and concerning the contemporary actual world. (PR 103)

It should be evident, in light of the preceding discussion, that by 'extensive continuum' we are to understand, in this context, not the Receptacle or mere extension as such, but either the spatio-temporal continuum peculiar to our world or, in general, the standpoint of any actual entity belonging to our cosmic epoch. I note this because many a commentator of Whitehead has cited these or similar passages in support of the contentions that the extensive continuum is manufactured, bit by bit, by actual entities and that, therefore, it has the ontological status of a derivative abstraction from actuality.[9] I have been defending the opposite theses, namely, that the extensive continuum is ontologically prior to the actual entities that come to be in it and that only a continuum of actualized extension can be considered as a derivative abstraction from actuality.

4.   Extension and solidarity

So far we have been considering the properties that extension gains through its actualization. We have yet to consider the aboriginal properties of extension, those had by any potential region prior to its actualization. Two such properties have already been mentioned, though: one, that extension is unbounded; the other, that it is indefinitely divisible, though undivided. To say that these properties belong to extension prior to actualization, however, is not to say that they can be made intelligible apart from the notion of actualization or the other categoreal notions of the organic philosophy. The organic categories, we must remember, form a coherent scheme. Thus, since extension is in itself undivided, the very notion of its divisibility requires the notion of the creativity whereby there is a becoming of actual entities dividing extension into proper regions. Moreover, divorced from creative experience—as manifested in either transition or concrescence—there is no meaning to the notion of indefinite divisibility; for only creative experience can take into account the divisibility of extension beyond its already actual divisions. Even more, the notion of potential regions of extension presupposes the notion of the creativity that would actualize such regions, and presupposes also the notion of the eternal objects of the objective species whose realization would constitute the definite boundaries required by all actualized, or proper, extensive regions. Finally, the notion of unbounded extension can have meaning only if its polar opposite, the notion of bounded extension, also has meaning. But the latter notion is not to be divorced from the notion of finite actualities.

However, though the boundlessness and the divisibility of the extensive continuum are not intelligible without the other organic categoreal notions, including the notion of actuality, is still remains true that they are two of its aboriginal properties, properties that are not the outcome of actualization. We must now seek other aboriginal properties of the extensive continuum, since these two do not by themselves explain how the solidarity of the universe is a function of that continuum.

That solidarity is, at least in part, a function of extension, there can be no doubt. The qualification 'at least in part' is introduced because extension by itself can only express the potentiality for solidarity; actual solidarity presupposes creativity and eternal objects as well as extension. Thus, on the one hand, the "extensive continuum expresses the solidarity of all possible standpoints" (PR 103); and on the other hand, it "is that general relational element in experience whereby the actual entities experienced, and that unit experience itself, are united in the solidarity of one common world" (PR 112).

In other words, actual entities are related to one another according to the determinations of the extensive continuum (PR 103); but this is only to say that their becoming atomizes the continuum and thereby makes actual the solidarity that was antecedently merely potential (PR 112). The extensive continuum, then, is to be understood as imposing on the actualities that atomize it the necessity that they function in, or be components of, one another. The continuum imposes community upon the actualities; and to be actual is to be emplaced within this community (AI 241). Thus, "the general common function exhibited by any one group of actual occasions is that of mutual immanence. In Platonic language, this is the function of belonging to a common Receptacle" (AI 258).

The sense in which actual entities are mutually immanent accounts for, indeed is nothing else than, their solidarity or connexity. But we must not forget that, in a different though related sense, actual entities are also mutually transcendent and that without their reciprocal transcendence there is no accounting for their discreteness and their individuality. Consequently, what we are now searching for are those properties of pure extension that will explain not just mere immanence but the mutual immanence of actual entities having non-overlapping extensive standpoints. We are searching, in effect, for those properties of extension that account for mutual transcendence as well as for mutual immanence, that account, in short, for the solidarity of discrete occasions. And these properties must belong to extension prior to actualization because according to Whitehead the discrete actualities that atomize extension are realizing a solidarity of standpoints that was antecendently potential (PR 103, 112).

Unfortunately, no explicit consideration of the properties in question is to be found in Whitehead's works. Whitehead does consider them, but in such a way that they appear to be properties of the spatio-temporal continuum. It happens that they are also that, but only because any property of pure extension must be also a property of actualized extension, the only exception being the boundlessness of pure extension, which contrasts with the definite boundary of any actual extensive region.

The properties I have in mind are considered by Whitehead in SMW, and are there termed the *separative*, the *prehensive*, and the *modal* characters of space-time. I shall explain them in detail shortly. But before I do that, I must justify my attribution of these characters to pure extension.

I begin by asserting what has yet to be shown: that the separative, prehensive, and modal characters that Whitehead attributes to space-time do solve the riddle of solidarity. However, if we restrict these characters to space-time, we will be able to provide an explanation for the solidarity of our cosmic epoch, but not for the solidarity of the universe at large. We must bear in mind, in this regard, that for Whitehead the

> general common function exhibited by any group of actual occasions is that of mutual immanence. . . . If the group be considered merely in respect to the basic property of mutual immanence, however otherwise lacking in common relevance, then—conceived as exemplifying this general connectedness—the group is termed a Nexus.
>
> Thus the term Nexus does not presuppose any special type of order other than the general metaphysical obligation of mutual immanence. But in fact the teleology of the universe, with its aim at intensity and variety, produces epochs with various types of order dominating subordinate nexūs interwoven with each other. (AI 258–59)

Since the members of any group of actual occasions are united by their mutual immanence, it follows that the actual universe—that is, the universe by way of actuality, as opposed to the universe by way of potentiality—is always a nexus, albeit an evolving or expanding one. Our own cosmic epoch is a subordinate social nexus within this universal non-social nexus. The special social order of our epoch may bestow certain special characters on the mutual immanence of its occasions; but, in the final analysis, the generic or metaphysical relation of mutual immanence cannot be explained in terms of features, such as space and time, that are peculiar to our epoch. For this reason, the mutual immanence of the actualities in the universal nexus cannot be explained in terms of separativeness, prehensiveness, and modality, unless these three characters are posited as properties of pure extension as well as of spatio-temporalized extension.

One advantage of attributing these three characters to extension, therefore, is that by so doing we will be able to elucidate the thesis of universal solidarity. This attribution, by the way, does not endanger the explanation of the solidarity of our cosmic epoch, since whatever is a property of extension antecedently to its spatio-temporalization by actual occasions remains a property of the resultant spatio-temporalized extension. Moreover, the attribution of these properties to pure extension finds further pragmatic or hermeneutic justification insofar as it also provides a key to some of the most difficult aspects of the organic philosophy; it solves practically every difficulty of interpretation occasioned not only by the doctrine of solidarity but also by such allied doctrines as those of transition, objectification, the objective reality of the future, and others. All this, of course, remains to be seen. But the point now is that we have something to gain by construing separativeness, prehensiveness, and modality as characters of pure extension.

In short, since there is much in Whitehead's philosophy that requires considering these characters to be aboriginal properties of extension and since, as we shall see, there is nothing about these characters or about extension itself that would prohibit it, I feel completely justified in thus considering them. We have, then, everything to gain and nothing to lose, in respect to achieving a coherent interpretation of Whitehead's organic philosophy, if we attribute separativeness, prehensiveness, and modality to extensive regions as such.

5. The theory of organic extensive aspects

My immediate task is to develop in some detail the doctrine that separativeness, modality, and prehensiveness are properties of pure extension. The doctrine thus developed, I hold, amounts to an elucidation of what Whitehead in SMW refers to as 'the organic theory of aspects', for which a more fitting title would be 'the theory of organic extensive aspects' (SMW 220). I first develop this theory without any appeal to textual considerations; then, in the next section of this chapter, I investigate whether it fits with what Whitehead in fact says, in SMW, about organic aspects, and about separativeness, modality, and prehensiveness.

In what immediately follows and in the rest of this essay, it will serve us well to have some systematic notation by which to refer to actual entities, and to the extensive regions that they embody, each its own. Accordingly, I use capital letters to designate actual entities; and, if I designate a given actuality by some such capital letter, say X, I use that same letter followed by an asterisk to designate the correlative extensive standpoint of that actuality. Thus, X^* is the extensive standpoint, or proper region, realized and embodied by X. In short, X^* is X's standpoint. I use capital letters followed by *two* asterisks to indicate potential extensive regions in their characters of being the standpoints of hypothetical actualities—actualities that might be but are not. Thus, Y^{**} refers to the extensive potentiality for the standpoint of Y, where Y is a hypothetical actuality. Finally, though the reason for this cannot be given immediately, I use the notation

w^*/X^* to indicate a subregion of X^*, having a particular kind of relationship to region W^*. In general, the slash notation (.../...) will be used to designate a subregion of the region, or subregion, designated by whatever is to the right of the slash. Thus, $v^*/w^*/X^*$ designates a subregion of w^*/X^*, which in turn designates a subregion of X^*. Such subregions, I should add, are not proper regions, but potential regions.

The theory of organic extensive aspects will now be developed under three successive headings, (a) separativeness, (b) modality, and (c) prehensiveness.

(a) *Separativeness*—To say that actual entities are discrete is to say that they are divided, each from the other (PR 471). But actual entities cannot be divided from one another unless the extensive regions that they embody are also divided from one another. Hence, proper extensive regions cannot include each other; they cannot even partially overlap so as to have common parts; they are, in short, mutually external.

We thus come to the notion that actual entities embody, or occupy, *separate* regions of extension. But notice that, as used here, the 'separateness' of proper regions does not preclude their possible contiguity. Any two proper regions are separate even if they are contiguous. It follows that all actualities, though finding their place in the one and only extensive continuum, are yet also separated in it. This is the separative property of extension. The discreteness of actual entities presupposes this property and also gives witness to it.

Indeed, the separativeness of extension is best understood as the metaphysical imposition of discreteness upon all actual entities. The extensive continuum is divisible; but, by reason of its separative character, it is actually divisible only into discrete or separate regions. When actual entities divide the continuum, they must conform to this separative principle; hence, they can only divide the continuum into separate, or mutually transcendent, regions. To be actual, therefore, means to be an entity occupying, or embodying, a discrete region of extension. (Of course, to be actual means more than that; but it means at least that.) For this reason, the extensive continuum may be regarded as expressing, in part at least, the general potentiality for discrete, or separate, actualities. We must look to creativity, as manifested in *macroscopic* processes, for the realization of this potentiality.

In terms of the notation previously introduced, we may explain the separative character of extension as follows. If A^{**} and B^{**} are two overlapping potential regions of extension, then the separative principle dictates that either one, *but not both*, could become the standpoint of an actual entity, and thus become a real or proper region. Thus, A^{**} could conceivably become A^*, and B^{**} could conceivably become B^*, but it is impossible that A^* and B^* could both obtain. Hence, A^* would always imply B^{**}; and B^* would always imply A^{**}. This is so, even when one potential region, say A^{**}, completely includes the other, say B^{**}. For, though the actualization of the former would necessarily involve the actualization of the latter, it still remains true that A^*, and only A^*, would count as the standpoint of actual entity A. B^{**} would be a subregion of A^*; but B^{**} would not itself be the standpoint of an actual entity. In other words, A^* would be a proper region; whereas B^{**}, though a part of A^*, would still retain its character of being a merely potential region—a region that could have served as the standpoint of a hypothetical actuality, but which in fact does not so serve. Thus, the existence of A^*, renders impossible, once and for all, the actualization of B^{**}.

All this was said earlier in respect to the distinction between extension as a potentiality for divisions of itself and extension as a potentiality for schemes of compossible standpoints. The point now is that the discreteness of extensive standpoints and of their correlative actualities presupposes, is the outcome of, and gives witness to, the separative property of extension.

Obviously, it is in virtue of the separativeness of extension that actual entities can transcend, or be external to, one another. In order to understand their mutual immanence, the modal and prehensive properties of extension must now be introduced.

(b) *Modality*—Modality is best introduced as that property of extension whereby each proper region mirrors within itself the entire extensive continuum. This means that each proper region mirrors *all* the proper regions—including itself—and *all* the potential regions of *its* universe. Here, by the universe of a proper region is meant the state of the universe relative to the origination of that region. Thus a proper region mirrors, in addition to itself, all the proper regions that were already in existence relative to its own origination. In like manner, a proper region mirrors all the extension that, relative to its own origination, was as yet unactualized, as yet mere extension. A proper region, therefore, mirrors within itself the entire extensive universe—the universe, that is, such as it was relative to that region's origination.

Disregarding for the moment the fact that each proper region mirrors the unactualized extension of its universe, we may construe the mirroring of the universe by a proper region as the latter's differentiation into a scheme of subregions that reproduces the scheme of proper regions into which that universe is actually divided. This differentiation is not subsequent to the origination of the proper region in question; rather, the region emerges as thus differentiated. Hence, the region is an element in the scheme of real divisions atomizing the continuum, and the region's internal modal differentiation mirrors this scheme. Consider, for example, an actual entity, say C, and two other actual entities that are in the actual world of C, say A and B. Then, by reason of the modality of extension, there exist three differentiated subregions within C^*, let us term them c^*/C^*, a^*/C^*, and b^*/C^*, which respectively mirror C^* itself, A^* and B^*, and which are so disposed that their locations, relative to one another, mirror the locations of C^*, A^*, and B^*, relative to one another.[10]

By the modality of extension, however, much more is meant than the mere mirroring of a proper region's relative location among other proper regions. Indeed, the notion of mirroring presupposes a more basic notion, namely, that modal subregions are differentiated, each from the others, and all from their parent region, because each refers to a different transcendent region. But even this notion of transcendental reference fails to bring out the full import of the notion of modality. To do it justice, we must assert that a modal subregion *is* the *modal presence*, in the parent region, of the transcendent region to which that subregion refers. This modal presence of one region in another is also termed the *aspect*—the modal extensive aspect, that is—of the former from the latter. Here, the term 'modal' is used in its root sense of 'manner'. Thus, in the previous example, a^*/C^* is the *mode*, or manner, in which A^* is present in C^*. In like manner, b^*/C^* is the *modal presence* of B^* in C^*, or, if you will, the modal aspect of B^* from C^*. Finally, c^*/C^* is the mode in which C^* is present in itself. It should be noted that c^*/C^*, termed the *self-aspect* of C^*, constitutes an exception to the rule of transcendental reference: c^*/C^* refers to the whole of C^*, at whose center it is located, but it does not refer to any proper region beyond C^*. However, c^*/C^* does refer to a^*/C^*, b^*/C^*, and the other modal differentiations of C^*. Thus, c^*/C^* is not completely exempted from the rule of transcendental reference: it refers beyond itself, but not beyond the region of which it is the self-aspect.

The foregoing characterization of modality comes to this: that each proper region is modally present in all other proper regions, or, equivalently, that each proper region is constituted by the modal presence in it of all other proper regions. But this characterization suffers from overstatement because, strictly speaking, a proper region can be modally present as such only in those proper regions that are subsequent to it in real time. Thus a more guarded characterization of modality must make it clear that some proper regions are present in another proper region only in the sense that they are potential divisions of the unactualized extension mirrored by the proper region in question. In other words, they are mirrored *qua* their potentialities, that is, *qua* potential regions, and not *qua* proper regions at all. This is one reason why we cannot really disregard the fact that each proper region mirrors the unactualized extension of its universe. Our initial characterization of modality must now be revised, so as to take this fact into account.

The mirroring of unactualized extension means, to continue with our example, that there is in C^* a modal subregion, let us term it $\&^{**}/C^*$, that refers to, and is the modal presence of, the unactualized extension of C^*'s universe. It also means that C^*'s relative location in its extensive universe is mirrored by the location of c^*/C^* relative, not only to b^*/C^*, a^*/C^*, and the other modally present proper regions, but also to $\&^{**}/C^*$. However, the importance of $\&^{**}/C^*$ lies in its introduction of pure extensive potentiality into the make-up of C^*. Because of this introduction, C—*qua* actuality in attainment—can take into account, can prehend, if you will, the extension that is being atomized by its contemporaries, as well as the extension that will be atomized by the actualities superseding C. In this manner, by reason of $\&^{**}/C^*$, the present world and the future world, each defined relative to C, are aboriginally immanent in C^*, but only in respect to their metaphysical extensive character. It should be added, however, that the division of $\&^{**}/C^*$ into the separate modal presences of C's present, and of C's future, is not, whereas $\&^{**}/C^*$ itself is, an aboriginal modal differentiation of C^*.

The further differentiation of $\&^{**}/C^*$ into the modal presence of the extension underlying the actualities that are contemporary with C, on the one hand, and into the modal presence of the extension that will underly the actualities in C's future, on the other, is to be ascribed to the intermediate creative phases of C's becoming. But this division will itself be based on the information provided by the modal presence in C^* of the proper regions correlative to the actualities in C's past, that is, in C's actual world. For, according to Whitehead,

> in so far as the relevant environment is dominated by any uniform type of coordination, any occasion will experience its past as 'anticipating' the prolongation of that type of order into the future beyond that past. But the future includes the occasion in question and its contemporary environment. In this way there is an indirect

immanence of its contemporary world in that occasion; not in respect to its particular individual occasions, but as the *general substratum* for that relation of order. This type of order will both relate the various parts of the contemporary world among themselves, and will also relate these parts to the occasion in question. (AI 253; italics mine)

The information in question allows C to determine, within certain limits of probability, which subregion of $\partial^{y}{**}/C^*$ refers to the transcendent extension that is serving as the *substratum* for C's contemporaries. The remaining subregion of $\partial^{y}{**}/C^*$ is then to be construed as referring to the transcendent extension that will house, so to speak, the actualities that must supersede C. Thus, an analysis of C, *qua* superject, would disclose $\partial^{y}{**}/C^*$ as differentiated into $pr^{**}/\partial^{y}{**}/C^*$, the modal presence of the extensive substratum of C's contemporary world, and $fu^{**}/\partial^{y}{**}/C^*$, the modal presence of the extensive substratum of C's general future.

Since, for Whitehead, each actual entity anticipates, and must have, an immediate successor, C's physical anticipation of its own immediate successor involves some subregion of $fu^{**}/\partial^{y}{**}/C^*$. For this reason, in the analysis of superject C, we would find a subregion, let us term it $!d^{**}/fu^{**}/\partial^{y}{**}/C^*$, that would be the modal presence of D^{**} in C^*, where D^{**} is the potential region that the becoming of D, C's immediate successor, will convert into a proper region or actual standpoint. The exclamation mark in this notation is intended to denote the special status that $!d^{**}/fu^{**}/\partial^{y}{**}/C^*$ has among the various subregions of $fu^{**}/\partial^{y}{**}/C^*$. It alone has been singled out, *via* anticipatory feelings, as the potential standpoint of C's immediate successor. The differentiation of $!d^{**}/fu^{**}/\partial^{y}{**}/C^*$ from the rest of $fu^{**}/\partial^{y}{**}/C^*$ is effected by C as subject, and involves more than the modal character of extension. Because of this differentiation, C anticipates its own immediate successor, and not just the general future.

The properties of unactualized extension are preserved by the nature of $\partial^{y}{**}/C^*$. Indeed, in respect to the principle of solidarity, the importance of $\partial^{y}{**}/C^*$ lies in its introduction into C^* of the metaphysical properties of pure extension. For it is by reason of $\partial^{y}{**}/C^*$ that the unactualized extension of the continuum is modally present in C^* without loss of its metaphysical properties of indefinite divisibility, modality, separativeness, and prehensiveness. These properties jointly give witness to the imposition of a metaphysical limitation on all contemporary and future occasions relative to C. Thus, though these occasions are not directly given for C, the fact that they must all conform to the principle of solidarity *is* given for C. In other words, what is given is the fact that all contemporary and future occasions, relative to C^*, whatever their individual characters, whatever their measure of freedom, must ultimately exist in solidarity with one another, with C, and with all the occasions in C's actual world (*i.e.*, in C's past). In respect to the future, this means that C can anticipate the modal presence of its region, and thus of itself, in all the proper regions yet to become.

Just as the unactualized extension of C's universe is mirrored in C^* with retention of its metaphysical properties, so, in like manner, are the proper regions of C's universe mirrored in C^* with retention of their metaphysical properties. This means, for example, that B^* is modally present in C^* with full retention of its own modal structure. Therefore, b^*/C^* is itself differentiated into a number of modal subregions, among which are $b^*/b^*/C^*$, $x^*/b^*/C^*$, and $\&^{**}/b^*/C^*$. These modal differentiations of b^*/C^* respectively refer to B^*'s own self-aspect, to the modal presence in B^* of X^*, the proper region of an actual entity in B's actual world, and to the unactualized extension of B's universe. In other words, $b^*/b^*/C^*$ refers to, and is the modal presence of, b^*/B^*; and $x^*/b^*/C^*$ refers to, and is the modal presence of, x^*/B^*; and finally, $\&^{**}/b^*/C^*$ refers to, and is the modal presence of, $\&^{**}/B^*$.

The upshot of this is that the modal presence of one proper region in another conveys into the structure of the latter the whole modal structure of the former. This has three important consequences. The first of these is that we are thus provided with an explanation of how the finite part can mirror the infinite whole. This explanation bases itself on the transitivity of modal presences: namely, that if X^* is modally present in B^*, and B^* is modally present in C^*, then X^* is modally present in C^*. Thus, the transitivity of modal immanences amounts, in this regard, to a principle of economy; for, inasmuch as X^* is modally present in C^* *qua* $x^*/b^*/C^*$, it is not necessary that X^* also be modally present in C^* *qua* x^*/C^*. Because of this, the infinite can be immanent in the finite.

Consider, for example, another proper region, P^*, whose correlative actuality is in the actual world of X. P^* is then modally present in C^* as $p^*/x^*/b^*/C^*$. But the point to notice is that the subregions of C^* associated with the modal presences of B^* and X^* and P^* are progressively smaller, and, even more important, that b^*/C^* includes $x^*/b^*/C^*$, which in turn includes $p^*/x^*/b^*/C^*$. In this manner, since extension is indefinitely subdivisible, a finite subregion of C^*, such as b^*/C^*, can introduce into C^* the modal presences of an indefinite number of proper regions.

The principle of modal economy is best conceived of as a principle of extensive perspective. In order to state this principle in general terms, let us say that one proper region, X^*, has 'primary modal presence' in another proper region, Y^*, when the subregion of Y^* that refers to X^* is of the general form x^*/Y^*. Let us then say that X^* has secondary, or second-order, modal presence in Y^*, when the subregion of Y^* that refers to X^* is of the general form $x^*/...*/Y^*$. Accordingly, let us also say that X^* has tertiary, or third-order, modal presence in Y^*, when the modal presence of the former in the latter is of the general form $x^*/...*/...*/Y^*$. In this manner, we can proceed to define fourth-order modal presences, fifth-order modal presences, sixth-order ones, and so on, indefinitely.

With this in mind, we can say that, because of the transitivity of modal presences, only a finite number of proper regions need obtain first-order modal presence in a given proper region—the only proviso being that these primary modal presences must jointly introduce into the region in question all of the remaining proper regions of that region's correlative universe. These remaining proper regions will have modal presences of some order or other, but will not have first-order modal presence in that region. It should be added that one region may be modally present in another more than once, and that these multiple presences may be of the same, or of different, modal order, but that in no case may a region have more than one primary modal presence in another region.

A proper region, then, is differentiated into a finite number of primary modal presences, including in that number its own self-aspect, and into the modal presence of the unactualized extension of its universe. The only metaphysical requirement is that the finite number of primary modal presences derivatively introduce the modal presences of all the other proper regions of that proper region's universe. Beyond this metaphysical determination, which proper regions achieve first-order modal presence is determined by the special laws of a cosmic epoch, or by the even more specialized laws of the subordinate societies within that epoch.

I have been discussing the first of three consequences of the transitivity of modal immanence. A second consequence of modal transitivity is that, in terms of it, we can explain the sense in which later proper regions are modally immanent in earlier ones. Consider, for example, an actual entity, say A, in the actual world of C. The unactualized extension of A's universe is mirrored in A^* by $\&^{**}/A^*$. But $\&^{**}/A^*$ is potentially divisible into subregions of itself. Any such potential subregion of $\&^{**}/A^*$ gives witness to the metaphysical properties of extension. Hence, any subregion of $\&^{**}/A^*$ refers to, and is the modal presence of, a potential region lying outside A^* in the unactualized extension of A^*'s universe. Because of this, C^* is, in a restricted sense, modally present in

A^*, though A^* came into existence prior to the becoming of C. That is to say, since A is in the actual world of C, there is in $\&^{**}/A^*$ a potential subregion, let us term it $c^{**}/fu^{**}/\&^{**}/A^*$, that refers to, and is the modal presence of, C^{**}—of C^{**}, and not of C^*, because C was not yet in existence, relative to A's own origination. In other words, when A was an actuality in attainment, $c^{**}/fu^{**}/\&^{**}/A^*$ referred to C^{**}, the transcendent standpoint of a hypothetical actuality. With the coming to be of C, however, C^{**} became C^*, and, hence, $c^{**}/fu^{**}/\&^{**}/A^*$ became referrent to C^*, so far as C itself is concerned. Nevertheless, even for C *qua* subject, $c^{**}/fu^{**}/\&^{**}/A^*$ refers to the extensive potentiality for C, and not to the particularity of C itself. This is a given fact for C because $c^{**}/fu^{**}/\&^{**}/A^*$ is modally present in C^* as $c^{**}/fu^{**}/\&^{**}/a^*/C^*$, and not as $c^*/a^*/C^*$.

Generally speaking, the fact that within $\&^{**}/A^*$ there are potential subregions, such as $m^{**}/\&^{**}/A^*$ and $n^{**}/\&^{**}/A^*$, in no way guarantees that any novel actual entities will come into existence precisely at those transcendent regions indicated by the potential subregions in question. It is metaphysically necessary that the unactualized extension of A's universe be perpetually divided by contemporary and future actualities, but it is not necessary that M^{**} and N^{**} become the standpoints for two such actualities; that is, it is not necessary that M^{**} and N^{**} become M^* and N^*, respectively.

This statement has to be qualified because an actual entity's anticipatory feeling of its immediate supersessor does have the character, by and large, of a self-fulfilling prophecy. An anticipatory feeling by A, to continue with our example, involves a subregion of $fu^{**}/\&^{**}/A^*$ that is differentiated from the rest of $fu^{**}/\&^{**}/A^*$ by means of an eternal object of the objective species. Let us assume that $!c^{**}/fu^{**}/\&^{**}/A^*$ constitutes such a modal differentiation and that it serves as the objective datum for A's anticipatory feeling of its own immediate descendant. This means that it is part of A's appetition that its immediate supersessor originate at C^{**}. This is only one aspect of the determination that an actual entity can exert on the future; but it is because of this aspect that A's immediate successor will originate at C^{**}, *provided* that this be compatible with the determination imposed on the future by the anticipatory feelings of A's contemporaries. For if A's anticipated descendant fails to materialize where it was anticipated by A, the reason for this is to be traced to incompatible claims laid on unactualized extension by A and some other actual entity contemporary with A.

The final consequence of the transitivity of modal immanence must now be noted. Since every modal presence mirrors the modal structure of the proper region to which it refers, it follows that the modally differentiated subregions of a given proper region mirror one another. In other words, the modal differentiations within a given proper region give witness to the mutual immanence of the transcendent regions to which they refer. We must realize, however, that some of the transcendent regions thus involved are merely potential in regard to the proper region whose modal differentiation we are considering. In the example we have been considering throughout this discussion, X is in the actual world of B, and B is in the actual world of C; consequently, the modal presences in C^* of X^* and B^* disclose, for C *qua* subject, that X^* mirrors the extensive potentiality for B^*, and that B^* mirrors the actuality of X^*. But the full disclosure for C, in this respect, is: (i) that X^* mirrors the extensive potentiality for B^* and C^*; (ii) that B^* mirrors the actuality of X^*, and the extensive potentiality for C^*; and (iii) that C^* mirrors the actuality of both X^* and B^*, as well as the actuality of C^* itself.

Modality, it follows from the foregoing discussion, is that character of extension whereby the ultimate solidarity of the universe is both imposed upon, and revealed to, each of its creatures. It imposes solidarity because no creature can exist that does not modally contain its universe. It discloses solidarity because each creature's own modal structure is mirrored by its modal presence in the other creatures. Thus, two creatures are present in a third as each mirroring the other, and both as mirroring the third. For this third creature, therefore, the universe discloses itself as a system of mutual relevance.

So much for the modality of extension. I must now examine the prehensiveness of extension.

(c) *Prehensiveness*—By 'prehensiveness' we are to understand that metaphysical property of extension whereby each proper region is the integral and indissoluble union of the modal aspects of all extensive regions, actual and potential. In this respect, therefore, each proper region is to be construed as the prehensive unity of its own modal self-aspect with the modal aspects of all other extensive regions, be these actual or merely potential. This prehensive unity of modal aspects is an ultimate fact, not to be explained by an appeal to anything more primitive than extension itself. It must be understood, however, that by itself extension can only account for the potentiality for prehensive unities. We must turn to creativity in order to account for the actual existence of a prehensive unity.

In this regard, the relation between extension and creativity should be understood as follows: extension is in itself undivided, but divisible; creativity is the underlying activity whereby actual entities come into existence and divide extension into regions of itself. Now, each emergent actuality realizes and embodies a region of extension; but extension itself imposes a threefold determination upon the extensive regions thus created. First, actual regions cannot overlap one another; they must be discrete or mutually transcendent—this determination gives witness to the separative property of extension. Second, actual regions must be modally present in one another; here, of course, we must remember that a modal presence refers either to an actual region as such or to the potentiality for such a region; with this in mind, we can assert that actual regions must be mutually immanent—this determination gives witness to the modal property of extension. Third, actual regions must be the indissoluble unities of their own intrinsic modal differentiations; an actual region is a unity, not merely in the sense of being numerically one, but in the more important sense of being the union, or integration, of many modal presences, including its own—this determination gives witness to the prehensive property of extension.

By reason of extension, therefore, each proper region begotten by the creativity must be separate from all other extensive regions, and it must also be the prehensive unity of the modal aspects within itself of all other regions. Thus, separativeness, intrinsic modal differentiation, and prehensive unity are all necessary, or metaphysical, properties of each proper region. Moreover, since each proper region implies, and is implied by, the actual entity that embodies it, it follows that separativeness, modality, and prehensiveness are all necessary properties of each actual entity. The point to notice, however, is that we must understand the extensive continuum as itself imposing these three properties on all the actualities that come to be in it. This, I contend, is what Whitehead means when he says that all actual entities are subject to the determinations of the continuum (PR 103). The organic theory of modal aspects is merely the elucidation of the determinations imposed by pure extension.

One outcome of these considerations is that separativeness, modality, and prehensiveness must all be considered under two different headings: first, under 'potentiality', wherein they are to be construed as properties of pure extension, imposing a threefold limitation upon the extenso-creative potentiality for proper regions; and second, under 'actuality', wherein they are to be construed as three necessary properties of every actual entity—namely, that it be discrete; that it modally contain its universe; and that it be integrally one. Thus, in respect to extensive properties, each actual entity is the realization of the extensive potentiality for a discrete region, and is the realization of the extensive potentiality for the modal immanence of other regions in that region, and is also the realization of the potentiality for the prehensive unity of these modal presences.

It should be emphasized, however, that the creation of a proper region *does not* involve three successive acts of creativity—the first, to create the proper region; the second, to differentiate it into modal subregions; and the third, to unify these modal differentiations. On the contrary, a proper region is created *all at once* as the discrete, prehensive unity of its own modal differentiations. This creation constitutes one essential aspect of the initial phase of existence in the history of a given actuality. It marks the birth of that actuality; but by no means does it constitute the whole of that actuality's existential history.

A terminological clarification is in order here. In SMW, the term 'prehension' is not used, as it is used in PR and subsequent books, to mean one of the component feelings of an actual entity, but is used, instead, as a synonym for 'event' or 'actual occasion' (SMW 101). Therefore, the prehensive unity of modal presences should not be confused with the felt unity of feelings which crowns and completes an occasion's becoming. The former unity is an aboriginal feature of the occasion and is an outcome of the transcendent process of transition. The latter unity—which presupposes, includes, and transcends the former—is the final individual achievement of the occasion and is primarily the outcome of the immanent process of concrescence.

With this terminological observation, my reconstruction of the theory of organic modal aspects comes to an end. My contention is that I have only worked out in some detail what is already implicit in Whitehead's writings. The theory of organic aspects, I hold, is part and parcel of the metaphysical theory of extension. I must now put this metaphysical theory, or my reconstruction of it, to a fourfold test: first, I must examine whether it is in fact compatible with what Whitehead says, in SMW, about separativeness, modality, and prehensiveness; second, I must investigate, if somewhat superficially, whether this metaphysical theory coheres with the cosmological theory of extension advanced in PR; third, I must see what light it throws on the thesis of solidarity; and fourth, I must examine how well it squares with other organic doctrines or categories immediately relevant to this thesis.

In the remaining sections of this chapter, I am concerned with the first two of these tests. The two others will be considered in the chapters that follow.

6. The theory of organic aspects in SMW

Whitehead's elucidation, in SMW, of the notions of separativeness, modality, and prehensiveness is rather brief; and it is conducted, for the most part, in connection with the nature of space and of spatial volumes only. Whitehead tells us, however, that for the sake of simplicity he is limiting his discourse to spatial volumes but that what he says in respect to spatial volumes is also true in respect both to temporal durations and to spatiotemporal regions (SMW 90–92). My elucidation of the three characters in question has assumed that they are aboriginal properties of pure extension and that, consequently, they must be properties of all actualized extension, including the spatio-temporalized extension of our cosmic epoch. Indeed, my discussion has added a step to the progression involved in Whitehead's discussion of this matter: his went from space to time, and from time to space-time; mine implicitly went from space-time to mere extension. As I check my conclusions against the text of SMW, this progression is, in effect, reversed.

We saw earlier that Whitehead distinguishes between the particular societies of actual entities that make up our cosmic epoch—what he often calls 'the world' or, insofar as it is the terminus of sense-perception, 'nature'—and the universal nexus within which that society is embedded;[11] we also saw that he distinguishes between mere extension and spatio-temporalized extension. I now want to emphasize that these distinctions are included among the organic doctrines advanced by Whitehead in SMW. Witness, in this connection, the following passages from that book:

> Nature exhibits itself as exemplifying a philosophy of evolution of organisms subject to determinate conditions. Examples of such conditions are the dimensions of space, the laws of nature, the determinate enduring entities, such as atoms and electrons, which exemplify these laws. But the very nature of these entities, the very nature of their spatiality and temporality, should exhibit the arbitrariness of these conditions as the outcome of a wider evolution beyond nature itself, and within which nature is but a limited mode. (SMW 130)

Realization is the becoming of time in the field of extension. Extension is the complex of events *qua* their potentialities. In realization the
potentiality becomes actuality. (SMW 179)

With these passages in mind, I can safely argue that separativeness,
prehensiveness, and modality are properties of space-time *because* they are
aboriginal properties of the extension that actual entities—or, as they are
termed in SMW, 'prehensive occasions', 'prehensions', or 'events'—have
atomized and spatio-temporalized.

We must remember, in this regard, that the extensive regions realized
and embodied by the actual entities of our cosmic epoch are four-dimensional hyper-volumes. It follows that the modal presence of one of these
entities in another is also a four-dimensional hyper-volume. In other
words, the standpoint of an actual entity of our epoch is a four-dimensional region, modally differentiated into smaller four-dimensional regions. The notion of a spatio-temporal system represents an abstraction
from the intrinsic modal differentiation of such an actuality (SMW 101).
Moreover, the subordinate modal structure of each first-order modal
presence introduces an alternative spatio-temporal system. The same is
true for all orders of modal presences.

If the above considerations are correct, we may expect Whitehead to
assert that spatio-temporal regions mirror one another; furthermore, so far
as space and time can be abstracted from each other, we may also expect
him to assert the same of temporal durations and of spatial volumes,
respectively. This is precisely what we find him contending in the following passages:

> In a certain sense, everything is everywhere at all times. For every
> location involves an aspect of itself in every other location. Thus
> every spatio-temporal standpoint mirrors the world. (SMW 128)

> [Modality] is the reason why space and time (if for simplicity we
> disjoin them) are given in their entireties. For each volume of space, or
> each lapse of time, includes in its essence aspects of all volumes of
> space, or of all lapses of time. (SMW 100)

> Also each duration of time mirrors in itself all temporal durations.
> (SMW 92)

> The volumes of space have no independent existence. They are only
> entities within the totality; you cannot extract them from their en-
> vironment without destruction of their very essence. Accordingly, I
> will say that the aspect of *B* from *A* is the *mode* in which *B* enters into

the composition of *A*. This is the modal character of space, that the prehensive unity of *A* is the prehension into unity of the aspects of all other volumes from the standpoint *A*. . . . It is evident that I can use Leibniz's language, and say that every volume mirrors in itself every other volume in space. (SMW 91–92)

I argued earlier in this chapter that the modal differentiations of a given region mirror one another. It follows from this that the modal aspects within a given spatio-temporal event must also mirror one another. Moreover, the same should hold true for the spatial volume and for the temporal duration of a given event—if we abstract these from each other. For example, the spatial volume of such an event should contain the modal aspects of all other spatial volumes; and these modal aspects should mirror each other. It happens that Whitehead makes this fact explicit both in relation to modal aspects in general, and to spatial aspects in particular:

> These aspects are aspects of other events as mutually modifying each the other. In the pattern of aspects they stand in their pattern of mutual relatedness. (SMW 210)

> Accordingly, the prime fact is the prehensive unity of volume, and this unity is mitigated or limited by the separate unities of the innumerable contained parts. We have a prehensive unity, which is yet held apart as an aggregate of contained parts. But the prehensive unity of the volume is not the unity of a mere logical aggregate of parts. *The parts form an ordered aggregate, in the sense that each part is something from the standpoint of every other part*, and also from the same standpoint every other part is something in relation to it. Thus if *A* and *B* and *C* are volumes of space, *B* has an aspect from the standpoint of *A*, and so has *C*, and so has the relationship of *B* and *C*. (SMW 91; italics mine)[12]

Whitehead does not explicitly treat the mutual mirroring of temporal aspects; but he has told us, we must not forget, that what is true of spatial volumes is also true of temporal durations. Therefore, the passages just quoted should be sufficient evidence that here too my characterization of the theory of organic aspects has been true to Whitehead's intent.

From my discussion of the organic theory of aspects, it also follows that the modality of spatio-temporal events (or of spaces and times, as abstracted from their mutual implication) cannot be divorced from their prehensiveness and separativeness. To do so would be to commit what Whitehead terms the 'fallacy of simple location': the belief that a thing "can be said to be *here* in space and *here* in time, or *here* in space-time, in a perfectly definite sense which does not require for its explanation any references to other regions of space-time" (SMW 69; see also 81).[13] The theory of organic aspects, in effect, lays down the groundwork for the repudiation of simple location. Consider, for example, an experient-event, say A; and assume that some sensum, or sense-object, is qualifying b^*/A^*. If we now abstract from the prehensiveness of A^* and from the separativeness of A^* and B^*, we are then left with a subregion of A^* having no other function than to serve as the locus for a sense-object. The sense-object would then be said to be simply located at b^*/A^*, since this extensive subregion of A^* would be deprived of its twofold character of referring to B^* and of being an element in the prehensive unity of A^*. Thus, the modal differentiations within an experient-event, if abstracted from their involvement with prehensiveness and separativeness—if abstracted, that is, from the scheme of extensive solidarity—give rise to the idea of simple location, inasmuch as they have ceased to function as the modal presences of events in each other.

The belief in simple location is reinforced by the fact that the modal presence of one event in another distorts neither the relative spatial volume, nor the relative temporal duration, of the former event. Hence, each modal presence within the spatio-temporal structure of a given event has a determinate location specifying the volume of space and the duration of time which are to be assigned to it. But it would be an ontological mistake to argue, on these grounds, that such an event has simple location in space-time.

If my reconstruction of the theory of organic aspects is adequate to Whitehead's intent, we may expect him to discuss the fallacy of simple location precisely in respect to the abstraction of modality from prehensiveness and separativeness. Once more, the text of SMW does not disappoint us:

> My theory involves the entire abandonment of the notion that simple location is the primary way in which things are involved in space-time. In a certain sense, everything is everywhere at all times. For every location involves an aspect of itself in every other location. Thus every spatio-temporal standpoint mirrors the world. (SMW 128)[14]

> Everything which is in space receives a definite limitation of some sort, so that in a sense it has just that shape which it does have and no other, also in some sense it is just in this place and in no other. Analogously for time, a thing endures during a certain period, and through no other period. I will call this the *modal* character of space-time. It is evident that the modal character taken by itself gives rise to

the idea of simple location. But it must be conjoined with the
separative and prehensive characters. (SMW 90)

The prehensive unity of the region *A* [consists] of the prehensive
unification of the modal presences in *A* of other regions. (SMW 92)[15]

This unity of a prehension [or event] defines itself as a *here* and a *now*,
and the things so gathered into the grasped unity have essential
reference to other places and other times. . . . In the first place, note
that the idea of simple location has gone. (SMW 98)

The standpoint *A* is, of course, a region of space-time; that is to say, it
is a volume of space through a duration of time. But as one entity, this
standpoint is a unity of realized experience. A mode of sense-object at
A . . . is the aspect from *A* of some other region *B*. Thus the sense-
object is present in *A* with mode of location in *B*. Thus if green be the
sense-object in question, green is not simply at *A* where it is being
perceived, nor is it simply at *B* where it is perceived as located; but is
present at *A* with mode of location in *B*. (SMW 99–100)

If we now ask how green can be perceived in *A** with mode of location at
B*, the answer is that green is *in A**, but with mode of location *at B**,
because green has ingressed at *b*/A**, the subregion of *A** that is the
modal presence of *B** in *A**.

According to my characterization of the theory of extension, all events
are together in the one continuum of extension; but this is not what is
meant by the prehensive togetherness of events. Events are divisions of
the one extensive continuum; but they are also separated from one
another, inasmuch as each occupies its own unique region of that
continuum. Thus, in respect to their status within the continuum, the
prime fact about events is that they constitute a *disjunctive* diversity.
However, the notion of mere disjunctive diversity is an abstraction from
the concrete relations of events. Events, we must remember, are also
modally present in one another and, as such, they are prehensively
together: all in each, and each in all. Hence, as modally present within the
spatio-temporal structure of a given event, all the other events are together
in that event, even if some are earlier than others.

The notion of separateness, it should be noted, may also apply to modal
presences within one event if these modal presences be all of the same
order. Nevertheless, this separateness of same-order modal presences is
mitigated by the double fact that they are all modal differentiations within
one self-same event and that any two such modal presences mirror one
another and are therefore together as lower-order modal components of
each other. Thus, the prime fact about the modal presences within a given

event is that they form a *conjunctive* diversity. However, the notion of mere conjunctive diversity is an abstraction from the concrete relations of *discrete* events. To avoid this abstraction, the conjunctive diversity of modal presences within a given event is always to be contrasted with the disjunctive diversity of events beyond the one in question. The conjunctive diversity mirrors, is a function of, and also refers to, the disjunctive diversity. This is what follows from my characterization of separativeness and prehensiveness; and this too, if in less detail, is what is being asserted by Whitehead in the following passages:

> Things are separated by space, and are separated in time: but they are also together in space, and together in time, even if they be not contemporaneous. I will call these characters the *separative* and the *prehensive* characters of space-time. (SMW 90)

> [The analysis of the total event] discloses a prehensive unification of the modal presences of entities beyond itself. (SMW 103)

The upshot of these considerations, then, is that my attribution of prehensiveness, separativeness, and modality to pure extension is in complete accord with what Whitehead has to say about these properties in connection with space and time, or with space-time. All further justification of my development of the theory of organic aspects is to be sought in the light it sheds on the doctrine of solidarity. That it does illuminate this doctrine should by now be obvious. Clearly, the separateness of proper regions accounts for the mutual transcendence of the actualities that embody them, each its own; and clearly also, the modal presences of extensive regions, each in the others, accounts for the mutual immanence of actual entities. Nevertheless, there are details to be worked out, particularly in respect to the doctrines of objectification and position. I consider these details in subsequent chapters. For the moment, I must complete my articulation of the metaphysical theory of the extensive continuum.

7. Modal presence and objectification

In Whitehead's writings subsequent to SMW, the notion of one event 'modally present' in another event is replaced by the notion of one actual entity 'objectified' in another actual entity. The sole exception is MT, where 'objectification' becomes 'expression'. That 'modal presence' and

'objectification' have approximately the same meaning is evident from the
fact that, just as in SMW we are told that the notion of 'simple location' is
incompatible with the doctrine that one event is modally present in
another (SMW 128, 94–104), so too in PR we are told that

> the notion of 'simple location' is inconsistent with any admission of
> 'repetition'. . . . In the organic philosophy the notion of repetition is
> fundamental. The doctrine of objectification is an endeavor to express
> how what is settled in actuality is repeated under limitations, so as to
> be 'given' for immediacy. (PR 208)

The approximate synonymity of 'modal presence' and 'objectification' is
evident also from the fact that, just as in SMW the effectiveness of an
event is understood in terms of the aspects of itself which enter into the
prehensive unities of other events (SMW 168), so too in PR the effectiveness of an actual entity is explained in terms of those objectifications of
itself which enter into the constitution of other actualities (PR 134, 336).

The notions of modal presence and objectification, it must be emphasized, are not ultimately interchangeable. Strictly speaking, it is extensive regions that are modally present in one another, and it is actual
occasions that are objectified in one another. But the two notions are
intimately related because, as we shall see later, the modal presences
differentiating an occasion's standpoint provide the extensive *loci* which
are to be embodied by the objectifications of the other occasions—by the
causal objectification of earlier occasions, by the presentational objectification of contemporary occasions, and by the anticipatory objectification of
later occasions. In other words, all objectifications within a given occasion
presuppose the modal subregions they embody, each its own; and the
extensive subregion embodied by an objectification is the modal presence,
in the given occasion's standpoint, of the proper region in which the
objectified occasion arose (if past), is arising (if contemporary), or will
arise (if future).

Although a modal presence may be distinguished from the objectification embodying it, often there is no need to do so. After all, the objectification includes the modal presence, so that in referring to the former
we are already referring to the latter. My point is that any talk about the
objectification of one occasion in another is implicitly talk about the modal
presence of one extensive region in another. However, in a discussion
aimed at the elucidation of the mutual immanence of discrete occasions,
the role played by the modal presences of regions, each in the others,
should not be left implicit. Why this is so will become increasingly evident

in later chapters. The relevant point now is that, after SMW, Whitehead talks about actual occasions being objectified in one another rather than about events being modally present in one another. But the basic doctrine remains the same: the final actualities, though individual and discrete, are internally related to one another.

8. The extensive continuum: as one, and as many

I return to the doctrine of objectification in the next chapter. At present, the near-synonymity of 'modal presence' and 'objectification' helps me to pinpoint yet another reason why the organic doctrine of the extensive continuum has been so little understood by Whitehead's commentators. In this regard, bear in mind the significations of 'extensive continuum' already considered: (i) *the* continuum of pure extension; (ii) *any* continuum of actualized extension; such a continuum could be either (a) a *single* actual standpoint, or (b) a *plenum* of actual standpoints; and (iii) the *spatio-temporal* continuum of actualized extension created by our cosmic epoch insofar as its component actualities form a plenum. To this list we must now add a new manifold signification: that of the extensive continuum as modally present, or objectified, in each of the events, or actual entities, that come to be in it. For according to Whitehead, each actual entity "includes the objectifications of the actual world and thereby includes the continuum" (PR 104).[16] Thus, the extensive continuum is both one and many: one as in itself; and many as modally mirrored in each actual entity.

Accordingly, in one sense, every actuality is in the continuum, and, in another sense, the continuum is in every actuality. In the language borrowed from Plato, this means that

> it is part of the essential nature of each physical actuality that it is itself an element qualifying the Receptacle, and that the qualifications of the Receptacle enter into its [*i.e.*, the physical actuality's] own nature. (AI 171; see also PR 104–05)

Now, since the actualities that qualify the Receptacle are extensive because each embodies a unique region of that Receptacle, and since these actualities qualify one another because they are objectively or modally present in one another, it follows that the Receptacle itself is objectively or modally present in each of the actualities that qualify it. Hence, the actualities qualify, and are qualified by, the Receptacle.

Notice that this much follows from the doctrine that the modal presence of one region in another preserves, or mirrors, the extensive structure of the former. To say this is to say that one actual entity is objectified in another without loss of its extensive relations. Thus, an act of experience, according to Whitehead,

> has an objective scheme of extensive order by reason of the double fact that its own perspective standpoint has extensive content, and that the other actual entities are objectified in it with the retention of their extensive relationships. These extensive relationships are more fundamental than their more special spatial and temporal relationships. (PR 105)

In order to achieve an adequate understanding of the above quotation, and particularly of the notion of an 'objective extensive scheme', let us consider a given actuality, say C. Now C is extensive simply because it embodies C^*. But this is not what is meant by C's 'objective scheme of extensive order'. C^* mirrors the state of the universe from which C arises; that is, it mirrors C's universe. But this means that C's extensive universe—whatever it may be in terms of actual and potential divisions—is modally, or objectively, present in C^*. In other words, C's extensive universe is a scheme of actual and potential divisions of itself; and this scheme—of which C^* is an actual element—is mirrored by C^*'s own scheme of modal differentiations. This modal structure of C^* is what is meant by C's 'objective scheme of extensive order'.

Thus, C has an objective scheme of extensive order, on the one hand, because C's own perspective standpoint is extensive, and, on the other, because the actualities in C's actual world, say A and B, for example, also have extensive standpoints, and these standpoints, as well as their mutual relationships, are objectified in C. In this respect, the objectifications of A and B in C are to be understood as the embodiments of a^*/C^* and b^*/C^*, respectively. They are more than that, but they are at least that. In this respect also, by C's perspective standpoint is meant either C^*, or c^*/C^*; if the former, the fact that C is an actual division of the continuum is being emphasized; if the latter, what is being emphasized is the fact that C's extensive relations to other actual divisions of the continuum are objectified for C. In either case, the two senses of 'perspective standpoint' involve one another. Thus, c^*/C^*, a^*/C^*, and b^*/C^* form a scheme of differentiations internal to C^*, and this scheme mirrors, is a function of, and refers to, the scheme of divisions into which C, A, and B have divided the extensive continuum.

We should not forget, in this account, that C's modal scheme mirrors all of the actual entities in C's universe, not just A and B, and that it also mirrors the unactualized extension of C's universe. We should also remember that this modal scheme is both a constituent *of*, and an object *for*, C as subject (PR 118–19). Hence, the scheme is *objectively real* for subject C. Moreover, when C perishes as subject, the modal structure of C^* remains a feature of C as superject (PR 441). Thus the superject of a subject can give witness to what, for its subject, was objectively real. The product gives witness to what the process experienced.

I summarize the present discussion as follows. So far as the extensive continuum is a potentiality for non-overlapping divisions of itself, we may construe it as a *scheme* of divisions, or of regions, of itself. Relative to the origination of a new occasion, the scheme is in part already actual, and in part merely potential. Now, since the modality of extension requires that each proper region mirror the universe from which it arises, it follows that each novel occasion reproduces within itself the actual divisions, as well as the potentiality for further divisions, of its universe. In so doing, however, each novel occasion also reproduces within itself the entire extensive continuum, so far as by the latter we understand 'a scheme of extensive order'. Thus, the scheme of which actual occasions are components is also a constituent of each actual occasion.

At the risk of seeming redundant, I stress once more that what is repeated, or objectified, within each actual entity is the scheme of extensive order, and not extension itself. Extension is the presupposed *wherein* of all creation, and thus cannot itself be created or repeated. Extension is eternal and infinite. Actual entities merely divide it into finite regions and thereby make actual what was antecedently merely potential.

9. A comment on the theory of extensive connection

My elucidation of the organic doctrine of extension, despite the length of this chapter, has been far from exhaustive. The reason for this is that my main concern here is with the *metaphysical* properties and functions of the extensive continuum. Therefore, it should not be surprising that I have not discussed the relationship of extensive connection to which Whitehead devotes so much time in Part IV of PR. For, though the theory of extensive connection is important for Whitehead's philosophy of science and for his epochal cosmology, it is not on the whole a metaphysical theory.

Metaphysics is strictly concerned with the necessary features of any and all cosmic epochs. Science and philosophical cosmology, on the other hand, must also concern themselves with the pervasive, but contingent, features of our cosmic epoch. Accordingly, the contingent fact that the actual entities of our epoch form a plenum is important to both science and cosmology. Also important to them is the *contingent* fact that in physical nature, as Whitehead construes it, energy is transmitted from one spatio-temporal region to another only if the two regions are contiguous with each other. It thus follows that the contiguity of actual occasions, what in PR is termed their 'immediate external connection', is an important doctrine for science and cosmology—important for them, that is, so far as they are viewed from the standpoint of Whitehead's organic philosophy. Nevertheless, according to the metaphysics—as opposed to the cosmology—espoused by the organic philosophy, it is not necessary that actual entities form a plenum; nor is it necessary, if they should form a plenum, that the transmission of physical energy be always from contiguous region to contiguous region.

Since this last aspect of Whitehead's metaphysics is one major reason for the relevance of the organic philosophy to quantum physics, and since it is an aspect largely ignored by Whitehead's commentators, I quote below what Whitehead has to say on the "physical importance of 'external connection'" (PR 468).

So long as the atomic character of actual entities is unrecognized, the application of Zeno's method of argument makes it difficult to understand the notion of continuous transmission which reigns in physical science. But the concept of 'actual occasions', adopted in the philosophy of organism, allows of the following explanation of physical transmission.

Let two actual occasions be termed 'contiguous' when the regions constituting their 'standpoints' are externally connected. Then by reason of the absence of intermediate actual occasions, the objectification of the antecedent occasion in the later occasion is peculiarly complete. There will be a set of antecedent, contiguous occasions objectified in any given occasion; and the abstraction which attends every objectification will merely be due to the necessary harmonizations of these objectifications. The objectifications of the more distant past will be termed 'mediate'; the contiguous occasions will have 'immediate' objectification. The mediate objectifications will be transmitted through various routes of successive immediate objectifications. Thus the notion of continuous transmission in science must be replaced by the notion of immediate transmission through a route of successive quanta of extensiveness. These quanta of extensiveness are the basic regions of successive contiguous occasions. *It is not necessary for the philosophy of organism entirely to deny that there is direct objectification of one occasion in a later occasion which is not contiguous to it.* Indeed, the contrary opinion would seem more natural for this doctrine. Provided that physical science maintains its denial of 'action at a distance', the safer guess is that direct objectification is practically negligible except for contiguous occasions; but that this practical negligibility is a characteristic of the present cosmic epoch, without any metaphysical generality. (PR 468–69; italics mine)

Since contemporary science no longer denies the possibility of action at a distance, the direct objectification of non-contiguous occasions is a doctrine whose possible cosmological applications deserve careful exploration. Here, however, we must limit ourselves to noticing that the availability of remote earlier occasions for direct objectification is precisely what we should expect given the modality of extension and the everlasting existence of completed actualities. The metaphysical doctrine, therefore, is that a past actual occasion—no matter how remote in real time or how remote in the extensive continuum—is always available for objectification in two distinct ways: (i) directly, as a crude initial datum; and (ii) indirectly, as objectified in an indefinite number of actual entities that are later than itself, and that are now themselves serving as initial data for objectification in novel actualities (PR 345–46, 435). For example let P, Q, and R be three successive occasions, serially ordered; then, relative to R's becoming, P was available for objectification both as in itself (*i.e.*, as the embodiment of P^*), and as objectified in Q (*i.e.*, as the embodiment of p^*/Q^*). This means that P will achieve objective immanence in R either as embodying $p^*/q^*/R^*$ only, or as separately embodying both $p^*/q^*/R^*$ and p^*/R^*. Whether or not P is contiguous to (or extensively connected with) Q, and Q to R, is of no consequence either to this example or to the metaphysical doctrine in question.

Another reason for not considering the theory of extensive connection is that it has very little to do with the metaphysical features of an actual entity. Indeed, the whole development of the theory tends to abstract from the atomicity of actual entities and from their mutual objective immanence.

> In this theory the notion of the atomicity of actual entities, each with its concrescent privacy, has been entirely eliminated. We are left with the theory of extensive connection, of whole and part, of points, lines, and surfaces, and of straightness and flatness. (PR 448)

Furthermore, the theory does not deal exclusively with the properties of this epoch's continuum; rather, it ranges from notions applicable to any continuum, to notions that are applicable to some continua but not to others, and finally to notions that are directly relevant only to certain pervasive features of our cosmic epoch.

It is entirely out of the question, therefore, that the elucidation of solidarity should require the elucidation of extensive connection. Unfortunately, Whitehead seldom distinguishes his metaphysical theory from its cosmological applications. Consequently, many crucial doctrines of his philosophy are not stated in their true metaphysical generality; instead, they are introduced and discussed in terms of the contingent features of our epoch. This is the case with the explanation of many crucial aspects of the doctrines of solidarity and objectification; thus, in PR, a major part of the explanation of these doctrines goes hand in hand with the explanation of extensive connection, thereby obscuring the fact that the former are metaphysical doctrines whereas the latter is not. It thus happens that in Whitehead's discussion of these doctrines the notion of a scheme of extensive order, which is the true metaphysical notion, is often replaced by the notion of a scheme of extensive connection, which is only a derivative cosmological notion. The latter notion introduces the additional assumption that the elements in the continuum's scheme of actual divisions are externally connected to one another, either mediately or immediately. So far as this is true of our cosmic epoch, it follows that the portion of the continuum that is relevant to the occasions of our epoch is objectified, in each of them, as a scheme of contiguous divisions.[17] Thus, for our epoch, the scheme of extensive order becomes the scheme of extensive connection (PR 442). The relation of the latter to the former is that of epochal species to metaphysical genus.

For the purposes of this essay, this is all that we need to know concerning the theory of extensive connection. I need to add only that for Whitehead the relation of modal, or objective, immanence is more primitive than that of immediate external connection: "contiguity, temporal and spatial, is definable in terms of the doctrine of immanence" (AI 260). Therefore, since the doctrine of immanence is, in effect, the doctrine of solidarity, the contiguity of occasions cannot be a presupposition of their solidarity.

10. *Brief comment on physical space-time*

Thus far my discussion of extension has remained aloof from any considerations of physical time and physical space. This is as it should be, for I am concerned with Whitehead's *metaphysical* theories of extension and solidarity and not with the *cosmological* theories of space-time and of solidarity in space-time. Nevertheless, something must be said in passing about the special characters of extension that are peculiar to our cosmic epoch and about how those characters give rise to Whitehead's epochal theory of time.

There is no metaphysical necessity that actualized extension should be measurable, or that it should be four-dimensional, or that it should form a plenum (PR 53, 103). It seems an empirical fact, however, that in our cosmic epoch the proper regions embodied by its component actualities are measurable, four-dimensional hyper-volumes that form a plenum or continuum of actualized extension (PR 53, 464). This means that a super-sessional route of occasions, such as the route formed, for example, by the occasions A, B, and C, constitutes a continuous region of actualized extension, where A^* is contiguous with B^*, and B^* with C^*. It also means that wherever this route of occasions is causally objectified it is prehended as forming a continuous extensive region, with objectifications of the same modal-order being externally connected, and those of a higher modal-order extending over, or including, those of a lower modal-order. The upshot of this is that, as objectified, the extensive standpoint of an actual occasion, such as B, can be divided into a temporally earlier half, which is contiguous (in some order of modality) with the objectified standpoint of A, and a temporally later half, which is contiguous (in some order of modality) with the objectified standpoint of C.

From the metaphysical point of view, however, it would be a mistake to think that the temporal divisibility of B's standpoint corresponds to the genetic divisibility of its becoming. It would be a mistake because B^* is created, *all at once*, in the first phase of B's becoming (PR 434–35). The becoming of B^* results from the ingression into B^{**} of a complex geometrical form establishing the boundary and extensive structure, in this case four-dimensional, of B^*. But the becoming of B is not over. Its phases of concrescence supersede the creation of its dative phase (PR 434). The qualitative forms generated by B's concrescence are ingressed into the different subregions of B^*; but the order and loci of their ingression do not correspond to the temporal divisibility of B^*. "The conclusion is that in every act of becoming there is the becoming of something with temporal extension; but that the act itself is not extensive, *in the sense* that it is divisible into earlier and later acts of becoming which correspond to the extensive divisibility of what has become" (PR 107; italics mine).

Once we realize that the temporal quantum associated with the standpoint of an occasion is created, *all at once*, in the first phase of that occasion's becoming, we have no difficulty in understanding why Whitehead holds that the real supersession of phases of concrescence is not in physical time.

> This genetic passage from phase to phase is not in physical time: the exactly converse point of view expresses the relationship of concrescence to physical time. It can be put shortly by saying, that physical time expresses some features of the growth, but *not* the growth of the features. (PR 434)

Since the temporal quantum associated with an occasion is created all at once, and since there can be no *actual* quantum of time later than the quantum in question *until* that occasion has completed its becoming, it follows that physical time itself (or temporalized extension) becomes by 'arrests' or 'epochs'. The temporal quanta do form a continuum; but the creation of this continuum is not a continuous becoming (PR 53); rather, it is constituted by abrupt and arrested stages—by *epochs*, if you will. This is the meaning of 'epoch' which gives Whitehead's epochal theory of time its name.[18]

11. Summary

I have been interpreting and developing the metaphysical doctrine of the extensive continuum so far as this doctrine is relevant to the task of elucidating the interrelated notions of 'solidarity', 'objectification', and 'position'. With that task in mind, I distinguished, from one another, several significations of 'extensive continuum' (but by no means all) and thereby determined which of these significations have true metaphysical import. With that same end in mind, I also established that *the* metaphysical continuum is eternal and infinite; that the actual entities that come to be in it create regions of extension, each its own, but that they do not create the extension of their regions; and that, apart from the actualities that atomize it into regions or divisions of itself, the continuum is divisible but undivided.

To that same end also, I argued that separativeness, modality, and prehensiveness are aboriginal properties of extension and only derivatively properties of time and space, or of space-time. By reason of these properties, I also argued, the continuum imposes a threefold determination on all actual entities: first, they must be discrete; second, they must be modally present in one another, at least in respect to the extensive potentialities from which they either have arisen, are arising, or will arise; and third, they each must be the indivisible unity of its own intrinsic modal, or objective, structure.

Finally, in order to prepare for the explication of solidarity, objectification, and position, I have shown that the extensive continuum—so far as we can consider it as a *scheme*, partly actual, partly potential, for compossible and modally connected divisions of itself—is itself held to be modally, or objectively, present in each of its actual divisions. In other words, I have shown that, though there is but *one* scheme of extensive order, the scheme is objectively present in all actual entities and is thus, in an important sense, numerically *many*.

Beyond the arguments and textual considerations brought forth in this chapter, my interpretation of the organic doctrine of metaphysical extension seeks its final justification in the light it sheds on the doctrines of solidarity, objectification, and position. Their elucidation is the main topic of the next three chapters.

SIX

Objectification, Position, and Self-Identity

My main task in this chapter is to bring my interpretation of metaphysical extension to bear on the interrelated organic doctrines of objectification, position, and self-identity. An adequate understanding of these three doctrines is almost tantamount to a complete understanding of the doctrine of solidarity. The pertinence of this task, therefore, should be obvious. Nonetheless, I must briefly postpone undertaking it, for another task, already once-deferred, must be completed first.

At the beginning of the preceding chapter I anticipated but deferred explicitly answering three major objections to the claim that the organic philosophy construes the solidarity of the universe as being grounded on the metaphysical functioning of an eternal extensive continuum. The first objection—that Whitehead often describes extensive continuity as being a derivative, contingent feature of our cosmic epoch—was in large measure defused as soon as I differentiated mere extensive continuity, which is necessary and primitive, from actualized or spatio-temporalized extensive continuity, which is contingent and derivative. However, the other two objections—to the effect that if the extensive continuum were an eternal reality and a metaphysical principle, it would have been discussed by Whitehead as a formative element and as a category—still retain some of their sting. Of course, the complete repudiation of all three objections is ultimately to be sought in the coherence, the consistency, and the intelligibility gained by the organic philosophy when interpreted in terms of the claim in question. But the articulation of the nature, properties, and functioning of the metaphysical continuum is now sufficiently developed to support an immediate attempt to empty these objections of most of their force. To this attempt, therefore, I now turn.

1. Three objections refuted

The formative elements of the temporal world, Whitehead states in RM, are the creativity, the multiplicity of eternal objects, and the primordial nature of God. The temporal world and its formative elements, Whitehead also states in that book, constitute the all-inclusive universe (RM 90). But if this is true, and if the only formative elements are those that Whitehead explicitly mentions in RM, my interpretation of solidarity is faced with a serious difficulty; for it rests on the assumption that there is a metaphysical continuum of extension which is presupposed by the becoming of every temporal actuality but which does not itself become. In other words, my interpretation of solidarity is in trouble because it assumes that the extensive continuum or Receptacle is a formative element, an assumption which seems clearly at odds with the acount of the formative elements given in RM.

This problem is compounded by the fact that the extensive continuum is not mentioned in the categoreal scheme of PR. In the final analysis, however, the problem is specious. After all, other important organic principles, such as supersession and conformation, also are missing from the categoreal scheme of PR. Moreover, the metaphysical functioning of the Receptacle—its imposition of mutual immanence on all the occasions that come to be in it—is clearly stated in AI (p. 258). Furthermore, if the Receptacle accounts for the "general metaphysical obligation of mutual immanence," it follows that the Receptacle itself must be a metaphysical principle. Finally, everything that Whitehead says in AI about the Receptacle—that the actual occasions come to be in it, that they find their emplacement within it, and that they qualify it and are themselves qualified by it—entails that the actual occasions do not create the Receptacle (AI 171–72, 241). But if not created by them the Receptacle must be eternal. Hence, since the Receptacle is presupposed by the becoming of every actual occasion, but does not itself become, it must be construed as a formative element as well as a metaphysical principle.

Accordingly, if what Whitehead says in AI about the Receptacle is given its due weight, the absence of the extensive continuum from both the list of formative elements and the categoreal scheme can signify no more than an oversight on Whitehead's part. Actually, it signifies less than that, for Whitehead does not completely overlook the metaphysical theory of extension in his earlier major works, SMW and PR. The theory permeates those works; but its discussion is largely absorbed into, and hence hidden in, the discussions of the spatio-temporal continuum and of the principle of creativity. What Whitehead neglects to do, in SMW and PR, is clearly to distinguish the metaphysical properties and functions of *mere* extension from the cosmological properties and functions of *spatio-temporalized* extension. He also neglects, in those books and in RM, to explicitly separate the metaphysical roles of extension and creativity. These neglects can be remedied, however, by reading SMW, RM, and PR in light of what is said in AI about the Receptacle and its metaphysical functions.

In this last regard, it is important to recognize that no one book by Whitehead contains an explicitly complete account of all the interrelated doctrines of the organic philosophy. Indeed, in the prefaces to most of his philosophical works Whitehead repeatedly testified to his habit of writing books which could be read independently of one another but which were meant to complement and supplement each other in giving expression to the philosophical system he was developing. It will be instructive to quote at length from those prefaces, for they support a basic assumption underlying the interpretative aspects of this essay: that the philosophy of organism is to be carefully culled from all of Whitehead's philosophical books, starting with PNK and ending with MT, and is not to be found in its entirety in any one of those books. Here are the relevant passages:

> [*The Concept of Nature*] forms a companion book to my previous work *An Enquiry Concerning the Principles of Natural Knowledge*. Either book can be read independently but they supplement each other. In part the present book supplies points of view which were omitted from its predecessor; in part it traverses the same ground with an alternative exposition. (CN, "Preface," p. vi)

> Since the publication of the first edition of this book [*i.e.*, PNK] in 1919, the various topics contained in it have been also considered by me in *The Concept of Nature* . . . and in *The Principle of Relativity*. . . . I hope in the immediate future to embody the standpoint of these volumes in a more complete metaphysical study. (PNK, "Preface to the Second Edition," p. ix)

> The train of thought which was applied to science [in] *Science and the Modern World* is here [*i.e.*, in RM] applied to religion. The two books are independent, but it is inevitable that to some extent they elucidate each other by showing the same way of thought in different applications. (RM, "Preface," p. vii)

> The three books—*Science and the Modern World, Process and Reality, Adventures of Ideas*—are an endeavor to express a way of understanding the nature of things, and to point out how that way of understanding is illustrated by a survey of the mutations of human experience. Each

book can be read separately; but they supplement each other's omissions or compressions. (AI, "Preface," p. vii)

[MT condenses] for publication those features of my Harvard lectures which are incompletely presented in my [previously] published works. (MT, "Preface," p. vii)

Of immediate interest to us is the fact that SMW, PR, and AI are meant to supplement each other's omissions and compressions. For this fact supports my contention that the omission from SMW and PR of an explicit account of the metaphysical functions of extension is remedied by the account of the Receptacle given in AI. In addition, this fact supports my contention that the metaphysical properties and functions of extension are implicitly under discussion when the doctrines of spatio-temporalized extension and of creativity are expounded in SMW, RM, and PR. Evidently, the absorption of one discussion into another, so that the former is mostly only implicit in the latter, is one of the means by which Whitehead compresses his exposition. Unfortunately, the compression is achieved at the cost of clarity and intelligibility; for the reader of SMW, RM, and PR, unless forewarned by a careful reading of AI, cannot be expected to distinguish from each other doctrines which the three earlier texts confound. No wonder, then, that Whitehead's metaphysical doctrine of extension has been for so long overlooked.

To avoid confusing the metaphysical extensive continuum with the spatio-temporal continuum, it must be borne in mind always that the Receptacle of AI *is* the extensive continuum of PR *provided* the latter notion is understood in its most general, unqualified, metaphysical sense. This identity has been evident throughout my earlier considerations of solidarity, for 'extensive continuum' and 'Receptacle' were there found to be used indifferently by Whitehead to refer to that which accounts for the mutual immanence of discrete occasions. But it has been evident also in the parallels between *some* of the accounts Whitehead gives of the extensive continuum and those he gives of the Receptacle. Thus, just as the Receptacle is said to be devoid of all geometrical form (AI 156), so too the extensive continuum is said to be, in its metaphysical generality, devoid of shapes, dimensions, and measurability (PR 103). Also, just as the Receptacle is said to qualify, and to be qualified by, occasions of experience (AI 171), so too the extensive continuum is said to include, and to be included in, actual occasions (PR 104–05). Finally, just as the major defining characteristic of our world is said to result from the Actual World's imposition of Space-Time on the Receptacle (AI 241–42), so too the major defining characteristic of our cosmic epoch is said to result from the spatio-temporalization of the extensive continuum imposed by the epoch's constituent occasions (PR 123, 147, 442–43).

Once the synonymity of 'Receptacle' with some uses of 'extensive continuum' has been established, the positing by Whitehead of an eternal, necessary, metaphysical extensive continuum can no longer be credibly denied. It is then a relatively easy matter to find, in SMW and in PR, passages where Whitehead, regardless of what their immediate context may suggest, is in truth describing—sometimes explicitly, sometimes implicitly—the properties and functions of the metaphysical extensive continuum. In fact, some of those passages have been noticed by other interpreters of Whitehead; but almost invariably they have dismissed them as inconsistent with what they took to be Whitehead's basic claims about the derivative, contingent nature of extensive continuity.[1] There is, of course, no inconsistency. What is derivative and contingent is the formation, in our cosmic epoch, of a continuum of spatio-temporalized extension. Moreover, the passages cannot be dismissed without robbing the thesis of solidarity of much of its coherence and intelligibility. The discussion of the preceding chapter in effect identifies and interprets many of the passages in question. It thereby rescues the metaphysical theory of extension from its confusion with the cosmological theory of spatio-temporalized extension.

Once AI alerts us to the fact that an eternal continuum of extension is posited by Whitehead as grounding the universe's solidarity, it becomes easier to notice the strikingly similar accounts Whitehead gives of extension and creativity. Indeed, so similar are the accounts as to strongly suggest that, for Whitehead, creativity and extension are indissoluble aspects of one ultimate reality—a reality underlying the becoming, the being, and the solidarity of all actual entities. To make this point clear, let me first cite the similarities in question.

First of all, the creativity and the extensive receptacle are each compared to, and contrasted with, the Aristotelian notion of matter. In each case, the organic notion is judged to be superior in metaphysical subtlety to the Aristotelian notion. In each case, also, it is obvious that what are being compared are the ultimate principles of different metaphysical systems. Second, the creativity and the extensive continuum are each described as being entirely formless; moreover, each is described as receiving forms insofar as it is embodied by actual occasions, and in a way not to be abstracted from those occasions. Third, creativity and extension are each described as characterizing, and as being characterized by, actual occasions. Thus, in respect to creativity, the creatures are said to condition it, and it is said to condition them. Thus, too, in respect to the Receptacle, the actual occasions are said to qualify it, and it is said to qualify the occasions. Fourth, the creativity and the extension are each said to be embodied by actual occasions. Fifth, actual occasions exhibit themselves both as individualizations of the one substrate activity and as divisions of the one extensive continuum. Sixth and last, each individualization of the substrate activity, and each division or proper region of extension, is described as acquiring the unity of an actual occasion.[2]

These similarities cannot eradicate the one essential difference between creativity and extension. For the creativity is the dynamic principle on which the essential genetic development of the universe is grounded, whereas the extensive continuum is the static principle on which the essential solidarity of the universe is grounded. Thus, the similarities we have just considered do not allow us to identify the creative principle and the extensive principle; but they do allow us to construe these principles as expressing two differentiable, but inseparable, aspects of the ultimate ground of the organic universe. This ultimate ground has no name of its own, other than the names used to designate its two indissoluble aspects. Accordingly, insofar as this ground is the whereby of all becoming, it is termed 'creativity'; and insofar as it is the wherein of all interconnected actual existence, it is termed 'extension'.

Of the terms associated with the organic notion of an ultimate ground, the term 'Receptacle' comes closest to being used as the proper name for that which is both creative and extensive. To be sure, this term is generally used by Whitehead as synonymous with 'extension' and 'extensive continuum'. Nevertheless, there is one passage in AI suggesting that Whitehead intended the term to signify not only the extensive continuum imposing solidarity on the actualities, but also the creativity manifesting itself in the actual process of creative advance:

> There is the one all-embracing fact which is the advancing history of the one Universe. This community of the world, which is the matrix for all begetting, and whose essence is process with retention of connectedness,—this community is what Plato terms The Receptacle. (AI 192)

This passage would seem to be a corrective against construing the Receptacle as a mere field for the emplacement and community of actual occasions (AI 240–41). For, as Whitehead tells us elsewhere, "The notion of nature as an organic extensive community omits the equally essential point of view that nature is never complete. It is always passing beyond itself. This is the creative advance of nature" (PR 443).

The Receptacle, then, must be construed as being creative and not just extensive. For it must account for the creative expansion of the universe and not just for its solidarity. Thus construed, however, the notion of the Receptacle conveys exactly the same principle as is conveyed by the Category of the Ultimate: that the universe is ever advancing beyond every completed multiplicity of its achieved elements, yet always retaining the achieved elements as components of the novel elements in achievement. Thus, by whatever name—creativity or Receptacle—we call the ultimate extenso-creative matrix of the organic universe, its function is to explain how the universe "expands through recurrent unifications of itself, each, by the addition of itself recreating the multiplicity anew" (PR 438).

Admittedly, there is a scarcity, though not a lack, of direct textual support for the thesis that creativity and extension are indissoluble aspects of one ultimate reality. But any interpretive thesis such as this one must be finally judged by the light it throws on the doctrines it was meant to interpret. In that respect, the thesis in question is not without merits. For if true, it would provide the most economical way of explaining the similarities between extension and creativity, without explaining away their radical differences. For example, it would explain why any one individualization of creativity must also be a division of extension and why the attainment of unity by the creative individualization is also the attainment of unity by the extensive region. Moreover, the truth of this interpretive thesis would explain how the modal immanence, in an actual occasion, of the unactualized extension of its correlative universe reveals to that occasion the creative potentiality, as well as the extensive potentiality, for the becoming of future occasions. Without such a revelation the organic doctrine of anticipatory feelings is sheer nonsense. Finally, if true, this interpretive thesis would explain why Whitehead did not bother to list the extensive continuum among the formative elements or include it in the categoreal scheme. For insofar as 'creativity' designates an ultimate reality which is extensive as well as creative, the list of formative elements and the categoreal scheme already include, albeit only implicitly, the doctrine of the extensive continuum.

The intimate association of creativity with extension, and Whitehead's habit of compressing his exposition at the cost of confounding different (though always related) doctrines, jointly account for the lack of explicit emphasis that SMW, RM, and PR place on the nature and function of the metaphysical extensive continuum. Specifically, they account for the confusion of metaphysical extension with spatio-temporalized extension, and for the apparent absence of the metaphysical continuum from the list of formative elements and from the categoreal scheme. Thus, when allowances are made for the idiosyncrasies and flaws of Whitehead's expository style, the three objections we have been considering are substantially disarmed. Any force they may still retain can be overcome only by the strength of the overall interpretation here being presented.

At a more general level, we may conclude that there are at least three reasons why the organic theory of the metaphysical extensive continuum has gone largely unnoticed or misunderstood in the received interpretations of Whitehead's philosophy. These reasons have all to do with the peculiarities of Whitehead's exposition. The first reason is that Whitehead's works are intended to complement and supplement one another, so that no one book—not even PR—provides a complete, systematic account of the organic philosophy. Many of the received interpretations, however, assume otherwise and rely too heavily on PR, by far the most poorly composed of Whitehead's works and the one with the least consistent terminology. The second reason is that Whitehead often compresses his exposition by confounding, in one discussion, his accounts of different, though related, notions. This is particularly the case when the notions are related either as species to genus, or as differentiable but inseparable aspects of one self-same reality or principle. As a rule, however, the received interpretations make no attempt to differentiate notions which Whitehead's own exposition has confounded. The third reason, put bluntly, is that Whitehead's self-admitted faults of exposition are often far from minor.[3] This last reason attests to the fact that the first two may well explain, but certainly do not excuse, the haphazard and unsystematic manner in which Whitehead has presented his views on the metaphysical extensive continuum.

If my interpretation and development of this much-neglected Whiteheadian theory is correct, it follows that the extensive continuum is to be understood not only as a metaphysical principle and as formative element but also as an aspect of an ultimate reality of which creativity is another aspect. The two aspects are distinguishable but inseparable; in their unity they constitute an extenso-creative matrix which is the ultimate ground for the becoming, the being, and the solidarity of all actual entities. Accordingly, no account of the organic philosophy can be thought complete until it has developed a coherent theory of the extenso-creative receptacle in which the dynamic solidarity of the universe is rooted. For our limited purposes, however, a sketch of the theory's main notions is sufficient. But any attempt to present such a sketch at this moment would be inopportune because a third aspect of the ultimate matrix—envisagement—has yet to be elucidated, and because the immediate concern is with the relevance of metaphysical extension to the doctrine of mutual immanence. Still, we would do well not to forget that any discussion of extension in abstraction from creativity, or of creativity in abstraction from extension, is necessarily provisional. Only the joint functioning of extension and creativity can adequately explain the universe's dynamic solidarity.

In the sections that follow, my discussion will focus on three main topics: (i) on how the extensive continuum accounts for the twofold reality of an actual entity—intrinsic and extrinsic (in this regard, I elucidate how the metaphysical properties of extension are presupposed by the different modes—causal, presentational, and anticipatory—in which actualities are objectified in one another); (ii) on the manner in which the metaphysical theory of extension explains how an actual entity can have a multiplicity of instantiations, yet be the self-same entity in each instantiation (in this respect, I elucidate the crucial organic doctrine of position); and (iii) on how the distinction Whitehead makes between position and definiteness is essential for understanding the self-identity and self-diversity which he attributes to all actual entities (in this regard, I examine the related notions of freedom, particularity, and individuality, and take a closer look at the twentieth through twenty-fourth Categories of Explanation).

2. The twofold reality of actual entities: intrinsic and extrinsic

My task now is to explain, in terms of the doctrine of the extensive continuum, how each actual entity has a twofold reality: the one, single and intrinsic; the other, multiple and extrinsic. This twofold reality of an actual entity, it should be noted, presupposes the identification of a subject-superject with each and every one of its numerically different objectifications in other subject-superjects. However, the defense of that identification must be postponed until we can discuss the doctrine of position.

By reason of the modality of extension, each actual entity is modally, or objectively, present in all other actual entities. This modal presence of a given occasion in all other occasions can be understood only in terms of the extensive potentiality from which the given occasion either had already arisen, in relation to occasions later than itself, or was arising, in relation to occasions contemporary with itself, or was subsequently to arise, in relation to occasions earlier than itself. In other words, if *A* is the actuality in question, then its standpoint, *A**, is modally present in any other actuality, say *X*, in one of three basic modes: (i) as *a*/.../X**, if *A* is earlier than *X;* (ii) as *a**/pr**/&**/X**, if *A* and *X* are contemporaries; and (iii) as *a**/fu**/&**/X**, if *A* is later than *X*. But the point to emphasize now is that *A*, by reason of its modal presences in other occasions, has a self-transcendent reality, as well as a self-immanent reality.

In terms of the organic theory of extensive modal aspects, this means that each actual entity, or event,

> corresponds to two . . . patterns [of aspects]; namely, the pattern of aspects of other events which it grasps into its own unity, and the pattern of its aspects which other events severally grasp into their unities. . . . There is thus an intrinsic and an extrinsic reality of an event, namely, the event as in its own prehension [*i.e.*, as its own prehensive unity within its own extensive standpoint], and the event as in the prehension of other events [*i.e.*, as its modal presence within the extensive standpoints of other prehensive unities]. (SMW 146)

Hence, if we take event *A* as our example, and if *M* and *N* are events in the immediate past of *A*, then *A* prehensively unifies within its own standpoint the modal aspects of *M* and *N*—namely, *m*/A** and *n*/A**, respectively. Thus, *m*/A** and *n*/A** are components of the pattern of modal aspects that *A* gathers into its own prehensive unity. This pattern of aspects belongs to the intrinsic reality of *A;* it is found entirely within, and it is partly analytical of, the extensive standpoint of *A*. But *A* also enters, *via* its own modal aspects, into the prehensive unity of other events. Thus, if *X* is an event in the immediate future of *A*, then *A* is modally present in *X* as *a*/X**. Now *a*/X** is one element in the pattern of modal aspects that *X* gathers into the prehensive unity of its own standpoint, *X**. Hence, *a*/X** is one example of the extrinsic reality of *A;* for *a*/X** is to be construed as the modal presence of *A* in an extensive standpoint other than its own; it is *A* as found beyond *A**.

The reality of an event as within its own standpoint and the reality of that same event as beyond its own standpoint involve one another. On the one hand, the manifold extrinsic reality of an event—its modal presences in other events—is a function of its own intrinsic reality, actual or potential: of its *actual* intrinsic reality if the other events are later than itself; and of its *potential* intrinsic reality if the other events are either earlier than, or contemporary with, itself. In the last two cases an event is modally present in other events because its own extensive standpoint existed in its own right, *as a potential region*, prior to the event's own becoming. Without the eternal existence of the (potential) extensive region which became the event's own proper standpoint, the event could not be modally present in its contemporaries or in the events in its past. In the first of the three cases, however, an event is modally present in later events because *it* exists in its own right. Thus, in the previous example, if a^*/X^* is the *locus* for one instance of the extrinsic reality of A, this is so because, when X comes into being, A is already existing in its own right as the embodiment of A^*. X must mirror, objectify, repeat, or modally include, the universe from which it arises. A is one element in the correlative universe of X; hence, A is mirrored, repeated, objectified, or modally included, within the standpoint of X. But, apart from its continuing existence, A would not be available for causal objectification in X. If A does not exist, there can be no repetition of A. The creativity for X can take A into account, and can repeat A, only if A exists in itself. The point to remember here is that the causal objectification of A in X does presuppose the perishing of A *qua* subject, but it does not presuppose the non-existence of A; A continues to exist *qua* superject. This explains how a^*/X^* can be a function of A, as well as of the emergence of X. It is in this sense, then, that the extrinsic reality of an event involves its intrinsic reality.

The intrinsic reality of an event, on the other hand, also involves that event's extrinsic reality; for an event's intrinsic reality "will also include the aspects of the event in question as grasped in other events" (SMW 146). Here we reason as follows. Since the extensive potentiality from which an event arises is modally present in the extensive standpoints of all other events—past, present, and future—and since all other extensive standpoints—actual or potential—are modally present within that event, it follows that, in respect to the extensive region that it has realized and embodied, the event's modal presences in other events are also modally present within the event in question itself. What we have here, in effect, is a special consequence of what we earlier referred to as the transitivity of modal presences (*supra*, p. 228 ff.). Because of this transitivity, each event mirrors itself as mirrored in other events. For this reason, so far as cognition is a significant element in the experience enjoyed by an event, "its knowledge of itself arises from its own relevance to the things of which it prehends the aspects" (SMW 207). Thus an event can take into account its entrance, actual or potential, into the constitution of all other events, past, present, or future; and thus also it can take into account its objective role, actual or potential, in the experiences enjoyed by all other events, past, present, or future. In this manner, each event "knows the world as a system of mutual relevance, and thus sees itself as mirrored in other things" (SMW 207).

In order to clarify the notion of an event seeing itself as mirrored in other things, let us consider the following example. First, let *A*, *B*, and *C* be three successive events in a linear order of events. Then, let *P*, *Q*, *R*, and *S* be four successive events in a different linear order of events. Finally, in respect to *B:* let *A* and *P* be in its immediate past; let *Q* and *R* be two of its contemporaries; and let *C* and *S* be in its immediate future. This example, by the way, will remain under surveyance throughout this chapter and the next two. Now let us examine how *B* mirrors itself as mirrored (a) in past events, (b) in future events, and (c) in contemporary events.

(a) The extensive continuum is eternal; hence, the extensive region that *B* is to actualize and embody—namely, *B***—is antecedent to the very existence of *B*. To be sure, this extensive region does not exist as a proper, or bounded, region prior to the existence of *B;* but it does exist as a potential region, or potential division, of the extensive continuum. Because of this, and because the unactualized extension of the universe relative to an event earlier than *B* must be modally present in that event, *B*** must be modally present in all events earlier than *B*. Thus, *!b**/fu**/&ᵛ**/A** is the modal presence in *A* of the extensive potentiality from which *B* is to arise, and is, to that extent, the modal presence in *A* of *B*. Similarly, *b**/fu**/&ᵛ**/P** is the modal presence of *B*** in *P**.

As used above, the symbol '*!*' is intended to denote that *A* has singled out *!b**/fu**/&ᵛ**/A** as the modal presence of the extensive region that its immediate descendant should embody or occupy. This notation is to be contrasted with that of *b**/fu**/&ᵛ**/P**, where the absence of the symbol '*!*' is intended to suggest that the modal presence of *B*** in *P** has no special significance in the experience enjoyed by *P*. In *P*'s experience, *b**/fu**/&ᵛ**/P** remains undifferentiated—though differentiable—from the rest of *fu**/&ᵛ**/P**. This is only another way of saying that, in the experience enjoyed by *P*, the particular extensive potentiality for *B* remains undifferentiated from the general extensive potentiality for future actualities. The exact opposite is the case in regard to the experience enjoyed by *A*. In *A*'s experience, *!b**/fu**/&ᵛ**/A** has been differentiated from the rest of *fu**/&ᵛ**/A** and serves as an element in the objective datum of *A*'s anticipatory feeling of *B*.

In any case, whether or not the modal presence of *B*** in events earlier than B has any special significance for the events in question, the fact remains that they all mirror what is to be an *essential* feature of B, that is, B's own extensive standpoint. To that extent, and to that extent only, B is modally present in all events earlier than itself. For this reason, when B comes into existence, not only are earlier events, such as A and P, modally present in it, but B-as-in-earlier-events is also modally present in B itself. We must remember, in this regard, that any event modally present in another event conveys its own modal structure into that other event. Hence, not only a^*/B^* and p^*/B^*, but also $!b^{**}/fu^{**}/\&^{**}/a^*/B^*$ and $b^{**}/fu^{**}/\&^{**}/p^*/B^*$, are modal constituents of B. Thus, B, in its subjective existence, can prehend itself as mirrored in the constitution of past events.

(b) An analogous situation obtains in respect to events that are in B's future. The total experience enjoyed by B includes the physical anticipation of its own immediate descendant, C. Thus, $!c^{**}/fu^{**}/\&^{**}/B^*$ is an important element in the objective datum of B's anticipatory feeling of C; it is the modal presence in B of C^{**}, the extensive region which B anticipates that its immediate descendant will actualize and embody. But to the extent that $!c^{**}/fu^{**}/\&^{**}/B^*$ is differentiated from the rest of $fu^{**}/\&^{**}/B^*$, it exhibits for B some of the details of the potential modal structure of C^{**}. Hence, the metaphysical necessity that B be modally present in C^{**}, should C^{**} become the seat of an actual event, has its own modal counterpart in the further differentiation of $!c^{**}/fu^{**}/\&^{**}/B^*$ into $b^*/!c^{**}/fu^{**}/\&^{**}/B^*$. Thus, $b^*/!c^{**}/fu^{**}/\&^{**}/B^*$ is the modal presence in B of B's own modal presence in C^{**}. Moreover, since B anticipates that its immediate descendant will occupy C^{**}, and since in this example C does occupy C^{**} (or rather C^*), it follows that $b^*/!c^{**}/fu^{**}/\&^{**}/B^*$ is indeed the modal presence in B of B's own modal presence in C.[4] B, therefore, sees itself as mirrored in C.

What is true of B in relation to C is also true of B in relation to all events that are later than itself. For to the extent that B differentiates $fu^{**}/\&^{**}/B^*$ into the modal presences of the potential standpoints of specific—if hypothetical—future events, it must also differentiate within these modal presences the modal presence of its own modal presence within those standpoints. Assuming, for example, that the modal presence of S^{**} in B has some special significance in the experience enjoyed by B, it would follow that B's anticipatory feeling of its own modal presence in S has, as an element of its objective datum, the modal subregion $b^*/s^{**}/fu^{**}/\&^{**}/B^*$. In principle, therefore, B can see itself as mirrored in the constitution of all future events.

(c) We turn now to B's contemporaries. The extensive potentialities for Q and R are modally present in B: the one as $q^{**}/pr^{**}/\&^{**}/B^*$, the other as $r^{**}/pr^{**}/\&^{**}/B^*$. To the extent that these modal presences are actually differentiated in B's experience from the rest of $pr^{**}/\&^{**}/B^*$, they are also further differentiated so as to mirror the extensive potentiality for the modal presence of B's own standpoint in the events, if there be any, having Q^{**} and R^{**} as their respective standpoints. In the example in question, since Q is anticipated by P, and since P is modally present in B, the modal presence of Q^{**} is more likely to be differentiated from the rest of $pr^{**}/\&^{**}/B^*$ than the modal presence of R^{**}. If so, this differentiated region would include $b^{**}/pr^{**}/\&^{**}/q^{**}/pr^{**}/\&^{**}/B^*$ as one of its own modal components. Hence, so far as $q^{**}/pr^{**}/\&^{**}/B^*$ and its modal components play a relevant role in the experience enjoyed by B, B would see itself as mirrored in the constitution of Q. But this finding cannot be limited to the case of Q alone; it must be extended in principle to include all of B's contemporaries. For whether or not the modal presences of the standpoints of its contemporaries play a significant role in B's experience, the fact remains that, by reason of the modality of extension, B can see itself as mirrored in all events contemporary with itself.

One upshot of the transitivity of modal presences, therefore, is that each event can know itself as mirrored in all other events, past, present, or future. But this is only to say that an event's extrinsic reality is itself modally present in the event in question. To continue with our example, this means that the intrinsic reality of B cannot be divorced from the extrinsic reality of B. For $!b^{**}/fu^{**}/\&^{**}/a^*/B^*$, $b^{**}/fu^{**}/\&^{**}/p^*/B^*$, $b^*/!c^{**}/fu^{**}/\&^{**}/B^*$, $b^*/s^{**}/fu^{**}/\&^{**}/B^*$, $b^{**}/pr^{**}/\&^{**}/q^{**}/pr^{**}/\&^{**}/B^*$, and $b^{**}/pr^{**}/\&^{**}/r^{**}/pr^{**}/\&^{**}/B^*$ are one and all modal constituents of B^* and, hence, objects for B *qua* subject and, hence also, elements in the completely determinate reality of B *qua* superject. Thus, B's intrinsic reality is in part a function of its extrinsic reality, actual or potential.

Conversely, in the example in question, the manifold extrinsic reality of B is shown to be a function either of superject B, or of B^{**}; of the former, in respect to events that are in the future of B; of the latter, in respect to events that are either in the past of, or contemporary with, B. In other words, B's extrinsic reality is, in part at least, a function of B itself *qua* superject, or of the extensive region (B^{**}) that the coming into being of B transforms into B^*. Thus, b^*/C^* and b^*/S^* are functions of the everlasting existence of superject B; whereas $!b^{**}/fu^{**}/\&^{**}/A^*$, $b^{**}/fu^{**}/\&^{**}/P^*$, $b^{**}/pr^{**}/\&^{**}/Q^*$ and $b^{**}/pr^{**}/\&^{**}/R^*$ are functions of B^{**}, the potential region that B transforms into an actual region by embodying it.

It follows from the preceding considerations that in Whitehead's philosophy of organism the reality of an event encompasses its extrinsic, as well as its intrinsic, existence. For each mode of existence involves the other, so that the reality of an event belongs not simply to one or the other mode, but rather to both modes. Thus, for Whitehead an event "is only itself as drawing together into its own limitations the larger whole in which it finds itself. Conversely it is only itself by lending its aspects to this same environment in which it finds itself" (SMW 132).

The twofold reality of an occasion or event, therefore, is a metaphysical tenet of the organic philosophy. We should never allow this finding to be obscured by the fact that, for some purposes, one mode of the reality of an occasion may be legitimately emphasized over the other. For example, when we consider an occasion *qua* subject, we are apt to emphasize its *intrinsic* reality—and rightly so, since what is important about the occasion *qua* subject is its existence as a creative process of experience entirely contained within a particular region of the extensive continuum. This particular region is the occasion's standpoint, and what the occasion *qua* subject directly experiences is entirely contained within its standpoint. The other occasions have been objectified within that standpoint so as to be both constituents of, and objects for, the occasion in question. Thus, in the subjective phases of its existence, the occasion experiences its own constitution and thereby experiences the world as modally present within the occasion itself (PR 309). This means that "experience is not a relation of an experient to something external to it, but is itself the 'inclusive whole' which is the required connectedness of 'many in one'" (AI 299). It also means that the complete experience is nothing other than what the actual entity is in itself, for itself" (PR 81). Accordingly, the subject is the occasion "conceived as what it is in itself and for itself, and not as from its aspect in the essence of another such occasion" (SMW 101). Considered merely as subject, therefore, an occasion has a mode of reality which is primarily intrinsic, primarily self-contained.

Despite what has just been said, however, it is also true that the intrinsic reality of an occasion *qua* subject already involves, and essentially so, its extrinsic reality. For the subject is also the actual occasion as in its teleological process of self-completion, and this process, according to Whitehead, is guided by the subject's aim at intensity of feeling in its own immediate present and in the relevant future (PR 41, 130, 341). Hence, the subject fashions itself in a certain way so that the causal objectifications (or abstractive repetitions) of its superject will influence future actualities in a certain way. This means, in effect, that the subject is taking into account the extensive potentialities for the extrinsic objectifications of its superject. Thus, the subject's existence involves a preparation for the extrinsic objectifications of its superject. Since this preparation has a bearing on the increasing definiteness achieved by the subject, any understanding of the subjective process whereby the superjective product is created necessitates a reference to the extrinsic reality of the occasion in question. The extrinsic reality of an occasion, therefore, is never irrelevant to what that occasion is *qua* subject, and this remains true no matter how much we emphasize the intrinsic reality of such a subject.

When, on the other hand, we consider an occasion merely *qua* superject, we are apt to emphasize its extrinsic reality, and this with good reason. To be sure, the superject is intrinsically real in the sense of existing as the embodiment of the extensive region that the subjective process of which it is the outcome has embodied. Indeed, the superject is the subject's extensive region with its same aboriginally determinate position, and with all the determinate definiteness that accrued it during, and by reason of, the subject's creative existence. But the superject is the dead product of that creative process; it is something in itself, but not for itself.

Thus, if this were all the reality to be assigned to the superject, it would be indistinguishable from non-entity. The superject, however, *is* distinguishable from non-entity, but only because it conditions the creative advance of the universe beyond itself. The creativity repeats, or causally objectifies, the superject in all subsequent actualities. This is why the organic philosophy denies that there is any hard and fast distinction between particulars and universals (PR 76). The many repetitions of an attained actuality constitute what Whitehead has in mind when he speaks of a superject, or satisfaction, as 'universalized' into a character of the creativity (PR 249). As repeated, the attained actuality is both a constituent of, and an object for, each of the actualities in which it is repeated. It thus becomes a universal character (albeit under different abstractions) of all future actualities (PR 344).

The repetitions, or causal objectifications, of the superject constitute its extrinsic, or objective, reality. Because of these transcendent functionings, the superject is distinguishable from non-entity. Each objectification gives witness to the continuing existence of the superject to which it refers, and from which it derives. The superject is the presupposed transcendent reality, conditioning and necessitating its plurality of objective presences in later actualities. In this respect, the extensive continuum

is the factor whereby the many objectifications of the superject are coordinated as the many transcendent functionings of one and the same attained
actuality. But the point to notice now is that, were it not for these
coordinated transcendent functionings, the intrinsic reality of the superject—what it is in itself—would be indistinguishable from non-entity.
Hence, when we consider the superjective existence of an actuality, what
we rightly emphasize are its extrinsic objectifications. The superject's
intrinsic reality is revealed only so far as its extrinsic manifestations give
witness to it. In respect to each of its objectifications, therefore, the
superject is like the far side of a shield: hidden, yet known (AI 293).

On the basis of the preceding considerations, we must conclude that in
the organic philosophy the final actualities of the universe have a twofold
reality: intrinsic and extrinsic. Thus, though for some purposes we may
wish to emphasize one or the other mode of its dual reality, each actual
occasion is the indissoluble union of both modes of reality, and is never
just the one as opposed to the other. The complete reality of an actual
occasion, therefore, encompasses its self-transcendent, as well as its self-
immanent, existence. Here 'self-transcendent existence' means 'existing as
within proper regions other than its own', and 'self-immanent existence'
means 'existing as within, or as the embodiment of, its own proper
region'.

3. The multiple location and unique position of an actual occasion

An immediate consequence of the twofold reality of occasions is that we
must assign to each occasion a multiplicity of *loci* in the extensive
continuum. Thus, in the example under surveyance, B is located not only at
B^*, but also at b^*/C^* and b^*/S^*. In fact, with due allowance for the different
modes of extensive immanence, we can say that B is located wherever it is
mirrored, or, to be more precise, wherever its extensive region is mirrored.
Accordingly, $!b^{**}/fu^{**}/\mathit{\&}^{**}/A^*$ and $b^{**}/pr^{**}/\mathit{\&}^{**}/Q^*$ are also locations
of B. In a certain sense, then, B is everywhere at all times. "For every
location involves an aspect of itself in every other location" (SMW 128).
Hence, according to Whitehead, we cannot attribute simple (*i.e.*, singular)
location to an actual occasion (SMW 128; PR 208). Every occasion must be
construed as having multiple, rather than simple, location. Thus, B^* is not
the only location of B, for B is also located in every region where B^* is
mirrored.

With the exception of B^*, however, all the regions at which B may be said to be located are *improper* regions, that is to say, they are subregions of proper regions, actual or potential, but are not themselves proper regions. They could be construed as *proper subregions* because each is either differentiated or differentiable from the other subregions of its parent region. But whether construed as proper subregions or as improper regions, they are alike regions of the extensive continuum, and B is severally located in each of them. Still, the differentiation of B^* from the other locations of B is important; for the self-immanent, or intrinsic, existence of B is primarily associated with B^*, and not with the improper regions where B is objectified. Thus, for example, the self-functioning of B is completely contained in B^*, particularly in b^*/B^*, though it does involve a reference to regions which lie beyond B^*. In addition, the objective reality of B for other occasions, past, present, and future, is a function of B^* (or of B^{**}).

Nevertheless, we must not push the special status of B^* too far; for, as we saw above, B^* mirrors the entire universe correlative with B, and thus mirrors itself as mirrored in other regions. Thus, in one sense, B is in B^* because it

> arises out of the data provided by this standpoint. But in another sense it is everywhere throughout the continuum; for its constitution includes the objectifications of the actual world and thereby includes the continuum; also the potential objectifications of itself contribute to the real potentialities whose solidarity the continuum expresses. Thus the continuum is present in each actual entity, and each actual entity pervades the continuum. (PR 104–05)

In our example, then, the continuum is present in B because B^* mirrors the universe from which B arose and thus mirrors the scheme of proper regions into which the continuum is actually divided or into which it could be divided. For the same reason, B mirrors its own transcendent locations. Similarly, B pervades the continuum because it is objectified in regions that transcend, and are transcended by, B^*.

Whitehead, it should be noted, emphasizes that one reason why an actual occasion cannot be simply located is that it must be located wherever its effects are, and its effects are always future occasions, insofar as it contributes to their determination. Here we must remember that what is immanent in such an effect is the abstractive repetition of the earlier occasion. This is why

> the notion of 'simple location' is inconsistent with any admission of 'repetition'. . . . In the organic philosophy the notion of repetition is

fundamental. The doctrine of objectification is an endeavour to express how what is settled in actuality is repeated under limitations, so as to be 'given' for immediacy. Later, in discussing time, this doctrine will be termed the doctrine of 'objective immortality'. (PR 208)

The immanence, *via* repetition, of the cause in the effect is the reason why in modern physics, as Whitehead understands it, a physical thing is not only what it is in itself, but also what it does to other things. Accordingly, for Whitehead:

Modern physics has abandoned the doctrine of Simple Location. The physical things . . . are each to be conceived as modifications of conditions within space-time, extending throughout its [*i.e.*, space-time's] whole range. There is a focal region, which in common speech is where the thing is. But its influence streams away from it with finite velocity throughout the utmost recesses of space and time. . . . For physics, the thing itself is what it does, and what it does is this divergent stream of influence. . . . The physical thing is a certain coordination of spaces and times and of conditions in those spaces at those times. (AI 201–02)

This conception of a physical thing is couched in terms that are adequate to the pervasive features of our cosmic epoch but are too specialized for metaphysical discourse. To translate it into metaphysical terms, we need only to substitute 'events' or 'actual occasions' for 'physical things', and 'extensive regions' for 'spatio-temporal regions'. We should also bear in mind, however, that for Whitehead "the effectiveness of an event beyond itself arises from the aspects of itself which go to form the prehended unities of other events" (SMW 168). To say this, of course, is to say that the effectiveness of an occasion arises from the abstractive repetitions of itself within the constitutions of other occasions (PR 134, 336). With this in mind, then, we can translate the substance of the passage from AI as follows: An event or actual occasion is not simply located. It is where it is; and it is also where its effects or objectifications are. Thus, an actual occasion is to be construed as a certain coordination of proper regions and modal subregions and of the conditions in those regions and subregions.

Both Whitehead's original passage and our translation of it put too much emphasis on the objectifications of an actuality in the occasions in its future. The actuality is also objectified, though not repeated, in occasions that are either earlier than, or contemporary with, itself. These other objectifications constitute another reason why the actuality cannot be construed as having singular location. The actuality has, in addition to its own unique self-immanent location, a multiplicity of self-transcendent locations in its past world, in its contemporary world, and in its future world. Accordingly, every actuality is, in one sense, the coordinate reality of all its locations.

The coordinate reality of an occasion's multiplicity of locations, it should be noted, is a function of the metaphysical properties of extension. In this respect, the metaphysical continuum grounds both the potentiality for, and the imposition of, the coordination of extensive regions required by the manifold reality of actual occasions. In other words, by reason of the separative, modal, and prehensive properties of the extensive continuum, the unique immanent location of a subject-superject and the many transcendent locations of its objectifications are all coordinated into the one manifold reality of a single actuality.

The metaphysical properties of extension must also account for the identification of an actual occasion with each and every one of its objectifications in other occasions. Without such an identification, the doctrine of multiple location is unintelligible. What needs to be explained, in this regard, is how a *particular*, as opposed to a universal, can have multiple instances. In the last analysis, such an explanation requires that the organic philosophy be able to provide a definition of 'particular' that is compatible with the doctrine of multiple location.

To understand how one self-same particular can have multiple instances, we must, first of all, carefully distinguish the notion of 'location' from the notion of 'position'. In the organic philosophy, for an entity to be located at a given extensive region is for that entity to occupy, embody, or qualify that region. Thus, in the example under surveyance, B is located at B^*. Also, whatever it is that embodies b^*/C^* may be said to be located at b^*/C^*. For example, there are contrasts located in b^*/C^* or in some part of b^*/C^* (PR 352). But the notion of location is applicable to all entities of all types, insofar as they each embody, occupy, or qualify an extensive region. The only exceptions are eternal objects in restricted or conceptual ingression, for in that guise they are qualifications of experience but not of extension. Accordingly, the location of an entity of whatever type is the extensive region it embodies or qualifies. The entity gives its character to the region, and the region gives its extensiveness to the entity.

The notion of position presupposes the notion of location but is much more complex than it. In the primitive and legitimate sense of the term, only actual occasions have position. An occasion's position specifies the *where* and *when* of its existence, relative to the existence of other actual occasions—*where* in the extensive continuum and *when* in the creative advance of actuality. The position of an actual occasion is the aboriginal element of its determinateness, the element which is common to all its phases of existence.

We must remember here that Whitehead analyzed the determinateness of an actual occasion into determinate *definiteness* and determinate *position* (PR 38). Now the definiteness of an actual occasion is its illustration of a selection of eternal objects ingressed as determinants of its subjective form (PR 38, 69, 233–34). In a derivative sense, the eternal objects functioning as determinants of an occasion's objective datum may also be construed as elements of its definiteness. But even if definiteness is construed in this wider sense, the definiteness of an occasion does not exhaust its determinateness. Indeed, by itself the definiteness of the occasion is but a shadow of the occasion's concrete reality (PR 93–94, 30). For an actual occasion "realizes form and is yet more than form. It refers to past, present and future" (MT 95).

What an actual occasion refers to are the other actualities—attained, in attainment, or merely potential—of its universe (PR 21–22; MT 115). It refers to them because its own extensive standpoint mirrors the state of the universe which gave it birth.

> An event has contemporaries. This means that an event mirrors within itself the modes of its contemporaries as a display of immediate achievement. An event has a past. This means that an event mirrors within itself the modes of its predecessors, as memories which are fused into its own content. An event has a future. This means that an event mirrors within itself such aspects as the future throws back on to the present, or, in other words, as the present has determined concerning the future. (SMW 102–03)

The modes to which Whitehead refers are the modal differentiations *within* the event's standpoint; but these modal differentiations bear an essential reference to regions, and hence to occasions (actual or potential), *beyond* that standpoint. Thus, the event or occasion is concerned with occasions that, in their intrinsic reality, lie beyond the occasion in question (MT 229–30; AI 231). But these same occasions, by reason of their extrinsic reality, are also modally, or objectively, present in the said occasion.

By virtue of the modal immanence of the actual occasions to which the occasion refers, the occasion has a determinate *position*, where " 'position' is relative status in a nexus of actual entities" (PR 38). In other words, the

modal or objective immanence in an occasion of all the occasions constituting its actual world is the reason why occasions "have a determinate status
relatively to each other. . . . It is the reason why it belongs to the essence
of each occasion that it is *where* it is" (MT 226–27). This means that the
objective composition of an actual entity—what it is by virtue of the
immanence in it of other occasions—assigns to it a determinate status in its
correlative actual world. Its objective composition forever enshrines and
exhibits its position. Therefore, "the actual entity, in virtue of being *what*
it is, is also *where* it is. It is somewhere because it is some actual thing with
its correlated actual world" (PR 93).

The use of the term 'where' as synonymous with 'status' and 'position' is
misleading; for, as I said earlier, the position of an actual occasion
encompasses its *when* in the creative advance, as well as its *where* in the
extensive continuum. The when of a completed occasion is itself analyzable
into two dates: one for the occasion's 'birth' and another for its 'death'. The
occasion's dates as well as its correlative location are defined relative to the
occasions objectified in it. Thus, by virtue of the other actualities
objectified in it, that is, by virtue of its position or status, an actual occasion
is "dated and located among the actual entities connected in itself"
(PR 352).[5]

The whole point of the doctrine of position, then, is that an actual
entity "has a status among other actual entities not expressible wholly in
terms of contrasts between eternal objects" (PR 350). The complete
contrast of eternal objects ingressed in an actual occasion constitutes the
determinate definiteness of that occasion. This definiteness is *part* of the
occasion's essence, but it cannot be the *whole* of its essence. Accordingly,
the occasion's definiteness is termed its *abstract essence*, whereas its
complete determinateness is termed its *real essence* (PR 93–94). Each actual
occasion has a unique real essence, but its abstract essence need not be
unique, since it is merely a contrast of eternal objects, and any such
contrast, as we saw in Chapter Four, is reproducible in principle.[6] Hence,
according to Whitehead,

> There is nothing self-contradictory in the thought of many actual
> entities with the same abstract essence; but there can only be one
> actual entity with the same real essence. For the real essence indicates
> 'where' the entity is, that is to say, its status in the real world; the
> abstract essence omits the particularity of the status. (PR 94)

From this it follows that the uniqueness of an occasion's real essence—the
uniqueness of its determinate constitution—is a function of its position
and not of its definiteness.

In turn, the position of an actual occasion is primarily a function of the actual occasions that are objectified in and for it. This point bears emphasizing because, according to Whitehead, "the determinateness and self-identity of one [actual] entity cannot be abstracted from the community of the diverse functionings of all entities" (PR 38). Now, the relevant types of entities, in this context, are eternal objects and actual entities. The other types function in a given actuality in a manner derivative from, or parasitic on, the functioning of eternal objects and actual entities. But, considered in themselves, the functionings of eternal objects in an actual entity will only give us the definiteness, or abstract essence, of that actuality. Therefore, it is the functionings, or objectifications, of all the other actualities in the said actuality which account for the latter's unique determinateness and self-identity. Accordingly, an actuality's position— its unique, nonshareable, determinateness—is a function of the objectifications within itself of the other actualities in its correlative universe. An actual entity's real essence, then, "involves real objectifications of specified actual entities" (PR 94). For this reason, an actual entity "cannot be described, even inadequately, by universals; because other actual entities do enter into the description of any one actual entity" (PR 76).

4. Position and the indicative scheme

Insofar as other actual occasions enter into the description of a given occasion, they specify the position of that occasion. In other words, the objectification within an occasion of its correlative universe is such as to indicate the position of the occasion in the extenso-genetic order of the universe. This is why Whitehead says that the constitution of an actual occasion assigns to it its status in the universe (PR 93). But this indication of the position of an occasion by the occasion's own determinate constitution cannot be divorced from the metaphysical properties of the extensive continuum. For the indication of an occasion's position by the occasion's own real essence requires that the universe be essentially a systematic environment imposing a coordination of mutual internal relations on its concrete constituents (PR 21–22, 394).[7]

Needed in this regard, therefore, is an *indicative system* rooted in the ultimate nature of the universe. The Receptacle, insofar as it is an extensive matrix imposing on its creatures the threefold determination of separativeness, prehensiveness, and modality, provides the requisite indicative system. For, by virtue of the metaphysical properties of extension, the discrete actualities of the universe are coordinated as the prehensive unifications of each other's modalities. Accordingly, the modal scheme of the extensive standpoint of an actual occasion is an indicative system assigning to that occasion, as well as to each of the occasions objectified in the occasion in question, its relative status in the universal nexus of occasions (PR 296). This "systematic scheme, in its completeness embracing the actual past and the potential future, is prehended in the positive experience of [the] actual entity" (PR 112). Therefore, the modal, or objective, scheme of its own standpoint can indicate to the actuality how the other actualities are extenso-genetically ordered in relation to one another and to itself.

To understand how the modal structure of an occasion's standpoint can have this indicative function, let us return to the example being surveyed throughout this chapter. In that example, we must remember, A, B, and C constitute a serial order of actual occasions, and P, Q, R, and S constitute another serial order of occasions. All the occasions in question are in the past of C, except for S, which is contemporary with C. (It is understood that C cannot be in the past of itself.) Also, Q and R are both contemporaries of B. Finally, A and P are contemporaries, and both are in the past of B and of Q. These relationships, with one addition, suffice for the task at hand, which is the analysis of C's proper region, or extensive standpoint, insofar as it functions as an indicative system. The addition in question is the introduction of D into the example—where D is an actual occasion in the immediate future of C, and belonging to the same serial, or supersessional, order as C.

In considering how the standpoint of C functions as an indicative system, we must bear in mind that the objectifications of the attained actualities in C's actual world "are systematically disposed in their relative status, according as *one* is, or is not, in the actual world of *another*" (PR 448). Moreover, we must also bear in mind "that the other actual entities are objectified with the retention of their extensive relationships" (PR 105). In the preceding chapter (Section 5), these two crucial aspects of the doctrine of objectification were developed as the related concepts of the different orders of modal immanence and of the transitivity of modal presences. Both concepts are essential to the understanding of how the modal structure of C's standpoint is significant of the relative genetic order, as well as of the relative extensive order, exhibited by the occasions in the actual world of C, and by C itself.

The modal structure of C*, which is positively prehended by C, yields the following information about the extenso-genetic order of the occasions under consideration. First, the fact that B is in the immediate past of C is indicated for C by the first-order modal presence, b^*/C^*, which B has in C^*. Second, the fact that A is not in the immediate past of C, but is in the immediate past of B, is indicated for C by the second-order modal presence, $a^*/b^*/C^*$, which A has in C^*. Third, $q^{**}/pr^{**}/\&^{**}/b^*/C^*$, $r^{**}/pr^{**}/\&^{**}/b^*/C^*$, $b^{**}/pr^{**}/\&^{**}/q^*/r^*/C^*$ and $b^{**}/pr^{**}/\&^{**}/r^*/C^*$ jointly indicate for C that Q is supersessionally earlier than R, but that both Q and R are contemporaries of B. Fourth, $a^{**}/pr^{**}/\&^{**}/p^*/q^*/r^*/C^*$, $p^*/b^*/C^*$, and $p^{**}/pr^{**}/\&^{**}/a^*/b^*/C^*$ jointly indicate for C that A and P are contemporaries, and that both are in the immediate past of B. Fifth, $!s^{**}/fu^{**}/\&^{**}/r^*/C^*$ and $s^{**}/pr^{**}/\&^{**}/C^*$ jointly indicate for C that S is one of its contemporaries, and that the origination of the becoming of S is immediately subsequent to the termination of the becoming of R. Sixth, $!c^{**}/fu^{**}/\&^{**}/b^*/C^*$ and $!d^{**}/fu^{**}/\&^{**}/C^*$ jointly indicate for C that its own becoming originated immediately after B terminated its becoming, and that the termination of C's becoming will be immediately followed by the origination of D's becoming. In this way, the 'when' of C's birth and the 'when' of its death are correlated to the birth and perishing of other occasions.

Similarly, other modal differentiations of C^* will indicate for C how all the occasions of its actual world are dated with respect to each other's birth or death. Thus, though the preceding analysis has not exhausted the indicative system inherent in the modal structure of C^*, it should suffice as an explanation of the general principle involved in the specification of the metaphysical dates to be assigned to actual occasions. A similar principle is involved in the indication of the correlative locations of the actual occasions in C's actual world, including the indication of C's own correlative location. For the correlative locations of the modal presences within C^* are such as to mirror the correlative locations of the proper regions to which the modal presences respectively correspond.

Thus, for example, the correlative locations of the actual occasions that occupy, or will occupy, B^*, C^*, and D^* are mirrored within C^* by the correlative locations of b^*/C^*, c^*/C^*, and $!d^{**}/fu^{**}/\&^{**}/C^*$. Thus, too, the correlative locations of A^*, B^*, and C^* are mirrored within C^* by the correlative locations of $a^*/b^*/C^*$, $b^*/b^*/C^*$, and $!c^{**}/fu^{**}/\&^{**}/b^*/C^*$. In like fashion, the correlative locations of C and S are mirrored within C^* by the correlative locations of c^*/C^* and $s^{**}/pr^{**}/\&^{**}/C^*$. In this manner, then, C's location relative to the occasions of its actual world—be those occasions earlier than, contemporary with, or later than, C—is also indicated by the modal scheme into which C's standpoint is structured. Moreover, since C is objectified in other actualities with retention of its own extensive relationships, C's own correlative location is also indicated by the modal structure of each of C's objectifications. For example, the modal structure of c^*/D^* exhibits the same correlative location for C as does the modal structure of C^*.

In this regard, it is important to distinguish between the notion of absolute location and the notion of correlative location; for each actual occasion has a multiplicity of *absolute* locations, but only one *correlative* location. For example, C is absolutely located in each of the following regions: C^*; $!c^{**}/fu^{**}/\&^{**}/B^*$; $c^{**}/pr^{**}/\&^{**}/S^*$; and c^*/D^*. Nevertheless, the modal structure of each of these regions exhibits one self-same correlative location for C. Thus, paradoxically as it may sound, an actual occasion has the same correlative location wherever it is located. It should be evident, therefore, that by the position of an actual occasion we are to understand the correlative where-when of its existence.

It has now been shown that the extensive standpoint of C, by reason of its scheme of modal differentiations, indicates for C its position, or correlative status, in the extenso-genetic order of the universal nexus. The same modal scheme also indicates for C the position, or 'where-when', of every actual occasion objectified in C. Now, throughout this entire discussion we have been assuming that the judgments concerning the positions of the different occasions were being made, or could have been made, by subject C. For, according to Whitehead, "It must be held that judgment concerns the universe as objectified from the standpoint of the judging subject. It concerns the universe through that subject" (PR 305; see also PR 309). But this does not mean that, with the perishing of subject C, the judgments concerning C's position, or concerning the positions of the occasions in C's actual world, can no longer be made. For they can be made by all, and are probably made by some, of the actual occasions in the future of C. In fact, any actual entity that has C as a member (*qua* attained actuality) of its actual world, will be able to make exactly the same judgments, and will base those judgments on exactly the same scheme of extensive modalities (PR 351–52).

Here I must emphasize again that actual occasions are objectified with the retention of their extensive relations or, equivalently, that the relationship of modal immanence is transitive. In other words, to continue with the example, it must be emphasized again that every causal objectification of C, in occasions later than C, objectifies with it the modal structure of C^*, and thus objectifies also the indicative system on which subject C had based its judgments. Therefore, any occasion in which C is causally objectified can also make the requisite judgments concerning the position of C or of any actual occasion in the actual world of C. Any such later occasion, say D, will be basing its judgments on the scheme of modal differentiations which is at once internal to C, and also modally present in D as a subordinate element of D's own scheme of modal differentiations; for the modal structure of c^*/D^* mirrors the modal structure of C^*.

This conclusion is the immediate consequence of the organic doctrine that the nexus constituting the actual world of an occasion is not destroyed when that occasion perishes but remains in existence to be reproduced in, and to be added to by, the novel actualities that transcend both it and its correlative occasion (PR 364–65). "An actual world is a nexus; and the actual world of one actual entity sinks to the level of a subordinate nexus in actual worlds beyond that actual entity" (PR 42). The objectification, in the later actualities, of a subordinate nexus, and of the actuality for which that nexus serves as an actual world, is the reason why earlier indicative systems reappear as subordinate elements of later indicative systems. Thus, "the possibility of diverse judgments by diverse actual entities, having the same content (of 'proposition' in contrast with 'nexus'), requires that the same complex of logical subjects . . . can enter as a partial constituent into the 'real' essences of diverse actual entities" (PR 293). Thus, too, "each actual world is a nexus which in this sense is independent of its original percipient. It enjoys an objective immortality in the future beyond itself" (PR 351–52).

The most important outcome of these considerations, it should be evident, is that an actual occasion exhibits one and the same determinate position, one and the same real essence, wherever it is located in regard either to its intrinsic reality or to any of the causal modes of its extrinsic reality. Except in some special cases, however, this doctrine does not hold true for the anticipatory and contemporary modes of an occasion's extrinsic reality. For in general those modes can only indicate the possible 'where' of an actual occasion but not its possible 'when'. But this restriction having been specified, the long and the short of this doctrine is that in each of its self-transcendent locations an actual occasion displays the same position, and hence the same real essence, as it displays in its self-immanent location. For example, the proper region C^*, which is where C is self-immanently located, and the modal region c^*/D^*, which is where one of the self-transcendent, causal objectifications of C is located, both tell the same tale about the position or real essence of C.

In this manner, the preceding considerations have provided an elucidation of how an actual occasion can have a multiplicity of locations yet have the same position wherever it is located. But, by the same token, since the real essence of an occasion is a function of its position, these considerations have also begun to elucidate the notion of an actual occasion with multiple location yet self-identical in each and all of its locations. Finally, since the position of an actual occasion is a function of the objectification within it of other actual occasions, these considerations have also elucidated why it is that, for Whitehead, the determinateness and self-identity of an actual occasion cannot be abstracted from the community of the diverse functionings of the actual occasions in the universe of that occasion (PR 38).[8]

5. Self-identity and positional uniqueness

One basic consideration remains: for the organic philosophy, each actual occasion is unique, and the particularity of each actual occasion is predicated on its uniqueness. Now an actual occasion can be unique if, and only if, its real essence is unique. In other words, an actual occasion can be unique if, and only if, it has a unique position in the extenso-genetic order of the universe. Hence, it must be shown that an actual occasion cannot share its position with any other actual occasion.

In this respect, it would seem that the uniqueness of an occasion's position can be sufficiently well grounded on the fact that no two actual occasions can embody the same proper region of the extensive continuum. This is tantamount to saying that the uniqueness of each occasion's position is guaranteed by the separative property of extension. For, by reason of their separate extensive standpoints, two actual occasions would differ from one another even if they had the same abstract essence and even if their respective processes of becoming had been jointly initiated and jointly terminated. The two occasions would have different positions, even while having the same dates of initiation and termination, because their correlative locations in the continuum would be different.

I take Whitehead to be making precisely this point when he writes,

> It is not wholly true that two contemporaries A and B enjoy a common past. In the first place, *even if the occasions in the past of A be identical with the occasions in the past of B*, yet A and B by reason of their difference of status, enjoy that past under a difference of perspective elimination. Thus the objective immortality of the past in A differs from the objective immortality of the *same past* in B. (AI 252; italics mine)

Clearly, what Whitehead is asserting here is that the one past common to A and B is objectified in those occasions under different abstractions. To that extent, A and B spring from qualitatively, as well as numerically, *different* objectifications of the *same* past. They both presuppose the exact-same community of attained actualities at the base of their respective natures. Accordingly, A and B have the same identical date of initiation. By an analogous train of reasoning, it could be shown that A and B could have a common future and hence a common date of termination. Nonetheless, even if A and B are construed as having identical birth-dates and identical death-dates, they would still have to be construed as having different positions because their correlative locations in the extensive continuum would be necessarily different. Thus, the necessary uniqueness of an actual occasion's position can be demonstrated by appealing solely to a metaphysical property of the extenso-creative matrix.

Now, immediately after the passage just quoted, Whitehead does go on to say that a contemporary of A, P in his example, need not be a contemporary of B, and that if P is in the past of B, "even the occasions in the past of A are not wholly identical with those in the past of B" (AI 253). But this assertion simply represents an attempt by Whitehead to apply the metaphysics of organism to the cosmology of relativity physics. Nothing in Whitehead's metaphysics, as I understand it, precludes the possibility of two contemporaries having identical pasts or identical futures. Indeed, it is my conviction that the metaphysics of organism gains in coherence and adequacy when it allows for the possibility of two or more occasions having identical birth-dates or identical death-dates. What is must disallow is the possibility of two or more occasions having identical correlative locations; for this latter possibility is incompatible with the indicative function of the extensive scheme and hence is incompatible with the manifold self-identity of actual occasions.

Nevertheless, for reasons that are not apparent to me, Whitehead sometimes makes, in effect, the stronger but arbitrary claim that no two actual occasions can share exactly the same actual world and, hence, that no two actual occasions can have either the same correlative date of initiation or the same correlative date of termination. Thus, in the fifth Category of Explanation, Whitehead asserts that

> no two actual entities originate from an identical universe; though the difference between the two universes only consists in some actual entities, included in one and not in the other, *and* in the subordinate entities which each actual entity introduces into the world. (PR 33–34; italics mine. See also PR 42)

In respect to the 'and' which I have emphasized in this quotation, notice that the later conjunct is superfluous, given the force of the earlier conjunct. For the difference in actual worlds is sufficient to guarantee the required difference in real essences. Hence, it is entirely possible that Whitehead may have worded this statement carelessly. For notice that if we substitute 'or' for the emphasized 'and', we gain a more significant reading of the passage in question. Moreover, read as a disjunction, this passage is compatible with my views on the issue; for the extensive standpoint of an actual entity is a subordinate entity introduced into the world by the becoming of that actuality.

In any case, whether we take my view on this matter, or Whitehead's, the outcome is the same: the position of an actual entity, and hence its real essence, is necessarily unique. Thus, to identify an actual occasion it is sufficient to indicate its determinate position. This means, in effect, that the self-identify of an actual occasion is a function of its position. Now, since the modal subregions embodied by the causal objectifications of a given occasion have each the same modal structure as the proper region embodied by the occasion in question, and since the position of an entity is a function of the modal structure of the extensive region it embodies, it follows that in each of its causal objectifications the actual occasion in question is indeed a reproduction of its identical self. Thus, one concrete actuality can have multiple reproductions of itself, each reproductive instance embodying a different extensive locus, yet each instance proclaiming its self-identity with all the other instances.

The doctrine of position, therefore, allows the organic philosophy to identify a concrete actuality, or superject, with each of its numerically different objectifications in later actualities. The same doctrine, with some qualifications, also provides for the identification of an actual occasion with each of its objectifications in occasions earlier than, or contemporary with, itself. For *at the very least* the correlative location of an actual occasion is exhibited by each and every one of its objectifications. Thus, that on which the uniqueness of an occasion's self-identity depends—its unique correlative location—is (or will be) mirrored in, and indicated by, every proper region of the extensive continuum. Of course, only in a small number of the occasions embodying those proper regions, each its own, will the indication of the said occasion's correlative location have any special significance. But the point to notice is that every actual extensive standpoint includes within itself a modal aspect of the proper region from which the occasion in question arose, is arising, or will arise and thereby includes something of the occasion's unique essence. For the unique real essence and self-identity of an occasion cannot be divorced from the uniqueness of its determinate position, and in turn the uniqueness of its position cannot be abstracted from the uniqueness of its correlative location. It follows that Whitehead means exactly what he so often says: actual occasions are discrete entities, but each is immanent in *all* the others—past, present, or future.

I have now shown not only that an actual occasion exhibits one and the same position in each of its multiple locations, but also that the position thus exhibited is unique to the occasion. I have shown, in addition, that the unique real essence or self-identity of an occasion is grounded on the uniqueness of the occasion's position. To that extent I have begun to demonstrate how a particular may have multiple instances of itself; for a particular occasion displays the same identity in each of its locations; thus the occasion, in each of its locations, is neither more nor less than an instance of itself. The organic conception of particularity cannot, therefore, be divorced from the organic doctrine of position.

6. *Aboriginal position and acquired definiteness*

The doctrine of position provides a ground not only for the self-same identity exhibited by an actual occasion in itself and in each of its objectifications but also for the self-same identity exhibited by an occasion throughout, and in each of, its successive phases of self-immanent existence: the dative phase, the conformal phase, the supplemental subjective phases, and the superjective phase. For the dative phase of an occasion is nothing more than its extensive standpoint as structured by the causal objectifications of the attained actualities of its correlative actual world (PR 104). Hence, an occasion's position, its positional essence, belongs to it from the earliest or aboriginal phase of its existence (RM 151). Moreover, since intrinsic supersession is a cumulative process in which the earlier phases are absorbed without loss into the later phases, it follows that the position of an actual occasion remains the same throughout all of its phases of existence, including its terminal phase—the superject (PR 470, 441). But to say this, given that an occasion's real essence is primarily a function of its position, is to say that an occasion's self-identity remains the same throughout the occasion's adventure of self-formation. For though an actual occasion gains increased definiteness with each phase of concrescence, it remains true that it is one self-same particular which is thus gaining definiteness.

In this respect, the sense in which an occasion's real essence is a function of its position requires further elucidation, since it might seem that the definiteness of an occasion is as much a part of its real essence as its position. However, the latter is true only if we are considering an actual entity as superject, that is, as completely determinate. In this regard as in many others, the distinction between an actuality as in attainment and that same actuality as attained is of the utmost importance. An attained actuality is the outcome of a creative process, which is the same actuality as in attainment. As attained, each actuality is completely determinate in every respect; but as in attainment, each actuality is a process of passing from partial to complete determinateness.

Notice that I am claiming that the process of attaining complete determinateness starts from a stage of partial determinateness and not from one of complete indeterminateness. The partial determinateness in question is the occasion's position. I hold, in effect, that each occasion is aboriginally determinate in respect to its position. In other words: if no determinate position, then no occasion whatsoever. The completely indeterminate is unspecificable, ineffable, and indistinguishable from non-entity. Thus, without its aboriginally determinate position, an actuality in attainment would not be the unique and specifiable particular that it is. To be sure, considered in its very first phase of existence, an occasion is only minimally determinate; but such minimal determination is the difference between entity and non-entity.

It should be emphasized, lest language mislead us, that it is not claimed that any given actuality other than God exists aboriginally. Rather it is held that for an occasion to exist at all, it must exist with determinate position. This is all that is meant by saying that an occasion's position is aboriginal.

An occasion in attainment, however, has no aboriginal definiteness. Indeed, the occasion in attainment *is* the process of attaining definiteness by means of a real supersession of real creative phases, each new phase adding to the definiteness already achieved by the earlier phases. Thus, in the first or aboriginal phase of its existence the merely real occasion has a determinate position whereby it is already the specifiable or indicatable particular that it is; but, as in this first phase, the merely real occasion is completely indeterminate in respect to definiteness. The acquisition of a determinate definiteness is the gradual and cumulative achievement of the phases subsequent to the dative phase. The merely real occasion first receives the conformal definiteness generated in the responsive phase. Next, the occasion is subjected to the primary conceptual feelings immediately derived from its conformal feelings. Finally, the occasion—now truly self-realizing and hence truly *actual*—proceeds to freely fashion the remainder of its own definiteness by a succession of originative and integrative feelings, culminating in the superjective satisfaction. It is *only* as a superject that the occasion is a completely determinate entity. Therefore, it is only as a superject that the occasion exhibits a fully determinate definiteness as well as a fully determinate position.

The superject's real essence *is* the indissoluble union of its position and its definiteness. If we now consider the superjective occasion in abstraction from the process which was its becoming, and to which it bears witness, we are apt to conclude that its definiteness and its position are equally necessary for that occasion's existence. But with this conclusion no meaning can be found for the notion of contingency, or for the notion of freedom, or for the notion of self-determination, in respect to that occasion. However, if we refrain from considering the superject under such an abstraction and consider it, instead, as the outcome of a creative process involving a real supersession of creative phases, we see that, though its position could not have been other than it is without it thereby being an altogether different particular, its definiteness could have been other than it is and it still would have been one and the same particular, albeit with a different definiteness.[9]

The sense in which an actual entity would have remained the *same* particular, even if it had acquired a completely different definiteness, is what permits us to speak of a subject and its superject as being one and the same entity. When we thus speak, we are *not* committing the genetic fallacy, since the subjective process and the superjective product both exhibit the same unique position, the same unique particularity, the same unique self-identity. In other words, to the extent that the particularity of an actual entity—its indicatable self-identity—is inextricably a function of its positional determinateness, the self-realizing subject and the self-realized superject are truly one and the same particular in two supersessionally successive stages of its intrinsic existential history. For the same reason, we can speak of the phases in an occasion's becoming as being each that self-same occasion as in *that* phase of its existence. However much two phases of an occasion may differ from each other in respect to definiteness, they do not differ in respect to position.

One important upshot of the distinction between aboriginal position and acquired definiteness, then, is that *each actual occasion becomes but does not change* (PR 92, 122–24; AI 262). In other words, given that an occasion's determinate position is of a piece with its dative phase, and given that all subsequent phases of the occasion's existence presuppose and incorporate the dative phase, it follows that the occasion's unique and specifiable *particularity* remains unchanged as the occasion passes through its successive phases of becoming. The occasion does become more definite, but the occasion does not thereby change its self-identity. Thus an actual entity, as in a later phase of its existence, differs from itself, as in an earlier phase, in respect to its degree of achieved definiteness; but in both phases it is one and the same entity because its unique position is common to all its phases of existence. In other words, whatever phase an actuality is in, it is specifiable as *that* entity with *that* unique relative status among the actualities of its universe. Thus we can speak of one self-same entity that either is in the process of acquiring definiteness or is, as the result of such a process, already completely definite. It is in this sense that the uniqueness and specifiability of an actual entity is primarily a function of its position and only secondarily a function of its definiteness.

To fail to distinguish between an actual entity's aboriginal position and its gradually acquired definiteness is to render meaningless the notion that, in some sense, each actuality freely determines itself, that is, freely determines what it is to be. For if position and definiteness are equally presupposed by the existence of an actual entity, then either an actual entity exists both with completely determinate position *and* with completely determinate definiteness, or it does not exist at all. But if for an actuality to exist at all is for it to exist as completely determinate in all respects, then in its existence there is no room left for its choosing what or how it is to be. It already is all that it can be. Furthermore, since it would make no sense to say that a non-existing actuality chooses what it is to be, we must come to the realization that, with this approach, there is no meaning to the notion that an actuality freely determines what it is to be or to the notion that it freely fashions its own immediate definiteness.

Only the distinction between an actuality with the minimal determinateness of position and that same actuality completely determinate in respect to both definiteness and position restores the requisite meaning—provided, of course, that we construe becoming as involving a real supersession of creative phases. Many interpreters of Whitehead have missed this point and thus have compromised, albeit unknowingly, the freedom Whitehead ascribes to actual entities (PR 390). Their failure in this regard is generally threefold. First, they have made little or no sense of the *real supersession* of phases whereby an actual entity comes to be. Second, they have failed to see the relevance, in this connection, of the two species of creative process; for it is the *macroscopic* process that produces an occasion with a determinate position, and with a partially determinate definiteness derived conformally from the objectification in that occasion of occasions which, relative to it, are already actual; whereas it is the *microscopic* process that, starting with the outcome of the macroscopic process as its datum, autonomously provides the forms of definiteness constituting the novel immediacy of that occasion. This latter process is nothing else than the actuality itself functioning as *causa sui*. Finally, these interpreters have failed to comprehend the full import of the contrast between an occasion's *position*, which is the aboriginal and given element of its essence, and an occasion's *definiteness*, which, with the exception of the subjective forms of simple conformal feelings, is the acquired and self-realized element of its essence.

7. From bare particular to fully-clothed individual

Another important upshot of the distinction between position and definiteness is that we can meaningfully distinguish between what an occasion is *qua bare particular*, its dative phase, and what an occasion is *qua fully-clothed individual*, its superjective satisfaction. The bare particular is the *merely real* occasion. The fully-clothed individual is the *attained actuality*. In between these two extreme stages lie, first, the *minimal* individuality of the occasion as in its phases of primary physical and conceptual feelings, and second, the *deepened* individuality of the occasion as an autonomous *actuality in attainment* (PR 173, 176, 22).[10] The two intermediate stages constitute the becoming of the occasion's definiteness. Thus they represent the process whereby the bare particular becomes a concrete individual through its progressive acquisition of fully-clothed feelings (PR 82).

The bare particular occasion, it is worth noting, becomes a fully-clothed individual without thereby altering its aboriginal particularity. In this sense, individuality is an enrichment of particularity. It is the particular as valuable *for* itself and as enriching itself through the autonomous creation of its own value. Not all particulars are capable of this enrichment. But all actual occasions, and some societies of actual occasions, do exhibit this capacity. To that extent, they exhibit in their own natures a passage from *mere particularity*—the particularity which is exhibited by *all* entities insofar as they exist *in* themselves—to *full individuality*—the individuality which is exhibited by only those entities that exist, or have existed, *for* themselves. Accordingly, every subject-superject and every personal living society is a particular with full individuality.

Notice that a particular is to be construed as a full individual only if it has a hand in the creation of its own real essence, where by real essence is meant the actual unity of determinate position and determinate definiteness. But notice, also, that each fully individualized particular first exists with mere positional determinateness, and then acquires its mostly self-fashioned individual definiteness. The distinction between an individual's position and its definiteness, we thus discover, provides a solid metaphysical foundation on which to build a theory of organic existentialism. Unlike the traditional theories of existentialism, however, the organic theory would not restrict the scope of self-creative freedom to human existence. In metaphysics there are no special dispensations. The freedom of human individuals differs in degree and in complexity, but not in kind, from the freedom of non-human individuals. In this essay, I can do no more than foreshadow the basic principles of an organic existentialist theory by explicating its metaphysical roots. But the importance I attach to the development of such a theory is one reason why I have labored to elucidate the real *supersession* of creative phases, the real distinction between *transition* and *concrescence*, and the real difference between *position* and *definiteness*.

For the moment, the point to emphasize is that an occasion's bare particularity precedes its fully-clothed individuality. In thus distinguishing between bare particularity and individualized particularity, I am merely trying to save an important metaphysical distinction from being completely lost in the vagaries and inconsistencies of Whitehead's all too fluid terminology. To help save and develop this distinction, I will next consider four different senses in which we may attribute individuality to an actual occasion.

The first sense merely signifies the numerical unity of an actual occasion. In respect to this sense of the word, each particular occasion is an individual from the very first phase of its existence. Obviously, this sense of individuality can be predicated of any entity, however complex, which can function as the objective datum of either a primary prehension or an integrative prehension. This sense of individuality is *not* the one I am here trying to save and develop, but it is not irrelevant to our understanding of actual occasions.

More to the point is the sense of individuality which signifies any entity that exists *for* itself. This sense of individuality can be properly predicated only of occasions in their subjective immediacy and, derivatively, of some societies of occasions. An occasion is an individual, in this second sense of the term, from the moment it exists as a subject with conformal feelings to the moment it exists as a subjective satisfaction, the last creative-subphase of its existence. Notice that the dative phase of the occasion is *not* an individual in this new sense of the term. This is one reason why Whitehead refers to the second phase of an occasion's existence as "the individu-alizing phase of conformal feeling" (PR 176). With this phase, the aborigi-nal particularity of the occasion has been *minimally* individualized. The occasion is now something for itself as well as in itself.

The minimal individuality of the occasion as in its conformal phase is to be contrasted with the deepened individuality of its supplemental, orig-inative, phases. In these phases, "each actual occasion contributes to the circumstances of its origin additional formative elements deepening its own peculiar individuality" (PR 22). Whitehead leaves no doubt that the more spontaneous, the more originative, the more autonomous these phases are, the more the occasion's individuality is deepened: "Spon-taneity, originality of decision, belongs to the essence of each actual occasion. It is the supreme expression of individuality . . . the freedom of enjoyment derived from the enjoyment of freedom" (AI 332). We have here the third sense of individuality predicable of an actual occasion. This sense signifies any entity that exists *for itself as in a process of autonomous self-formation.* Again, this third sense of the term can be properly predicated only of occasions in their immediate, actual, teleological process of self-realization and, derivatively, of some societies of actual occasions. This means that this sense of the term applies to an occasion only after the derivation of its initial subjective aim from its hybrid physical feeling of God. The deepening of individuality, therefore, begins *after* the primary phase of conceptual valuation, of which the feeling of subjective aim is the dominant component. Accordingly, individuality begins to deepen with the phase of conceptual reversion and achieves its maximum depth in the phase of subjective satisfaction. Thus, this sense of individuality, White-head tells us, properly applies "to an actual entity in its immediacy of self-attainment when it stands out as for itself alone, with its own affective self-enjoyment. The term 'monad' also expresses this essential unity at the decisive moment, which stands between its birth and its perishing" (AI 227).

The third sense of individuality belongs to the occasion as concrescence and is susceptible of incrementation. The fourth sense, on the other hand, belongs to the occasion as *concrete* and is *not* susceptible of incrementation. In this last sense, individuality signifies any entity that is *the completely determinate product of a completed process of self-causation.* Once more, this sense of individuality can be predicated only of actual occasions and, derivatively, of some societies of actual occasions. But an occasion is an individual, in this fourth sense of the term, only in the superjective phase of its existence. Similarly, in this sense of the term a society is an individual only if it has ceased to endure. An individual thus conceived is determinate in every respect and is intolerant of any addition (PR 72). In this last sense, then, the individuality of an actual occasion is "the outcome of whatever can be ascribed to it in the way of quality or relationship" (PR 122). What can be ascribed to it in the way of *quality* is its *definiteness;* what can be ascribed to it in the way of *relationship* is its *position.* The attained actuality is the final, individual synthesis of position and definiteness.

To reconcile the last three senses of individuality we must notice that, in every occasion, minimal individuality is necessarily superseded by concrescent individuality, which in turn is necessarily superseded by concrete individuality. We can thus subsume all three senses under a general sense of individuality which is attributable to, and only to, entities that either are, or have been, or are about to be self-realizing. In this manner, we bring the notion of individuality, as Whitehead apparently intended, into near-synonymity with the interrelated notions of actuality and self-realization. In particular, the distinction between the third and fourth senses of individuality can then be construed as corresponding respectively to the distinction between an actuality in attainment and an attained actuality (PR 326) or, equivalently, to the distinction between the self-realizing subject and the self-realized superject (PR 340).

In equating the individuality of an occasion with its self-realization, we must not allow ourselves to forget that an occasion's self-realization starts from the occasion's *given* phases of existence—the phases produced by the macroscopic process of efficient causation. Self-realization is self-completion. The entity which is completing itself has been thrown into existence by the transcendent creativity of transition. As the product of transition, the entity finds itself existing with a completely determinate position but with a minimally determinate definiteness. It is a particular, barely clothed in the subjective forms of its conformal feelings, and endowed with an initial subjective aim inherited from God. Its self-causation starts from that aim (PR 373–74). Thus, "an actual entity in the temporal world is to be conceived as originated by physical experience with its process of completion motivated by consequent, conceptual experience initially derived from God" (PR 524). What is to be completed is the determination of the entity's definiteness. Accordingly, the entity's process of self-completion—its concrescence or self-realization—is its autonomous passage from the incomplete definiteness of the conformal phase to the complete definiteness of the satisfaction. In this sense, "definition is the soul of actuality: the attainment of a peculiar definiteness is the final cause which animates a particular process; and its attainment halts its process" (PR 340). With this attainment, the occasion finally exists as a fully-clothed particular—clothed with the complex definiteness of its final, integral subjective form (PR 82). "The point to be noticed is that the actual entity, in a state of process during which it is not fully definite, determines its own ultimate definiteness. This is the whole point of moral responsibility" (PR 390).

8. Self-identity and self-diversity

Throughout the preceding discussions of the actual entity's manifold reality, of its multiple locations, of its aboriginal and unique position, and of its gradual, autonomous acquisition of definiteness, I have been trying to elucidate certain ultimate notions of Whitehead's metaphysics which bear directly on the related organic conceptions of solidarity, particularity, and individuality. Of special interest are the contrasting notions of the self-identity and the self-diversity of an actual entity. These notions find systematic, but cryptic, expression in the organic categoreal scheme, but are most evident in the twentieth through twenty-fourth Categories of Explanation—most evident, that is, if allowances are made for what these categories imply, but leave unstated, about the nature of actual entities.

Taken together, the twentieth through twenty-fourth Categories constitute an attempt to reconcile the self-identity of an actual entity with the self-diversity of roles it plays in its own self-formation and in the formation of all actual entities later than itself. When the full import of these categories is adequately interpreted, they explain how an actual entity can remain self-identical in respect to the successive phases of its self-immanent existence and in respect to the manifold modes of its self-transcendent existence. But they explain, in addition, how an actual entity can be self-diverse in respect to the many phases of its becoming and in respect to the many objectifications of its being. Finally, they explain how an actual entity can be involved in its own creation without performing the impossible feat of bringing itself into actual existence from sheer non-existence.

The earlier considerations of this chapter, together with the examination of the principle of process in Chapter One, and of the principles of relativity, ontology, and creativity in Chapters Two and Three, have already provided a significant elucidation of the twentieth through twenty-fourth Categories of Explanation. However, since these five Categories are crucial for the final understanding of the particularity, individuality, and solidarity of actual entities to be developed in the next two chapters, it will be helpful to end the present chapter with an explication of their full metaphysical import.

As their explication unfolds, it will be evident that these five Categories illuminate, and are illuminated by, the four basic principles studied in the first three chapters. This should not come as a surprise. The organic categories complement and supplement one another. For that reason, whatever a given category leaves implicit is as important as what it makes explicit. Each category provides either a partial glimpse of the particular individuality of actual entities or a partial glimpse of the solidarity of actual entities. Taken together, the organic categories give expression to Whitehead's fundamental vision of the universe as a solidarity of creative individuals. My point is that to understand Whitehead's vision we must read his categories as supplementing each other's omissions and compressions.

In the categoreal scheme, the twentieth Category of Explanation reads as follows:

> That to 'function' means to contribute determination to the actual entities in the nexus of some actual world. Thus the determinateness and self-identity of one entity cannot be abstracted from the community of the diverse functionings of all entities. 'Determination' is analysable into 'definiteness' and 'position', where 'definiteness' is the illustration of select eternal objects, and 'position' is relative status in a nexus of actual entities. (PR 38)

The first thing to notice is that this category bears the imprint of the relativity principle. This fundamental principle, let us remember, is the fourth Category of Explanation and tells us, in effect, "that no entity can be abstracted from its capacity to function as an object in the process of the actual world. 'To function as an object' is 'to be a determinant of the definiteness [and position] of an actual occurrence'" (PR 371).[11] The twentieth Category of Explanation, on the other hand, after defining 'the functioning of an entity' in terms of 'the determination it contributes to an actual entity', goes on to express a principle which is almost the exact converse of the relativity principle: that no actual entity can be abstracted from the functioning in it of all entities of all types.[12] For this reason, the twentieth Category of Explanation may be regarded as a corollary to the principle of relativity.

The twentieth Category, it should next be noticed, fails to make explicit that by 'function' we are to understand not only any realized contribution to the determinateness of an actuality, but also any activity whereby such a contribution is realized. That 'to function' also has the latter sense is in fact made explicit by Whitehead in the next three Categories of Explanation. Nonetheless, the point I wish to emphasize now is that if we limit the meaning of 'function' to the former sense only, then 'to function' simply means 'to be a realized determinant of an actuality'. This limitation unnecessarily abstracts the realized determinant from the activity which procured its realization. This is precisely what Whitehead wishes to avoid by broadening the sense of 'to function'. To capture the full sense of the term, it is necessary to explain that 'to function' also means 'to be an activity effecting the determination of an actual entity'.

In view of the discussions of the preceding sections, it should be obvious that the second sense of 'to function' remains unstated in the twentieth Category because Whitehead is there considering the actual entity as completely determinate and thus as abstracted from the activity of realization which was its own becoming. What the Category emphasizes is that the determinateness and self-identity of the *completed* actuality cannot be abstracted from the objective functionings of all earlier actualities, which jointly determine its position, nor from the objective functionings of all unrestrictedly ingressed eternal objects, which jointly determine its definiteness. But the Category leaves implicit both the presupposed macroscopic process of transition whereby the past actualities acquire their objective functioning, and the presupposed microscopic process of concrescence whereby a selection of eternal objects acquire their objective functioning. In other words, the twentieth Category leaves unstated both the transcendent creative process by which the past actualities are causally objectified so as to be constituents of the new actuality's objective content, and the immanent creative process by which the new actuality autonomously selects the eternal objects which, once it has unrestrictedly ingressed them, will be constituents of the actuality's own subjective form. Moreover, by considering the actuality as already completed, the Category fails to make explicit the full contrast between the actuality's *given*, *aboriginal* position and its *self-realized*, *acquired* definiteness, as well as the parallel contrast between transition and concrescence.

By leaving unstated the contrasting contributions which transition and concrescence make to the determination of an actual occasion, the twentieth Category of Explanation obscures the fact that every occasion is both other-caused and self-caused, both other-realized and self-realized. Or, to put it in the language most pertinent to our immediate concern, the twentieth Category obscures the fact that every actuality is both other-functioned and self-functioned. For this reason, to make explicit that transition and concrescence are creative activities contributing to the determination of an actual entity is to bring attention to the second sense of 'to function'. In this respect, however, the activity of transition is *merely a vehicle for the objective functioning of the earlier actualities*, whereas the activity of concrescence, though a vehicle for the objective functioning of eternal objects, is *nothing less than the new actuality functioning in respect to itself*. Because of this self-functioning, when the new actuality is completely determinate or satisfied, it will be the case that every entity in its correlative universe, *including the actuality itself*, will have functioned in its determination. This is precisely why the completed actuality "cannot be abstracted from the community of the diverse functionings of *all* entities" (PR 38; italics mine).

Finally, it should be noticed that every actuality is other-functioned in respect to its position, but is primarily self-functioned in respect to its definiteness. The imprint of the ontological principle on the twentieth Category of Explanation is thus revealed. Indeed, the distinction between the position and the definiteness of an attained actuality is practically the distinction between the contributions which efficient causation and final causation have made, respectively, to the determinateness of that actuality. Accordingly, the twentieth Category may be construed as a corollary to the ontological principle also.

The next three Categories of Explanation explicate some of the points that are implicit in the twentieth Category. These Categories read as follows:

> (xxi) An entity is actual, when it has significance for itself. By this is meant that an actual entity functions in respect to its own determination. Thus an actual entity combines self-identity with self-diversity.
> (xxii) That an actual entity by functioning in respect to itself plays diverse roles in self-formation without losing its self-identity. It is self-creative; and in its process of creation transforms its diversity of roles into one coherent role. Thus 'becoming' is the transformation of incoherence into coherence, and in each particular instance ceases with this attainment.
> (xxiii) That this self-functioning is the real internal constitution of an actual entity. It is the 'immediacy' of the actual entity. An actual entity is called the 'subject' of its own immediacy. (PR 38)

The joint effect of these three Categories is to define 'actuality' in terms of 'self-function'. For though the immediate definition of 'actuality' is given in terms of 'self-significance', 'self-significance' is itself defined in terms of 'self-function'. Indeed, the twenty-first Category could, and should, be construed as the organic *principle of actuality*. It provides a definition of 'actuality' that closely parallels the definition of 'entity' provided by the principle of relativity. It defines being an *actuality* in terms of being *self-functioning*, just as the relativity principle defines being an *entity* in terms of being *other*-functioning. Each actuality, therefore, is significant for itself, just as each entity is significant for other entities.

The principle of actuality and the other two Categories now under examination may be construed as corollaries to the ninth Category of Explanation, the principle of process. According to this principle, let us remember, the self-realizing subject *creates* the self-realized superject. Thus, in formulating the process principle, Whitehead is mindful of the fact that every "actual entity is to be conceived both as a subject presiding over its own immediacy of becoming, and a superject which is the atomic creature exercising its function of objective immortality" (PR 71). Indeed, the preceding eighth Category of Explanation states, as we saw in Chapter One, "that two descriptions are required for an actual entity: (a) one which is analytical of its potentiality for 'objectification' in the becoming of other actual entities, and (b) another which is analytical of the process which constitutes its own becoming" (PR 34). The whole point of the process principle, therefore, is to establish that *how* the occasion as subject becomes creates *what* that *same* occasion as superject *is*, "so that the two descriptions of an actual entity are not independent" (PR 34). All this we saw in the earlier chapter. My point now is that the principle of process is concerned with the peculiar genetic relation between (and thus with both) the actuality in attainment and the attained actuality.

In contrast with the principle of process, the three Categories now being examined are concerned almost exclusively with the self-functioning subject and not with the self-functioned superject. Their main topic is the process which is the occasion's own internal, or immanent, creation. They focus on the occasion as a self-forming, self-determining, self-significant, concrescent subject. Put another way, they deal with the occasion insofar as it is an individual in the third sense of 'individuality' specified above. However, as the last sentence of the twenty-second Category reminds us, and as we have seen in connection with the principle of process, the concrescent subject aims at, and supersessionally gives way to, the concrete superject. The actuality in attainment is, after all, the becoming of the attained actuality. The attained actuality is *what has become* (PR 107, 207). Therefore, we cannot, except provisionally and for reasons of emphasis, equate being actual with being an activity of self-functioning.

Whitehead's true doctrine, I have argued, is that every actual entity is *both* a self-realizing subject *and* a self-realized superject. In this regard, it is as much of a mistake to abstract the actuality of the subjective process from the actuality of the superjective product as it is to abstract the actuality of the superjective product from the actuality of the subjective process (PR 129). Accordingly, we must construe an entity as actual if, and only if, it either is, or *has been*, self-functioning. The subject is actual because it is the occasion existing as in its phases of self-functioning activity; the superject is actual because it is that self-same occasion existing as in its final, immortal phase. In other words, the superject is actual because it is the same occasion that *was* self-functioning in its supersessionally earlier phases of subjective existence. Thus, to paraphrase Whitehead: an actuality is self-functioning, and whatever is self-functioning is an actuality; an actual entity is at once the subject of self-functioning, and the superject which is self-functioned (PR 340). My point is that the principle of actuality should read: an entity is actual when it has, *or has had*, significance for itself; by this is meant that an actual entity functions, *or has functioned*, in respect to its own determination.

The principle of actuality and the principle of process alike obscure the fact that by the self-creation of an actual occasion Whitehead means no more than its self-completion. These two principles, therefore, must always be interpreted in light of the ontological principle—the principle of *efficient*, and final, causation (PR 36–37). Accordingly, the self-functioning of an occasion is simply the process of autonomous decisions by which the occasion completes the determination of its definiteness through the acquisition of subjective forms and the integration of feelings (PR 249). But the occasion thus functioning in respect to its own determination was first brought into existence by a process of transition determined by the transcendent decisions of the earlier occasions and of God (PR 248). The self-functioning of an actual occasion, then, is its self-causation; but no actual occasion is entirely self-caused; each is also the product of efficient other-causation (PR 134, 228, 320).

In this respect, as we saw in Chapter Three, the definition of 'actuality' which Whitehead gives in terms of 'decision' is far clearer and much less ambiguous than the definitions of it which he gives in terms of 'self-realization' and 'self-function':

> Just as 'potentiality for process' is the meaning of the more general term 'entity', or 'thing'; so 'decision' is the additional meaning imported by the word 'actual' into the phrase 'actual entity'. 'Actuality' is the decision amid 'potentiality'. It represents stubborn fact which cannot be evaded. The real internal constitution of an actual entity

progressively constitutes a decision conditioning the creativity which transcends that actuality. (PR 68–69)

A stubborn fact in this regard is the immortal actuality of a superject (PR 196–97, 335–36, 366). There is no tearing the self-functioning of an actuality in attainment from the attained actuality of the stubborn facts in its past nor from the attained actuality of the stubborn fact which it is itself about to become. The earlier facts decide its dative phase and, *via* aesthetic conformation, its phase of conformal feelings and its phase of conceptual reproduction (PR 227, 249). In turn, its own existence as superject will constitute a new stubborn fact deciding the dative phases of occasions in its future. In this manner, "an actual entity arises from decisions *for* it, and by its very existence provides decisions *for* other actual entities which supersede it" (PR 68). These decisions are, in both cases, *transcendent* decisions. In between the transcendent decision *from* which it arises and the transcendent decision *from* which its successors arise, the actual entity exists as completing itself by its *immanent* decisions respecting the determination of its own final definiteness (PR 227, 248–49).

Accordingly, what an improved formulation of the principle of actuality should make clear is that the actuality of the self-functioning subject is the actuality associated with *immanent* decision, whereas the actuality of the self-functioned superject is the actuality associated with *transcendent* decision. Similarly, what an improved formulation of the principle of process should make clear is that *how* the self-functioning subject *becomes*, in respect to the determination of its definiteness, creates, *in part*, what the self-functioned superject *is*. The other part of the superject's *being* is, of course, its other-functioned, determinate position, the position it shares with every phase of the process of which it is the outcome. Both principles should make clear the full nature of each actual entity insofar as it is other-functioned, self-functioning, self-functioned, and other-functioning. In other words, they should make clear the four stages constitutive of an actual entity's existential history: (i) the datum or decision received; (ii) the process of concrescence or subjective self-realization; (iii) the satisfaction or self-realized superject; and (iv) the causal objectifications or decisions transmitted (PR 227).

An actual occasion's position is the one element of its nature which is common to all four stages of its existential history. Precisely because its position is invariant, the occasion remains self-identical throughout the different stages of its existence. On the other hand, the occasion's definiteness is different in each stage of its history: it is completely absent in the dative phase; minimally determinate in its conformal phase; progressively enriched and increasingly determinate in the subjective phases; completely determinate in the satisfaction; and abstracted from in varying ways in its causal objectifications. Precisely because its definiteness is variable, the occasion exhibits *self-diversity* throughout the different stages of its existence. Thus, the invariant position and the variable definiteness of an actual occasion are the very reasons why its nature combines self-identity with self-diversity.

By reason of the initial indeterminateness of its definiteness, the self-same occasion must play a diversity of roles in respect to its self-formation. As autonomous subject, it has to provide itself with a determinate definiteness that transforms the initial incoherence of its conformal feelings into the final coherence of its satisfaction. But the phase by phase acquisition of its final definiteness and coherence means that the occasion in a later phase of its becoming is diverse from itself in an earlier phase. The occasion is *not* changing, but it *is* becoming.[13] When its definiteness has been rendered fully determinate, the occasion *has* become. It is now a determinate satisfaction with unavoidable consequences.

With the attainment of its satisfaction, the occasion loses the self-diversity inherent in its function of *self-formation* but gains the self-diversity inherent in its function of *other-formation*. The latter mode of self-diversity is not even alluded to in the three Categories of Explanation we have been examining. Nonetheless, it is all but explicit in other Categories of Explanation—the fourth, the sixth, the eighth, the eighteenth, the twenty-fourth and the twenty-fifth. Our immediate concern is with the twenty-fourth Category. It reads as follows:

> (xxiv) The functioning of one actual entity in the self-creation of another actual entity is the 'objectification' of the former for the latter actual entity. The functioning of an eternal object in the self-creation of an actual entity is the 'ingression' of the eternal object in the actual entity. (PR 38)

This Category, which we previously examined in Chapter Three, is yet another corollary to the principles of relativity and ontology.

The relativity principle tells us that all entities of all types have objective functioning. Read in abstraction from the four immediately preceding Categories of Explanation, the twenty-fourth Category simply provides specific terms with which to refer to the objective functionings of actual entities and eternal objects—'objectification' and 'ingression', respectively. But read in the light of the full metaphysical import of the twentieth through twenty-third Categories, the twenty-fourth Category serves as a reminder that the *position* of an actual entity is determined by the *objectifications* in it of the already completed actualities of its correlative universe, and that the *definiteness* of an actual entity is determined by the *ingression* into it of eternal objects selected by the subject from the data of its conceptual prehensions. The former determination is the outcome of the *efficient* process of transition; the latter determination is the outcome of the *teleological* process of concrescence. Accordingly, the twenty-fourth Category serves as a reminder that every actual entity is at once the product of the efficient past and the product of its own teleological self-causation (PR 134, 228, 320). For this reason, this Category is a corollary to the ontological principle as well as to the relativity principle.

Thus far we have considered the twenty-fourth Category of Explanation in the guise of a reminder that "each occasion has its physical inheritance and its mental reaction which drives it on to its self-completion," and that each occasion thereby unites "its formal immediacy with objective otherness" (AI 244–45). But we may view it, in addition, as a reminder that the self-same reality of an individual actuality can—indeed, *must*—be considered both *formally* and *objectively* (PR 336). This is why, according to Whitehead,

> in enquiring about any one individual we must ask how other individuals enter 'objectively' into the unity of its own experience. This unity of its own experience is that individual existing *formally*. We must also enquire how it enters into the 'formal' existence of other things; and this entrance is that individual existing *objectively*, that is to say—existing abstractly, exemplifying only some elements of its formal contents. (S 26–27)

My point is that Whitehead, in formulating the first half of the twenty-fourth Category, is mindful of the fact that every actual entity is *subject-superject*, and of the correlative fact that every actual entity, *in virtue of its existence as superject*, is causally objectified in every actuality later than itself (PR 130, 134, 165).

Each causal objectification of the superject is a numerically different instance of its particular self-identity. In this sense, the self-diversity of the completed occasion is its manifold extrinsic reality. But the self-diversity which is to be attributed to the superject in its objective functionings goes beyond the fact of numerical diversity. This is so precisely because each causal objectification abstracts from the full formal content of the superjective satisfaction (S 25–26; PR 337). Since the form and degree which the abstraction takes can vary from one objectification to another, it follows that the causal objectifications of any given occasion *may* differ from each other qualitatively in addition to *having* to differ numerically.

What I now wish to emphasize, in this regard, is that the causal objectifications of any given superject *may* differ from each other in respect to the *definiteness* they each exhibit, but *cannot* differ from each other in respect to the *position* they each exhibit. The reason for this is twofold. First, the causal objectificiation of one occasion in another can be construed as the self-revelation of the former for the latter only if the objectification exhibits for the latter the self-identity of the former (PR 347). Second, numerically different objectifications can be construed as the causal objectifications of one self-same occasion only if they each exhibit the self-identity of that occasion. Accordingly, since the self-identity of an occasion is a function of its determinate position, it follows that the causal objectifications of that occasion cannot abstract from its determinate position. This conclusion is implicit in Whitehead's claim that "actual entities are objectified with the retention of their extensive relationships" (PR 105); for, as we saw earlier, the position of an actual occasion is a function of the extensive structure of its dative phase.

The abstractions involved in the causal objectifications of an actual occasion, it should now be obvious, are in each case an abstraction from its determinate definiteness. Causal objectification, let us remember, is the transmission of a component feeling, and not of the total satisfaction (PR 364). This means that the occasion is reproduced in the guise of being the subject of one or another of its component feelings, and not in the guise of being the subject of the final, integral feeling that is the satisfaction. The simpler the component feeling by which the occasion is objectified, the greater the abstraction there is from the occasion's total definiteness, or subjective form. In this manner, the distinction between an occasion's position and its definiteness enables us to understand how one and the same occasion may be causally objectified in many different modes (PR 34). In other words, the distinction permits us to understand the self-identity and the self-diversity of each attained actuality.

I have now come full circle in my examination of the organic doctrine of position. I began by considering its relevance to understanding an occasion's manifold extrinsic reality and, after examining its relevance to understanding an occasion's supersessional phases of intrinsic reality, I have returned to the original topic. In effect, I have been advancing an interpretation of this doctrine that permits us to understand how an actual occasion can be self-identical throughout all its phases of self-immanent existence, and how each causal mode of an occasion's self-transcendent existence can be self-identical with, yet numerically different from, the superject of which it is a function. But this interpretation permits us to understand, in addition, how organic particulars, of whatever category of existence, can be repeated with retention of their individual determinateness and self-identity.

In this last regard, we must remember that prehensions, subjective forms and nexūs, as well as actual occasions, are described as particulars by Whitehead.[14] However, only actual occasions are self-realizing particulars, for the realization of prehensions, subjective forms, and nexūs is always parasitic on the self-realization of actual occasions. Now, in order to provide a general explanation for the reproduction, with retention of self-identity, of particulars of all categoreal types, the organic philosophy must hold that *a particular is any entity whose essential character assigns to it a determinate position in the extenso-genetic order of the universe*. With this definition, each actual occasion is obviously a particular, since its real essence assigns to it a position which belongs to no other particular *of the same categoreal type*. Moreover, with this definition, prehensions, subjective forms, and nexūs may also be construed as particulars, since their real essences respectively assign to each of them a determinate position. The position of these non-self-realizing particulars is in each case derivative either from the position of the actual occasion of which the particular in question (a subjective form or a prehension) is a constituent, or from the positions of the several actualities by which the entity in question (a nexus) is constituted.

It must be maintained, in this regard, that the complex subjective form of an actual occasion embodies the self-aspect of that occasion (*e.g.*, the complex subjective form of C is the embodiment of c^*/C^* and also, transcendentally, of $c^*/c^*/D^*$); accordingly, the subjective form of a given occasion must be assigned the same position as is assigned to that occasion. Similarly, the prehensions belonging to, or originated by, a given occasion have the same position as that occasion, that is to say, they have the same position as their subject. Finally, nexūs can be dated and located relatively to one another; but their dates and locations are functions of the positions of their component actualities (PR 351–52). Thus, all organic particulars can be dated and located.

Insofar as actual occasions are reproduced in later occasions, their component subjective forms and prehensions, as well as the nexūs which they constitute, are also reproduced in the later occasions. But by virtue of their determinate positions, each and every one of the particulars in question—be it an actual occasion, a subjective form, a prehension, or a nexus—retains its determinate self-identity in each reproductive instance. In this manner, the doctrine of position enables us to understand how the organic particulars can be among the reproducible elements of the organic universe. For, according to Whitehead, as we saw earlier,

> The oneness of the universe, and the oneness of each element in the universe, repeat themselves to the crack of doom in the creative advance from creature to creature, each creature including in itself the whole of history and exemplifying the self-identity of things and their mutual diversities. (PR 347–48)

9. Summary

We have been examining the related doctrines of objectification, position, and self-identity in light of the interpretation of metaphysical extension advanced in the preceding chapter. The examination has yielded a number of important conclusions.

First, when allowances are made for the fact that Whitehead's philosophical works are meant to supplement each other's omissions and compressions, the extensive continuum emerges as a formative element of the temporal world, and hence as a metaphysical principle of the organic philosophy. Indeed, the strikingly similar accounts which Whitehead gives of extension and creativity indicate that the two are to be construed as indissoluble aspects of the ultimate reality underlying the becoming, the being, and the solidarity of all actual entities. Creativity is the dynamic principle on which the essential genetic development of the universe is grounded; extension is the static principle on which the essential solidarity of the universe is grounded. But the two principles condition one another. In their unity they constitute an extenso-creative matrix which is at once the whereby of all becoming and the wherein of all interconnected existence.

Second, in virtue of the metaphysical properties of extension, each actual occasion has a twofold reality: the one, single and intrinsic, is the self-immanent reality of its formal existence; the other, multiple and extrinsic, is the self-transcendent reality of its objective existence. But, also by reason of the metaphysical properties of extension, the two modes of an occasion's reality involve one another, so that the occasion is never simply one or the other mode, but is always both. Thus, the complete reality of an occasion encompasses both its self-immanent, and its self-transcendent, existence. The former mode of existence is its reality insofar as it occupies its own proper region of the extensive continuum; the latter mode is its reality insofar as it occupies modal components of proper regions other than its own. The proper regions from which occasions have arisen, are arising, or will arise, involve one another modally. This means that the intrinsic reality of one occasion involves the extrinsic reality of all occasions, including the occasion's own extrinsic reality. Thus, by reason of the modality of extension, all actual occasions are objectively each in the others—at least in respect to the proper regions of extension which they embody, or will embody, each its own.

Third, an actual occasion has a multiplicity of absolute locations in the extensive continuum; but, in each of those locations, the occasion exhibits one and the same position in the extenso-creative order of the universe. An actual occasion cannot share its position with any other actual occasion, for the self-identity of each occasion is a function of its unique position. In turn, the position of an occasion is a function of the unique modal, or objective, structure of the proper region serving as the extensive standpoint of its self-immanent reality. This means that the unique particularity attributable to an actual occasion cannot be abstracted from the metaphysical properties of eternal extension. Moreover, it is by reason of the transitivity of modality that the self-transcendent reality of an actual occasion reveals, in each instance, the exact self-same position revealed by its self-immanent reality. Thus, it is by reason of the modal property of extension that the objectifications of an actual occasion are each an instantiation of the occasion's unique self-identity. Finally, it is only by reason of this property that the extensive standpoint of each actual occasion constitutes an indicative system assigning a different unique position to each occasion objectified therein, as well as to the occasion to which the standpoint belongs.

Fourth, the position of an actual occasion grounds the self-identity exhibited by an occasion throughout its successive phases of self-immanent existence. It is an aboriginal feature of the occasion, of a piece with its dative phase. In contrast, the definiteness of an occasion is a feature which it gradually acquires in the subsequent phases of its becoming. Only in the superjective satisfaction, therefore, are the position and definiteness of an actual occasion equally determinate. To lose sight of the distinction between an occasion's aboriginal position and its acquired definiteness is to render meaningless the autonomous self-causation which the organic philosophy attributes to every actual occasion. It is also to render meaningless

Whitehead's claim that actual entities become but do not change. For what Whitehead means is that an actual occasion, through its autonomous process of self-completion, becomes more definite without thereby altering its positionally-grounded self-identity.

Fifth, the distinction between an occasion's aboriginal position and its acquired definiteness allows us to develop a contrast, mostly implicit in Whitehead's writings, between an occasion *qua* bare particular and that same occasion *qua* fully-clothed individual. Individuality can then be understood as an enrichment of particularity. Since this enrichment is the product of self-causation, and since it is exhibited by some social nexūs, as well as by actual entities, the contrast in question provides a metaphysical foundation on which to build a theory of organic existentialism. To be an individual, in the sense most relevant for such a theory, is *to exist for oneself as in a process of autonomous self-formation*. This, for Whitehead, is the necessary basis of moral responsibility.

Sixth, every actual entity combines self-identity with self-diversity. The twentieth through twenty-fourth Categories of Explanation constitute an attempt to give categoreal expression to this important doctrine. The self-identity of an actuality in its phases of intrinsic reality, and in every instance of its extrinsic reality, is a function of its invariant position. The self-diversity of an actuality from phase to phase, and from objectification to objectification, is a function of its variable definiteness. The five categories in question also provide an understanding of the nature of actual entities in terms of objective and formal functioning. An actual entity is rendered determinate by the functioning in it of all entities in its universe, including its own functioning in respect to itself. Thus, to be actual is to be, or to have been, self-functioning; but no actual entity is merely self-functioning or self-functioned; it is also other-functioned and other-functioning.

These six conclusions are presupposed by any adequate understanding of the individuality and solidarity of actual entities. The final development of such an understanding is the general topic of the next two chapters.

SEVEN

Extensional Solidarity and the Dative Phase

My elucidation of the manifold reality and self-same position exhibited by an actual occasion has almost exhausted the elucidation of solidarity itself. For I have now shown to a great extent how discrete actualities can be mutually immanent. Nonetheless, a number of interrelated explanatory and interpretive tasks remain to be completed. First of all, I have to explain how the entire correlative universe of an actual occasion is ontologically presupposed by, and involved in, the becoming and the being of that actual occasion. This requires showing not only that each previously completed actuality functions, however negligibly, in the becoming of the novel occasion, but also that every formative element of the temporal world plays an essential role in that becoming. Second, a fifth formative element—or, equivalently, a third aspect of the Ultimate— must be carefully explicated, and its relevance to the organic conception of solidarity must be gradually explored. Third, I must develop further the essential role played by extension in Whitehead's metaphysical theory. In particular, I must explain (i) how extension establishes and preserves the internal relatedness of an actual occasion to its correlative universe, and (ii) how the metaphysical properties of extension are presupposed by any adequate analysis of an actual occasion. Fourth, I must demonstrate the relevance of the organic theory of extension to the organic theories of perception and knowledge. Fifth, I must distinguish three interrelated senses of solidarity: extensional, objective, and functional. Finally, sixth, I must explain how the organic philosophy reconciles the solidarity of all actual existents with the autonomous individuality of every actual existent.

These remaining tasks do not lend themselves easily to a linear fulfill-ment. They involve topics whose interrelatedness is largely a function of the categoreal coherence exhibited by the organic metaphysics. To pro-vide the discussion with some semblance of order, in this chapter and in the next I shall reconstruct the existential history of C, the now familiar occasion of the example under surveyance throughout the previous chap-ter. The first order of business, and one to which I shall devote much of the present chapter, is the reconstruction of the emergence of C's dative phase. There should be no doubt that this is the best place to start; for according to Whitehead, "it is impossible to scrutinize too carefully the character to be assigned to the datum in the act of experience. The whole philosophical system depends on it" (PR 238). Thus, in this chapter, a careful scrutiny of the emergence and nature of the dative phase will permit me to fulfill the first three tasks just outlined, and also to explain the meaning of extensional solidarity. In the next and final chapter, the understanding of the dative phase achieved through that scrutiny will enable me to complete the remaining tasks.

1. The relevance of attained actualities and extension

I begin by considering the pure potentiality from which C is to arise. The pure potentiality comprises the creativity, the multiplicity of eternal objects, and a potential region of the extensive continuum. This potential region will be termed C^{**}. Now C^{**} is a potential division, or a potential proper region, of the extensive continuum. It is an extensive quantum that could become the standpoint of an actual occasion. However, considered in itself, the extensive continuum offers no reason why C^{**} should be transformed into C^*, the standpoint of C. Or to speak with wider gener-ality:

> In the mere extensive continuum there is no principle to determine what regional quanta [*sic*] shall be atomized, so as to form the real perspective standpoint for the primary data constituting the basic phase in the concrescence of an actual entity. (PR 104)

Nevertheless, in keeping with the ontological principle, there must be a reason for the transformation of C^{**} into C^*, or simply, for the becoming of C^*, since that transformation, or that becoming, constitutes a decision amid potentiality, or, in other words, a selection from incompatible possibilities for regional realization.

This decision is precisely what pure potentiality can never provide because, according to the ontological principle itself, every decision is to be referred to one or more actualities (PR 68). It is a mistake, then, to expect that an actual occasion could arise exclusively from what the universe is by way of pure potentiality. "A new creation has to arise from the actual world as much as from pure potentiality; it arises from the total universe and not solely from its mere abstract elements" (PR 123). Accordingly, the reason for the initiation of C's becoming, or what is the same, the reason for the transformation of C^{**} into C^*, is to be sought in the attained actualities of the actual world correlative with C (PR 105).

The reason being sought must explain (a) why the origination of C's becoming occurs just when it does, rather than earlier or later, and (b) why C embodies C^* rather than some other extensive region. Now (a) means that the transcendent decision bringing about the transformation of C^{**} into C^* must be referred to an actual occasion whose completion is immediately antecedent to the initiation of C's becoming; and (b) means that the occasion in question must be a determinant, though not necessarily the only determinant, of the extensive standpoint of its successor. In the example under consideration, B is the requisite occasion. Thus, the superjective existence of B is somehow the immediate efficient cause of the transformation of C^{**} into C^*, where C^* may be construed as symbolizing both the extensive standpoint embodied by C, and the dative phase of C's existence (PR 104, 124).

To say that B is the immediate cause of C is not to deny that every superject in the actual world of C is an efficient cause of C. But most, if not all, of the occasions in C's actual world were superjects before B itself became a superject. Yet the initiation of C's becoming did not occur until immediately after B had completed its becoming. Hence, in respect to the creation of C, the causal efficacy of the other occasions somehow presupposes the superjective existence of B. Thus, to speak again with wider generality, "the whole antecedent world conspires to produce a new occasion. But some one occasion in an important way conditioned the formation of a successor" (MT 225–26).

The question now is: How does superject B constitute a reason for the transformation of C^{**} into C^*? We want to know, in effect, how the termination of B's becoming can be the cause of the creation of C at C^*. Of course, any explanation of how B is the immediate cause of C must involve an appeal to the principle of creativity. According to that principle, the ultimate character of the universe is such that every disjunctive many must be reduced, *via* reproduction, to a conjunctive many within a novel one (PR 31–32). The problem now is to explain the *when* and *where* of the novel one—*C*, in our example. Fortunately, the *when* of *C*'s becoming, or of the initiation of *C*'s becoming, *is* explained by the principle of creativity itself. For the termination of *B*'s becoming constitutes *B* into the newest member of a new disjunctive many. But this new disjunctive many must be immediately reduced to a conjunctive many within a novel one.

> For the fundamental inescapable fact is the creativity in virtue of which there can be no 'many things' which are not subordinated in a concrete unity. Thus a set of all actual occasions is by the nature of things a standpoint for another concrescence which elicits a concrete unity from those many actual occasions. (PR 321–22)

Hence, every actual occasion must have an immediate successor (PR 107). But this means that the termination of *B*'s becoming is indeed the cause of, or the reason for, the initiation of *C*'s becoming. In short, the creative process of immediate transition from *B* to *C* is the unavoidable outcome of the ultimate character of the universe (PR 322).

I have yet to explain how *B* can be the reason for the *where*, or extensive locus, of *C*'s becoming. Whitehead, it should be noted, never attempted such an explanation. But his theory of the metaphysical extensive continuum, as interpreted and developed in this essay, does provide ample basis for the required explanation. To achieve this explanation, we must bear in mind two things: first, that the subjective aim of an actual occasion "is at intensity of feeling . . . in the immediate subject, and . . . in the *relevant* future" (PR 41); and second, that an actual occasion can feel the different potential regions, or subregions, constituting its own regional standpoint (PR 482–83, 262). Thus, the existence of feelings of bare regions, explicitly asserted by Whitehead, justifies our assumption that the anticipatory feeling associated with the subjective aim of an occasion involves some subregion of the modal presence, in that occasion, of the unactualized extension of its correlative universe. In our example, this means that *B* feels *!c**/fu**/&**/B** as the objective reality of the transcendent extensive region to be actualized and included by its immediate successor, *C*. The anticipated standpoint of *C* is the one most consonant with *B*'s subjective aim as originally derived from *B*'s hybrid feeling of God's primordial nature. Accordingly, God is a second actuality anchoring the transcendental decision to transform C^{**} into C^*.

Two aspects of the theory of metaphysical extension are immediately relevant to the task at hand: first, that *!c**/fu**/&**/B** refers transcendentally to C^{**}; and second, that all standpoints, whether actual or potential, "are coordinated as diverse determinations of one extensive continuum" (PR 103). This means that any two actual standpoints must exhibit as much coordination, or mutual modal mirroring, as it is in the ultimate nature of the universe to allow. But the universe is dynamic, always advancing from creature to creature, or what is the same, from novel standpoint to novel standpoint. Hence, the actual coordination of standpoints is an ongoing affair. Moreover, since a completed actuality cannot be changed, lest it lose its self-identity, all actual coordination of standpoints must refer to the adjustment of emerging standpoints, so as to coordinate them with the standpoints of the already attained actualities. The new is harmonized with the old.

In our example, this means that unless C be originated at C^*, the standpoint of C would not be completely coordinated with the standpoint of B; for the standpoint of B includes a modal differentiation, $!c^{**}/fu^{**}/\&^{**}/B^*$, that refers to C^{**} and imputes to it the function of being the standpoint of C. Thus, if C were not to embody C^*, there would be a lack of adjustment between what B^* mirrors as the standpoint of C and what would in fact be the standpoint of C. In other words, the anticipatory objectification of C in B would distort or misrepresent the true location of C if C did not in fact emerge where B anticipated it. Such a distortion, it must be remarked, would be inevitable if C^{**} had already been actualized, in part or in whole, by some of B's contemporaries. This is another reason for saying that there can only be as much coordination as the universe will allow. But barring those unfortunate conditions, the coordination of actual standpoints inherent in the ultimate nature of the universe would require and bring about the origination of C at C^*.

We must assume, therefore, that the creative transition from B to C will, under normal conditions, originate C at the extensive region where B anticipated it (i.e., C) would be originated. To that extent, then, B's superjective existence is the reason for, or the cause of, the transformation of C^{**} into C^*. We thus come to the conclusion that B is the immediate efficient cause of both the *where* and the *when* of C's becoming.

2. *The relevance of creativity and envisagement*

B can function as the immediate cause of C only insofar as its superjective existence and internal modal structure are taken into account by the macroscopic process that produces the dative phase of C's existence. In other words, the transition from B to C presupposes that the Creative Receptacle takes into account the state of the universe relative to the termination of *B*'s becoming. This means that the Creative Receptacle, or existential matrix, is *sensitive*, if I may so use the word, to its own successive states of actual and potential determinateness. This sensitivity of the matrix to itself is what Whitehead referred to as an *envisagement* belonging to the underlying activity of the universe (SMW 148–49). For reasons that will gradually appear, but which are almost obvious, I interpret envisagement as a *third* aspect of the existential matrix. This envisaging aspect of the matrix has been all but explicit in my earlier discussions of transition and efficient causation. I must now attempt to make its relevance fully explicit.

Attained actualities can function as efficient causes of a new occasion only if their superjective existence is taken into account by the macroscopic process begetting the dative phase of the new occasion. More generally, the universe as a whole—including its eternal objects and its extensiveness, as well as its actualities—can be involved in the becoming of a new occasion only if it is taken into account by the transcendent creative activity begetting the new occasion's dative phase. In other words, the transition from newly settled universe to newly emergent occasion presupposes that an individualizing manifestation of the eternal creativity takes into account the state of the universe relative to the origination of the new occasion. This taking into account of the universe by the transcendent creativity is not to be understood as belonging to, or as being part of, the new occasion's own subjective experience. For the occasion's subjective experience presupposes the existence of the occasion's dative phase, and the dative phase itself presupposes, and results from, the transcendent creativity's taking into account of a newly completed state of the universe. Therefore, the notion of *taking into account* must be construed as signifying an essential aspect of the universe's extenso-creative or existential matrix—the aspect whereby each transcendent, or individualizing, manifestation of the universe's creativeness is determined, limited, and enabled by the state of the universe relative to that manifestation.

Whitehead construes the universe's taking into account of its own states as a *threefold envisagement* belonging to the eternal creativity itself, independently of its individualized embodiments:

> the underlying activity, as conceived apart from the fact of realization, has three types of envisagement. These are: first, the envisagement of eternal objects; secondly, the envisagement of possibilities of value in respect to the synthesis of eternal objects; and lastly, the envisagement of the actual matter of fact which must enter into the

total situation which is achievable by the addition of the future.
(SMW 149)

The future to be added by the underlying creativity is, of course, a new
actual occasion. The actual matter of fact that must enter into the total
achievable situation is composed of the attained actualities already in
existence relative to the origination of the new occasion's earliest phase of
existence. The envisagement of possibilities of value in respect to the
synthesis of eternal objects has God's primordial nature as its terminus.
Accordingly, this mode of envisagement is only a special case of the
creativity's envisagement of matter of fact. It is the creativity's envisagement of the primordial conceptual fact. In this primordial fact, which
results from the primordial act of conceptual valuation, the eternal objects
constitute a well-ordered realm of possibilities. But the eternal objects are
not created by the primordial act. The primordial, or divine, activity
merely orders and evaluates them into a structured conceptual realm of
possible values. Thus, the eternal objects exist independently of the
primordial nature; as independently existing, however, they do not constitute a true realm, but do form a multiplicity which is eternally envisaged by the underlying creativity. Nonetheless, without the creativity's
envisagement of God's primordial nature, the individual eternal objects
would lack discriminable relevance to the actual matter of fact that must
enter into the composition of the occasion to be begotten (SMW 247–50).

The threefold envisagement whereby the universe as a whole determines the initial stage of a new occasion is an implicit presupposition of
the Category of the Ultimate. Envisagement is presupposed, in other
words, by the metaphysical functioning of the Creative Receptacle. For it
is not enough that the Receptacle be an extensive and creative reality; it
must also be an envisaging reality, capable of taking into account its own
factual states and its own potentialities. The point is that the Receptacle,
the Creativity, the Ultimate—or whatever else we may wish to call it—
must be able to take into account, or envisage, the existence of every new
disjunctive plurality of completely attained creatures before it can create,
relative to each new disjunction, the dative phase of a new creature. The
dative phase thus created, since it is a finite extensive region containing
within itself the objectification of the plurality in question, is the *real
potentiality* for that plurality of attained creatures to be synthesized into
the constitution and subjective experience of a novel creature. This real
potentiality, we must not forget, is a function of the metaphysical properties of extension; for "extension, apart from its spatialization and tem-

poralization, is that general scheme of relationships providing the capacity that many objects can be welded into the real unity of one experience" (PR 105). Thus, envisagement, extension, and creativity are all presupposed as aspects of that ultimate reality whereby the many become one and are increased by one.

Returning to the reconstruction of C's existential history, and using 'envisaging creativity' as synonymous with 'envisaging creative receptacle', I remark once more that the creativity's envisagement of the new multiplicity of attained actualities brought about by the perishing of B is crucial for the understanding of the process of transition from B to C. For B *qua* superject is in itself completely inactive. Its efficacy in bringing about the where and when of C's dative phase presupposes that its existence and modal structure is envisaged by the creativity (AI 230). To the envisaging creativity, the existence of superject B, and hence of a new disjunctive many, is the cue for the production of a new occasion; also, to the envisaging creativity, the modal structure of B's standpoint is the reason for creating that novel occasion at C^{**}, which thus becomes C^*, a new proper region of extension. That B's efficacy is dependent on the creativity which envisages it, and which creates C's dative phase, is one reason why Whitehead says that transition is the vehicle of the efficient cause (PR 320). The other reason is that transition, through abstractive repetition or causal objectification, carries the actual cause into the actual effect, there to condition the phases of concrescence (PR 320–21).

3. The relevance of eternal objects of the objective species

The creativity's envisagement of the multiplicity of eternal objects, particularly of those of the objective species, is also presupposed by the transition from B to C. For the creation of C^*, the new proper region which is at once the dative phase and the extensive standpoint of C, involves the ingression of eternal objects that establish the boundary and actual modal structure of the region in question. To understand why this is so, we must remember that the creation of C's standpoint is subject to the metaphysical determinations of the extensive continuum (PR 103). Accordingly, the standpoint of C must be a *proper* region, which means that it must have a boundary proper to itself (PR 546, Corrigenda; PNK 122). Also, the standpoint of C must be *separate*, which means that it must transcend, and be transcended by, all the other proper regions of extension. Finally, C's standpoint must be the *integral* (or *prehensive*, as the word is used in SMW) unity of the *modal* presences within itself of all of the other extensive regions beyond itself. In short, C^* must be discrete, bounded, and integral, yet modally differentiated so as to mirror the state of the universe that gave it birth.

It follows that C^{**} can be transformed into C^* only through the realization of what previously were its potential boundary and its potential modal structure. In regard to the notion of modal structure, notice that C^{**} potentially mirrors *any* state of the universe, but that C^* must mirror the actual state of the universe giving birth to C. In other words, and speaking with greater generality, the potential modal structure of a potential region changes with each creative advance of the universe; but the actual modal structure of a proper region must permanently mirror the state of the universe relative to the creation of that proper region. But this means, to return to the example, that the modal structure of C^* is the realization of the general potentiality for modal mirroring inherent in C^{**}, insofar as that general potentiality is particularized by the state of the universe correlative with C's birth.

The realization transforming C^{**} into C^*, or transforming a potential modal structure into a real one, involves the ingression of eternal objects of the objective species. For the modal mirroring within C^* of C's universe, we must remember, is tantamount to the objectification within C^* of C's universe. Accordingly, since the main function of the eternal objects of the objective species is to objectify the universe for an occasion, it follows that the transformation of C^{**} into C^* involves their ingression (PR 445–46). In this respect, then, the transformation of C^{**} into C^* is the realization of a contrast of eternal objects of the objective species. But it is also more than that; for the contrast and the modal properties of the extensive standpoint jointly effect the causal objectification in C of C's actual world.

Always assuming the necessary involvement of the envisaging creativity, I can now explain how the modal scheme of extension, and the eternal objects of the objective species, jointly function so as to causally objectify, in and for an actual occasion, the attained actualities in that occasion's universe. In this respect, however, I must point out that a mere reading of what Whitehead has to say about the eternal objects of the species in question could well mislead one into thinking that they alone are responsible for the causal objectifications of actual entities; for that is what the following passage would seem to suggest:

> Thus a member of this species can only function relationally: by a necessity of its nature it is introducing one actual entity, or nexus,

> into the real internal constitution of another actual entity. Its sole
> avocation is to be an agent in objectification. It can never be an
> element in the definiteness of a subjective form. The solidarity of the
> world rests upon the incurable objectivity of this species of eternal
> objects. (PR 445–46)

But the last sentences quoted should warn us that there is at least one
other factor involved in causal objectification; for the solidarity of actual
occasions, as Whitehead tells us in so many different places, is necessarily
a function of the extensive continuum or Receptacle.[1] Indeed, for
Whitehead,

> if we take the doctrine of objectification seriously, the extensive
> continuum at once becomes the primary factor in objectification. It
> provides the general scheme of extensive perspective which is
> exhibited in all the mutual objectifications by which actual entities
> prehend each other. (PR 118)

Accordingly, my task now is to explain how these two eternal factors of
potentiality—the multiplicity of eternal objects of the objective species
and the infinite continuum of extension—cooperate in achieving the causal
objectification of one occasion in, and for, another occasion.

To fulfill this task, all of the considerations of Chapter Five, but in
particular those of Section 8, must be borne in mind. In that section, I
discussed the manifold signification of 'extensive continuum', and also the
senses in which the extensive continuum, when considered as a scheme of
extensive divisions or regions, may be said to be both one and many: one
as in itself; and many as modally mirrored in the extensive standpoints of
actual occasions. In other words, *the one infinite* continuum of extension is
atomized by actual occasions into a scheme of extensive standpoints
(PR 104–05); but each extensive standpoint is itself *a finite* continuum of
extension modally mirroring the scheme of divisions, actual or potential,
of *the infinite* continuum. Considered in this sense, then, the continuum is
a scheme of divisions, or of extensive relations, which must find
exemplification in each actual occasion and in the objectifications by
which actual occasions prehend each other (PR 118). "The 'extensive'
scheme is nothing else than the generic morphology of the internal
relations which bind the actual occasions into a nexus, and which bind the
prehensions of any one actual occasion into a unity, coordinately
divisible" (PR 441; see also PR 438–39).

Since the extensive scheme, in virtue of its manifold reality, expresses the solidarity of all possible standpoints, it follows that for each *potential* standpoint the scheme is the "one relational complex in which all potential objectifications find their *niche*" (PR 103; italics mine). This means that if we are considering C^{**} as a potential standpoint for the immediate successor of B, then C^{**} is, at that juncture of the universe's creative advance, potentially differentiated into potential modal subregions that mirror the new scheme of actual standpoints brought about by the superjective existence of B. Thus, developing further the notation I have been using, let $(b^*)^{**}/C^{**}$ and $(r^*)^{**}/C^{**}$ stand for the potential modal presences within C^{**} of B^* and R^*, respectively. In addition, since B^* and R^* have their own modal structures, their potential modal presences within C^{**} themselves potentially mirror other potential modal presences, such as $(a^*/b^*)^{**}/C^{**}$ and $(q^*/r^*)^{**}/C^{**}$. These four potential modal differentiations of C^{**}, as thus designated, suffice for the present purpose; they constitute the *niches* for the causal objectifications, in C^*, of B, R, A, and Q, respectively.

The whole thrust of the doctrine of extensive modalities, or of organic aspects, comes to this: if C^{**} is realized, if it becomes the standpoint of an actual occasion, its potential scheme of modalities also must be realized. Now, at that juncture of creative advance which is the transition from B to C, the potential modal scheme of C^{**} includes the potential modalities I have just designated. Hence, the transformation of C^{**} into C^* must also transform the potential scheme of C^{**}, which includes the designated modalities, into the real scheme of C^*, which includes b^*/C^*, r^*/C^*, $a^*/b^*/C^*$, and $q^*/r^*/C^*$, the causal objectifications of B, R, A, and Q, respectively.

This conversion of the potential modal scheme in C^{**} into the real scheme of causal objectifications in C^* can be achieved only through the unrestricted ingression of eternal objects of the objective species. But, as unrestrictedly ingressed, the sole function of these eternal objects is to *crystallize*, as it were, the modal scheme of C^{**} in relation to the state of the universe giving birth to C. The eternal objects ingressed do *not* create the extensive relationships of the scheme; rather, the extensive relationships of the scheme, and the occasions already actual, determine *what* eternal objects are ingressed and *where* they are ingressed. For example, $(b^*)^{**}/C^{**}$ determines the complex eternal object which would convert it into b^*/C^*; for if b^*/C^* is to mirror B, then the eternal object in question must be the same one which establishes the boundary and modal differentiations of B^*. This eternal object may be construed as a character transmitted from B^* to C^* (or to b^*/C^*, to be more exact) by reason of the ultimate relatedness of extensive regions. "But the character is gained through the relatedness and not the relatedness through the character" (R 18–19).

The character in question is a complex geometrical form, the organic analogue to a Platonic mathematical form (PR 446). This geometrical form, both as ingressed in B^* and as ingressed in b^*/C^*, has one self-consistent function: to indicate which divisions of the extensive scheme were already completely actual at the moment of B's birth. Through this indication, the date of B's birth is permanently captured by the extensive scheme internal to B^* and also by the extensive scheme internal to b^*/C^*. In both cases, then, the scheme provides the requisite indication of B's self-same position in the extenso-genetic order of the universe.

Thus, the self-identity of B as embodying B^*, and of B as embodying b^*/C^*, is due to the crystallization of the extensive scheme through the ingression of geometrical forms that effectively distinguish actual extensive regions from potential ones. Without this differentiating function of the ingressed forms, the extensive scheme could not possibly indicate the position of B, no matter which location of B we are considering. For by itself, divorced from the ingression of eternal objects of the objective species, the scheme is a system of potential regions mirroring one another, and, to that extent, capable of indicating the correlative *locations* of *hypothetical* occasions, but not capable of indicating the *position* of *actual* occasions. It follows that eternal objects of the objective species are necessary ingredients in the causal objectifications of earlier occasions in later ones.

But the extensive scheme, as we have just seen, is also a necessary ingredient. For the extensive scheme internal to a region provides the niches, or molds, for the realization of the geometrical forms involved in causal objectification. This is why Whitehead says that the extensive relations *mold* the causal objectifications of attained actualities in, and for, the actualities in attainment (PR 470). For example, by reason of its extensive relations with B^* and C^{**}, $(b^*)^{**}/C^{**}$ is the niche, or mold, for the potential objectification of B in C^{**}. In turn, b^*/C^* is the modal subregion embodied by the objective reality of B in C, after the transformation of C^{**} into C^*.

The necessary involvement of the extensive scheme in causal objectification manifests itself in yet another way. For without the transcendental references of the modal subregions of an extensive standpoint, each modal subregion referring to the transcendent region which it mirrors, the geometrical forms realized in that standpoint could have no other function than to be characters of the occasion embodying that standpoint. In other words, if a geometrical form ingressed in one occasion objectifies another occasion, this is due to that geometrical form being ingressed in a modal subregion that refers transcendentally to the region embodied by the intrinsic reality of the objectified occasion. In this fashion, the transcendental reference of a modal subregion explains how an eternal object, be it of the objective species or of the subjective species, can "be an ingredient of one event under the guise, or aspect, of qualifying another event" (SMW 146). For example, it is the transcendental reference which $(b^*)^{**}/C^{**}$ bears to B^* that accounts for the fact that when B_1, the contrast of geometrical forms establishing the boundary and position of B, is realized in that modal niche, it functions as an ingredient of C under the guise of qualifying B. Thus, the modal subregion lends its transcendental reference to the forms that embody it.

The notion of transcendental reference, it should be noted, is essential to Whitehead's conception of the actual occasion. For him, the actual occasions "are the primary units of the actual community and the community is composed of the units. But each unit has in its nature a reference to every other member of the community, so that each unit is a microcosm representing in itself the entire all-inclusive universe" (RM 91).[2] This reference from one occasion to all occasions cannot be explained in terms of the functioning of eternal objects; for the relational essences of eternal objects tell no tales as to their ingression in particular actualities (PR 391). Thus, only the extensive scheme can account for the transcendental reference that each causal objectification bears to the superject it is reproducing. Without such reference, the contrast of geometrical forms expressing the position of the objectified superject would fail in its function. This is why Whitehead says that the position of an actual occasion is "not expressible wholly in terms of contrasts between eternal objects" (PR 350).

The notion of transcendental reference presupposes not only the Ultimate's extensive aspect but also its envisaging aspect. Notice in this regard that the transcendental reference from one formal extensive standpoint to other formal extensive standpoints cannot possibly be experienced because the experiential domain of each actual occasion is one and the same with its own finite extensive standpoint. Thus, in our immediate example, the transcendental reference from b^*/C^* to B^* cannot be experienced by C because C's experience is limited to C^* and the contents of C^*. In other words, since only one term of the referential relation—i.e., only b^*/C^*—falls within C's formal standpoint, C cannot *experience* the transcendental reference of its own formal standpoint to the formal standpoint of B. For the same reason, C cannot experience the transcendental reference of $a^*/b^*/C^*$ to A^*, or of r^*/C^* to R^*, or of $q^*/r^*/C^*$ to Q^*.

Nonetheless, the transcendental reference from the modal subregions of C^* to extensive regions beyond C^* is a necessary condition for the nature and significance of C's own process of experience. As Whitehead says,

> Each experient enjoys a perspective apprehension of the world, and equally is an element in the world by reason of this very prehension, which anchors him to a world transcending his own experience. For, it belongs to the nature of this perspective derivation, that the world thus disclosed proclaims its own transcendence of that disclosure. To every shield, there is another side, hidden. (AI 293)

The problem, then, is to explain the relevance of the side that is hidden, for the hidden side is in some sense taken into account—is intuitively known—in and by each occasion of experience.

The solution to this problem is to construe C's process of becoming as involving an individualization of envisagement, as well as involving an individualization of creativity and a division of extension. As with the individualization of creativity, the individualization of envisagement requires that we distinguish between an individualizing, and an individualized, manifestation of the eternal envisagement. The individualizing manifestation is transcendent in respect to C's subjectivity and is an essential aspect of the macroscopic creative process by which C is begotten. In fact, we speak of the *envisaging creativity* of transition precisely because each individualizing manifestation of creativity is necessarily accompanied by an individualizing manifestation of envisagement. On the other hand, the individualized manifestation is immanent to C's subjectivity and is an essential aspect of the microscopic creative process by which C autonomously completes itself. Indeed, since each individualized manifestation of creativity is necessarily accompanied by an individualized manifestation of envisagement, we could speak also of the envisaging creativity of *concrescence*. However, because the individualized creative envisagement is owned by, and is an essential aspect of, subject C, it is customary to refer to it as C's subjective experience (PR 232–37, 24, 65, 252–53, 423).

What needs to be emphasized, however, is that what has been individualized is the eternal envisagement *of* the whole universe, *by* the whole universe, and *from* the whole universe. Accordingly, the individualizing macroscopic process by which C is begotten is here construed as involving an envisagement *of* the whole universe, and *by* the whole universe, but either *from* C^{**}, during the first process-subphase, or *from* C^*, during the remaining phases of transition. In turn, the individualized microscopic process by which C autonomously completes itself is here construed as involving an envisagement of the whole universe *by* C and *from* c^*/C^*. Finally, C's subjective experience is here construed as a complication and enrichment of the individualized envisagement owned by C. It is the enriched, complicated envisagement of C^*, by subject C, and from c^*/C^*.

The complications and enrichments are due, on the one hand, to the modal, prehensive, and separative properties of C^* and, on the other, to the autonomous self-definition of C insofar as it embodies c^*/C^*. The subjective side of C's experience embodies c^*/C^*, while the objective side embodies all regions of C^* that are external to c^*/C^*. Thus, C's own process of experience is necessarily confined within the bounded region that is C^*. Nonetheless, C's envisagement of the universe beyond C^* grounds, or is one and the same with, C's intuition that the universe objectively disclosed within its experience transcends that disclosure. For example, C experiences the objective reality of B as embodying b^*/C^*, but it envisages the transcendental reference of b^*/C^* to B^* and also the formal reality of B as embodying B^*. Thus, the objective disclosure, or self-revelation, of B in and for C's experience proclaims B's own transcendence of that disclosure. B as transcendent, like the other side of a shield, is hidden from experience, yet known.

One advantage of recognizing envisagement as a third aspect of the Ultimate, or as a fifth formative element of the temporal world, is that we can then understand each act of experience as involving, and as partly growing out of, an individual envisagement of the connectedness between the universe within and the universe without. Apart from the individual envisagement of this connectedness—the same connectedness, let us remember, that the organic categories are intended to elucidate (AI 293)—the doctrine that each causal objectification refers transcendentally to the superject of which it is a reproduction would have to be abandoned. Accordingly, the solidarity of the universe rests not only upon the incurable objectivity of eternal objects of the objective species, but also on the extensive, creative, and envisaging aspects of the Ultimate. This explanation of solidarity and causal objectification thus illustrates the truth that the actual creatures, although genuine individuals, cannot be disjoined from the Ultimate (SMW 99; RM 91–92; IS 243).

4.   *The relevance of eternal objects of the subjective species*

From the preceding considerations we may safely conclude that both the
extensive scheme and the objective species of eternal objects are necessary
factors in causal objectification. Thus far, however, the discussion has
concentrated on causal objectification through geometrical form. But that
is not the whole story of causal objectification; for eternal objects of the
subjective species also function in the objectification of attained
actualities. In other words, the causal objectification of an attained
actuality involves the transmission, or reproduction, not only of its
determinate extensive structure, which specifies its position, but also of its
determinate subjective form, which specifies its definiteness.[3]

It has been noted already that causal objectification may abstract from
the definiteness of the superject being objectified, but that it cannot
abstract from the extensive structure specifying the position of that
superject. A superject cannot be said to have been causally objectified in a
later occasion unless its unique position, which is the essential part of its
real essence, has been reproduced in that later occasion (SMW 97). Thus,
causal objectification by extensive structure, or geometrical form, is more
fundamental than causal objectification by qualitative definiteness.
Nevertheless, some degree of objectification by qualitative definiteness, or
subjective form, would seem to be necessary (PR 230). Otherwise, one
actual occasion would be causally objectified in another as a bare *it*—an *it*
with determinate position, but with no determinate definiteness
whatsoever. Such a bare *it* would have no effect on the concrescence of the
later occasion, since it would have no subjective form that could require
conformation from the later occasion. However, it does seem that, for
most cases of causal objectification, the element of qualitative definiteness
is negligible, whereas the element of extensive determinateness is never
negligible. This, I contend, is why Whitehead says that the effectiveness,
or causal objectification, of one event in another is trivial, *except* for the
systematic aspects of geometrical shapes (SMW 168–69).

In regard to the attained actualities in the near past of a novel occasion,
however, objectification by subjective form is of the utmost importance,
since it establishes the qualitative conditions to which the novel occasion
must conform. The extensive scheme, it must be noted, is crucial also to
this aspect of causal objectification; for it establishes the modal niche which
is to be embodied by the reproduced subjective form. In order to explain the
joint function of the extensive scheme and the eternal objects of the
subjective species, let us consider again the causal objectification of *B* in *C*.

Now let B_2 stand for the subjective form of one of B's feelings. The definiteness of that subjective form is due to the unrestricted ingression into b^*/B^* of an eternal object of the subjective species; let us call it x. In such a role, x is said to be functioning *subjectively* (PR 446). In the causal objectification of B in C, x is unrestrictedly ingressed into $b^*/b^*/C^*$. In this manner, an element of B's definiteness is transmitted from B's intrinsic reality to the mode of B's extrinsic reality by which B is immanent in C. As ingressed into $b^*/b^*/C^*$, however, x is functioning *datively* for C (PR 249), and *relationally* between the intrinsic realities of B and C (PR 446). As thus functioning, x expresses the definiteness of B_2 as exhibited by the causal objectification of B in and for C.

Notice that the ingression of x into C under the guise of qualifying B can be explained only through the modal character of $b^*/b^*/C^*$ and b^*/C^*, and through the transcendental reference that those two subregions bear to b^*/B^* and B^*, respectively. For this fact makes evident the indispensable role played by the extensive relations that the eternal extensive continuum imposes on all actualities. "These extensive relations do not make determinate *what* is transmitted; but they do determine conditions to which all transmission must conform" (PR 441). It must be maintained, therefore, that the reproduction of B_2, as abstractly representing B's subjective definiteness, and the reproduction of B_1, as concretely indicative of B's position, *together with the modal region b^*/C^** (which includes $b^*/b^*/C^*$) *and with the transcendental reference which that region bears to B^**, constitute the causal objectification, or objective reality, of B in and for C. Thus, B can transcend itself and become immanent in C only by reason of the metaphysical cooperation of eternal extension with eternal objects of both the subjective, and the objective, species. Moreover, it is only by reason of this metaphysical cooperation that this particular mode of the self-transcendence of B is the self-revelation of B for C (PR 347).

What is true of B is, in that respect, true of all occasions in the past of C. Each such occasion reveals itself to C in one mode or another of abstraction from its final definiteness, but without the slightest abstraction from its aboriginal position. Now, *that* each occasion in C's past must be objectified in C is determined by the metaphysical properties of eternal extension. But *how*, or in what mode of abstraction from its definiteness, each occasion is objectified in C is *not* determined by the properties of extension. Instead, the mode in which an occasion in C's past is objectified in C is due largely, though not exclusively, to *transcendent decisions* made by the earlier occasion itself. Physical purposes, let us remember, are the feelings by means of which occasions decide *how* they are to be objectified in the future beyond themselves.

The relative efficacy of different physical purposes is subject to the categoreal condition that all the causal objectifications given for an occasion must be such as to provoke conformal feelings that are compatible for aesthetic synthesis in that occasion. For this reason, the physical purposes of different occasion's in *C*'s past are not equally efficacious in determining the objectifications of their respective parent occasions. As a general rule, the physical purposes of occasions in *C*'s immediate past will be more efficacious than those of occasions in its remote past. This means that the more remotely past the occasion is, the more its objectification abstracts from its final definiteness, and the less that abstraction is made in accord with its physical purposes. The exact opposite is the case with immediately past occasions.

Of the occasions in *C*'s immediate past, however, *B* has by far the most efficacious physical purposes. *B* is preeminent, in this respect, because it is the only occasion that physically anticipates *C* as its own immediate descendant. This means, as we saw earlier, that *B* constrains the envisaging creativity begetting *C* in a manner that is not open to any other actual occasion. Accordingly, *B* is causally objectified in *C** in strict accordance with *B*'s transcendent decisions in that regard. The causal objectification of the other actualities in *C*'s past, on the other hand, have their physical purposes partially overridden in a process of mutual adjustment that ensures their compatibility for aesthetic synthesis. This partial overriding of the individual physical purposes of the occasions in *C*'s past signals the presence of a stabilizing factor in the general metaphysical situation.

5. The relevance of God's primordial nature

Thus far I have explained how the transition from *B* to *C*, or the transformation of *C*** into *C**, presupposes that the transcendent creativity envisages both the disjunctive plurality of attained actualities and the disjunctive multiplicity of eternal objects. I must explain now how this transition, or this transformation, presupposes also that the transcendent creativity envisages the primordial nature of God. The discussion of the threefold envisagement that Whitehead attributes to the eternal creativity will thus be completed.

Let us notice, first of all, that the transformation of *C*** into *C** involves the realization of a complex contrast of geometrical forms establishing the boundary and extensive structure of C^*. But the complex eternal object expressing the manner of this contrast must subordinate within itself other complex eternal objects, each expressing the manner of the contrast of geometrical forms associated with the extensive structure and boundary of an actual occasion causally objectified in C^*. This means that the creative advance from occasion to occasion involves the realization of the members of an infinite abstractive hierarchy of eternal objects of the objective species (SMW 237–38, 244–45). Each novel occasion realizes an eternal object from this hierarchy—an eternal object which is 'proximate' to the ones realized by the immediately antecedent occasions, since it contains them as its components of an immediately lower grade of complexity.

In our example, this means that the transformation of C^{**} into C^* presupposes the ingression of a complex geometrical form that integrates the complex geometrical forms ingressed in the attained actualities of C's correlative universe. But the attained actualities of C's universe cannot decide which complex geometrical form is to synthesize their respective geometrical forms. Thus, the ingression into C^* of the appropriate geometrical form gives witness to the fact that the transcendent creativity takes into account the relevant abstractive hierarchy as conceptually prehended in God's primordial nature.

The envisagement of God's primordial nature by the transcendent creativity is necessary, in addition, because the physical purposes of the attained actualities in C's correlative universe cannot by themselves determine how those actualities are to be jointly objectified in C^*. As jointly objectified, these actualities must be compatible for aesthetic synthesis in C's experience of them (PR 101, 173, 227). In this respect, any incompatibility would be due to the definiteness, and not to the position, of the objectified actualities. Now, the definiteness by which an attained actuality is objectified is due, conditions permitting, to its physical purposes. But there is no reason why the physical purposes of the attained actualities should not give rise to objectifications that would be incompatible for aesthetic synthesis. Thus, there may be conditions forbidding that some of the attained actualities be jointly objectified according to the determinations of their respective physical purposes. These adverse conditions necessarily become more probable in the creative advance from occasion to occasion; eventually, therefore, the physical purpose of an attained actuality "meets with incompatibilities, and is attenuated, or modified, or eliminated from further endurance" (PR 422).

Despite the failing efficacy of physical purposes, however, every attained actuality in the correlative universe of *C* must be objectified by some element, however negligible, of its definiteness; and all the objectified actualities in the datum for *C* must be compatible for *aesthetic* synthesis in *C*'s experience of them.

> The objectified particular occasions together have the unity of a datum *for* the creative concrescence. But in acquiring this measure of connection, their inherent presuppositions of each other eliminate certain elements in their constitutions, and elicit into relevance other elements. Thus objectification is an operation of *mutually adjusted abstraction*, or elimination, whereby the many occasions of the actual world become one complex datum. (PR 321; italics mine)

The problem is that the ultimate adjustment of the objectifications in the datum for *C* cannot be due entirely to the failing, or vanishing, efficacy of the physical purposes of the objectified occasions. Nor can it be due to *C*'s immanent decisions; for *C*'s concrescence presupposes the already adjusted datum.

Accordingly, in the transition from *B* to *C*, there is a fundamental indetermination as to how the occasions in *C*'s actual world are to be objectified into the complex datum for *C*; but neither those occasions, nor *C* itself, can provide the decision solving that indetermination. But this decision must be attributed to some actuality, lest the ontological principle be violated. Hence, we must come to the conclusion that only God's primordial nature can provide the transcendent decision solving this indetermination. For God's primordial nature, as we saw in Chapter Four, is constituted by an infinity of conceptual feelings severally relevant to all realizable basic conditions. Thus, there is in God a complex conceptual feeling indicative of how the attained actualities of *C*'s universe are to be objectified in *C*'s dative phase in a manner that renders them compatible for synthesis in *C*'s aesthetic experience of them. In this way, God's primordial nature "solves all indeterminations of transition" (PR 315).

But the efficacy of God's transcendent decision again presupposes the envisaging creativity as its vehicle. Moreover, the envisaging creativity also objectifies God's primordial nature in *C**. This objectification is by means of those of God's conceptual feelings that are immediately relevant to the character given to *C* by the causal objectifications of the temporal occasions in *C*'s universe. When subject *C* feels God through a hybrid physical feeling, it feels God as thus objectified (PR 343). Since *C* derives its initial subjective aim from this hybrid feeling, it follows that God is a partial determinant both of the transition to *C*, and of the concrescence of

C (PR 374). God's primordial nature, then, "is a character of permanent rightness, whose inherence in the nature of things modifies both efficient and final cause, so that the one conforms to harmonious conditions, and the other contrasts itself with an harmonious ideal" (RM 61).

That God's primordial nature conditions both efficient and final causation is a conclusion we first reached in our extended discussion of the ontological principle (Chapter Three, Section 6). Its reconsideration at this time is intended to emphasize that, "apart from God, the remaining formative elements would fail in their functions" (RM 104). But the complete truth is that even God would fail in his functions without the remaining formative elements. The Ultimate—with its creative, extensive, and envisaging aspects—the multiplicity of eternal objects, and the primordial nature of God are all equally necessary for the existence of C, or of any other temporal occasion. Nonetheless, our immediate concern is with the crucial role that God's primordial nature plays in each of the macroscopic processes by which the universe begets its individual occasions. More specifically, our immediate concern is with the role that the primordial nature plays in the universe's begetting of C^*, the absolutely first phase of C's existence.

In this last regard, some of the points already made require additional development and emphasis. First it must be noticed that B's physical anticipation of C cannot decide the precise *manner* of the contrast of geometrical forms by which C^{**} is to be bounded and structured. B cannot provide the requisite decision because it cannot possibly prehend the complete *matter* of the contrast in question. The matter of that contrast, let us remember, is jointly determined by the already attained actualities of C's correlative universe. But some of the attained actualities in the past of C—for example, Q and R—are contemporaries of B, and B cannot prehend the complete extensive structure of its own contemporaries. Therefore, B lacks the information presupposed by any decision determining the manner of the requisite contrast.

In the second place, C's correlative world of attained actualities *cannot* determine the *manner* of the contrast which is to constitute the boundary and structure of C^*, even though it *does* determine the *matter* of that contrast. The reason for this incapacity is that any given matter for contrast may be contrasted in an indefinite number of manners. Thus, neither B's physical anticipation of C, nor the fact that C's correlative actual world determines the potential modal structure of C^{**}, can decide the precise manner of the contrast of geometrical forms whereby C^{**} is transformed into C^*.

In the third place, this last conclusion is not intended to deny my earlier claim that B's physical anticipation of C, and B's own completion, respectively account for the where and when of C's becoming. But we have to distinguish between the metaphysical structure of C's extensive standpoint, which would be the same no matter what cosmic epoch C belonged to, and the cosmological structure of that standpoint, which is a function of the type of geometry defining the cosmic epoch to which C in fact belongs. Thus, assuming that C belongs to our cosmic epoch, the contrast of geometrical forms by which C^* is bounded and structured not only assigns to C its determinate metaphysical position in the extenso-genetic order of the universe, but also assigns to it its cosmological place in the spatio-temporal order of our cosmic epoch. This means, on the one hand, that the realized contrast, call it C_1, crystallizes the potential modal structure of C^{**} and thereby transforms it into C^*, the standpoint of C and the immortal indicator of C's extenso-genetic position. But this also means, on the other hand, that C_1 gives to C^* a determinate spatio-temporal structure analyzable into a factor of spatial volume and a factor of temporal endurance (PR 195). The determinate spatio-temporal structure depends, whereas the determinate positional structure does *not* depend, on the precise *manner* of contrast C_1. Had the manner been different, the spatio-temporal structure of C would have been different, but its extenso-genetic position would have been the same. The point, then, is that C's correlative actual world, which includes B, is both necessary and sufficient for the position of C (given that C has in fact become, and leaving C's completion-date out of the picture), whereas it is only necessary for the spatio-temporal structure of C.

Implicit in this last point is the fact that the determinate features of an actuality cannot all be metaphysical or necessary. Some measure or other of contingency is the mark of the genuinely actual. But what is contingent is not to be equated with what is accidental or arbitrary. Rather, the contingent structural and qualitative features of ontologically basic entities give witness to the reality of the autonomous decisions that are essential to all realization. Indeed, autonomous decisions are the hallmark of all entities that are genuinely actual. All such decisions, according to the ontological principle, are made *for* some actuality or other, either *by* the actuality itself or *by* some other actualities. The fourth point to emphasize now is that the decisions determining the contingent features of C's dative phase are made by actualities other than C, for C cannot make any decisions until it exists as an autonomous subject. But if the transcendent decisions attributable to the actual occasions in C's past are not sufficient to account for the contingent structural features of C's dative phase, then the missing requisite decisions must be attributed to the eternal actuality that is God's primordial nature.

The final point to emphasize, then, is that some complex primordial feeling—a divine conceptual feeling including, but not limited to, the *primordial counterpart* of what is to be C's initial subjective aim—is inherently relevant to the particular circumstances of C's potential birth. This complex divine feeling constitutes a primordial transcendent decision respecting: (i) the *manner* of C_1, the contrast of geometrical forms by which the extensive standpoint of C is to be bounded and structured; (ii) the mode in which the primordial nature is itself to be causally objectified in and for C; and (iii) the particular way in which the objectifications of the attained actualities in C's correlative universe are to be mutually adjusted so as to permit the derivation of conformal feelings that are compatible for aesthetic synthesis. Because the transcendent creativity involved in the transition from B to C envisages the divine feeling in question, as well as envisaging the rest of the actual world correlative with C's potential birth, its determination by that world is complete and coherent. It is only as thus coherently and completely determined that the individualizing manifestation of creative envisagement provoked by B's completion can successfully fulfill its function of begetting the dative phase of C—can, in other words, coherently function as the vehicle of all transcendent decisions, whether temporal or eternal, concerning the transformation of C^{**} into C^*.

The threefold role played by the primordial nature in the begetting of C's dative phase exhibits God as the ultimate source of all contingent order. He is the actuality by reason of which there is physical law (PR 434). For example, the factors of spatial volume and temporal endurance selected for C are determined by the primordial counterpart of C's initial subjective aim (PR 434, 195). Nonetheless, we must never lose sight of the fact that the actualization of any contingent form of order is a social and cooperative affair, one requiring the autonomous decisions of actual occasions as much as the autonomous decisions of the divine actuality. Indeed, at any particular juncture of the universe's creative advance, the primordial nature provides only that measure of determination that is not already provided by the attained actualities of the universe.

In addition, we must never forget that what the universe is by way of actuality exhibits an extenso-genetic order of mutually immanent individuals that is *not* contingent. This metaphysical, or necessary, order of actuality is presupposed by the development, maintenance, and even *failure* of any contingent form of order. "In the world, there are elements of order and disorder, which thereby presuppose an essential interconnectedness of things. For disorder shares with order the common characteristic that they imply many things interconnected" (AI 292). More to the point, every actual contingent form of order implies both the possibility of alternative forms of order and the possibility of actual disorder. But to the metaphysical order of the universe there is neither alternative nor exception. God and the occasions of the actual world are equally in the grip of that necessary order which it stands in the ultimate nature of the universe to impose (PR 529). The birth of *C*, or of any other actual occasion, is subject to the general metaphysical order of things, as well as to the particular and contingent order which its actual world imposes on it.

6. *The occasion as internally related to a knowable universe*

I have completed an account of the origination of *C*'s dative phase that is consonant with Whitehead's claim that a new creation has to arise from the *total* universe—from the world of attained actualities and from every eternal factor of potentiality (PR 123). Indeed there is nothing in the universe correlative to *C*'s birth that fails to function in the creation of *C*'s dative phase. The envisaging creativity, the continuum of extension, *B*'s anticipatory feeling of *C*, the disjunctive plurality of attained actualities, the multiplicity of eternal objects, and the primordial nature of God are all alike involved in the creation of *C*'s dative phase. Thus, as Whitehead says repeatedly, the entire universe conspires to produce the new occasion (RM 113; PR 340; MT 225).

In addition, and primarily by reason of the modality of extension, the entire universe finds its objective reality within *C**; for not only are all attained actualities causally objectified in *C**, but also the extensive standpoints of occasions contemporary with *C*, or in the future of *C*, are all modally present in *C**.[4] Indeed, the causal objectification in *C** of all occasions in *C*'s past is only a special case of the modal immanence in *C** of the entire universe correlative with *C*'s birth. The particular physical purposes and anticipations of the attained actualities in *C*'s universe, together with the metaphysical imposition of modal immanence by the Creative Receptacle, constitute the reason why the efficient causation whereby *C** is begotten "is nothing else than one outcome of the principle that every actual entity has to house *its* actual world" (PR 124).

What *C* houses, of course, is not *its* universe *simpliciter*, but rather *its* universe as *objectified*. To be sure, *C* "springs from *that* universe which there *is for it*" (PR 124). Nonetheless, the state of the universe from which *C* springs—*i.e.*, the state of the universe which gives birth to *C*—is both outside and inside *C*. The occasion originates from an external totality and also embodies it (PR 22). For the attained actualities of the external world are objectified within *C**, and these "objectifications express the causality by which the external world fashions the actual occasion in question" (PR 489). Hence, by reason of its dative phase, *C* is *internally related* to its correlative universe in a twofold way: first, because its initial phase of existence is created by *that* state of the universe, and is thus dependent on it; and second, because *that* universe is objectively reproduced within *C* itself as the aboriginal and essential element of *C*'s character. In short, *C* is internally related to its correlative universe because the essential element of *C*'s determinateness, its *position*, is a function of that universe.

C's correlative universe, it must be noted, is a fleeting momentary state of the universe, which, nevertheless, is permanently captured in the crystallized modal structure of *C*'s own extensive standpoint. For the universe is never at a standstill. Even as *C* is undergoing its phases of concrescence, the universe which gave it birth is changing by the addition of new attained actualities.[5] But the modal structure of *C*'s standpoint does preserve, for *C*'s own experience, and for the experience of subjects in *C*'s future, the objective reality of *C*'s correlative universe. Whether as directly experienced by *C*, or as objectified for later subjects, *C*'s extensive structure tells the same tale about the universe which gave birth to *C*. Thus, the metaphysical chronology and topology of the universe are forever captured and enshrined in the extensive standpoints of its actual occasions.

In effect, *C** is a metaphysical hologram of *C*'s correlative universe. Thus, the holographic conception of reality—the conception which physicist David Bohm, psychologist Karl Pribram, and other contemporary scientists are beginning to find so illuminating in their respective disciplines—has been an essential, but generally unacknowledged, ingredient of Whitehead's metaphysical thought since 1924, if not earlier. The analogies between the holographic conception and Whitehead's doctrine of modal or objective immanence, it must be noted, are far from being superficial. For example, just as the information contained in an entire hologram is contained also, though less clearly and less completely, in any one of its parts, no matter how small, so too the information which is contained in *C** as a whole is contained also, in varying degrees of incompleteness, in each of the modal subregions of *C**, no matter how small.

The degree to which the information contained in a modal subregion of C^* approximates in completeness the information contained in C^* as a whole is partly a function of the subregion's order of modality. Thus, b^*/C^*, r^*/C^* and all causal objectifications that have a primary modal presence in C^* contain each almost as much information as is contained in C^* as a whole. The reason for this is that the occasions that are causally objectified in C^* with primary modal presence are those, and only those, that are in the past of C, but are *not* in the past of any occasion that is in the past of C. Because the occasions in question are those in the immediate past of C, their objectifications in C^* contain each practically the same information about the universe's actual topology and chronology that C^* as a whole contains. The only information missing is that which the occasions in question could not have respecting each other because of their mutual contemporaneity. In other words, the causal objectification of each occasion in C's immediate past presents for C the entire history of the universe up to the birth of the occasion in question, thereby leaving out only some of the information concerning the complete determinateness of its own contemporaries.

The information contained in causal objectifications that have a secondary modal presence in C^* will be proportionately less than that contained in objectifications with primary modal presence. Thus, $a^*/b^*/C^*$ and $q^*/r^*/C^*$ contain each slightly less information than is contained in b^*/C^* and r^*/C^*, respectively. Similarly, $p^*/q^*/r^*/C^*$ will contain even less information than $q^*/r^*/C^*$. In this manner, as we consider objectifications of progressively lower modalities, the information they each contain will be progressively less complete than that contained in C^* as a whole. It is important to notice, however, that the information contained in any modal subregion, no matter how small the region or how low its modality, concerns the extenso-genetic structure, in part actual and in part potential, of the universe as a whole. Accordingly, even a modal subregion of $\&^{**}/C^*$ contains information concerning the extenso-genetic relations that all actualities must exhibit in respect to each other. In other words, every modal subregion of C^* reveals for subject C the necessary, systematic interconnectedness of all actual existents—reveals, in short, the metaphysical necessity of extenso-genetic solidarity (PR 498–99).

Two additional points must be made concerning the information contained in the metaphysical hologram that is C^*. First, what is true concerning extenso-genetic relations, which are metaphysical, is true also concerning spatio-temporal relations, which are cosmological. I am speaking, of course, only of actual occasions belonging to our cosmic epoch. If C

is one such occasion, then, by reason of the modal structure of C^*, it holds "in its essence its spatio-temporal relationships (both within itself, and beyond itself) throughout the spatio-temporal continuum" (SMW 180).

The second point is that what is true concerning the universe's structural features is true also concerning the universe's qualitative features. But the information which C^* contains regarding the qualitative features, or definiteness, of past actual occasions is determined *primarily* by cosmological principles, even though these are constrained by metaphysical ones. Nonetheless, the similar fact obtains that, in respect to the *definiteness* of things, causal objectifications with a higher order of modal presence contain more information than those with a lower order. For example, occasions in the immediate past of C, in virtue of the greater efficacy of their physical purposes, will be causally objectified in C^* with little abstraction from the determinate definiteness of each. This is particularly the case with B because, in addition to being in the immediate past of C, it also physically anticipates C as its own immediate descendant. Thus, for metaphysical reasons, the causal objectification of B in C "is peculiarly complete" (PR 468). In addition, for reasons that do not appear to be metaphysical, if C belongs to our cosmic epoch, then the immediately past occasions that are in the immediate extensive vicinity of C^{**} will be objectified in C^* with peculiar completeness also (PR 469). Thus, to speak with greater generality, in our cosmic epoch "there will be a set of antecedent, contiguous occasions objectified in any given occasion; and the abstraction which attends every objectification will merely be due to the necessary harmonization of these objectifications" (PR 468).

The interpretation, development, and application of Whitehead's organic epistemology, it should be noted, cannot be divorced from the doctrine that the extensive standpoint of each actual occasion is, in effect, a metaphysical hologram of the state of the universe begetting the occasion in question. For, according to Whitehead, "judgment concerns the universe as objectified from the standpoint of the judging subject" (PR 305). More accurately, judgment concerns the universe as objectified from *and within* the extenso-genetic standpoint of the judging subject. This means, for example, that the complete history of the universe, up to the moment in which it begets C, is captured in the structural and qualitative features of C^*, the dative phase and extensive standpoint of C. Thus, the universe that begets C is knowable by C, and by all occasions in the future of C, precisely because it is immortally captured in the texture of C^*. This is why, in the organic philosophy, "the problems of efficient causation and of knowledge receive a common explanation by reference to the texture of actual occasions" (PR 290). This is also why, "according to this philosophy, the knowable is the complete nature of the knower, at least such phases of it as are antecedent to that operation of knowing" (PR 92).

I find reason later to qualify the last quoted statement. For the moment, however, what needs to be emphasized is the metaphysical and epistemological importance of each occasion's dative phase. Each such phase is begotten *by*, and contains the objectification *of*, a particular state of the universe's cumulative history. Thus, by reason of its dative phase, each actual occasion is *internally related* to its correlative universe; and, for the same reason, the universe correlative with each occasion is *knowable*, though not necessarily known (PR 236), by the occasion in question.

7. *The dative phase as the real potentiality for subjective experience*

The importance of an occasion's dative phase is not limited to the fact that, in virtue of it, the occasion is internally related to, and can come to know, its correlative universe. For, in addition, the dative phase is the *real potentiality* for the occasion's subjective phases. What the occasion can be *qua* subject is both conditioned and enabled by its dative phase. To make clearer this role of the dative phase, let us return to the examination of *C*'s existential history.

The creation of *C*'s dative phase, I have said repeatedly, may be construed as the transformation of *C*** into *C**. Now *C*** is a potential region of the Receptacle, a region that harbors within itself the pure extensive, creative, and envisaging potentiality for the becoming of an actual occasion. But no actual occasion can arise from *pure* potentiality. Hence, the pure potentiality represented by *C*** must be limited and conditioned by the objectifications of settled occasions before it can serve as the *real* potentiality for a new actuality. This limiting and conditioning of *C*** is what transforms it into *C**. Thus, *C** is the real potentiality for an actual, or self-realizing, occasion to spring from it (PR 546; Corrigenda). Yet *C** is also the occasion itself as *merely real*.

Before *C* can be self-realizing, however, it must exist as a subject—that is, it must exist *for itself* as well as in itself. But to exist as a subject is to exist as exhibiting some measure of qualitative definiteness. In other words, there can be no subject without subjective form. Therefore, self-realization presupposes that the macroscopic process that begets the dative phase of an occasion also begets, in an immediately subsequent phase, the subject *for which* the aboriginal dative phase is a complex object.

We saw earlier, in Chapter Three, that the subject is born with the phase of conformal feelings. The point to emphasize now is that the dative phase is the real, or *natural*, potentiality for the phase of conformal feelings. In this respect, Whitehead says, comparing his Creative Receptacle to Aristotle's prime matter,

> that the limitation of pure potentiality, established by 'objectifications' of the settled past, expresses that 'natural potentiality'—or, potentiality in nature—which is 'matter' with that basis of initial, realized form presupposed as the first phase in the self-creation of the present occasion. The notion of 'pure potentiality' here takes the place of Aristotle's 'matter' and 'natural potentiality' is 'matter' with that given imposition of form from which each actual thing arises. All components which are *given* for experience are to be found in the analysis of natural potentiality. Thus, the immediate present has to conform to what the past is for it, and the mere lapse of time is an abstraction from the more concrete relatedness of 'conformation'. (S 36)

To speak with greater accuracy, however, Whitehead's statement must be modified in two important respects. First, the dative phase or natural potentiality is presupposed as the *first preliminary* phase to the concrescence of feelings which is the genuine self-creation of an actual occasion. In this regard, the thing to remember is that an occasion has more than one given phase—has *three* given phases, to be exact: the dative phase proper, the phase of conformal feelings, and the phase of conceptual reproductions. Genuine self-creation begins only with the phase of conceptual reversion. Thus, "what is actual arises from its given phases" (S 21).

The second modification concerns the connection between natural potentiality and what is given for experience. For it is important to realize that experience is given both objective and subjective components. All *objective* components that are given for experience are indeed to be found in the analysis of natural potentiality. But the *subjective* components for experience—the subjective forms of the conformal feelings and the initial valuations of the conceptual reproductions—are *not* to be found in the analysis of natural potentiality. Rather, they are to be found in the analysis of the subject to which they belong, and whose initial phases of existence they constitute. Nonetheless, the eternal objects determining the definiteness of the subjective forms and valuations in question are also to be found in the natural potentiality, or in the causal objectifications, provoking the physical and conceptual conformation. Thus, each of the eternal objects concerned has two ingressions: one in the objective side of experience, and another in the subjective side. In the former side, it expresses the definiteness of an objectified past occasion; in the latter, it expresses the initial definiteness of the novel subject.

Strictly speaking, therefore, the dative phase of an occasion is the natural potentiality for that occasion's conformal feelings and conceptual reproductions. In turn, these primary physical and conceptual feelings, together with the dative phase which they in fact include, constitute the real potentiality for any genuine concrescence of feelings. For notice that there can be no concrescence, or growing together, of feelings until there are feelings to concrescence or integrate. Thus, the three given phases of an actual occasion are best construed as *preliminary* to its genuine concrescence or self-creation. Here, as always, we must remember that by the self-creation or self-causation of an occasion Whitehead means its self-completion.

The immediate concern, however, is with the dative phase and not with the other two preliminary phases. It is evident that the natural potentiality from which a subject arises is also the dative phase to which it must be conformed. It is evident also that the dative phase is the past itself as reproduced in and for the novel occasion, whereas the remaining phases of the occasion constitute the present as superseding and including its given past (S 35–36). Finally, it is evident the dative phase is the ultimate real potentiality for the successive phases of feeling that arise from it and refer to it.

8. The dative modal scheme as the real potentiality for aesthetic integration

Much less evident is the importance of the dative phase's modal structure for the synthesis of the feelings that arise from it. This is an aspect of the dative phase which I have not previously emphasized, because my main concern has been to exhibit how the metaphysical properties of extension explain the mutual immanence of discrete actualities. In other words, I have been concerned with the organic theory of extension primarily in respect to how any two occasions can be, in one sense, outside each other's extensive standpoint, while also being, in another sense, inside each other's extensive standpoint. But the same theory explains, in addition, how different prehensions belonging to one occasion can be synthesized into one integral prehension without losing their individual differences, and in a manner such that both their differences and their integration are recoverable from the final satisfaction, or from the objectification, of the occasion in question.

In this respect, the metaphysical properties of eternal extension may be construed as giving rise to a scheme of extensive relations that grounds all internal relations obtaining either *between*, or *within*, actual occasions. Thus, "the 'extensive' scheme is nothing else than the generic morphology of the internal relations which bind the actual occasions into a nexus, and which bind the prehensions of any one actual occasion into a unity, coordinately divisible" (PR 441). How extensive relations underlie the reciprocal internal relations by which two or more occasions form a nexus should be fairly obvious by now. For example, B and C are internally related to each other because their respective standpoints, B^* and C^*, are modally present in each other. This means that b^*/C^* grounds the objective reality of B in and for C, and that $!c^{**}/fu^{**}/\&^{**}/B^*$ grounds the objective reality of C in and for B. Each occasion prehends the objective reality of the other occasion. Also, each occasion is partly constituted by the objective reality of the other. In short, by reason of the extensive scheme, the bonds binding B and C to one another are bonds between discrete individuals—individuals divided from, or external to, one another. Nonetheless, the bonds are such that B and C are internally related to one another (PR 470–71).

To explain how the extensive scheme binds the prehensions of any one occasion into a coordinately divisible unity, I must, first, develop further my articulation of the modal structure of an occasion's self-aspect, and second, elucidate those notions of the coordinate division theory that bear on the thesis of solidarity. I begin the first of these tasks by noting that heretofore we have been equating the dative phase of an occasion with its aboriginal objective content. Henceforth, however, we must be careful to distinguish the two by noting that the self-aspect of an occasion is part of its dative phase, but is *not* part of its objective content. For example, c^*/C^* is part of C's extensive standpoint and is thereby a component of C's dative phase; but c^*/C^* is not part of C's objective content because it constitutes the modal presence of C^* within itself. Thus, unlike the other modal subregions of C's standpoint, c^*/C^* does *not* objectify any aspect of the universe external to C^*. Therefore, since whatever is part of C's objective content must objectify some component or other of the universe external to C^*, c^*/C^* is *not* part of C's objective content.

Indeed, so far is c^*/C^* from being a component of C's objective content that its true nature is best construed as the extensive aspect of the real potentiality for C's *subjective content*. For all qualitative features of C's subjectivity must be understood as resulting from the unrestricted ingression into c^*/C^* of eternal objects of the subjective species. This means, in effect, that the subjective forms of C's prehensions embody each some subregion or other of c^*/C^*. Thus, c^*/C^* serves as the extensive standpoint of C's subjectivity. Thus, too, the definiteness of C is the qualitative definiteness of c^*/C^*.

The point is that the *subjective* content of C's experience embodies, or has a seat in, the *self*-aspect of C's extensive standpoint. In turn, the *objective* content of C's experience embodies, or has its seat in, what may be termed the '*other*-aspect' of C's extensive standpoint. The other-aspect is the subregion obtained by subtracting, as it were, c^*/C^* from C^*. If we now let '$\&/C^*$' designate the other-aspect of C^*, then c^*/C^* and $\&/C^*$ house, respectively, the subjective and objective contents of C's experience. In this manner, the contrast between c^*/C^* and $\&/C^*$ grounds the necessary contrast between the subjective and objective sides of C's concrete experience. Of course, what is metaphysically true of C must be true of every actual occasion. Therefore, the general conclusion is that the structural contrast between the self-aspect and the other-aspect of an occasion grounds the necessary contrast between the subjective and objective sides of the occasion's concrete experience.

We must not lose sight of the fact that the qualitative definiteness of an occasion's self-aspect is *not* an aboriginal feature of its existence; for it has no such definiteness as a mere component of the occasion's dative phase. For example, *qua* component of C's dative phase, c^*/C^* is entirely devoid of qualitative definiteness; moreover, it has only the structural determinateness that belongs to it insofar as it is a proper subregion of C^*. The reason for c^*/C^*'s absence of qualitative definiteness, and for its poverty of structural determinateness, is that it mirrors the contents of C^{**} relative to C's birth. In this regard, we must remember, first, that C^* mirrors the entire universe giving birth to C, and second, that the universe which gives birth to C includes C^{**}. In an important sense, therefore, c^*/C^* is the modal presence within C^* of C^{**}, rather than of C^* itself. That, in brief, is the reason why C's dative phase is devoid of subjective content.

To say that c^*/C^* is devoid of qualitative definiteness is to say that it is devoid of *empirical* properties; but it is not to say that c^*/C^* is devoid of *metaphysical* properties. As the modal presence of C^{**} within C^*, c^*/C^* has determinate metaphysical properties in virtue of the fact that it mirrors the potential modal structure of C^{**} relative to the origination of C's dative phase. Notice, in this regard, that the potential modal scheme of C^{**}

includes c^{**}/C^{**}, the modal presence of C^{**} within itself. Thus, c^{**}/C^{**}, has a potential modal structure mirroring the potential modal structure of C^{**} at the particular juncture of the universe's creative advance. However, whereas the origination of C^* as a whole crystallizes the modal structure of C^{**} through the unrestricted ingression of eternal objects of the objective species, the origination of c^*/C^* does *not* crystallize the potential modal structure of c^{**}/C^{**}—at least not through the ingression of eternal objects of the objective species.

This last qualification is important because the potential modal structure of c^{**}/C^{**} is *indirectly* crystallized, albeit in a very limited sense, by the transcendental reference which c^*/C^* bears to $\partial\!\!\!/\,/C^*$. The reason for this reference is that each modal subregion of $\partial\!\!\!/\,/C^*$, whether real or potential, is modally mirrored in c^*/C^*. For example, b^*/C^* is modally mirrored by a subregion of c^*/C^* which we shall signify by $(b^*/C^*)^{**}/c^*/C^*$. Similarly, $s^{**}/pr^{**}/\partial\!\!\!/^{**}/C^*$ and $d^{**}/fu^{**}/\partial\!\!\!/^{**}/C^*$ are modally mirrored by $(s^{**}/pr^{**}/\partial\!\!\!/^{**}/C^*)^{**}/c^*/C^*$ and $(d^{**}/fu^{**}/\partial\!\!\!/^{**}/C^*)^{**}/c^*/C^*$, respectively. This modal mirroring by c^*/C^* of the real and potential modal structure of $\partial\!\!\!/\,/C^*$ results from the fact that c^*/C^*, since it is the modal presence of C^{**} within itself, must mirror C^{**} as mirroring C's correlative universe. In other words, all the metaphysical extensive relations between the potential modal structure of C^{**} and the extensive regions beyond C^{**} must be mirrored within C^* by the metaphysical extensive relations between the potential modal structure of c^*/C^* and the modal subregions of $\partial\!\!\!/\,/C^*$. Thus, for example, just as b^*/C^* mirrors and refers transcendentally to B^*, so too $(b^*/C^*)^{**}/c^*/C^*$ mirrors and refers transcendentally to b^*/C^*.

The point is that c^*/C^* exhibits a derivatively crystallized modal structure in virtue of its potential subregions mirroring and referring transcendentally to the modal subregions constituting the crystallized modal structure of $\partial\!\!\!/\,/C^*$. Since the modal structure of $\partial\!\!\!/\,/C^*$ is unalterable, the generic morphology of c^*/C^*'s potential scheme of modal differentiations is also unalterable, so far as the *termini* of its transcendental references is concerned. But c^*/C^*, unlike $\partial\!\!\!/\,/C^*$, has no determinate modal structure made up of proper subregions with boundaries and internal structures rendered fully determinate through the unrestricted ingression of geometrical forms. This indeterminacy of c^*/C^*'s modal structure is precisely what makes possible the synthesis of its primary, or conformal, feelings in and by subsequent integral feelings. On the other hand, the measure of derivative determinacy attributable to c^*/C^*'s potential modal scheme is precisely what makes possible the unambiguous conformation of C's subjectivity to each individual objectification in C's objective content. Let us examine how c^*/C^*'s potential modal scheme functions in the origination of conformal and integral feelings.

First, let us notice that eternal objects of the objective species cannot ingress into c^*/C^*, lest they transform it into a second objectification of C's correlative universe and thereby rob C of its subjectivity. Therefore, the only determinate internal structure that c^*/C^* can come to have must result exclusively from the unrestricted ingression into it of simple and complex eternal objects of the subjective species. Here 'internal structure' means simply the internal differentiation of c^*/C^* in terms of simple and complex qualities. The qualities in question are qualities of C's subjectivity—that is to say, they are qualities of what C is for itself *qua* subject (AI 325; PR 354). They are also qualities of what C will be for others *qua* objectified superject. But the point to emphasize now is that the eternal objects whose ingressions into c^*/C^* determine the qualities of C's subjectivity are the determinants of the subjective forms of C's feelings (AI 325). Together they constitute the definiteness of C's final complex subjective form.

Second, let us remember that the final subjective form of an actual occasion is progressively built up by the supersessionally successive phases of feelings constitutive of the occasion in question, each feeling contributing its own individual subjective form. Moreover, the subjective form of each feeling must embody some subregion or other of the occasion's self-aspect. But which subregions of the occasion's self-aspect are embodied by which of the occasion's subjective forms is not a matter of chance. The relevant determining factors, in this regard, are the potential modal scheme of the occasion's self-aspect, the objectifications of other actualities including God, and the occasion's own immanent decisions. For example, which subregions of c^*/C^* are embodied by which of C's subjective forms is determined partly by the generic morphology of c^*/C^*'s potential modal scheme, partly by the objectifications in $\&/C^*$ and partly by C's own immanent decisions.

In respect to conformal subjective forms, however, only the first two determinants are at work; for an occasion cannot make any immanent decisions until it exists as an autonomous subject. For example, when the macroscopic process begets C's initial subjectivity in conformation to the objectifications in $\&/C^*$, the regional seat of each conformal subjective form is jointly determined by the individual objectification from which that subjective form is derived, and by the modal subregion of c^*/C^* mirroring the proper subregion embodied by that objectification. Indeed, the two determining factors are but two inseparable aspects of the one ultimate determining factor, which is the reciprocal extensive relationship obtaining between the two subregions in question. Thus, if the objectified occasion is, say, B, then the determining factor is the reciprocal extensive relationship between b^*/C^*, the proper modal subregion embodied by B's causal objectification, and $(b^*/C^*)^{**}/c^*/C^*$, the modal presence of b^*/C^* in c^*/C^*. For this reason, the subjective form of C's conformal feeling of B embodies $(b^*/C^*)^{**}/c^*/C^*$ and thereby refers transcendentally to its appropriate objective datum—the objective reality of B as embodying b^*/C^*.

It is important to remember here that each individual objectification in C's "total objective datum dictates its conformal qualitative reproduction in the subjective form" (AI 327). For this reason, corresponding to the distribution of objective data in ∂/C^*, there is a distribution of conformal subjective forms in c^*/C^*, each such subjective form unambiguously referring to its own individual objective datum in ∂/C^*. "Thus the distribution of subjective form among the separate prehensions refers primarily to the conformal origins of subjective form derived from the various components of the total objective datum" (AI 327). In this manner, the derivative determinacy of c^*/C^*'s potential modal scheme dictates the regional distribution of C's conformal subjective forms.

In respect to the subjective forms of integral feelings, however, the crucial determining factor is constituted by the immanent decisions of C *qua* autonomous subject; for neither the objectified occasions in ∂/C^*, nor the potential modal scheme of c^*/C^*, dictates how C's initial conformal feelings are to be integrated (AI 328). Nonetheless, any aesthetic integration that subject C decides to generate will necessarily make use of some aspect or other of c^*/C^*'s potential modal scheme. By way of illustration, let us consider an extremely simple integral feeling, one integrating two conformal feelings that have for their data the objectifications of extensively contiguous occasions. Say that B and R are two such occasions; then, b^*/C^* and r^*/C^* are extensively contiguous subregions of ∂/C^* and, correspondingly, $(b^*/C^*)^{**}/c^*/C^*$ and $(r^*/C^*)^{**}/c^*/C^*$ are extensively contiguous subregions of c^*/C^*. These last two subregions are embodied, respectively, by the subjective forms of C's conformal feelings of B and R. Since they are extensively contiguous, these two subregions constitute, through their aggregation, a third potential subregion of c^*/C^*. Let us designate this third subregion by $[(b^*/C^*)^{**}+(r^*/C^*)^{**}]^{**}/c^*/C^*$. Now, if C chooses to integrate its conformal feelings of B and R, it will do so by unrestrictedly ingressing into $[(b^*/C^*)^{**}+(r^*/C^*)^{**}]^{**}/c^*/C^*$ an eternal object of the subjective species having the appropriate relational essence to synthesize within it-self the eternal objects already ingressed at $(b^*/C^*)^{**}/c^*/C^*$ and $(r^*/C^*)^{**}/c^*/C^*$. The contrast of subjective forms which thereby results is the complex subjective form of an integral feeling whose immediate data are the two conformal feelings it subordinates within itself, but whose ultimate objective datum is the contrast of B and R as embodying b^*/C^* and r^*/C^*, respectively.

It is necessary to emphasize here, if only in passing, that the synthesis of the objectifications of B and R into a *felt contrast* is a derivative functional synthesis. The two objectifications are synthesized only insofar as the subregions they embody constitute the *terminus* of the transcendental reference of $[(b^*/C^*)^{**} + (r^*/C^*)^{**}]^{**}/c^*/C^*$. In other words, the complex subjective form of the integrating feeling, since it embodies both $(b^*/C^*)^{**}/c^*/C^*$ and $(r^*/C^*)^{**}/c^*/C^*$, refers transcendentally to a potential subregion of $\&/C^*$ constituted by the aggregation of b^*/C^* and r^*/C^*. By reason of this transcendental reference, the two objectifications embodying the two subregions, each its own, are felt *as* in the unity of a contrast. Thus, whereas the nexus of the two objectifications is an aboriginal datum for every subjective phase of C's becoming, their contrast, since it is generated by C itself in one of its subjective phases, can be a datum only for those of C's subjective phases that are supersessionally later than the one in which it is generated.

The generalization of this last conclusion is of the utmost importance for the understanding of Whitehead's metaphysics. The objectifications in an occasion's dative phase *have the unity of a nexus* by reason of their mutual immanence. Moreover, the dative phase as a whole, which includes the modal presence of all unactualized extension, *has an extensive unity* grounded on the separative, modal, and prehensive properties of extension. But the dative phase of an occasion *does not have the unity of a contrast*. It *gains* the unity of a contrast only by reason of the occasion's autonomous origination of integral feelings. Thus, the final unity of the occasion's total objective datum *is* the unity of a felt contrast corresponding to, and sustained by, the final unity of the occasion's total subjective form (PR 433–34). The point is that we must not confuse the dative phase's aboriginal unity, which is a *given for* the subjective concrescence, with its final unity as a felt contrast, which is *produced by* the subjective concrescence. To the extent that many received interpretations are vitiated by this confusion, they tend to misconstrue the process of transition by which the aboriginally unified dative phase is begotten.[6]

But I have digressed. It needs to be emphasized now that, in virtue of the total modal scheme of C^*, the integral prehension under analysis exhibits a mutual internal relation between the seat of its complex objective content and the seat of its complex subjective form. In other words, the aggregate subregion of $\mathcal{c}/C^*$ housing the prehension's objective content, and the aggregate subregion of c^*/C^* housing the prehension's subjective form, refer transcendentally to each other. There is no ambiguity of reference in either direction. Moreover, the unambiguous mutual reference of the two subregions is a metaphysical fact antecedently to the generation of the prehension. Thus, the mutual transcendental reference of the two subregions constitutes the extensive potentiality for the morphological unity of the prehension in question. The completed prehension is the concrete realization of that potentiality.

As a matter of fact, with the possible exception of pure conceptual prehensions, the concrete unity of every prehension, whether conformal or integral, is rendered possible by, and includes, the morphological unity of its objective and subjective seats. The importance of the morphological unity of each prehension is that it survives the death of the subject to which it belongs. Were it not for this ultimate metaphysical fact, the superjective existence of an occasion would provide no information whatever regarding the specific feelings enjoyed by that same occasion during its subjective existence. The morphology of the superject's extensive standpoint, with its fusion of metaphysical and empirical elements, is precisely what makes possible the imaginative reconstruction of the subjective process of experience. The reconstruction is logically possible, though not necessarily empirically possible, for any occasion in which that superject is causally objectified, and is limited by the degree to which the objectification abstracts from the superject's definiteness. The morphology of extensive standpoints, we may thus conclude, is the reason why each superject preserves within itself the history of its own process of becoming. In other words, it is the reason why each experience-product gives witness to the experience-process of which it is the outcome.

The extensive scheme of an occasion's standpoint, it is now evident, provides subregional niches not only for the objectifications of other occasions but also for the simple and complex qualities defining the occasion's own subjective content (PR 470). Moreover, the occasion's extensive scheme grounds not only the morphological unity of each of its constituent prehensions, but also the morphological integration of its supersessionally earlier prehensions in and by its supersessionally later ones. Similarly, the scheme grounds the morphological integration of the subjective forms that is presupposed by the integration of prehensions, and grounds also the derivative functional integration of the diverse components of the occasion's total objective content.

To be sure, all integration—whether of complete prehensions, or of their subjective forms, or of their data—results from the autonomous immanent decisions of the occasion *qua* subject. But the fact remains that the extensive scheme of the occasion's standpoint conditions every integration that the subject chooses to make. Thus, though Whitehead never makes this point sufficiently explicit, the occasion's internal extensive scheme is *one* indispensable ground (there are others) of the "mutual relations (a) between the objective content of a prehension and the subjective form of that prehension, and (b) between the subjective forms of various prehensions in the same occasion, and (c) between the subjective form of a prehension and the spontaneity involved in the subjective aim of the prehending occasion" (AI 325). Additional indispensable grounds are the occasion's subjective aim, the primordial counterpart of that aim, and the relational essences of the eternal objects unrestrictedly ingressed into the occasion's standpoint.

9. The dative scheme's relevance to genetic and coordinate analyses

The fact also remains that—since it is an essential ingredient of the occasion's dative phase, and since all other phases of the occasion's existence presuppose, refer to, and incorporate the dative phase—*an occasion's internal extensive scheme is an essential feature of every phase of the occasion's existence*, including the superjective phase or satisfaction (PR 470, 441). Because of this every completed occasion can be analyzed both genetically and coordinately (PR 433–48). An occasion's genetic analysis is one and the same with the imaginative reconstruction of the occasion's subjective process. It is the analysis of the occasion as in concrescence. An occasion's coordinate analysis emphasizes the potential divisibility of the completed occasion's extensive standpoint. It is the analysis of the occasion as already concrete. Both modes of analysis, it bears repeating, are predicated on the fact that the occasion's extensive scheme is the crucial morphological factor shaping the occasion's "qualitative content and objectifications of other particulars into a coherent finite experience" (PR 470).

In its genetic analysis, an actual occasion "is seen as a process; there is a growth from phase to phase; there are processes of integration and of reintegration. At length a complex unity of objective datum is obtained, in the guise of a contrast of actual entities, eternal objects, and propositions, felt with corresponding complex unity of subjective form" (PR 433–34). To understand how the genetic analysis of an occasion can be derived from the objectification of its satisfaction, we must bear in mind that no integral feeling ever abolishes the individual particularities of the feelings it integrates within itself, that no integral subjective form ever abolishes the individual particularities of the subjective forms it subordinates within itself, and that no felt contrast ever abolishes the individual particularities of the entities unified in that contrast. For example, the integral feeling we have been examining does not abolish the individual particularities of *C*'s initial conformal feelings of *B* and *R;* nor does the integral subjective form abolish the individual particularities of the conformal subjective forms; nor, finally, does the unity of the integral feeling's complex objective datum abolish the individual particularities of the objectifications of *B* and *R.*

This is not to deny the morphological unity of the integral feeling in question. Nor is it to deny that a real particular contrast of subjective forms, and a real particular contrast of objectifications, have been originated by the autonomous decisions of subject *C.* But the unique *individual essence* of each eternal object, on the one hand, and the unique *position* of each actual entity, on the other, ground not only the unique (though reproducible) self-identities of eternal objects and actual entities themselves, but also the unique (and also reproducible) self-identity of each nexus, each prehension, each subjective form, each proposition, each contrast and each multiplicity. Whitehead gives *partial* expression to this fundamental organic doctrine in the Categoreal Obligation of Objective Diversity, which states that "there can be no 'coalescence' of diverse elements in the objective datum of an actual entity, so far as concerns the functions of those elements in that satisfaction" (PR 344). But the doctrine is not limited to the contrasting elements in a complex objective datum. It applies to all modes of synthesis, regardless of the elements synthesized (PR 344, 347–56). The general doctrine, then, is that the individual particularities of the synthesized elements necessarily infect the individual particularity of their synthesis (PR 348–49).

Notice that, aside from eternal objects and multiplicities thereof, the self-identity of every entity of a categoreal type is 'positional' and thereby is dependent on the *indicative* function of an extensive scheme. Accordingly, the individual particularities of the objectifications, subjective forms, feelings, and other components of an actual entity cannot be divorced from the extensive scheme of the actuality's regional standpoint. This is another reason why the actuality's extensive scheme is the principal informational source from which its subjective process can be imaginatively reconstructed.

We should not be surprised by the relevance of an occasion's extensive scheme to the occasion's genetic analysis. The modal scheme of an occasion's dative phase *determines* the transcendental reference, or intentionality, of every subjective form accruing to that occasion *qua* subject, and *conditions* the integrations of subjective forms by which all aesthetic syntheses are achieved. That same dative modal scheme is a feature of the occasion's satisfaction and of every causal objectification of that satisfaction in and for later occasions. Therefore, an occasion's dative modal scheme is the aspect of its concrete nature that is most relevant to its genetic analysis. This is one reason why for genetic analysis "the primary fact about an occasion is its initial 'dative' phase" (PR 448).

The key to an occasion's genetic analysis is provided by the mutual reference of the modal scheme of its self-aspect and the modal scheme of its other-aspect. For the mutual reference of the two schemes ensures that the pattern of the satisfaction's "subjective form cannot be absolutely disjoined from the pattern of the objective datum" (PR 356–57). Indeed, any determinate component of either pattern necessarily refers transcendentally to some determinate component of the other pattern. Accordingly, there is an obvious procedure, or principle, by which the individual prehensions of an occasion can be discovered.

> The principle, according to which a prehension can be discovered, is to take any component in the objective datum of the satisfaction; in the complex pattern of the subjective form of the satisfaction there will be a component with direct relevance to this element in the datum. Then in the satisfaction, there is a prehension of this component of the objective datum with that component of the total subjective form as its subjective form. (PR 359)

This procedure is relatively straightforward in respect to the discovery of an occasion's initial conformal feelings; for it is aided by the derivative determinacy of the self-aspect's modal scheme and by the fact that no quality can be attributed to the subjective form of a conformal feeling that is not also a quality of the definiteness of that feeling's objective datum. Thus the reconstruction of an occasion's conformal feelings can be extremely accurate.

Unfortunately, because of the general indeterminacy of the self-aspect's dative modal scheme, and because integral feelings can overlap both in regard to the seats of their subjective forms and in regard to the seats of their objective data (PR 359), the discovery of an occasion's integral prehensions is much more difficult. Whitehead would seem to have this difficulty in mind when he says,

> There is some arbitrariness in taking a component from the datum with a component from the subjective form, and in considering them, on the ground of congruity, as forming a subordinate prehension. The justification is that the genetic process can be thereby analyzed. If no such analysis of the growth of that subordinate prehension can be given, then there has been a faulty analysis of the satisfaction. (PR 360)

We may conclude, therefore, that the discovery of an occasion's integral prehensions, though difficult, is indeed possible.

The genetic analysis of an occasion must reconstruct each successive phase of the occasion's aesthetic process. Thus, taking the dative phase as a given for the purposes of the analysis, it first reconstructs the phase of conformal feelings. Next, it reconstructs the phases of conceptual reproduction and reversion. Finally, it reconstructs the successive phases of integral feelings, beginning with a phase made up of the simplest integral feelings, passing through phases of progressively more complex integral feelings, and ending with the satisfaction itself, which is the final, all-encompassing, most complex integral feeling belonging to—indeed, it is the same as—the completed occasion. In the genetic analysis, therefore, each reconstructed phase groups together all the prehensions of a similar degree of complexity that have been discovered by the procedure just discussed.

However, if we were to take any one of the discovered feelings by itself and consider it as a feeling in terms of which the completed occasion could be causally objectified in some other occasion, we would be thereby considering what Whitehead calls a *coordinate division* of the first occasion. The coordinate analysis of an occasion, when that analysis is understood to be *metaphysical* rather than cosmological, is the analysis of the occasion into every constituent prehension, or coordinate division, by which it could be causally objectified in other occasions. In other words, the metaphysical coordinate analysis of an actual entity "is analytical of its potentiality for 'objectification' in the becoming of other actual entities" (PR 34). When we thus analyze an occasion, therefore, "we are analyzing the complexity of the occasion in its function of an efficient cause. It is in this connection that the morphological scheme of extensiveness attains its importance" (PR 448).

The morphological scheme is important for an occasion's coordinate analysis not only because it permits the discovery of its constituent prehensions, but also because each constituent prehension embodies one or another regional component of the scheme (PR 436–37). In fact, the term 'coordinate division', when it is not used as synonymous with 'coordinate analysis', signifies 'a coordinate region of the extensive scheme'. This is why Whitehead uses 'morphological analysis' and 'extensive analysis' as synonymous with 'coordinate analysis' (PR 331, 335). Thus, strictly speaking, a coordinate division is any quantum of extension coordinately related, or relatable, to other extensive quanta in virtue of the fact that all such quanta are modally present each in the others. In the broadest sense of the term, therefore, a coordinate division is any division of the extensive continuum: it may be a proper region, or a merely potential region, or a proper modal subregion, or a potential modal subregion. For example, B^*, C^*, and D^{**} are coordinate divisions composing part of the macrocosmic, or universal, scheme of extensive regions, and b^*/C^*, c^*/C^*, and $d^{**}/fu^{**}/\&^{**}/C^*$ are coordinate divisions composing part of the microcosmic scheme of extensive regions that is internal to C^*.

The metaphysical coordinate analysis of a completed occasion, however, is in terms of coordinate divisions that are each embodied by one or another of the occasion's constituent prehensions. Any such coordinate division will include both a subregion of the occasion's self-aspect and a subregion of its other-aspect. For example, let C be the occasion under analysis, and let its conformal prehension of B be the constituent prehension chosen for consideration; then, the coordinate division embodied by that prehension will be a potential modal subregion of C^* including both $(b^*/C^*)^{**}/c^*/C^*$ and b^*/C^*. "Thus we reach perceptive bonds involving one sub-region of the basic region of the perceiver, and one subdivision of the basic region of the perceived" (PR 440).

In thus interpreting what Whitehead means by a coordinate division and by the analysis of an occasion into coordinate divisions, I have made an effort to separate the metaphysical aspects of Whitehead's theory of coordinate analysis from the cosmological notions with which Whitehead mixes them. For the exposition of that theory, in PR, is concerned mostly with issues bearing on the cosmologically relevant theory of extensive connection. The latter theory, as we saw in Chapter Five, is concerned primarily with the special features of the realized continuum characterizing our cosmic epoch. Indeed, the theory of extensive connection is an attempt to rectify some of the defects of the method of extensive abstraction which Whitehead had used in his earlier works on the philosophy of nature (PR 339–40). In keeping with that end, the theory of extensive connection explicitly disregards the atomicity and mutual externality of the actual entities constituting our cosmic epoch (PR 449–59); thus, it does explicitly what the method of extensive abstraction had done implicitly (PR 440).

To that same end, the cosmological theory of coordinate analysis entirely disregards the morphological unity and determinate particularity of the individual prehensions constituting a completed occasion. For cosmological analysis, *any* potential subregion of the occasion's standpoint is a coordinate division of it, provided that the coordinate subregion in question include both a subregion of the occasion's self-aspect and a subregion of its other-aspect. In such an analysis, therefore, no attention is paid to the integrity of the proper modal subregions in the occasion's dative phase. Accordingly, the analysis yields an infinite number of potential modal subregions, each arbitrarily relating some component of the occasion's total objective datum with some component of its total subjective form.

In an occasion's metaphysical coordinate analysis, however, the lines of division are determined by the proper modal subregions of the occasion's dative phase. True, the satisfaction—or, more accurately, its objectification—is the primary fact given for coordinate analysis (PR 448). But it is the (objectified) satisfaction's dative modal scheme that determines where the divisions are made, for it assigns to each component objectification its position in the extenso-genetic order of actuality.

> In this way we obtain an analysis of the dative phase in terms of the 'satisfactions' of the past world. These satisfactions are systematically disposed in their relative status, according as *one* is, or is not, in the actual world of *another*. Also they are divisible into prehensions which can be treated as quasi-actualities with the same morphological system of relative status. (PR 448)

My point is that we need not concern ourselves here with those aspects of the theory of coordinate analysis which are derived from the fact that the "morphological system gains special order from the defining characteristic of the present cosmic epoch" (PR 448). What needs to be emphasized, instead, is that the dative modal scheme of an actual occasion is the principal factor of its terminal constitution enabling the discovery of its constituent prehensions and thereby enabling both the genetic and the coordinate analyses of the occasion. The former analysis reconstructs the growth of the individual prehensions and groups them into successive phases according to their complexity and order of growth. The latter analysis disregards the growth of the individual prehensions, emphasizes the modal subregions which they embody, each its own, and treats the prehensions as individual disjuncts in an exhaustive disjunction of the occasion's potential modes of objectification. The two most concrete ways in which an occasion may be analyzed, we must conclude, are possible only by reason of the occasion's dative modal scheme.

10. *Extensional solidarity and the philosophy of organism*

A coordinate division, as the preceding discussion has begun to make clear, is any extensive region considered in respect to its coordinate status in a scheme of extensive regions that are correlatively ordered by their modal presences in one another. Each coordinate division is either a *relatum* in a scheme of divisions internal to an actual entity, or it is a *relatum* in a scheme of divisions made up of the mutually transcendent standpoints of individual actualities. The former scheme is microcosmic, the latter is macrocosmic. There are at least as many microcosmic schemes as there are individual actual entities—more in fact, because the total microcosmic scheme of an actuality's standpoint is indefinitely analyzable into subordinate microcosmic schemes. For example, the total microcosmic scheme internal to C^* subordinates within itself the microcosmic schemes internal to b^*/C^*, r^*/C^*, and $s^{**}/pr^{**}/\&^{**}/C^*$, respectively. However, there is only one actual macrocosmic scheme of divisions, though it is ever expanding by the addition of novel standpoints.

The microcosmic scheme internal to an actual occasion, we must not forget, mirrors the macrocosmic scheme of which that occasion's standpoint is a coordinate division. Thus the microcosmic scheme is the modal presence within the occasion of the macrocosmic scheme of which that occasion's standpoint is a component. This intimate linkage between each microcosmic scheme and the macrocosmic scheme of extensive standpoints is a crucial presupposition of Whitehead's thesis of solidarity. For, by reason of the modal derivation of each microcosmic scheme from the one macrocosmic scheme, all the individual microcosmic schemes are internally related to each other, so that, in the end, *all microcosmic schemes are coordinated as aspects of the one macrocosmic scheme.*

Whitehead gives clear expression to the linkage between the one macrocosmic scheme and the many microcosmic schemes in at least two passages of PR. In one passage, the cosmological aspects of coordinate division color his language, but they do not obscure the metaphysical import of what he says:

But this scheme of *external* extensive relationships links itself with the schemes of internal division which are *internal* to the several actual entities. There is, in this way, one basic scheme of extensive connection, which expresses on one uniform plan, (i) the general conditions to which the bonds, uniting the atomic actualities into a nexus, conform, and (ii) the general conditions to which the bonds, uniting the infinite number of coordinate subdivisions of the satisfaction of any actual entity, conform. (PR 438–39)

In the other passage, the linkage is expressed in its metaphysical purity by explicitly appealing to "the solidarity of the extensive continuum" (PR 438).

This solidarity embraces not only the coordinate divisions within each atomic actuality, but also exhibits the coordinate divisions of all atomic actualities from each other in one scheme of relationship. (PR 438)

We thus come to understand what may be called the *extensional solidarity* of the universe.

By extensional solidarity I mean, first, the fact that the universe's eternal *extensiveness*—in virtue of the discreteness, prehensiveness, and mutual immanence of its regions—provides the morphological ground for all internal relations *within* and *between* actual entities. Whitehead's philosophy of organism obtains its name from that fact. For each actuality and each nexus of actualities is an *organization* of extensive regions united by their reciprocal extensive relations—relations at once of mutual transcendence, of mutual immanence, and of mutual transcendental reference. Every actuality, and every nexus, is more than that. But it is at least *that*. It follows that the fundamental metaphysical organisms posited by Whitehead's philosophy cannot be abstracted from the eternal extensiveness of the universe. For, as Whitehead says,

This extensiveness is the pervading generic form to which the mor-phological structures of the organisms of the world conform. These organisms are of two types: one type consists of the individual actual entities; the other type consists of nexūs of actual entities. Both types are correlated by their common extensiveness. (PR 439/CPR 287)

Without extensional solidarity, it is now clear, there can be no organization of coordinate regions. And without the organization of coordinate regions, it is also clear, there can be no actualities and no nexūs. The philosophy of organism, it then follows, cannot be abstracted from its metaphysical theory of extension without thereby severely distorting and truncating its most fundamental metaphysical doctrines.

By extensional solidarity I mean, in addition, four interrelated metaphysical doctrines bearing on the morphology of internal relations. The first doctrine is that the universe's eternal extensiveness expresses the solidarity of all extensive standpoints or, equivalently, of all *real potentialities* (PR 103–05), so that "extension is the most general scheme of real potentiality, providing the background for all other organic relations" (PR 105). The second doctrine is that the universe's eternal extensiveness grounds the systematic scheme of extensive relations that is exemplified in the *formal*, or intrinsic, reality of each occasion, so that the scheme is an essential ingredient of the *real potentiality* from which every occasion *arises* and of the *attained fact* which every occasion *is* (PR 441). The third doctrine is that the systematic scheme of extensive relations is exemplified not only in each actuality considered formally but also in each actuality considered *objectively*, or extrinsically, so that the universe's eternal extensiveness "provides the general scheme of extensive perspective which is exhibited in all the mutual objectifications by which actual entities prehend each other" (PR 118). The fourth doctrine is that the systematic extensive scheme inherent in the real potentiality for an occasion of *experience*, since it constitutes the objectification of the entire continuum of eternal extension and of every attained actuality already existing therein, is the "general relational element in experience whereby the actual entities experienced, and that unit experience itself, are united in the solidarity of one common world" (PR 112).

By extensional solidarity I mean, finally, that every region outside an occasion's regional standpoint contributes its own modal reality to the extensive scheme internal to that standpoint. Since the standpoint contributes its own modal self-aspect to its own internal extensive scheme, it follows that the standpoint requires all extensive regions, including itself, in order to be what it is and in order to have the internal scheme that it has. Thus, paraphrasing the original definition of solidarity by H. Wildon Carr, we can say that *extensional solidarity* means that diverse extensive regions, by their respective modal presences in a given region, bring to pass the internal modal scheme of that region, without thereby sacrificing either their individual integrity, or their transcendence of that region. The extensional solidarity of the universe, thus understood, is one aspect of the potentiality for, as well as being an ingredient in, the solidarity of the universe in each of its actual entities.

EIGHT

Solidarity and Individuality

I now bring this essay to its conclusion by examining how the extensional solidarity of the universe is presupposed by the organic theories of perception and knowledge and by explaining how the autonomous individuality of every actual entity is required by the solidarity of all actual entities. Two additional organic senses of solidarity will be thus illuminated. In addition, the general character of the remaining phases of *C*'s existential history will be carefully studied.

1. The conformal phases: from objectivity to subjectivity

The extensive scheme of an occasion's regional standpoint provides the morphological basis for the supersessional passage from the objectivity of the dative phase to the subjectivity of the conformal phases. As objectified within the dative phase, the occasion's correlative universe is a complex datum for feeling. In the dative phase proper, however, there is as yet no feeler, no subject, to feel the complex datum. The macroscopic process has begotten the nascent occasion's initial objective content, but it has yet to beget its initial *subjective* content. For the macroscopic process is not over. Its second process-subphase begets the occasion's initial subjective content by physically conforming the appropriate modal subregions of the occasion's self-aspect to the definiteness of the individual objectifications in the complex datum. Each individual conformation at once gives subjective content to the new occasion and completes the two-stage origination of a simple physical feeling. In this manner, the novel subject and its primary physical feelings are born simultaneously; for the primary feelings emerge as constituting the novel subject in its aboriginal phase of existence.

Notice that the subject is born *subjected* to percepta in the mode of causal efficacy (PR 271). Thus, the subject's primitive phase of experience is that of itself as conformed to others because of those others (S 43; AI 325–26). The conforming subject, strictly speaking, is the occasion's self-aspect now transformed into the subjective field of the nascent experience. The others conformed to, on the other hand, are the individual objectifications in the occasion's other-aspect, which is now transformed into the objective field of experience. The subjective field is the regional seat of the perceiving subject or 'mind', whereas the objective field is the field of perception correlative with that perceiver. But the nascent experience-process encompasses both the perceiving mind *and* the perceived field. In fact, "the field of perception and the perceiving mind are abstractions" from the concrete experience (SMW 282). Accordingly, perception in the mode of causal efficacy is the concrete experience of the perceiving mind's conformation to the objectifications in its correlative perceptual field. It is the experience of a subject enjoying itself as the immediate effect of the objects it perceives.

Here I am parting company with the letter, but definitely not with the spirit, of many but by no means all of Whitehead's writings on the nature of the perceiving subject. For Whitehead usually explicitly identifies the perceiving subject with the total occasion in process of becoming. The more coherent organic doctrine, however, is that the *subject*—in the strictest and most phenomenologically relevant sense of that term—is *not* the total occasion but is, instead, the occasion's ingredient self-aspect insofar as that proper modal subregion is rendered definite by the subjective forms accruing to it by reason, initially, of the efficacious past and, subsequently, of its own autonomous, teleological self-formation. The subject, to speak with even greater precision, is the occasion's self-aspect enjoying its growing definiteness and alive with its activity of purposeful self-definition. If we abstract the self-aspect from the enjoyment, from the growing definiteness, and from the teleological activity, we are left with the modal standpoint of the perceiving subject or mind. If we refrain from such an abstraction, the self-aspect is embodied by, and is thereby a component of, the perceiving subject. In the concrete, therefore, the self-aspect is that component of the perceiving subject whereby the latter's enjoyment and self-definition have the essential character of occurring *here-now* in relation to the scheme of extenso-genetic order exhibited by its correlative field of perception.

To illustrate my meaning, let c/C stand for the subject ingredient in occasion C. Then, c^*/C^* is not only subject c/C's regional standpoint, but is also that component of subject c/C whereby the latter has the essential character of occurring here-now in relation to entities—actual or potential—which either occurred there-then in c/C's past, or are occurring there-now in c/C's present, or will occur there-then in c/C's future. The status of existing there-then in the past, or there-now in the present, or there-then in the future, correlative with the status of subject c/C as existing here-now, is assigned to the entities in question by the scheme of extenso-genetic order exhibited by $\mathscr{O}/C^*$, the perceptual field correlative with the perceiving subject c/C. Thus, in addition to indicating the individual status of each causal objectification given for c/C, the extensive scheme of $\mathscr{O}/C^*$ permits the differentiation of c/C's perceptual field into three interrelated subfields: $fu^{**}/\mathscr{O}^{**}/C^*$, the subfield of the future; $pr^{**}/\mathscr{O}^{**}/C^*$, the subfield of the present; and $(\mathscr{O}^*)^{**}/C^*$, the subfield of the past, which last subfield is the smallest potential subregion of $\mathscr{O}/C^*$ resulting from the aggregation of all causal objectifications in $\mathscr{O}/C^*$. Notice that $(\mathscr{O}^*)^{**}/C^*$ and $\mathscr{O}^{**}/C^*$ constitute an exhaustive analysis of $\mathscr{O}/C^*$.

My contention, I must hasten to add, is *not* that an occasion as a whole cannot be construed as a subject or mind. Rather, my contention is that the subjectivity of the whole occasion *is* the subjectivity of its self-aspect, that the self-causation of the entire occasion *is* the self-causation of its self-aspect, and that the autonomous individuality of the total occasion *is* the autonomous individuality of its self-aspect. In respect to any one occasion, therefore, we certainly do *not* have two subjectivities, nor two processes of self-causation, nor two autonomous individuals. What we do have, instead, are two different ways of construing the one subjectivity, the one process of self-causation, the one autonomous individual. In one way, the subject is an ingredient in the ongoing experience-process, an ingredient conformed to, conditioned by, and autonomously defining itself in response to, other determinate ingredients in that same experience-process. Let us refer to the subject thus construed as the *empirical subject*. In another way, the subject *is* the total ongoing experience-process as internally related to a universe that is, in its entirety, both beyond and within the experience-process. Let us refer to the subject thus construed as the *metaphysical subject*.

The two ways of construing the subjectivity of a given occasion are intimately related by the fact that the *empirical* subject embodies the self-aspect of the *metaphysical* subject. Thus, in a metaphysically grounded sense, the empirical subject *is* what the metaphysical subject is *for itself.* For this reason, if the experience-process is sufficiently complex to involve intellectual self-analysis, "the mental cognition is seen as the reflective experience of a totality, reporting for itself what it is in itself as one unit occurrence" (SMW 207). For the same reason, "the primary situation disclosed in cognitive experience is 'ego-object amid objects'" (SMW 211). The ego-object *is* the empirical subject, which is surrounded by the objects in its perceptual field. But the metaphysical subject *is* the total experience-process as including within itself

> an impartial world transcending the 'here-now' which marks the ego-object, and transcending the 'now' which is the spatial world of simultaneous realisation. It is a world also including the actuality of the past, and the limited potentiality of the future, together with the complete world of abstract potentiality, the realm of eternal objects, which transcends, and finds exemplification in and comparison with, the actual course of realisation. (SMW 211)

Accordingly, the metaphysical subject is a unit experience-process encompassing the objective reality of its correlative universe, and existing for itself as an empirical subject engaged in the self-defining activity of subordinating the individual objects of its given world to the emerging unity of its own feelings.

As this last remark implicitly suggests, there is another metaphysical basis for connecting and justifying the two senses in which an actual occasion may be understood as a subject. For, as an occasion progresses through the supersessional phases of its experience-process, the empirical subject's autonomous origination and integration of subjective forms determines a corresponding origination and integration of feelings whereby the many individual objectifications in its perceptual field become subordinate contributors to the emerging unity of experience (PR 232–37). In effect, the progressive achievement of unity by the feeler, or empirical subject, is of a piece with the progressive achievement of unity by the total experience-process, or metaphysical subject, which includes the feeler, the feelings, and the objects felt. The *aesthetic synthesis* is the unity of the empirical subject, whereas the *experient synthesis* is the unity of the metaphysical subject. But the experient synthesis is brought about by the autonomous aesthetic synthesis. Thus, "the 'aesthetic synthesis' is the 'experient synthesis' viewed as self-creative, under the limitations laid upon it by its internal relatedness to all other actual occasions" (SMW 227).

Since the aesthetic synthesis subordinates the objective data as contributors to the satisfaction, it follows that in the subjective satisfaction the unity of the subject construed empirically finally coincides with the unity of the subject construed metaphysically. In this final coincidence of the two senses in which an occasion may be understood as a subject, we have the reason why the empirical subject may be said to *own* the experience-process in which it is an ingredient; for the determinate unification of the total experience-process depends on, and results from, the empirical subject's autonomous, teleological activity of self-unification. This dependence of the metaphysical unification on the empirical unification is the main reason why the empirical sense of subjectivity must be considered as phenomenologically basic.[1] It will be noted, finally, that corresponding to the empirical sense of subjectivity, there is a sense in which the subject is *in* the experience; whereas, corresponding to the metaphysical sense of subjectivity, there is a sense in which the experience is *in* the subject.

The two interrelated senses to be ascribed to the term 'subject'—and to its technical synonym, 'mind'—constitute another example of the systematic ambiguity which, by reason of either the modality of extension or the principle of relativity, necessarily attaches to all terms designating the metaphysical entities posited by the organic philosophy. In the case of 'subject', so far as the term is intended to denote the intrinsic reality of the occasion as experience-process, the ambiguity results from the fact that the regional standpoint of the occasion is modally present within itself. To neglect the ambiguity of the term is to court interpretative disaster; for if it is not kept in mind when reading Whitehead's pronouncements on subjectivity and experience, it will be easy to miss much of the import of the reformed subjectivist principle grounding the entire organic epistemology. I shall return to this matter later. For the moment, however, my immediate concern is not to let the ambiguity of 'subject' obscure the nature of the conformal phases in an occasion's becoming.

The phase of conformal physical feelings constitutes the birth of the empirical subject. The experience-process has begun and it exists for itself as an empirical subject perceiving the individual causal objectifications in its perceptual field. In itself, the experience-process is the inclusive whole within which the perceiving empirical subject is vaguely differentiated from the objects perceived. This intra-experiential differentiation, though qualitatively vague by reason of the absence of analytic mentality, is *structurally determinate*, being metaphysically grounded on the modal contrast between the seat of the perceiver, the self-aspect of the occasion's standpoint, and the seat of the perceived, the other-aspect of that standpoint. Accordingly, the creative passage from the objectivity of the dative phase to the subjectivity of the conformal phase cannot be divorced from the extensive scheme of the occasion's regional standpoint.

The standpoint's extensive scheme is presupposed also by the *vector* and *causal* characters of the conformal, or perceptual, feelings with which the empirical subject is born. For this subject, through no activity or choice of its own, finds itself existing informed with qualities that are not only *conformal with*, but also *referrent to*, the individual definiteness of the objectifications it is born perceiving. Thus, in the conformal phase, the nascent occasion, still fully in the grip of the macroscopic process of efficient causation, exists for itself as an empirical perceiver whose innate definiteness has been *transmitted* to it *from*, and to that extent *caused by*, the very objects it is perceiving. Here we must remember, as Whitehead says we should, "that in physics 'vector' means definite transmission from elsewhere" (PR 177). Accordingly, the empirical subject, since it is still in the grip of the individualizing manifestation of creativity, enjoys its conformal subjective forms as having been transmitted to it from elsewhere—namely from the objectifications it perceives—and thus as completing the two-stage creation of *vector* feelings that belong to it and that are simultaneously *causal*, conformal, and perceptual (PR 176–77). In virtue of its innate vector feelings, then, the empirical subject is born perceiving the efficient causes of its own initial state of conformal definiteness.

My point is that neither the vector character, nor the causal character, of an occasion's conformal feeling would be possible in abstraction from the transcendental reference which the occasion's subjective field bears to its objective field. True, the objectifications in the objective field *are* the efficient causes of the empirical subject's innate definiteness because they, or the superjects of which they are the reproductions, are the determinants of what the macroscopic transition begets in the responsive phase. But the objectifications are perceived by the empirical subject as the efficient causes of its own innate definiteness only in virtue of the transcendental reference which its conformal subjective forms bear to the definiteness of those objectifications. The definiteness of the perceived objectifications is composed of their own subjective forms or feeling-tones. Therefore, the empirical subject's perception in the mode of causal efficacy is its "perception of the settled world in the past as constituted by its feeling-tones, and as efficacious by reason of those feeling-tones" (PR 184).

To provide a final illustration of my interpretation of conformal feelings, I return to the examination of occasion C. The second process-subphase of the macroscopic transition begetting C creates subject c/C as the feeler of many unintegrated physical feelings, one feeling for each individual objectification in $\&/C^*$. One such feeling, for example, conforms c/C's initial definiteness to the definiteness of b/C, the causal objectification of B in C. This causal objectification, let us recall, embodies b^*/C^* and exhibits both the *position* and *definiteness* of superject B—the former concretely, the latter under some measure of abstraction. In this last regard, the point to emphasize is that, without any distortion of its unique particularity or self-identity, B is objectified in C not in the full definiteness of its satisfaction, but only as the feeler of one of its component feelings. B_2, we should recall also, is the subjective form of the feeling by which B is objectified in C; and x is the eternal object of the subjective species whose unrestricted ingression into $b^*/b^*/C^*$ constitutes the definiteness of B_2 as objectified in C.

The reason why c/C is said to be begotten as *conformally* feeling b/C is that the subjective form of that feeling, let us call it C_2, is defined by the unrestricted ingression into $(b^*/b^*/C^*)^{**}/c^*/C^*$ of eternal object x—the same eternal object which, as unrestrictedly ingressed into $b^*/b^*/C^*$, is expressing the definiteness of B_2. In its new ingression, x is expressing the initial sympathy of c/C for b/C, or, speaking metaphysically, of C for B (PR 446–47). The eternal object x, which is also an element in the subjective form of B's intrinsic reality, is now having a double but self-consistent function within C: as ingressed into $b^*/b^*/C^*$, it expresses part of *what* b/C is for c/C (or of *what* B is for C); and as ingressed into $(b^*/b^*/C^*)^{**}/c^*/C^*$, it expresses *how* c/C feels b/C (or how C feels B). In the former role, x is functioning *datively for* the newborn subject; in the latter role, x is functioning *subjectively in* the newborn subject (PR 249–50; AI 235–36). "Thus this eternal object in C's experience will have a two-way mode of functioning. It will be among the determinants of B for C, and it will be among the determinants of C's way of sympathy with B" (PR 446–47).[2]

Notice that in the creation of C's conformal feeling of B, an eternal object ingressed as a partial determinant of the definiteness of the objectification b/C, and previously ingressed as partial determinant of the definiteness of superject B, is again ingressed, this time as a partial determinant of the definiteness of C's subjectivity (PR 364, 446–47). In virtue of the fact that the *loci* of its three ingressions are modally interrelated, the one eternal object is functioning relationally *between* B and C, and is functioning relationally also *within* C (PR 446, 249). The eternal object's relational functioning *between* the two occasions is really a two-way mode of functioning: as a determinant of superject B, and as a determinant of the causal objectification of B in and for C. But the eternal object's relational functioning *within* C is also a two-way mode of functioning: as a determinant of the objective datum of C's feeling of B's objectification (or of c/C's feeling of b/C), and as a determinant of the subjective form of that feeling (PR 249, 446–47).

It must be emphasized that the three ingressions of the one eternal object could not function relationally in abstraction from the modal properties of the regions they qualify. By reason of the modality of those regions, however, the three ingressions may be viewed as a two-step 'transmission' of quality (or feeling-tone, or emotion, or energy) from the past occasion to the present occasion. In the first step, the quality is 'transmitted' from the past as *beyond* the new occasion, to the past as *within* the new occasion. In other words, the quality is 'transmitted' from B as embodying B^*, to B as embodying b^*/C^*. In truth, the quality merely 'accompanies' the past occasion to its new instantiation in and for the new occasion. For the one eternal object characterizes the definiteness of two instances of B: the first instance is the original superject, which is *outside* C; the second instance is the reproductive causal objectification, which is *inside* C. Thus, the first step in the transmission of the quality is merely a concomitant of the objectification of B in and for C. In the second step of its transmission, however, the quality 'passes' from the past as already objectified in C, to the newborn subjectivity of C. It passes, in short, from b^*/C^* to c^*/C^*. In its second step, therefore, the transmission occurs *within* the one novel occasion of experience. It is a transmission *from* the objective field, and *to* the subjective field, of one and the same experience-process. This second transmission completes the creation of the conformal feeling whereby subject C (or subject c/C) is born enjoying a form of subjective definiteness inherited from B (or from b/C) by reason of the efficacy of B.[3]

The first phase of the subjective process, I have said repeatedly, is the phase of conformal feelings. It is the individualizing phase in the becoming of a new occasion. "The datum includes its own interconnections, and the first stage of the process of feeling is the reception into the responsive conformity of feeling whereby the datum, which is mere potentiality, becomes the individualized basis for a complex unity of realization" (PR 173). In the conformal phase the occasion is an individual because it exists *for* itself, as well as *in* itself. Nevertheless, in this phase the individuality of the occasion is deficient because the newborn subject exhibits, as yet, no autonomy of function and no originality of response to its datum. Thus, the complete individualization of the occasion awaits the third process-subphase of the macroscopic transition begetting that occasion. It awaits, in other words, the emergence of conceptual feelings derived by the macroscopic process from the physical feelings of the conformal phase. For included among the feelings of conceptual reproduction thus originated is the occasion's initial subjective aim, and this aim makes possible the feelings of conceptual reversion at once grounding and exhibiting the newborn subject's autonomy and originality.

The phase of conceptual reproduction not only provides the new subject with its initial subjective aim but also effects the mental conformation of the subject to its datum. Accordingly, the phase of simple physical feelings and the phase of conceptual reproductions may be construed as the conformal phases of the subjective process. The former phase completes the occasion's physical pole and thereby internally relates its nascent subjectivity to the actual course of universal history. The latter phase initiates the occasion's mental pole and thereby internally relates its emergent autonomy to the primordial ground of all novelty and creative order. Jointly the two phases constitute the energizing of the real present by God and the actual past (AI 362, 256, 269).

The autonomous, originative stage of the subjective process begins with the second phase of the mental pole—the phase of conceptual reversion. In other words, the subject's autonomous generation of feelings of conceptual reversion marks the beginning of the microscopic process of concrescence. Thus, the mental pole's earlier phase of conceptual reproduction is the last phase of the macroscopic process of transition. With its completion, the individualizing manifestation of the eternal creative envisagement has run its course. But it has begotten a novel subject owning a now fully individualized manifestation of the creative envisagement and thereby endowed with originative autonomy. The subject thus begotten exhibits the full individuality of that which exists for itself as engaged in a process of autonomous teleological self-formation, under conditions imposed by the determinate circumstances of its birth.

2. The integrative phases: extension and the modes of perception

Under the determining influence of God and the actual past, the macroscopic transition effects the bipolar constitution, or creation, of the novel concrescent subject (PR 374). "If we prefer the phraseology," writes Whitehead, "we can say that God and the actual world constitute the character of the creativity for the initial phase of the novel concrescence. The subject, thus constituted, is the autonomous master of its own concrescence into subject-superject" (PR 374). But regardless of how we may wish to phrase it, the point remains that the macroscopic transition begets a self-creating creature. The microscopic concrescence is the teleological process by which the creature autonomously completes itself.

The two processes, macroscopic and microscopic, are not to be confused with one another. The earlier one is *determined* by the macrocosmos it *envisages*, whereas the later one is only *conditioned* by the microcosmos it *perceives*. The one is the vehicle for the deterministic efficient causation of the universal nexus or macrocosmic organism; the other is the vehicle for the autonomous final causation of the microcosmic organism (PR 326–27). Nonetheless, the two processes are supersessionally successive episodes in the becoming of one and the same occasion.[4] The earlier one begets a new subject with a completely determinate *position*, but with an only partially determinate *definiteness;* the later one is the subject itself autonomously completing its own definiteness and thereby integrating its inherited repetitive feelings under the originative ones of its own creation.

The complex details of the theory of concrescent subjectivity—details intended to do justice to the breadth, the depth, and the richness of human experience—are well beyond the scope and concerns of this essay. Only two aspects of the theory of concrescence are immediately relevant to the essay's basic interpretive theses: first, the general character of perceptual and cognitive experience insofar as the primitive and derivative components of its objective content are underlaid by the morphology and the relationships of its extensive scheme; and second, the autonomous individuality of the concrescent creature insofar as it completes the solidarity of the universe in that creature. I examine the latter aspect of the theory in later sections. Here and in the next section I concentrate on the former.

My immediate contention is that each autonomous concrescence remains conditioned, in each of its phases, by the extensive relations of its standpoint. These relations, according to Whitehead, form a systematic scheme which is involved not only in the real potentiality from which every actual occasion arises, but also "in the attained fact which every actual occasion *is*" (PR 441). Accordingly, the phases intervening between the real potentiality, or dative phase, and the attained fact, or final satisfaction, also involve the standpoint's scheme of extensive relations. Indeed, as we saw earlier, the extensive relations of the scheme bind the prehensions of the concrescent subject into an integral unity, coordinately divisible. There is thus a fourfold involvement of a standpoint's extensive scheme in the becoming and being of the occasion embodying that standpoint: (i) in the occasion's datum, (ii) in its conformal phases, (iii) in its concrescent phases, and (iv) in its concrete superject. This fourfold involvement is aptly summarized by Whitehead as follows:

> We have now traced the main characteristics of that real potentiality from which the first [subjective] phase of a physical occasion takes its rise. These characteristics remain inwoven in the constitution of the subject throughout its adventure of self-formation. The actual entity is the product of the interplay of physical pole with mental pole. In this way, potentiality passes into actuality, and extensive relations mould qualitative content and objectifications of other particulars into a coherent finite experience. (PR 470)

We have seen already how the occasion's extensive scheme underlies the subject's experience of the causal efficacy of its past world. But the extensive scheme plays a fundamental role also in the concrescent subject's experience of its contemporary world and of its future world. In this respect the theory of extension is intended to answer the question: How can the present and the future, relative to an experiencing subject, be objectively real for that subject? Here it must be remembered that contemporary occasions are not causally related, and that there are no *existing* future occasions, relative to an experiencing subject. Moreover, the objectively real is always, in some sense, *given*. For, according to Whitehead:

> Two conditions must be fulfilled in order that an entity may function as an object in a process of experiencing: (1) the entity must be *antecedent*, and (2) the entity must be experienced in virtue of its antecedence; it must be *given*. Thus an object must be a thing received, and must not be either a *mode* of reception or a thing *generated* in that occasion. (AI 229)

The problem, then, is: How can the present and the future be given in virtue of their antecedence? The only possible answer is that what is given for the subject's experience is the objective reality of the eternal extensiveness in which any contemporary or future occasion must find its emplacement. For, since the continuum is eternal, the objective realities of its unactualized regions can be given in virtue of their antecedence. Moreover, what is thus given is something which is an essential factor of any occasion, past, present, or future.

The problem is solved, then, by the doctrine that the continuum of extensive potentiality is a datum for every actual occasion (PR 103–05, 123). The objective reality of the whole world—past, present, and future—is a function of the manifold objective reality of the scheme of extensive relations: every objectification, be it in the causal mode, or in the presentational mode, or in the anticipatory mode, must find its niche in this scheme (PR 103). "The prehension of this scheme is one more example that actual fact includes in its own constitution real potentiality which is referent beyond itself. The former example is 'appetition'" (PR 112–13).

Since all actual occasions are related according to the metaphysical determinations of the extensive scheme, it follows that

> all possible actual entities in the future must exemplify these deter-
> minations in their relations with the already actual world. The reality
> of the future is bound up with the reality of this continuum. It is the
> reality of what is potential in its character of a real component of what
> is actual. (PR 103)

Returning to our example, this means that $fu^{**}/\&^{**}/C^*$ is the portion of C's extensive standpoint that refers itself to the extensive potentiality to be actualized by the occasions in C's future. The assumption must be made, however, that $fu^{**}/\&^{**}/C^*$ gives witness to the transcendent envisaging and creative potentiality as well as to the transcendent extensive potentiality. This is one reason for construing the Receptacle as being at once envisaging, creative, and extensive. Construed in that manner, $fu^{**}/\&^{**}/C^*$ is the objective reality of C's future, insofar as that future is given to C in virtue of its antecedence.

Nevertheless, C's anticipatory feelings may and do add content to this given presence of the future. For example, C's prehension of $!d^{**}/fu^{**}/\&^{**}/C^*$ involves a special mode of ingression of eternal objects of both species: those of the objective species, to indicate that the immediate successor of C will embody D^{**}, and will modally mirror C; those of the subjective species, to indicate the factor of individual definiteness by which C, through its physical purposes, aims to be causally objectified in D^{**}. In this respect, there is an anticipatory objectification of D in C that is effected by C itself but that presupposes an aboriginal extensive datum. As anticipated by C, the objective reality of D, its immediate successor, is a synthesis into $!d^{**}/fu^{**}/\&^{**}/C^*$ of eternal objects as not-being, and as requiring the transition from C to D by which non-being becomes being (SMW 246).

The objective reality that Whitehead repeatedly attributes to the future is thus to be understood in terms of the theory of the extensive scheme (PR 327; IS 241–43). For "the systematic scheme, in its completeness embracing the actual past and the potential future, is prehended in the positive experience of each actual entity" (PR 112). Thus, seen in the light of the doctrine of extension, as advanced and developed in this essay, the following account of the future's objective reality can be read with greater understanding:

> An 'object' is a transcendent element characterizing that *definiteness* to which our 'experience' has to conform. In this sense, the future has *objective* reality in the present, but no *formal* actuality. For it is inherent in the constitution of the immediate, present actuality that a future will supersede it. Also conditions to which that future must conform, including real relationships to the present, are really objective in the immediate actuality.
> Thus each actual entity, although complete so far as concerns its microscopic process, is yet incomplete by reason of its objective inclusion of the macroscopic process. It really experiences a future which must be actual, although the completed actualities of that future are undetermined. In this sense, each actual occasion experiences its own objective immortality. (PR 327–28)[5]

The extensive scheme, needless to say, plays a similar role in regard to the objective reality of the world contemporary with an experiencing subject (PR 96). Thus, to return to my example, $pr^{**}/\&^{**}/C^*$ is the portion of C's standpoint that refers itself to the extenso-genetic potentiality being actualized by the occasions forming C's contemporary world. In other words, $pr^{**}/\&^{**}/C^*$ is the presentational objectification, in C, of C's contemporary world, insofar as that world is given in virtue of its antecedence. This modal subregion of C's standpoint is itself an extensive continuum exhibiting, for C, the metaphysical properties of the contemporary world, but *not* exhibiting the many real actualities in that world, except insofar as their occupation of extensive regions is a necessary element of their respective characters (PR 96–97). "The objectification of the contemporary world merely expresses that world in terms of its potentiality for subdivision and in terms of the mutual perspectives which any such subdivision will bring into real effectiveness" (PR 104).

Thus, as initially given, the objectification of C's contemporary world is reduced to a potential extensive scheme defining (i) the geometrical perspectives of C, "and (ii) possibilities of mutual perspectives for other contemporary entities *inter se*, and (iii) possibilities of division" (PR 96). In its original presentation, then, "the contemporary world is perceived with its potentiality for extensive division, and not in its actual atomic division" (PR 96). But *C*'s presentational feelings may add both geometrical pattern and qualitative definiteness to the original presentational datum. Indeed, if *C* is an occasion with a sufficiently complex mode of experiencing, it may construct a representation of what its contemporary world should be like, based on the information provided by its feelings of the actual past which it shares with that contemporary world (AI 251–53; PR 256). For, to the extent that *C*'s immediate environment is dominated by any uniform type of coordination, or by laws of inheritance massively exemplified by the members of its cosmic epoch, *C* "will experience its past as 'anticipating' the prolongation of that type of order into the future beyond that past. But this future includes the occasion in question and its contemporary environment" (AI 253). *C*, then, can transmute the structural and qualitative patterns of the immediate past into representative characteristics of its contemporary world; for "there is a basis in fact for the association of derivates from significant regions in the past with the geometrical representatives of those regions in the present" (AI 280–81).

For example, by reason of its prehension of the causal objectification of *R*, *C* may differentiate, by means of a geometrical form, $s^{**}/pr^{**}/\mathring{\&}^{**}/C^*$ from the rest of its presentational datum. The basis for that differentiation is provided by $!s^{**}/fu^{**}/\mathring{\&}^{**}/r^*/C^*$, which is the objectification in *C* of *R*'s anticipation of its immediate successor, *S*. (In this example, it must be remembered, *S* and *C* are contemporaries.) In addition, since "each historic route of like occasions tends to prolong itself, by reason of its weight of uniform inheritance derivable from its members" (PR 88), *C* may transmute a quality shared alike by *P*, *Q*, and *R*, into a character of *S*, or rather, of $s^{**}/pr^{**}/\mathring{\&}^{**}/C^*$. With the characters it has gained through transmutation, $s^{**}/pr^{**}/\mathring{\&}^{**}/C^*$ is the objective reality which *S* has for a later phase of *C*'s experience.

It should be noted that *C* may objectify an entire nexus of contemporary occasions by means of this procedure of transmutation (PR 483–85). Notice that the given make-up of $pr^{**}/\mathring{\&}^{**}/C^*$ offers no obstacle to transmutation.

> For the contemporary entities do not enter into the constitution of the percipient subject by objectification through any of their own feelings. Thus their only direct connection with the subject is their implication in the same extensive scheme. Thus a nexus of actual entities, contemporary with the percipient subject, puts up no

alternative characteristics to inhibit the transference to it of characteristics from antecedent nexūs. (PR 484)

We thus see how the interpretation of extension advanced in this essay affords an explanation of how contemporary occasions can be objectively real for one another. It must be emphasized, however, that beyond the mere extensive datum, the objective reality of contemporary and future occasions results from elaborations on the datum which are generated by the subjective concrescence itself. Only the objective reality of the past is entirely a given.

The transmutative activity whereby the subject employs sensa, derived from the objectifications of past occasions, to differentiate its presentational field (or its subfield of the present) into contrasting regions is termed *physical imagination* (IS 245).

> This physical imagination has normally to conform to the physical memories of the immediate past; it is then called sense-perception, and is nondelusive. It may conform to the physical memories of the more remote past: it is then called the image associated with memory. It may conform to some special intrusive element in the immediate past such as, in the case of human beings, drugs, emotions, or conceptual relationships in antecedent mental occasions: it is then variously called delusion, or ecstatic vision, or imagination. (IS 245)

The point is that the images associated with perceiving, remembering, imagining, dreaming, and hallucinating are all experienced as differentiating one and the same presentational field. Hence these images, though not necessarily what they symbolically refer to and represent, are always experienced as contemporary with the experiencing subject. In the case of human mnemonic experience, for example, the memory image—say a magazine-cover depicting a harbor scene—is experienced by the subject here-now as existing there-now, but also as being a copy of, and referring to, the perceptual-image of an earlier experience-product belonging to the same enduring subject to which the present occasional subject belongs. Thus the memory-image "is the image in the present, but its equally present character of being a copy arises from its comparison with the objectification of the past which is the true memory" (IS 244).

Perception in the mode of presentational immediacy, we thus see, is *not* limited to the subject's sensory-perception of aspects of its contemporary world but *includes* also its sensory-*recollection* of aspects of its past world, its sensory-*anticipation* of possible aspects of its future world, and its sensory-*construction*—under whatever influence, or to whatever end—of possible aspects of possible worlds: worlds dreamt, or worlds phantasized, or worlds hallucinated, or worlds hypothesized. Accordingly, remembering, anticipating, imagining, dreaming, and hallucinating are but different sub-modes of presentational immediacy. These sub-modes differ from each other in respect either to the source, or to the meaning, of the sensa they involve; but, in any given occasion, they all involve one and the same presentational field. Thus, the psychologically commonplace fact that any one self-same moment of human experience is likely to contain an objectively harmonious integration of images or sensa of different sub-modalities—usually of recollections, perceptions, and anticipations, but most dramatically, if unusually, of hallucinations and veridical perceptions—is exactly what we should expect, given the organic theory of presentational immediacy.

Notice that the presentational field is the modal presence, within the metaphysical subject, of the region of the eternal extensive continuum that is atomized by the contemporaries of that subject. Thus, the presentational field correlative with a given empirical subject, $pr^{**}/\&^{**}/C^*$ in the case of empirical subject c/C, is given by reason of the metaphysical properties of eternal extension. Notice, too, that the modal givenness of the extensiveness of the occasion's contemporary world is the *true* presentational objectification and is an aboriginal feature of the occasion. Notice, finally, that perception in the mode of presentational immediacy involves the empirical subject's autonomous embellishment of presentational objectification with the sensa it derives from the causal objectifications it is perceiving in the mode of causal efficacy. Therefore, though presentational objectification is no less primitive than causal objectification, perception in the mode of presentational immediacy is *derivative from*, and thus supersessionally *subsequent to*, perception in the mode of causal efficacy.

To speak with greater precision, I should say that perception in the mode of presentational immediacy is subsequent to physical memory; for perception in the mode of causal efficacy exhibits two distinct sub-modes: (i) *physical memory*, which is the empirical subject's perception of the *actual* causal efficacy of its past world; and (ii) *physical anticipation*, which is the empirical subject's perception of the *potential* causal efficacy of itself in the future, and of its contemporary world in that same future (IS 243–44; PR 271; AI 234, 246–51). But physical anticipation must be supersessionally later than physical memory, since it presupposes the empirical subject's structural and qualitative embellishment of that portion of its objective field that is the modal presence, within the metaphysical subject's standpoint, of the eternal extension to be realized and embodied by future occasions. Because the autonomous activity of the empirical subject is presupposed by both presentational immediacy and physical anticipation, it follows that at least some phases of presentational immediacy will be supersessionally earlier than some phases of physical anticipation (AI 266). This is necessarily the case because the last subjective phase of an occasion's becoming is marked by the heightened importance of physical anticipation. As Whitehead says: "The final phase of anticipation is a propositional realization of the essence of the present-subject, in respect to the necessities which it lays upon the future to embody it and to re-enact it so far as compatibility may permit. Thus the self-enjoyment of an occasion of experience is initiated by an enjoyment of the past as alive in itself and is terminated by an enjoyment of itself as alive in the future" (AI 248–49).

Notice that c/C's enjoyment of itself as alive in the future involves, but is not reducible to, its regional feeling of $c*/c*//!d**/fu**/\&\text{-}**/C*$. For the region in question would exhibit the qualitative definiteness with which c/C aims at being objectified in its immediate successor. Notice, too, that c/C's physical anticipation involves an embellishment of $fu**/\&\text{-}**/C*$, the modal subregion that is the *true* anticipatory objectification of the potentiality for the future beyond c/C. But the structural and qualitative embellishment of the modal subregion involves the ingression of eternal objects conceptually derived from the occasion's initial physical feelings of past occasions and God. Therefore, though anticipatory objectification is no less primitive than causal objectification, physical anticipation is *derivative from*, and thus supersessionally *subsequent to*, physical memory.

Causal efficacy and presentational immediacy are the two pure modes of perception posited by Whitehead (PR 255). A perceptual feeling belongs to a pure mode if its immediate objective datum is located in exactly one of the three subfields of perception. Thus, if the feeling is one of causal efficacy, its objective datum is located either in the subfield of the past, or in the subfield of the future, but not in both; if the feeling is one of presentational immediacy, its objective datum is located in the subfield of the present (PR 188–89). Pure perceptual feelings obtain only in the earliest phases of subjective experience because all feelings, including perceptual feelings of different modalities and sub-modalities, must be gradually integrated as the subjective experience progresses toward its final satisfaction (PR 255). The integration of different modalities of perceptual feelings constitutes the mixed, or impure, mode of perception termed *symbolic reference*.

The importance of symbolic reference for the organic theory of human perception and cognition cannot be exaggerated, since, according to Whitehead, "when human experience is in question, 'perception' almost always means 'perception in the mixed mode of symbolic reference'" (PR 255–56). To the extent that our knowledge is based on human perception, then, the epistemology advanced by the organic philosophy cannot be understood in abstraction from the complex theory of symbolic reference. However, this is not the place to consider the subtleties of the latter theory. For our purposes, it will suffice to provide an illustration of how perception in the mixed mode of symbolic reference presupposes the modal relations and transcendental references inherent in the extensive scheme of an occasion's standpoint.

The integrability of the two pure modes of perception, and the ability of an element of either mode to function as a *symbol* referring to a corresponding *meaning* in the other mode, equally presuppose the existence of components common to both pure modes (PR 255, 274). The common components are sensa and extensive *loci* (S 49; PR 256, 259). That there should be sensa in common is not surprising, for the sensa of presentational immediacy are derivative from the sensa of causal efficacy. For example, c/C's pure perceptual feeling of S as embodying $s^{**}/pr^{**}/\&^{**}/C^*$, and its pure perceptual feeling of R as embodying r^*/C^*, share a particular sensum because the definiteness of the objective datum of the presentational feeling is partly derived from the definiteness of the objective datum of the causal feeling. What may seem surprising is that the objective data of the two feelings do exhibit certain extensive *loci* in common. How can this be if one objective datum is in the subfield of the past, and the other is in the subfield of the present?

The only possible answer is that the *locus* of the causal objective datum and the *locus* of the presentational objective datum are modally immanent in one another. By reason of this mutual immanence, the direct perception of either *locus* involves an indirect perception of the other *locus* as a modal presence in the directly perceived *locus*. For example, in the causal feeling, r^*/C^* is directly perceived, whereas $s^{**}/pr^{**}/\&^{**}/C^*$ is only indirectly perceived in that feeling by reason of $!s^{**}/fu^{**}/\&^{**}/r^*/C^*$; similarly, in the presentational feeling, $s^{**}/pr^{**}/\&^{**}/C^*$ is directly perceived, whereas r^*/C^* is only indirectly perceived in that feeling by reason of $(r^*)^{**}/s^{**}/pr^{**}/\&^{**}/C^*$. Put in simpler terms, this means that, in C's experience, the objective reality of R is perceived directly in causal efficacy and indirectly in presentational immediacy, whereas the objective reality of S is perceived directly in presentational immediacy and indirectly in causal efficacy. Thus, what is perceived directly and distinctly in one mode is perceived indirectly and indistinctly in the other mode (PR 256–59, 262).

To the extent that a causal feeling and a presentational feeling relevantly involve a common extensive ground, in the sense of 'common' just described, they can be synthesized in an integral feeling, and they can function in that feeling as correlated symbol and meaning. For example, if the presentational *locus* of S is the common ground in question, then, in C's perception in the mode of symbolic reference, the objective reality of S is perceived as symbolically referring to the objective reality of R: S as symbol may signify R as being S's immediate efficient cause; or S as symbol may signify R as being an earlier moment of the enduring object of which S is the current, or present, moment. The actual relation of symbolization is decided by C, but is grounded, so far as mere reference is concerned, on the metaphysical properties of the extensive scheme in general, and of the presentational *locus* of S's objective reality in particular. But the point to emphasize now is that the correlative location of S, so far as it is a component of the presentational field, "is a common ground for the symbolic reference, because it is directly and distinctly perceived in presentational immediacy and is indistinctly and indirectly perceived in causal efficacy" (PR 257).

3. *Perception, knowledge, and objective solidarity*

In human experience, symbolic reference is the mode of perception which normally serves as the datum for conscious cognition. What we consciously know about the world is either revealed in, or inferable from, what we perceive in the mode of symbolic reference. What we thus *know* are enduring entities constituting an enduring world with a determinate past and an indeterminate future. What we consciously *perceive* are sensa illustrating spatial regions that, though always contemporary with us as perceivers, are generally significant not only of the contemporary world as such but also of its actual past and its potential future. The actual past and the potential future, thus signified, are *not* in any way inferred; they are *directly* perceived also, but in the mode of causal efficacy. Thus, though they emerge into consciousness only vaguely and indistinctly, the existence of an actual past and the existence of a potential future are never an issue for, and indeed are presupposed by, the common practices and beliefs of mankind. The man in the street may not know *how* he knows these things, but he knows *that* he knows them.

Nevertheless, in the modern period of philosophy there has never been a shortage of thinkers willing to claim that the existence of an actual past and a potential future can be known, if at all, only at the tail end of a long and laborious chain of complex inferences sanctioned solely by the fashionable epistemology of the day. This astonishing claim, according to Whitehead, results from the fact that heretofore modern epistemologies, however different they may be in other respects, are alike in their misguided attempt to construe perception in the mode of presentational immediacy as the sole perceptual datum for conscious cognition (PR 125; AI 170). Denuded of its basis in causal efficacy, however, presentational perception is reduced to a barren, meaningless display of sensa differentiating from one another the spatial regions they each embody. The regions and their sensa can have no significance whatsoever because there is nothing to signify (PR 216). Reality has been reduced to a momentary display of sensa illustrating regions for a momentary ego (AI 170). The illustrated regions are externally related to each other and are silent, individually and collectively, as to the existence of an actual past or a potential future.

Moreover, insofar as they are abstracted from the metaphysical scheme of extensive relations, the sensa and the regions they embody have lost all claim to independence and objectivity. Their joint reality can in no way transcend its present disclosure. What is perceived is, for all intents and purposes, a state of the perceiver; at best, what is perceived is something that could not exist independently of the perceiving ego. Accordingly, aside from the sensa and the regions in which they inhere, there is nothing for the momentary ego to know.

For Whitehead, the fact that modern epistemologies unwittingly trap the would-be knower in the solipsistic prison of the present moment constitutes, in effect, a *reductio ad absurdum* of at least one of their common assumptions (PR 78, 85, 125, 240). Whitehead believes this theoretical predicament arises from the attempt by epistemologists to adopt the subjectivist bias given to modern philosophy by Descartes, while still retaining as metaphysically primary a number of Aristotelian notions that are ultimately incompatible with that bias (PR 238–43). The bias in question constitutes a metaphysical doctrine as to the primary data for metaphysical philosophy and amounts to the doctrine that "subjective experiencing is the primary metaphysical situation which is presented to metaphysics for analysis" (PR 243).

The philosophy of organism accepts the subjectivist doctrine, or bias, as the legitimate starting point of metaphysics. But it rejects the inherited metaphysical trappings with which the doctrine was immediately clothed. In this regard, Descartes and his rationalist and empiricist successors, under the influence of scholastic habits of thought, assumed—explicitly or implicitly, consciously or unconsciously—that the experient subject must be an Aristotelian primary substance. In their eyes, therefore, the subjectivist bias became the doctrine "that those substances which are the subjects enjoying conscious experiences, provide the primary data for philosophy, namely, themselves as in the enjoyment of such experience" (PR 241). They also assumed with Aristotle that a primary substance is always a subject and *never* a predicate (PR 239). Accordingly, for them the analysis of any substance that is a subject enjoying conscious experiences could never yield even a single component substance, for that would be tantamount to predicating one substance of another substance. Since they also accepted the Aristotelian assumption that the relation of quality-inhering-in-substance is an ultimate metaphysical principle, this meant for them that the analysis of a substantial subject enjoying experiences could yield only the qualities inhering in that substance (PR 239, 241).

Taken together the last two assumptions "are the foundation of the traditional distinction between universals and particulars" (PR 239). This distinction, which Descartes and his successors accepted as metaphysically ultimate, provides a natural bridge for passing from a subjectivist doctrine as to the primary data for metaphysics to a subjectivist doctrine concerning the datum for subjective experience (PR 238–39). For, given the assumptions under discussion, that datum can be no more than a cluster of qualities, or universals, inherent in the experiencing subject. This doctrine *as to the datum for subjective experience* is termed by Whitehead, not without equivocation,[6] the *subjectivist principle*—namely, "that the datum in the act of experience can be adequately analyzed purely in terms of universals" (PR 239). This principle has the immediate, though generally ignored, consequence of rendering illegitimate the attempt by modern epistemologists to construe perceptual experience as the awareness, by one substance, that a universal quality is qualifying another substance (PR 240–41). The subjectivist principle makes perceptual experience, thus construed, a theoretical impossibility because the only qualities that a perceiving substance can perceive are those by which it is itself qualified (PR 77, 209).

Nor does the subjectivist principle allow the claim that the privately perceived qualities represent, and even resemble, other particular substances. For representative perception "can never, within its own metaphysical doctrines, produce the title deeds to guarantee the validity of the representation of fact by idea" (PR 85). In the first place, the validating comparison between fact and idea, or between substance and sensum, is impossible in principle. The mind perceives only the idea, or sensum; the fact, or substance, is hopelessly beyond perception. In the second place, no mere sensum qualifying the perceiving mind can possibly appear to that mind as representing, let alone resembling, a particular substance existing in total independence of that mind and completely beyond its perceptual domain. For a Cartesian mind, since it is an unextended substance, has no internal extensive scheme by which its qualifying sensa could gain objectivity and significance through the embodiment of regions with transcendental reference. Thus, any consistent account of the sensa appearing to a Cartesian mind must construe them as meaningless qualifications of subjectivity (PR 118). Moreover, the qualifications of an unextended substance must be themselves unextended; therefore, sensa cannot possibly resemble the properties of material or extended substance. Of course, one mind's sensa *may* resemble another mind's sensa; but neither mind could ever know of the other's existence, let alone whether the other mind's sensa resemble its own.

In the third place, the subjectivist principle invalidates the claim that the perceiving mind somehow *interprets* its private qualifications as signifying the existence and properties of other substances. For there is no earthly reason why the perceiving mind should be the least tempted to interpret its private qualifications as signifying entities of which it is absolutely and irremediably ignorant. Indeed, there can be neither a basis, nor a need, for interpreting the sensa that are given to it. How could it learn to interpret sensa? To what end would it interpret them? Since sensa constitute the sole datum for its solipsistic experience of the present moment, there is for it neither a past from which to learn nor a future for which to prepare.

The subjectivist principle, we may conclude, invalidates the claims not only of representational theories of perception but also of interpretational theories of cognition. For, if we assume its truth, any sensum we perceive, such as a patch of red, "is silent as to the past or the future. How it originates, how it will vanish, whether indeed there was a past, and whether there will be a future, are not disclosed by its own nature. No material for the interpretation of sensa is provided by the sensa themselves, as they stand starkly, barely, present and immediate. We *do* interpret them; but no thanks for the feat is due to them" (AI 232).

Needless to say, every proponent of the subjectivist principle covers up its solipsistic implications by appealing either to the goodness of God or to the mysterious workings of human nature (or animal faith). This is not the place to explain why these appeals are ultimately unsatisfactory. The relevant point, for our immediate purposes, is that Whitehead construes such appeals as unsuccessful attempts to save modern epistemological theory from the disastrous consequences of assuming that the datum for subjective experience is composed exclusively of universals.

Descartes and his successors, according to Whitehead, compounded the theoretical difficulties of their epistemological outlook by unwittingly construing the activity of experiencing as a merely *passive* witnessing by the subject of the sensa given for it—a witnessing entirely devoid of any subjective self-definition in response to the witnessed sensa. This doctrine of *mere* sensation is what Whitehead refers to as the *sensationalist principle* of modern epistemologies—namely, "that the primary activity in the act of experience is the bare subjective entertainment of the datum, devoid of any subjective form of reception" (PR 239). Thus, the sensationalist principle effectively denies to the perceiving subject any involvement in the creation of its own essence. The subject *is* experiencing, but it is *not* becoming. In fact, it cannot become because a substance's *complete* essence is an aboriginal feature of its existence. There is no adding to it; there is no subtracting from it. For that reason, the subject *cannot* have a hand in creating any part of its own essence.

A substantial subject's essence, then, is as much a complete given for that subject as is each sensum it experiences. Moreover, though the subject's sensa change from moment to moment, its essence is not thereby changed, for the sensa form no part of its essence. Sensa are merely accidental qualifications of the subject. They change, and the subject experiences their change (or so it is claimed[7]), but the subject remains unchanged. The paradox is thus established that a substantial subject, or substantial mind, is an unchanging subject of change (PR 116, 120, 122).

One upshot of the sensationalist principle is that the experiencing subject lacks an *individual* essence. Its entire essence is *generic*. It has exactly the *same* essence that all experiencing subjects have. Strictly speaking, therefore, the only knowledge a substantial subject can have regarding itself, so far as knowledge is at all possible for it, is *that* it is an experiencer experiencing whatever sensa happen to be given for it. If for argument's sake we grant it memory and anticipation, it can know also what its sensa or qualifications have been in the past and what it anticipates they will be in the future. But its history of perceived qualifications, Leibniz notwithstanding, is entirely contingent and forms no part of its essence. Therefore, a substantial subject's self-knowledge is not in any way improved if it is supposed to have escaped the solipsism of the present moment. A mental substance's knowledge of itself is minimal and trivial because the nature of its existence approximates the vacuity of a material substance's existence. The latter does not experience at all, but the former experiences only the accidental qualifications of its own being. Material substance knows nothing; mental substance knows only that it is an experiencer experiencing its accidental qualification by universals.

According to Whitehead, the sensationalist and subjectivist principles jointly constitute what he terms the *sensationalist doctrine* of modern epistemologies (PR 238). To adopt the sensationalist doctrine is, in effect, to veil from the experiencing subject not only the world in which it is supposed to exist, but also its own unique individuality—the former because in principle it is beyond its experiential domain; the latter because in principle it cannot exist. Given the sensationalist doctrine, therefore, direct knowledge is trivial and inferred knowledge is totally without rational justification or validation. Thus, a thoroughgoing skepticism regarding all knowledge based on sense-perception is the only logical outcome of the sensationalist doctrine's adoption.

Historically, the sensationalist doctrine as to the knowable is an offspring of the subjectivist doctrine as to the datum for metaphysics. Hume descends from Descartes. To Whitehead's understanding, however, the subjectivist doctrine is *not* at fault. For it gives rise to the sensationalist doctrine only if it is uncritically interpreted and developed in terms of traditional Aristotelian modes of thought. Thus, for Whitehead the fault lies not with the subjectivist doctrine but with the Aristotelian doctrines with which it has been unnecessarily associated. "All modern philosophy hinges round the difficulty of describing the world in terms of subject and predicate, substance and quality, particular and universal" (PR 78).

According to Whitehead, the Aristotelian modes of thought causing the difficulties of modern philosophy lose all claim to any metaphysical primacy as soon as the subjectivist doctrine is adopted (PR 241). For if the whole edifice of knowledge is to be built on the foundation of subjective experiencing, and if we do experience and know a world of particulars, then that world, and each particular entity within it, must somehow qualify, or be a component of, our present moment of subjective experience. Moreover, our present moment of experience must be qualified not only by the world contemporary with us but also by the actual past and potential future of that world. For either the immediate moment of experience "affords knowledge of the past and the future, or we are reduced to utter scepticism as to memory and induction" (SMW 62). In addition, if we are to be experienceable and knowable by at least some of the particulars that we experience and know, then at least *some* particulars must have the same ontological status that we have. Thus, in some sense or respect, our present moment of experience qualifies other moments of subjective experience, even as they, in some sense or respect, qualify it. Since we never really doubt that we experience and know a world of particulars with an actual past and a potential future, or that we are experienced and known by some of the particulars we experience, all this means that the particulars that enjoy subjective experiencing must be conceived as having a *capacity* for being components of one another and, so far as that capacity is realized, as predicable of each other.

The true point of divergence between Whitehead's organic philosophy and the epistemological tradition begun by Descartes, it then follows, is "the false notion suggested by the contrast between the natural meanings of the words 'particular' and 'universal'" (PR 79). For, as we saw in Chapter Two, actual entities—the ultimate particulars posited by the organic philosophy—share with all entities of all sorts the capacity for being repeated so as to function as components or qualifications of other actual entities. In other words, actual entities fall, as all entities do, under the scope of the principle of relativity—the organic principle that "directly traverses Aristotle's dictum, '(A substance) is not present in a subject.' On the contrary, according to this principle an actual entity *is* present in other actual entities" (PR 79).

Strictly speaking, only completed actual entities are repeatable, and then only in and for actual entities later than themselves. Nonetheless, in regard to the extensive standpoints they respectively embody, each its own, actual entities are modally immanent in one another. To that extent at least, every actual entity is predicable of all others. Thus, "if we allow for degrees of relevance, and for negligible relevance, we must say that every actual entity is present in every other actual entity. The philosophy of organism is mainly devoted to the task of making clear the notion of 'being present in another entity'" (PR 79–80).

Much of the present essay has been devoted to the same task; so it need not be argued here that one actual entity is present in another actual entity only as objectified in and for it, the objectification being causal, presentational, or anticipational. What needs to be emphasized now is that the organic philosophy construes the entities that enjoy subjective experience not as substances, each completely independent of all the others, but as actual entities, each dependent on all the others for *part*, though by no means all, of its individual essence. By thus construing the entities which are the primary data for metaphysical analysis, the organic philosophy is able to avoid the subjectivist principle as to the datum for subjective experience. For now that datum can be understood to include other actual entities as well as eternal objects, that is, other particulars as well as universals.

What is revealed in the datum, thus understood, is *not* a mere aggregate of particulars; rather, it is a *systematic community* of objectified actualities exhibiting themselves as being at once mutually immanent and mutually transcendent. There is no explaining the systematic character of the community, nor the unique self-identity of each of its members, without recourse to the common indicative scheme exhibited by the total datum and by every individual actuality in the datum. Thus, the importance of the indicative scheme displayed in an actuality's datum cannot be exaggerated. For one thing, the indicative scheme implicates, in the *essence* of the actuality of which the datum is the dative phase, the self-identity—either actual or potential—of all actualities, past, present, or future. For another, the indicative scheme implicates the other actualities as *formally* transcending the actuality in which they are *objectively* given. By reason of the indicative scheme, then, the objectified actualities composing a specified datum are revealed as formally transcending the actual occasion arising from, and including, that datum. This means that the objectifications of other actualities are the "factors in experience which function so as to express that the occasion originates by including a transcendent universe of other things. Thus it belongs to the essence of each occasion of experience that it is concerned with an otherness transcending itself. The occasion is one among others, and including [the objectifications of] the others which it is among" (AI 231).

The systematic scheme is important, in addition, because it implicates the actuality under consideration in the essence of all other actualities. The scheme reveals that something of the actuality's own individual essence—at the very least, a modal aspect of its own extensive standpoint—is or will be an objective constituent of every other actuality. To be sure, the actuality's formal reality transcends, and is transcended by, the formal reality of the other actualities. But its objective reality contributes to their formal reality, just as their objective reality contributes to its own formal reality. Thus, by reason of the nature and texture of its datum, the actuality experiences its own objective functioning—actual or potential—in the experience of all other actualities. This, of course, is simply another way of saying that, because of the modal property of extension, the actuality "sees itself as mirrored in other things" (SMW 207).

The datum's indicative scheme, then, not only implicates all other actualities in the individual essence of the actuality in question, but also implicates the actuality in question in the individual essence of every other actuality. The datum, in short, reveals the mutual implication of *all* actualities. This means that the actuality's own membership in the universal community of actualities is revealed to it by the indicative scheme of its own datum (SMW 63; AI 250).

The universal community *is* the world, and the world is composed alike by the experiencing actuality and the experienced actualities. For the datum exhibits the experiencer and the experienced as having equal metaphysical status (SMW 124; PR 123). It exhibits *all* actualities as members of a *common world* because it exhibits the world as a *common constituent* of every actuality. The importance of this function of the datum is evident in Whitehead's contention that if the world were not exemplified in the constitution of each experiencing subject, different subjects could not experience and know a common world (SMW 123–24; PR 224). The world must be internally related to every subject, and every subject must be internally related to the world. "For an actual entity cannot be a member of a 'common world', except in the sense that the 'common world' is a constituent of its own constitution" (PR 224).

It bears emphasizing that a subject's world comprises not only the actualities contemporary with the subject, but also every actuality in the subject's past, plus the potentiality for all actualities in the subject's future (SMW 211; AI 246–57). The *whole* world—past, present, and future—is *objectively* contained in the subject's datum (SMW 36–37; PR 227–28, 309–10). There is no solipsism of the present moment because the actual and potential history of the world is constitutive of the experiencing subject (PR 347–48). The determinate there-then of the subject's past, the ongoing there-now of its contemporaries, and the indeterminate there-then of its future are all to be found objectively in the crannies of the subject's here-now (SMW 102–03; AI 246–47, 251–53). This conclusion, according to Whitehead, "is essential for any form of realism. For there is in the world for our cognisance, memory of the past, immediacy of realization, and indication of things to come" (SMW 103).

Whitehead sometimes misleadingly refers to the organic philosophy's conception of the datum for subjective experience as the *reformed* subjectivist principle (PR 238, 252). In truth, however, the organic conception of the datum constitutes an outright *repudiation*, rather than a reformation, of the subjectivist principle; for it denies categorically (as well as categoreally) that the datum for subjective experience consists exclusively of universals. On the contrary, the datum is conceived by the organic philosophy necessarily to include the objectifications of other particulars. Indeed, the datum for a subject's experience *is* the objectification of the entire world correlative with that subject. The datum, thus conceived, is the *objective content* of subjective experience (PR 230).

> Of course, strictly speaking, the universals, to which Hume confines the datum, are also 'objects'; but the phrase 'objective content' is meant to emphasize the doctrine of 'objectification' of actual entities. If experience be not based upon an objective content, there can be no escape from a solipsistic subjectivism. (PR 230–31)

Thus, it is clear that the organic philosophy *rejects* the subjectivist principle and *replaces* it with an *objectivist* principle (SMW 123–28). This conclusion is made explicit by Whitehead when he says, "Descartes' discovery on the side of subjectivism requires balancing by an 'objectivist' principle as to the datum for experience" (PR 243).

What *has* been reformed by the organic philosophy is the subjectivist doctrine concerning the data for metaphysical analysis (PR 288–90). The organic subjectivist doctrine does take the data in question to be the entities that enjoy subjective experience. In that respect it does not differ from the Cartesian subjectivist doctrine. But it differs radically from the Cartesian doctrine in construing the entities that enjoy subjective experi- ence as being immanent in one another and, for that reason, as being both dependent on, the predicable of, one another (PR 219–20). On the or- ganic subjectivist doctrine, then, the data for metaphysical analysis are not substances but actual entities; and these are construed to be such that any one of them contains the objective reality—causal, presentational, or anticipational—of all the others. According to the organic philosophy, therefore, all actualities appear together in the subjective experience of any one actuality because every actuality, by reason of its dative phase, contains all the other actualities as its components (PR 288–90). In other words, "the organic philosophy interprets experience as meaning the 'self- enjoyment of being one among many, and of being one arising out of the composition of many'. Descartes interprets experience as meaning the 'self-enjoyment, by an individual substance, of its qualification by ideas'" (PR 220/CPR 145).

Whitehead aptly summarizes his position on both the subjectivist doc- trine and the subjectivist principle when he says,

The philosophy of organism admits the subjectivist doctrine (as here stated), but rejects the sensationalist doctrine; hence its doctrine of the objectification of one actual occasion in the experience of another actual occasion. Each actual entity is a throb of experience including the actual world within its scope. The problems of efficient causation and of knowledge receive a common explanation by reference to the texture of actual occasions. (PR 290)

Of course, the rejection of the sensationalist doctrine involves the repudiation not only of the subjectivist principle but also of the sensationalist principle (PR 238). What is of interest to us now, however, is that the rejection, or 'reformation', of the subjectivist principle is implicitly linked by Whitehead, in the passage just quoted, to the organic doctrine of objectification. For it is only as objectified that other actual entities are components of a particular actuality's datum. But, since the objectifications of the actualities in the subject's past are by far the most important components of its datum, this means that the repeatability of completed actualities is a crucial presupposition of Whitehead's conception of the datum for subjective experience. This is why Whitehead says that "the reformed subjectivist principle adopted by the philosophy of organism is merely an alternative statement of the principle of relativity" (PR 252).

My point is that the relativity principle, understood as asserting the repeatability of all entities of all sorts, is what permits Whitehead to claim that "all things are to be conceived as qualifications of actual occasions" (PR 252). It is also what allows him to hold that "the way in which one actual entity is qualified by other actual entities is the 'experience' of the actual world enjoyed by that actual entity, as subject" (PR 252). Is it any wonder then that Whitehead takes the principle of relativity to be the basic *explanatory* doctrine on which his metaphysical system is founded (PR 76)? Nevertheless, the principle of relativity, so far as it asserts the repeatability of completed occasions, itself presupposes, as well as partly elucidates, the even more fundamental Category of the Ultimate—presupposes, that is, an eternal reality, at once creative, extensive, and envisaging, that is ever manifesting itself in individual creative processes wherein and whereby, in each instance, the many already completed actualities of the universe become one and are increased by one. Thus, the reformed subjectivist principle both presupposes and partly elucidates the Category of the Ultimate.

In particular, the character which the organic philosophy assigns to the datum for subjective experience presupposes the extensiveness of the Creative Receptacle. In the first place, it is only by reason of the metaphysical properties of extension, or of the indicative scheme which they ground, that the self-identity of completed actualities can be repeated in actualities later than themselves. For the positional essence, and thus the self-identity, of an actual occasion is one and the same with the crystallized extensive structure of its regional standpoint and, for that reason, can be repeated in every extensive region wherein that standpoint is modally present. In the second place, an occasion's datum contains not only the causal objectifications, or reproductions, of the actualities in the occasion's past but also the modal presences of the extensive standpoints from which other occasions are either arising or will arise. In other words, it is only because of the modality of extension that the datum displays for the subject the potentiality for contemporary and future actualities in addition to displaying the settled actualities of the past. Finally, it is only in virtue of the modality of extension that the causal and presentational fields of pure perception are, on the one hand, *differentiated* from one another, and, on the other, perceived as *implicating* each other in a common extensive scheme.

Since each occasion, so far as it enjoys intellectual operations of cognition, ekes out its knowledge of the world by symbolic reference from one pure mode of perception to the other (PR 126), it follows that the crystallized extensive structure of an occasion's standpoint is precisely the occasion's feature—its 'texture', if you will—in reference to which, according to Whitehead, "the problems of efficient causation and of knowledge receive a common explanation" (PR 290). But this conclusion means, in effect, that the organic theories of efficient causation and of knowledge presuppose, as well as partly elucidate, the solidarity of the universe. In particular, they presuppose what we may term the *objective solidarity of the universe in, and for, each of its actual creatures*. In other words, they presuppose the ultimate fact that each actual entity, without loss of its individual self-identity, contributes its own objective reality to the constitution and self-identity of every other actual entity. Indeed, for any specified actuality, the other actualities, by contributing their objectified selves, at once cause the dative phase, compose the objective content, and specify the positional essence, of the actuality in question. Thus, for the organic philosophy, the character of the datum for an actuality's subjective experience cannot be divorced from, and is practically of a piece with, the objective solidarity of the universe in and for that actuality.

Each actual instance of objective solidarity is best construed as the crystallization and enrichment of a corresponding eternal instance of pure extensional solidarity. Here by pure extensional solidarity I mean the solidarity of the eternal continuum of extension in each of its potential regions. For example, the entire continuum of eternal extension is modally present in C^{**}. When C^{**} is transformed into C^*, the pure extensional solidarity of the universe in C^{**} is *not* abolished; rather, through the ingression of eternal objects of the objective species, it is crystallized so as to forever enshrine objectively the state of the universe begetting C; in addition, through the ingression of eternal objects of the subjective species, it is enriched with aspects of the determinate definiteness of the settled actualities in C's correlative universe. Thus, the transformation of the universe's pure extensional solidarity in C^{**} into its objective solidarity in C^* is the means by which the state of the universe that begets the dative phase of C also reveals itself to C's phases of subjective experience.

The objective self-revelation of the universe for the perceptual experience of each of its component actualities is the organic doctrine by which Whitehead hopes to solve all the major philosophical problems of causation and knowledge, as well as of perception. Whether this hope is ultimately justified, I cannot explore here. But it bears emphasizing once more that the doctrine is in principle denied to all metaphysical theories that do not repudiate the purported metaphysical ultimacy of Aristotelian categories. As Whitehead puts it,

> The perceptive constitution of the actual entity presents the problem, How can the other actual entities, each with its own formal existence, also enter objectively into the perceptive constitution of the actual entity in question? *This is the problem of the solidarity of the universe.* The classical doctrines of universals and particulars, of subject and predicate, of individual substances not present in other individual substances, of the externality of relations, alike render this problem incapable of solution. (PR 88–89; italics mine)

Whitehead's own solution to this vexing metaphysical problem is ultimately based on three closely interrelated doctrines: first, that actual entities are repeatable particulars (relativity principle); second, that each actual entity has to house its universe (ontological principle); and third, that the extensive regions embodied by actual entities, each its own, are modally immanent in one another (principle of extensional solidarity). Clearly, each of these Whiteheadian doctrines constitutes an explicit repudiation of one or more of the classical doctrines at issue. A metaphysical Rubicon has been crossed.

4. *Functional solidarity and autonomous individuality*

The organic philosophy's repudiation of the subjectivist principle is of a
piece with its doctrine that each actual occasion directly perceives the
objective reality of the world in which it exists. This doctrine provides for
a realistic epistemology partially grounded on the objective self-revelation
of the universe to each occasion of human experience. In turn, the organic
philosophy's repudiation of the sensationalist principle is of a piece with
its doctrine that each actual occasion has a hand, an autonomous hand, in
creating its own individual essence. This doctrine provides for a viable
theory of ethical responsibility partially grounded on the subjective self-
realization of every occasion of human experience. Of course, this is not
the place to develop either an organic epistemology or an organic ethics.
But just as the considerations of the preceding sections have illuminated
the metaphysical foundations of the organic theories of perception and
knowledge, so too the considerations of the present and following sections
should illuminate, if only dimly and implicitly, the metaphysical foundations of an organic theory of ethics.

My concern now is with the autonomous process of teleological self-
determination by which an already begotten occasion at once *completes* its
subjective definiteness and *integrates* its macroscopically given multiplicity
of conformal feelings. But I am concerned with this process only insofar as
it completes and crowns the solidarity of the entire universe in the creation
of the occasion in question. For the full import of the concept of universal
solidarity is that *all* actualities must contribute to, or function in, the
determination of every actuality. In other words, the thesis of solidarity is
equivalent to the assertion that, in respect to any specified actuality, *all*
actual entities in the universe correlative with that actuality, *including the
specified actuality itself*, must contribute to the complete determination of
the actuality in question. Thus, not only must all *other* actualities function
objectively in the determination of the specified actuality, but also the
specified actuality *itself* must function *formally* in its own determination.

The full import of the thesis of solidarity, then, is that every actual
entity is partly other-created and partly self-created. It must be admitted,
however, that this is not the meaning of 'solidarity' which Whitehead
usually has in mind when he expounds the solidarity of the universe.
Indeed, what Whitehead most frequently means by 'solidarity' is what
here has been termed 'objective solidarity', namely, the mutual immanence of all actual entities. Precisely for that reason, the main task of this
essay has been to elucidate the objective solidarity of the universe in each

of its creatures. But that task has required the elucidation of an even more basic sense of solidarity, the sense here referred to as 'extensional solidarity', namely, the necessary modal presence of each extensive region in *all* extensive regions, itself included. This more basic sense of solidarity is the one Whitehead usually has in mind when he is discussing the eternal extensive continuity of the universe as an aspect of the pure potentiality for all actual entities, the aspect whereby all real potentialities are coordinated with one another. Thus, in Whitehead's own usage the term 'solidarity' signifies either the solidarity of extensive regions or the objective solidarity of actual entities.

Nevertheless, the relationship between the extensional and objective senses of solidarity itself suggests a more encompassing conception of the solidarity of actual entities. For, as we saw earlier, objective solidarity represents a crystallization and enrichment of extensional solidarity; but objective solidarity does *not* represent an enrichment of the modal presence of an occasion's standpoint within itself. Let us remember that such a standpoint, at the completion of the dative phase, already displays an other-aspect that has been crystallized and enriched by the objectification of all attained actualities in the occasion's correlative actual world. In contrast, at the end of the dative phase, the standpoint's self-aspect remains devoid of qualitative content. Of course, the subsequent conformal phases *do* give qualitative content to the standpoint's self-aspect, so that, at the conclusion of the process of transition, a subject conformed to its correlative actual world has been begotten. But the qualitative enrichment of the self-aspect, so far as it is produced by the process of transition, is minimal, repetitive, entirely derivative, unintegrated, and lacking in determinateness. Accordingly, since the self-aspect's further enrichment, integration, and determination result from the subject's autonomous self-completion, we can construe the occasion's concrescence as the process whereby the extensional solidarity of the universe in that occasion's standpoint acquires its final qualitative enrichment and aesthetic determination and is thus transformed into a concrete fact of actual togetherness.

My point is that the extensional solidarity of the universe represents an aspect—creativity, envisagement, and the multiplicity of eternal objects are the other aspects—of the pure potentiality for the *functional solidarity* of all actualities in every actuality. My point, in addition, is that the actualization of functional solidarity, in respect to any specified actuality, requires both the macroscopic process of transition whereby all other actualities function objectively in the determination of the actuality in question and the microscopic process of concrescence whereby the said actuality itself functions formally in its own determination. By the *functional solidarity of actualities*, therefore, I mean simply the ultimate fact that every actual entity owes its final and complete determination partly to the transcendent functioning of all other actualities and partly to its own immanent functioning.

Admittedly, the *phrase* 'functional solidarity' does not appear even once in Whitehead's philosophical writings. My contention, nonetheless, is that the *conception* of functional solidarity—each actuality functioning in all, and all functioning in each—permeates every aspect of Whitehead's metaphysical thought.[8] I hold, indeed, that the basic metaphysical intuition underlying the whole of Whitehead's metaphysics is that "each task of creation is a *social* effort, employing the *whole* universe" (PR 340; italics mine). That all actualities *can*, and *do*, function in the creation of any one actuality is the fundamental intuition which the entire categoreal scheme of the organic philosophy is intended to elucidate. All else is an elaboration of details: details about the metaphysical presuppositions of functional solidarity; details about the basic kinds of metaphysical functioning to be distinguished; details about the basic sorts of metaphysical entities that function in each task of creation; details about the metaphysical principles constraining each creative effort; details about the metaphysical traits exhibited by each creature; and details about the implications of functional solidarity for science, epistemology, ethics, aesthetics, theology, and civilization.

But the details are all-important. For only their coherent articulation and empirical adequacy can objectively validate the intuition of functional solidarity. One important 'detail', in respect to each social effort to create a new actuality, is precisely the need to distinguish between the joint contribution made by all other actualities, their *objective* functioning, and the contribution made by the new actuality itself, its *formal* functioning. Indeed, the elaboration of this distinction is a recurrent theme in Whitehead's exposition of the organic philosophy; for the contrast between the objective and formal modes of functioning reappears in, and is partially elucidated by, the explanations and discussions of each of the following contrasts: (i) repetition and novel immediacy; (ii) objectification and subjective form; (iii) causal objectification and subjective aim; (iv) objective content and autonomous subject; (v) position and definiteness; (vi) transcendent decision and immanent decision; (vii) datum and self; (viii) dative phases and subjective phases; (ix) transition and concrescence; and (x) efficient causation and final causation.

Of these contrasts, by far the most important metaphysically, because it subsumes all the others, is that between efficient causation and final causation. In fact, according to Whitehead, "one task of a sound metaphysics is to exhibit final and efficient causes in their proper relation to each other" (PR 129). But to carry out this task it is necessary to exhibit the processes of efficient causation and final causation in their proper relation to one another. In turn, exhibiting efficient causation and final causation in their proper relationship is tantamount to exhibiting objective functioning and formal functioning in their proper relation to each other. In other words, the functional solidarity of actualities is of a piece with the ultimate fact that each actuality results partly from a process of efficient causation and partly from a process of final causation. Only by thus realizing the full import of the solidarity thesis can we finally understand why Whitehead says that the ontological principle—the principle of efficient, and final, causation—constitutes "the first step in the description of the universe as a solidarity of many actual entities" (PR 65). Thus, the universe is a solidarity of actual entities because every actual entity results partly from the objectification of all other actualities, particularly of those already completed, and partly from the autonomous activity whereby the actuality in question modifies, specifies, and realizes its own subjective aim.

It is precisely by reason of its self-functioning that an actuality is a *genuine* individual, *i.e.*, something existing *for* itself as in the process of autonomously determining its own essential character. To be an individual, in this sense, is to freely choose and determine, amid given conditions, what one is ultimately to be. This most profound sense of individuality will be gradually elucidated throughout the subsequent discussion. What must be stressed now is that an individual's given conditions and its autonomously acquired character are indissolubly linked aspects of the functional solidarity of the universe in each of its actual creatures. For the organic philosophy, therefore, the *solidarity* of actual existents, and the *individuality* of each actual existent, are *not* antithetical notions. Rather, autonomous individuality is required by, and represents the crowning fulfillment of, universal solidarity.

The thesis of functional solidarity is thus found to underlie the organic philosophy's reconciliation, at the metaphysical level, of two fundamental philosophic notions: individual absoluteness and individual relativity. "Here 'absoluteness' means the notion of release from essential dependence on other members of the community in respect to modes of activity, while 'relativity' means the converse fact of essential relatedness" (AI 54; single quotation marks around *relativity* have been added). The individual *relativity* of an actual entity—its essential, or internal, relatedness to all other actualities—is one and the same with the *extenso-objective* functioning of the universe in the standpoint of that actuality. The individual *absoluteness* of an actual entity—its essential freedom of self-determination—is one and the same with its autonomous process of *formal* functioning. Equivalently, an actuality's relativity is the determinate *position* imposed on it by its correlative universe, while its absoluteness is the determinate *definiteness* it freely confers on itself. Now, my contention is that the relativity of an actuality's position and the absoluteness of an actuality's definiteness are *not* accidentally juxtaposed features of the actuality's complete nature. Rather, both features are foreordained by the functional solidarity which, by reason of the eternal Creative Receptacle, it stands in the nature of the universe to impose on all its actual creatures.

I do not mean, let me add, that the *individual* essence of an actual entity—its unique synthesis of position and definiteness—is eternally foreordained. What I mean, instead, is that the imposition of functional solidarity by the eternal Creative Receptacle is the ultimate reason for the fact that *every* actual entity exhibits in its nature "the interweaving of absoluteness upon relativity" (AI 339). My point, then, is that there is a *generic* essence common to all actual entities, namely, that each exhibits an absoluteness of self-formation issuing from, and subordinating within its aesthetic concrescence, a standpoint of universal relativity (AI 227). Thus, since the relativity of actualities is one and the same with their mutual objective immanence, my point is simply that all actualities have this much in common: each "unites its formal immediacy with objective otherness" (AI 245). My more basic contention, however, is that the universe's ultimate imposition of functional solidarity is the reason why "the absolute self-attainment of each individual is bound up with a relativity which it issues from and issues into" (AI 376).

Two important qualifications must now be added. The first one, explicitly formulated by Whitehead, is that an occasion's conformal feelings limit and balance its absolute individuality or, equivalently, its absolute freedom of self-formation (AI 235). The absoluteness is limited by the fact that the subject is born conformed to its correlative datum. The subject's aboriginal conformal feelings thus mediate between the relativity of the dative phase and the absoluteness of the integrative phases. This means, as we saw earlier, that any subjective form that the subject gives to itself must be compatible for synthesis with the conformal subjective forms it has inherited from its datum. Accordingly, "there is no such fact as absolute freedom; every actual entity possesses only such freedom as is inherent in the primary phase 'given' by its standpoint of relativity to its actual universe" (PR 202/CPR 133).

But, as we saw earlier also, there *is* freedom. The same datum to which the subject is conformed also provides it with an initial subjective aim requiring the subject's autonomous decisions for its final specification and realization. Thus, "the datum both limits and supplies" (PR 168). The datum qualifies the subject's freedom, but it does not banish it (PR 435). The freedom of the subject, we may conclude, is *relatively* absolute. It is conditioned by the datum and by the conformal feelings, both physical and conceptual, imposed by that datum; but "however far the sphere of efficient causation be pushed in the determination of components of a concrescence . . . there always remains the final reaction of the self-creative unity of the universe" (PR 75). This self-creative unity of the universe *is* the absolute individual—*is*, in other words, the autonomous subject as fully owning a now fully individualized manifestation of the envisaging creativity.

The second qualification is that the autonomous activity of an actual occasion is primarily concerned with the definition and integration of its self-aspect, though it extends derivatively to the transmutative enrichment of its other-aspect or datum. This means, in effect, that the autonomous activity of self-determination belongs to, and is an essential aspect of, the empirical subject. But the empirical subject is not only the self that grows from the datum and in response to the datum; it is also the self that is *other* than the datum. This qualification is for the most part only implicit in Whitehead's writings. But it is of the utmost importance because, without it, Whitehead's metaphysical analysis of experience would be inconsistent with the phenomenology of ordinary human experience.

I am trying to do justice here to the phenomenological fact that a conscious human subject does not normally identify itself with, nor does it understand itself as composed of, the objects it consciously experiences—except, of course, in respect to its own body.[9] Indeed, insofar as the human subject construes itself as a mind, it does not identify itself even with the body it calls its own. Now, the fact in question is one of which Whitehead was well aware when he criticized the subjectivist principle and its major philosophical proponents. For example, he took Hume to task for attempting to interpret a perceived object, such as a grey stone, as a feature of the perceiver.

Hume . . . looked for a universal quality to function as qualifying the mind, by way of explanation of its perceptive enjoyment. Now if we scan 'my perception of the stone as grey' in order to find a universal, the only available candidate is 'greyness'. Accordingly for Hume, 'greyness', functioning as a sensation qualifying the mind, is a fundamental type of fact for metaphysical generalization. The result is Hume's simple impressions of sensation, which form the starting point of his philosophy. But this is an entire muddle for the perceiving mind is not grey, and so grey is now made to perform a new role. (PR 241–42)

Thus for Hume, as Whitehead understands him, the perceived objects are what the perceiving mind knows about itself, so that, tacitly, "the knowable facts are always treated as qualities of a subject—the subject being the mind. His final criticism of the notion of the 'mind' does not alter the plain fact that the whole of the previous discussion has included this presupposition" (PR 209).

Whitehead's criticism of Hume boils down to this: Hume's analysis of experience discards the object-subject contrast inherent in every occasion of experiencing. It ignores the objective 'otherness' of the grey stone and even of the grey abstracted from the stone. In effect, Hume's analysis collapses the objective aspect of experience into its subjective aspect. As a result, the analysis of experience becomes the analysis of the experiencer, and the analysis of knowledge becomes the analysis of the knower.

In contrast with Hume's, the organic doctrine is that the empirical subject and its datum are alike ingredients in the one occasion of experience. The actual occasion, or metaphysical subject, does include both the datum and the empirical subject; but the empirical subject does *not* include the datum. To be sure, the empirical subject does finally subsume the datum under the unity of its aesthetic synthesis. But this aesthetic appropriation of the datum by the empirical subject does not abolish the distinct otherness of the datum (PR 86). The appropriated datum *is* a subordinate component of the aesthetic synthesis; but it is *not* a component of the synthesis of subjective forms which alone constitutes the definiteness of the empirical subject.

There is, of course, no possibility of really abstracting the synthesis of subjective forms from the synthesis of feelings (or positive prehensions) or the synthesis of feelings from the extensive synthesis of objectifications and modalities in the occasion's standpoint. But that is to say only that the empirical subject, like the metaphysical subject, is not an independent or substantial individual. The empirical subject no more can be abstracted from the metaphysical subject in which it is ingredient than the metaphysical subject can be abstracted from the universe of which it is a component.

My point, then, is that the empirical subject's subsumption of the datum under its prehensive synthesis does not abolish the contrast between prehending subject and prehended object, nor between perceiver and perceived, nor between knower and known. Yet this is precisely the point which Whitehead obscures when he says that "the knowable is the complete nature of the knower, at least such phases of it as are antecedent to that operation of knowing" (PR 92). Surely, when I have perceptual knowledge of a grey stone it is not myself that I know but something other than myself. It is no less of a muddle to have the empirical subject include the objectifications it prehends than it is to have a substantial mind include the sensations it perceives. In both cases the objective side of experience is being collapsed into the subjective side.

In trying to save the applicability of Whitehead's metaphysics to the phenomenology of ordinary human experience, I do not wish to suggest that our habitual ways of construing conscious human experience should dictate, absolutely and uncritically, our metaphysical constructions. Far from it! Our ordinary ways of construing ordinary human experience must be explained—not explained away; but ordinary human experience can be metaphysically reinterpreted and its conscious phenomenology altered insofar as the guiding metaphysical notions bring into focus aspects of experience not previously noticed. Indeed, when conducted in terms of the organic metaphysics, the interpretation of ordinary human experience, or of ordinary human subjectivity, yields a phenomenology succinctly captured in Ortega y Gasset's dictum, "I am I and my circumstances." For the metaphysical subject *is* the empirical subject and its objective circumstances. Conversely, the empirical subject *is* the metaphysical subject functioning formally so as to complete itself in a purposed response to those aspects of its constitution that were determined by the objective functioning of its correlative universe.

In the end, my 'empirical subject' is simply Whitehead's 'subject', but only when the latter term is defined in respect to the intra-experiential contrast between *publicity* and *privacy*. First notice, in this regard, that the contrast between publicity and privacy is explicitly characterized by Whitehead as being internal to each actuality or occasion of experience:

> In the analysis of actuality the antithesis between publicity and privacy obtrudes itself at every stage. There are elements only to be understood by reference to what is beyond the fact in question; and there are elements expressive of the immediate, private, personal, individuality of the fact in question. The former elements express the publicity of the world; the latter elements express the privacy of the individual. (PR 443)

Notice too that "every prehension has its public side and its private side. Its public side is constituted by the complex datum prehended; and its private side is constituted by the subjective form through which a private quality is imposed on the public datum" (PR 444).[10] Accordingly, the public and private sides of experience are to be construed as featuring, respectively, a complex extensive synthesis of objectifications or modal presences and an ongoing generation and integration of subjective forms.

The public side of experience is generated primarily by the process of transition, though it is subsequently enriched transmutatively by the process of concrescence. The public is constituted by the objectification of the universe in, and for, each actuality. There can be intersubjective agreement in respect to the public because the public is the objective reality of the universe in its multiple instantiations. Objectification is publication.

The private side of experience is generated primarily by the process of concrescence, though it also includes conformal subjective forms generated by the process of transition. In fact, the concrescence transforms the derivative, even alien, flavor of the conformal subjective forms by absorbing them into the private synthesis of autonomously originated subjective forms (PR 131–32, 323). Thus, even though the repetitive process of transition infects the private side of experience with qualities derived from the public side, it remains true "that the genetic process of concrescence introduces the elements which emphasize privacy" (PR 481). Immediacy of self-realization is privacy.

The public and private sides of experience respectively embody the other-aspect and self-aspect of the actuality. Accordingly, the two sides are mutually related by the modality of extension. This modal relationship is one factor—creativity, envisagement, and the multiplicity of eternal objects are the other factors—enabling and necessitating the prehensive, or aesthetic, subordination of the public side to the private side. Thus, the prehensive synthesis is the experiential link between the extensive synthesis of objectifications embodying the other-aspect, and the synthesis of subjective forms embodying the self-aspect. Finally, the position and subjective aim of the actuality jointly ground the identity and unity of its process of concrescence, so that the synthesis of subjective forms is of a piece with the synthesis of prehensions, and the synthesis of prehensions is of a piece with the subordination of the public datum to the private immediacy.

With all this in mind, consider now the definitions Whitehead gives of 'superject' and 'subject' in relation to the contrasting notions of publicity and privacy:

An actual entity considered in reference to the publicity of things is a 'superject'; namely, it arises from the publicity which it finds, and it adds itself to the publicity which it transmits. It is a moment of passage from decided public facts to a novel public fact. Public facts are, in their nature, coordinate.

An actual entity considered in reference to the privacy of things is a 'subject'; namely, it is a moment of the genesis of self-enjoyment. It consists of a purposed self-creation out of materials which are at hand in virtue of their publicity. (PR 443)

Clearly, this conception of the subject abstracts the absoluteness of self-realization from the relativity with which it is necessarily interwoven. This means that when we are considering the actuality *qua* subject, we are considering it *primarily* as an autonomous individual creating its own definiteness through the generation and synthesis of its constitutive subjective forms.

My point is that when we consider the actuality *qua* subject, we consider it *qua* immediate self, and *not* as the prehensive fusion of datum and self, which, when completed, is the superject proper. In other words, we consider the individual absoluteness of the actuality in abstraction from the relativity of the actuality. Surely, this is precisely what Whitehead is saying in the following passage:

The individual immediacy of an occasion is the final unity of subjective form, which is the occasion as an absolute reality. This immediacy is its moment of sheer individuality, bounded on either side by essential relativity. The occasion arises from relevant objects, and perishes into the status of an object for other occasions. But it enjoys its decisive moment of absolute self-attainment as emotional unity. As used here the words 'individual' and 'atom' have the same meaning, that they apply to composite things with an absolute reality which their components lack. These words properly apply to an actual entity in its immediacy of self-attainment when it stands out for itself alone, with its own affective self-enjoyment. The term 'monad' also expresses this essential unity at the decisive moment, which stands between its birth and its perishing. (AI 227)

The subject, we must conclude, is the actuality as in its phases of autonomous individuality and thus as existing *for* itself as being *other* than the complex datum to which its individuality is essentially related.

This qualification of the doctrine that absoluteness is necessarily interwoven with relativity becomes important only in respect to higher-grade actualities. For higher-grade actualities are characterized by increased operations of conceptual reversion, and thus by increased autonomy and novelty of subjective content (PR 390). But greater autonomy and novelty require an increase in the number of integrative phases. In turn, the greater the number of integrative phases through which the subject passes, and the more the subject's definiteness is enriched by novelty, the more the subject's absoluteness of self-realization tends to obscure the relativity from which it originates. Thus, the subjectivity of a higher-grade occasion, or of a higher-grade society with personal order, can appear to itself as an independent reality—a substance, if you will—perceiving, but only *externally* related to, its given environment.

Whitehead claims that the deepening of individuality, or subjectivity, reaches its greatest depth with the emergence of consciousness. With this claim, therefore, Whitehead sets the stage for the organic explanation and interpretation of an important aspect of the everyday phenomenology of human experience—the apparent substantial individuality of the conscious subject. With the same claim, Whitehead formulates the organic conception of the philosophical task:

> Philosophy is the self-correction by consciousness of its own initial excess of subjectivity. Each actual occasion contributes to the circumstances of its origin additional formative elements deepening its own peculiar individuality. Consciousness is only the last and greatest of such elements by which the selective character of the individual obscures the external totality from which it originates and which it embodies. An actual individual, of such higher grade, has truck with the totality of things by reason of its sheer actuality; but it has attained its individual depth of being by a selective emphasis limited to its own purposes. The task of philosophy is to recover the totality obscured by the selection. It replaces in rational experience what has been submerged in the higher sensitive experience and has been sunk yet deeper by the initial operations of consciousness itself. (PR 22)

I add the suggestion that the illumination of perception in the mode of causal efficacy (to reveal the universal relativity of existence), the investigation of the principles—metaphysical, cosmological, and human—of symbolic reference, and the deconstruction of the pre-conscious phases of aesthetic synthesis constitute three major steps towards the fulfillment of the philosophical task.

A final point: the external totality from which the empirical subject originates and which the metaphysical subject-superject embodies must be recovered—but not at the cost of misconstruing the independent individuality of the subject as a mere illusion. For the subject, whether construed empirically or metaphysically, is genuinely *causa sui* in respect to the qualitative clothing of its feelings, the manner of its aesthetic synthesis, and the specification and realization of its subjective aim. This element of independent self-creation is too important to be denied. For, as Whitehead says,

> in the case of those actualities whose immediate experience is most completely open to us, namely, human beings, the final decision of the immediate subject-superject, constituting the ultimate modification of subjective aim, is the foundation of our experience of responsibility, of approbation or of disapprobation, of self-approval or of self-reproach, of freedom, of emphasis. This element in experience is too large to be put aside merely as a misconstruction. It governs the whole tone of human life. (PR 74)

Thus the independence of the individual subject is illusory only if it is taken to be truly absolute, only if its teleological self-determination is taken to preclude the universal relativity from which, and towards which, it issues. The truer picture, in Whitehead's vision of reality, is that the functional solidarity of the universe requires both the heteronomous efficient causation by which the subject is begotten in essential interdependence with its universe, and the autonomous final causation by which the subject completes itself and aesthetically subordinates its universe to the fullness of its own individuality. "The crux of philosophy is to retain the balance between the individuality of existence and the relativity of existence" (IS 201).

5. Autonomy and the evaporation of indeterminacy

Whether we construe the organic subject metaphysically or empirically, its autonomous individuality is completely at odds with the sensationalist principle. Beyond its conformal origins, the organic subject is *never* a passive witness to the objectifications given for it. Rather, its prehensive activity as a self-determining agent at once completes the determination of its own individual definiteness and transforms the objectified universe into a felt contrast (PR 233). Thus, whereas the particular experience of a substantial subject has no bearing on its essence, the particular experience of an actual entity *qua* subject is constitutive of its *individual* essence (PR 228). There is no tearing the organic subject from its experience because its experience is part and parcel of *what* it is and *where* it is. It follows that "Descartes' notion of an unessential experience of the external world is entirely alien to the organic philosophy" (PR 220).

Moreover, the autonomous individuality of the organic subject is incompatible with the sensationalist principle because, since the subject's experience is constitutive of its essence, it can only experience once (PR 43). The organic subject, unlike the substantial subject and unlike a personally ordered society of higher-grade occasions, *cannot* enjoy a history of changing reactions to changing circumstances (AI 262; PR 122). The organic, or occasional, subject "has no such history. It never changes. It only becomes and perishes" (AI 262). The organic subject cannot change because its self-identity is a function of its aboriginally given position. Its becoming is the completion of its definiteness and ceases with its attainment. Thus, in the organic philosophy, 'change' can refer only to the qualitative differences between successive occasions belonging "to some one society of a definite type" (PR 123). Thus, too, "it is fundamental to the metaphysical doctrine of the philosophy of organism, that the notion of an actual entity as the unchanging subject of change is completely abandoned" (PR 43).

Let me now complete this elucidation of the universe's functional solidarity by examining the general character of an occasion's formal functioning. I first note the nature and extent of the occasion's indeterminacy at the outset of its formal functioning. Then, I provide a brief summary of the bipolar origination of the indeterminate subject. Finally, I take a closer look at the integrative phases by which the autonomous subject completes the determination of its own individual definiteness.

The initial indeterminateness of an occasion is analyzable into (i) indeterminacy in respect to the qualitative clothing of its feelings, (ii) indeterminacy in respect to the integration of its feelings, and (iii) indeterminacy in respect to the specification of its subjective aim. This threefold indeterminacy of the occasion is the legacy of its bipolar origination. It is *how* the occasion is thrown into existence by its correlative universe.

The physical pole produces the occasion as in its conformal phase. In that phase, the occasion is *one* indeterminate subject with *many* simple physical feelings awaiting integration and awaiting the creation of novel subjective forms by which the integration is effected (PR 335). In turn, the first stage of the mental pole produces the occasion as in its phase of conceptual reproduction and thereby complicates the occasion's indeterminacy. The occasion is now *one* indeterminate subject with *many* unintegrated conceptual feelings, as well as with *many* unintegrated conformal feelings. The first stage of the mental pole does endow the occasion with its initial conceptual feeling of subjective aim, derived from the occasion's hybrid conformal feeling of God. But the initial subjective aim is itself indeterminate by reason of its generality; it presents the occasion with a range of alternative possibilities for self-definition, all equally general and all equally compatible for synthesis with the occasion's objective content (PR 342–43). Thus, as in its phase of conceptual reproduction, the bipolarly constituted occasion is indeterminate in respect to its subjective aim, as well as in respect to the qualitative clothing and synthesis of its received feelings. But the three modes of indeterminacy involve one another; *what* final, fully-definite *self* shall arise from the datum, and *how* the received feelings are to be *clothed* and *integrated*, are indissoluble aspects of one and the same problem.

The creative solution to this problem is sparked by the phase of conceptual reproduction. For the valuations of this phase, which are the subjective forms of the initial aim and the other conceptual feelings, carry into the occasion the germ of self-referential appetition whereby the urge towards its own self-completion is constituted (PR 380; AI 224). This is why an actual occasion "is to be conceived as originated by physical experience with its process of completion motivated by consequent, conceptual experience initially derived from God" (PR 524). In this manner, the first stage of "the mental pole introduces the subject as a determinant of its own concrescence" (PR 380). Thus, to the legacy of *indeterminacy*, the bipolar constitution of the incomplete subject adds the legacy of *freedom*. "The subject, thus constituted, is the autonomous master of its own concrescence into subject-superject" (PR 374). The autonomous subject must now solve the three-sided problem of its inherent indeterminateness.

The solution to the problem begins with the subject's autonomous modifications of its initial subjective aim (PR 343). These modifications begin with the second stage of the mental pole, the phase of conceptual reversion. In that phase, the subject conceptually prehends eternal objects that are *proximate*, in one or more abstractive hierarchies, to those already unrestrictedly ingressed in the data and subjective forms of its conformal feelings. These conceptual reversions are what make possible "the subsequent enrichment of subjective forms, both in qualitative pattern, and in intensity through contrast" (PR 381). But though the eternal objects serving as data for the conceptual reversions are necessarily compatible for synthesis with those already defining the subjective forms of the occasion's conformal feelings, they are *not* necessarily compatible with each other in respect to their obtaining joint, unrestricted ingression into the occasion. For that reason, they represent, singly or in sets, alternative and incompatible ways in which the generality of the initial subjective aim may be specifically realized. They represent, in other words, conflicting ideals of subjective self-definition.

The solution to this conflict of ideals or, equivalently, the solution to the problem of indeterminateness, is not to be found in the transcendent decisions provided by the settled world nor in the transcendent decisions provided by God. Rather, the immediate subject "from the spontaneity of its own essence must supply the missing determination for the synthesis of subjective form" (AI 328). It must choose for itself. It must decide *what* it is to *be*, amid the unavoidable circumstances of its birth. Thus the mental pole, in this regard, "is the subject determining its own ideal of itself by reference to eternal principles of valuation autonomously modified in their application to its own physical objective datum" (PR 380).

The subject's chosen ideal of itself is the final cause animating its concrescence. This ideal becomes more specific as a result of the particular immanent decisions constituting each successive phase of the concrescence. The subject evolves, for each product-phase-to-be, an appropriate *subjective end* guiding the ingression of eternal objects and the integration of feelings during the creation of that phase. The subjective end of a given phase-in-process is the initial subjective aim as transformed by the specifications that have accrued to it in the preceding phases and at the outset of the current phase-in-process (PR 342). In this manner, the initial subjective aim, "in its successive modifications, remains the unifying factor governing the successive phases of interplay between physical and conceptual feelings" (PR 343).

Until the satisfaction is reached, however, at the completion of each phase the subject is still confronted with conflicting alternatives concerning its own final self-definition. Thus, until it reaches its last creative subphase, the subject cannot choose once and for all *what* it shall *be*. The subject's progressive definition of its ideal of itself, and the subject's progressive creation of itself, are consequent on each other in the advance from phase to phase, and coincide completely only in the satisfaction. The subjective concrescence, therefore, is to be understood as "the growth and attainment of a final end. The progressive definition of the final end is the efficacious condition for its attainment" (PR 227–28).

This progressive definition of the final end, and thereby of the final self, is the basic ground for the occasion's incoherence, its self-diversity. The transformation of incoherence into coherence, according to the twenty-second Category of Explanation, is the task of the subjective concrescence, ceasing in each instance with its attainment. In the concrescence, therefore, the final end, or subjective aim, "starts with conditioned alternatives, and by successive decisions is reduced to coherence" (PR 342). The occasion's subjective self-diversity is thereby abolished. Accordingly, each phase in the subjective process represents a retreat from the initial generality of the subjective aim, and a retreat from the initial indeterminacy of definiteness, and a retreat from the initial incoherence of feelings. Conversely, each immanent decision by the subject represents a step towards the complete specification and realization of its subjective aim, and a step towards the complete determination of its final definiteness of subjective form, and a step towards the final integration of all its feelings, physical and mental, in the one positive feeling that is the satisfaction.

The three-sided problem of indeterminacy has been solved. Thus, "the actual entity, in becoming itself, also solves the question as to *what* it is to be" (PR 227). Thus, too, the subject's reactions to its objective content "are the subjective forms of the feelings, elaborated into definiteness through stages of process" (PR 234). Thus, finally, the subject "admits or rejects eternal objects which by their absorption into the subjective forms of the many feelings effect [their] integration" (PR 233–34). In short, the problem which the subject "solves is, how the many components of the objective content are to be unified in one felt content with its complex subjective form. This one felt content is the 'satisfaction', whereby the actual entity is its particular individual self" (PR 233). In its *subjective* satisfaction, the occasion, according to Whitehead,

> has attained its individual separation from other things; it has absorbed the datum, and it has not yet lost itself in the swing back to the 'decision' whereby its appetition becomes an element in the data of other entities superseding it. Time has stood still—if only it could. (PR 233)

With the attainment of its *superjective* satisfaction, however, the occasion loses its formal functioning and gains its capacity to function objectively in the occasions in its future. It has perished subjectively only to become immortal objectively. Its completion thus marks the twofold fact that *in it* the many have become one and that *with it* the many have been increased by one. "The creative action is the universe always becoming one in a particular unity of self-experience, and thereby adding to the multiplicity which is the universe as many" (PR 89). The creative action is the functional solidarity of the universe incarnating itself in its creatures. But each creature is created creator of itself. Accordingly,

> definition is the soul of actuality: the attainment of a peculiar definiteness is the final cause which animates a particular process; and its attainment halts its process, so that by transcendence it passes into its

objective immortality as a new objective condition added to the riches of definiteness attainable, the 'real potentiality' of the universe. (PR 340)

In this manner, the *completion* of functional solidarity effects the *renewal* of objective solidarity.

6. Concluding remarks

I must now bring to its conclusion my elucidation of the thesis of solidarity. In the preceding discussion I have been concerned primarily with showing how the extensive standpoint of an actual occasion is a generic scheme of extensive relations that is involved in the transcendent decision whereby the past is a datum for the occasion and in the immanent decision whereby the occasion subsumes the original objectivity of the datum under its own aesthetic synthesis. The aesthetic synthesis is the final outcome of the universal solidarity of actual functionings, including the self-functioning of the occasion under consideration. But the aesthetic synthesis presupposes its given extensive synthesis of objectified data. For "the 'aesthetic synthesis' is the 'experient synthesis' viewed as self-creative, under the limitations laid upon it by its internal relatedness to all other actual occasions" (SMW 227). This internal relatedness of the experiencing occasion to all other actual occasions is a function of the occasion's extensive standpoint, wherein are coordinated the objectifications of the other occasions. Thus, the extensive synthesis of objectified data is the real potentiality for the aesthetic synthesis. For there is no phase in the aesthetic synthesis that does not presuppose its given extensive synthesis.

In this respect, the extensive synthesis is not by itself the solidarity of all occasions, because it is something in itself, but not for itself; it is repetition without immediacy; it is other-functioning without self-functioning. In short, by itself, the extensive synthesis lacks the immediacy of self-functioning, which, when conjoined with the universality of other-functionings, constitutes the solidarity of the universe in the occasion under consideration. Thus, the solidarity of the world presupposes that the extensive synthesis serving as the standpoint of an occasion is itself synthesized with, and subsumed under, the aesthetic synthesis which arises from it. But in the process of aesthetic synthesis, the extensive standpoint of the experiencing occasion "is that general relational element in experience whereby the actual entities experienced, and that unit experience itself, are united in the solidarity of one common world" (PR 112).

The solidarity of the universe has another side to it that has not been discussed in this essay. I mean the special solidarity of functioning which the temporal actualities achieve in the consequent nature of the eternal actuality. In this respect, Whitehead argues that the solidarity of the temporal world is deficient by reason of incompatibilities which result in losses of qualitative content, of felt values and, ultimately, of relevance of functioning. But Whitehead finds "no reason, of any ultimate metaphysical generality, why this should be the whole story" (PR 517). Accordingly, he goes on to fashion a final interpretation of universal solidarity involving the doctrine that every temporal occasion also functions objectively in God's consequent nature, but—and here is the important difference—without loss of subjective immediacy, and with little or no loss of objective content. Since this is a special case of the general doctrine of solidarity, I have chosen not to discuss it here.[11]

My elucidation of the thesis of solidarity is now complete. I have shown that actual occasions are indeed mutually transcendent and mutually immanent: mutually transcendent, in regard to their respective intrinsic realities; and mutually immanent, in regard to their respective extrinsic realities. I have shown, in other words, that the intrinsic reality of one occasion is permeated by the extrinsic reality of all other occasions. I have shown, in addition, how the mutual immanence of discrete occasions is primarily a function of their belonging to a common continuum of extension. For it is the extensive continuum, with its separative, prehensive, and modal properties, that coordinates, within the intrinsic reality of one occasion, the self-transcendent functionings of all other occasions. Finally, I have shown how the immanence of earlier occasions in later ones is to be understood in terms of the abstractive repetition of particulars. For a particular occasion *can* be repeated, with retention of its self-identity, because, wherever it is repeated, it exhibits the self-same position that is its unique birth-mark.

It follows that my elucidation of the thesis of solidarity has fulfilled the three requirements of adequacy that I explicitly set for it in the first chapter of this essay. But the ultimate requirement for this interpretation of the thesis of solidarity, a requirement which I hope it has also fulfilled, is that it throw some light, some much needed light, on the fundamental intuition on which Whitehead built his philosophy of organism—an intuition partially captured, and partially lost, in each of the following statements:

. . . the universe is a process of attaining instances of definite experience out of its own elements. Each such instance embraces the whole, omitting nothing, whether it be ideal form, or actual fact. (RM 112)

The world expands through recurrent unifications of itself, each, by the addition of itself, automatically recreating the multiplicity anew. (PR 438)

There is one all-embracing fact which is the advancing history of the one Universe. This community of the world, which is the matrix for all begetting, and whose essence is process with retention of connectedness,—this community is what Plato terms The Receptacle. . . . (AI 192)

Notes

Chapter One: Solidarity and the Categories

1. The notion of connectedness, or of connexity, also applies to eternal objects *per se*; that is to say, eternal objects among themselves are in one sense mutually transcendent and in another sense mutually immanent. The senses in question are analogous, but by no means identical, to the senses of 'mutual transcendence' and 'mutual immanence' that are applicable to actual entities. That connexity applies also to eternal objects is one reason why their study in this essay is mandatory.

It must be noted here that 'connexity' seems to be, for Whitehead, a wider notion than that of 'solidarity'. For, though the two terms are generally used interchangeably, 'solidarity' is normally predicated only of actual entities, whereas 'connexity' is predicated of all entities of whatever type (MT 13, 91–92). In this respect, the starting point of the organic philosophy is the assumption

> that each entity, of whatever type, essentially involves its own connection with the universe of other things. This connection can be viewed as being what the universe is for that entity either in the way of accomplishment or in the way of potentiality. It can be termed the perspective of the universe for that entity. For example, there are the perspectives of the universe for the number three, and for the color blue, and for any one definite occasion of realized fact. (MT 91)

The *perspective* of the universe for a given entity, it should be obvious, *is* the given entity's *connectedness with* the universe there is for it.

If the entity in question is an actuality, then the perspective of the universe for that actuality may be said to be the latter's *solidarity* with its correlative universe. We may also speak of the universe's solidarity *in* that actuality. Finally, if we wish to emphasize the connectedness of the actuality with what its correlative universe is by way of *accomplishment*, past, present, or future, we may speak of the solidarity of that actuality with *all* actualities. It will be evident, as this essay progresses, that the term 'solidarity' has various interrelated meanings for the organic philosophy. For now, we are emphasizing only its signification of the mutual immanence of discrete actualities.

2. Even the most cursory reading of the secondary literature will reveal the general neglect to which these additional senses of immanence have been subject. Two recent instances of the claim that Whitehead was being careless whenever he spoke of mutual immanence (or of mutual prehensions, or of mutual internal

relations) may be found in Charles Hartshorne's *Insights and Oversights of Great Thinkers* (Albany: State University of New York Press, 1983), p. 164, and in George L. Kline's "Form, Concrescence and Concretum," in *Explorations in Whitehead's Philosophy*, ed. Lewis S. Ford and George L. Kline (New York: Fordham University Press, 1983), pp. 134–35. William P. Alston may be cited as one who has taken seriously, but has rejected as untenable, Whitehead's doctrine of the mutual immanence of all actual occasions. See the following three articles by Alston: (1) "Whitehead's Denial of Simple Location," *Journal of Philosophy*, 48 (1951), 713–721; (2) "Internal Relatedness and Pluralism in Whitehead," *Review of Metaphysics*, 5 (1952), 535–558; and (3) "Simple Location," *Review of Metaphysics*, 8 (1954–1955), 334–341.

3. Victor Lowe, "Whitehead's Gifford Lectures." *The Southern Journal of Philosophy*, 7, (1969), pp. 332–33. A more complete account of these six principles can be found in George Bosworth Burch's compilation of Whitehead's Harvard Lectures for 1926–27. Burch's notes have been edited by Dwight C. Stewart and published in *Process Studies*, 4, (1974), 199–206. The notes also appear as Appendix 3 in Lewis S. Ford's *The Emergence of Whitehead's Metaphysics: 1925–1929* (Albany: State University of New York Press, 1984), pp. 309–16. Burch renders the principle of solidarity as: "Every actual entity requires all other entities, actual or ideal, in order to exist" (*Process Studies*, p. 204; *Emergence*, 312–13).

4. *Proceedings of the Aristotelian Society, 1917–18*, p.32.

5. The organic categoreal scheme presented by Whitehead in PR should not be considered as a final and accurate formulation of the metaphysical principles and categories of the organic philosophy. In fact, as presented in PR, the organic categoreal scheme is both redundant and incomplete. In respect to its redundancy, Whitehead himself tells us that the third and fifth Categoreal Obligations can be eliminated from the scheme because they are only special cases of the second and fourth Categoreal Obligations, respectively (PR 348, 382). In addition, other instances of redundancy become obvious when we compare the twenty-seventh Category of Explanation with both the tenth and twelfth Categories of Explanation; the twenty-fourth Category of Explanation with the sixth through eighth Categories of Explanation; the twenty-fifth, with the eighth, Category of Explanation; and the twenty-sixth Category of Explanation with the second Categoreal Obligation.

In respect to the incompleteness of the categoreal scheme of PR, Whitehead acknowledged, in conversation with A.H. Johnson, the omission from the scheme of metaphysical notions such as continuity, emergence, and God's primordial Nature [Johnson's *Whitehead's Theory of Reality*, (1952; rpt. New York: Dover, 1962), p. 177]. To these three omissions I would add, as a minimum, the omission of the Receptacle or eternal extensive continuum (AI 258–59; PR 112, 118, 470–71), the omission of supersession (IS 240), and the omission of objective immortality (IS 243). In this regard, I take the notion of continuity alluded to in Whitehead's conversation with Johnson as a reference to the metaphysical doctrine of conformation and not as a reference to the eternal extensive continuum (AI 235–36, 325–27). In other words, I take Whitehead to have in mind the qualitative, rather than the extensive, continuity of nature. If I am wrong on this point, then the doctrine of conformation is also omitted from the categoreal scheme, and the views I present here on the metaphysical theory of eternal extension are strengthened all the more.

My immediate point is that the organic categoreal scheme is to be viewed as unfinished business. However, the systematic development of the scheme is not my concern in this essay. Moreover, and more to the point, even in its present state the scheme's metaphysical categories and principles exhibit a remarkably high degree of coherence.

6. Immediately after saying, in the definition of Speculative Philosophy already quoted in the text, that every element of our experience should be interpretable in terms of the scheme of metaphysical ideas, Whitehead goes on to say that by 'interpretation' he means

> that everything of which we are conscious, as enjoyed, perceived, willed, or thought, shall have the character of a particular instance of the general scheme. Thus the philosophical scheme should be coherent, logical, and, in respect to its interpretation, applicable and adequate. Here 'applicable' means that some items of experience are thus interpretable, and 'adequate' means that there are no items incapable of such interpretation. (PR 4)

It follows that any misinterpretation of one or more of the scheme's principles necessarily endangers the applicability and adequacy of the total scheme. It follows also that any further development of Whitehead's metaphysical ideas should always be judged by its effect, positive or negative, on the coherence, applicability, and adequacy of the total scheme.

7. A good introduction to the affinities between Whitehead's metaphysics and what some characterize as the emerging science of wholeness may be gleaned from John P. Briggs and F. David Peat's *Looking Glass Universe* (New York: Cornerstone Library, 1984), which attempts to popularize the more speculative views of Bohm, Pribram, and Prigogine, and also of Rupert Sheldrake. For more on this matter, readers should consult the bibliographical entries presented in this essay under Bohm, Pribram, Prigogine, Sheldrake, and Stapp. In addition, the following are of interest: Charles Hartshorne, "Bell's Theorem and Stapp's Revised View of Space-Time," *Process Studies*, 7 (1977), 183–91; William B. Jones, "Bell's Theorem, H.P. Stapp, and Process Theism," *Process Studies*, 7 (1977), 250–61; Henry J. Folse, Jr., "Complementarity, Bell's Theorem, and the Framework of Process Metaphysics," *Process Studies*, 11 (1981), 242–58; and David Ray Griffin's review of Rupert Sheldrake's *A New Science of Life: The Hypothesis of Formative Causation*, and David G. Trickett's review of David Bohm's *Wholeness and the Implicate Order*, both reviews in *Process Studies*, 12 (1982), pp. 34–40 and 50–54, respectively.

8. Ulric Neisser's account of memory provides an example of this kind of explanation. Thus, in connection with visual memory, he introduces the hypothesis that "we experience familiarity *to the extent that the present act of visual synthesis is identical to an earlier one*" (italics are Neisser's). This is taken from page 98 of his book, *Cognitive Psychology* (New York: Meredith Publishing Co., 1967).

9. My bracketed remark is intended to attenuate the ambiguity of Whitehead's phrasing. His meaning is that each act of becoming must terminate in a created creature, or there is no becoming at all. See PR 105 to 107, particularly 106, for a less ambiguous statement of the meaning of the phrase 'that something becomes'.

10. I have argued for this interpretation of causal objectification in "Whitehead's Principle of Relativity," *Process Studies*, 8 (1978), 1–20. But in the development of this essay's text I am adopting the convenient fiction that none of my articles on Whitehead's metaphysics have appeared in print. In this way, I can

present the views expressed in those articles in the context of the broader concern with solidarity that originally spawned them.

11. In private conversation.

12. See also PR 65–66, 338–39.

13. Particularly misleading is the account of simple physical feelings, also known as conformal feelings, that Whitehead gives in PR 361–65. A much better account—written after the distinction between feeling as subjective form and feeling as positive prehension is clear in Whitehead's mind—is to be found in AI 324–29. This is one indication, Lewis Ford to the contrary, that much of PR's Part III was written *before* Part II. For Ford's views on this matter, see his *Emergence of Whitehead's Metaphysics* (Albany: State University of New York Press, 1984), pp. 205–07, 213–221. My own interpretation of simple physical feelings is here developed in Chapter Two, Sections 4 and 5, in Chapter Seven, Sections 7 and 8, and in Chapter Eight, Section 1.

14. See, for example, Johnson, *Whitehead's Theory of Reality*, p. 183.

15. For an additional illustrious example see: William A. Christian, *An Interpretation of Whitehead's Metaphysics* (1959; rpt. New Haven: Yale University Press, 1967), pp. 326, 343 (also chapters 6, 7, 8, 9, and 11).

16. See Christian, p. 37, and Ivor Leclerc, *Whitehead's Metaphysics* (London: George Allen and Unwin Ltd., 1958), pp. 68–70.

17. PR 101, 208, 335, 362; RM 112; AI 250–51.

18. See, for example: Charles Hartshorne, "Whitehead's Novel Intuition," in *Alfred North Whitehead: Essays on His Philosophy*, ed. George L. Kline (New Jersey: Prentice-Hall, 1963), p. 22; Leclerc, *Whitehead's Metaphysics*, pp. 69–70, 79, 93; and Donald W. Sherburne, *A Whiteheadian Aesthetic* (New Haven: Yale University Press, 1961), p.9.

19. Leclerc, *Whitehead's Metaphysics*, p. 71.

20. The language I am forced to use at this time may suggest that the subjective process is *temporally* earlier than the superjective product. This is not the case. But I cannot make my meaning fully clear until the categories of supersession and position have been fully interpreted. Suffice it to say, for now, that the subjective process is *supersessionally*, but not temporally, earlier than the superjective product, and that the subject and the superject exhibit one and the same *position* in the extenso-genetic order of the universe. I shall argue later, in Chapter Six, that an occasion's position remains unchanged throughout all the phases of the occasion's existence, and that it thus serves as one ground for the identity of the occasion *qua* subject with the occasion *qua* superject.

21. The freedom of an actual occasion entails that its process could have been different. If the process had been different, the occasion would have had a different final definiteness, but it would have been the *same* occasion. The sense in which it would have been the same occasion is relevant to the doctrine that every actual occasion is a subject-superject; for, if the genetic fallacy is to be avoided, the doctrine requires that in some specifiable sense the subject be the same entity as the superject. The identity is specifiable in virtue of the unique and unchanging position of each actual occasion. This topic is developed in detail in the last three chapters of this essay (see previous note).

22. The views presented so far in this section, and also those presented earlier in Section 4, appear, with slight modifications, in my "Whitehead's Principle of

Process," *Process Studies*, 4 (1974), 275–84. I know of no published refutation of the arguments contained in that article and here. To date, references to the article by other commentators has been very favorable, though with some reservations in a few instances. See, for example: Robert Fancher, "Of Time, the Self, and Rem Edwards," *Process Studies*, 7 (1977), 40–43; William J. Garland, "Whitehead's Theory of Causal Objectification," *Process Studies*, 12 (1982), 180–91; George L. Kline, "Form, Concrescence and Concretum," in *Explorations*, ed. Ford and Kline, pp. 104–46; George R. Lucas, Jr., "The Compositional History of Whitehead's Writings," *International Philosophical Quarterly*, 24 (1984), 312–25; and David L. Schindler, "Whitehead's Inability to Affirm a Universe of Value," *Process Studies*, 13 (1983), 117–31.

It should be noted that Kline, although agreeing with my claim that becoming produces being, does not acknowledge that each actual occasion is both subject and superject, or, in Kline's terminology, both concrescence and concretum. The interpretations of supersession and position that I advance in this essay, if correct, constitute an implicit repudiation that views such as mine "imply that concrescence and concretum are *temporally* successive phases of an enduring entity, such that one phase can be 'not yet' and the other 'no longer' although the entity itself is fully present" (p. 145, n. 35, italics added; see also p. 146, n. 36).

I do not want to give the impression that my article on the principle of process has vanquished the view that the being of an actual entity *is* its becoming. Unrepentant proponents of that view still abound. For a recent example of it, see Charles Michael Johnson, "On Prehending the Past," *Process Studies*, 6 (1976), 255–69.

23. Whitehead muddies the waters further by saying that actual occasions "'perpetually perish' subjectively, but are immortal objectively" (PR 44). With the possible exception of God, whom the organic philosophy construes as an actual entity in unending concrescence, no actual entity can perpetually perish subjectively. The subjectivity of an actual occasion perishes exactly once. In a different sense of *perishing*, however, the objectivity of a superjective satisfaction *does* perish perpetually. In this other sense of the word, an occasion's "perishing is its assumption of a new metaphysical function in the creative advance of the universe" (AI 262). Its new function is to be an energizer of the complex macrocosmic begetting of each novel occasion in its future (AI 356; PR 44). In this sense, then, the perpetual perishing of an attained actuality is its *perpetual causal objectification* in every actuality whose becoming finds that attained actuality already in existence. *Objective perishing* is perpetual because of the necessary involvement of every completed occasion in the macroscopic processes of transition by which the occasions in its future are begotten. This is why, in one sense of the term, *transition* "is the 'perpetually perishing' which is one aspect of the notion of time" (PR 320).

The synonymity of 'transition' and 'perishing', I may add in passing, is one of the many reasons why I reject as unfounded Ford's contention that Whitehead abandoned the distinction between transition and concrescence in favor of concrescence as constituting the whole of an occasion's process of becoming. 'Perishing'— which has the root meaning of 'passing' or 'going through' (*per ire*)—is synonymous with 'transition' and 'passage'. Thus, Whitehead cannot have given up, in the middle of writing PR, a doctrine which appears explicitly in AI. For Ford's contention that Whitehead abandoned the doctrine of transition in the midst of writing PR, see the following: "Some Proposals Concerning the Composition of *Process and Reality,*" *Process Studies,* 8 (1978), 145–56; "The Concept of Process: From Transition to Concrescence," in *Whitehead und der Prozessbegriff,* eds. Harold Holz and Ernest Wolf-Gazo (Freiburg and Munich: Verlag Karl Aber, 1984) pp. 73–101; and *Emergence,* pp. 188–90, 194–97; 199–203, 213, 215, 241, 255.

24. The existence of *B*'s dative phase means that *A* has been superseded by *B*; but *B* will not be superseded by *C*, nor by any other actuality, until *B* has achieved the status of a superjective satisfaction. In one sense, therefore, the conformal phases of *B* also belong to the supersession that is intrinsic to *B*. However, since an occasion is not actual, or self-realizing, until its phase of conceptual novelty (or conceptual reversion), actuality *A* cannot be said to have been superseded by *actuality B* until the process of transition to *B* is over. For this reason, the occasion's intrinsic supersession of phases is normally equated with its process of concrescence, and its phases of transition are normally collapsed into one overarching relation of extrinsic supersession. Actuality *B* is begotten as immediately superseding actuality *A*; once begotten. it then fashions its own ultimate definiteness in the intrinsic supersessional process which is its own concrescence; then, having achieved its superjective satisfaction, it is immediately superseded by actuality *C*.

The uses of 'until' and 'then' in these remarks should not be taken to imply that the becoming of an actual entity *takes* physical time, or that it *lasts* for a certain period of such time. There is no chronometry of becoming. Supersessional relations are chronological relations and do not—indeed, cannot—constitute a continuum, let alone a measurable continuum. Physical time is chronometrical, and is merely a convenient way in which the extensive quantum embodied by an actual occasion can be correlated with, and quantitatively compared to, the extensive quanta embodied by other occasions, actual or hypothetical. However, some features of the chronology of becoming are reflected into the chronometry of what has become, is becoming, or will become (PR 442).

25. See John B. Cobb, Jr., "Freedom in Whitehead's Philosophy: A Response to Edward Pols," *Southern Journal of Philosophy,* 7 (1969), 409–13. For an explicit denial that there are any successive genetic phases within actual entity, see also, in the same issue, Charles Hartshorne, "Whitehead and Ordinary Language," p. 437.

26. This is the position taken by Christian in *Interpretation of Whitehead's Metaphysics*; see pp. 80–81. More recently, however, Christian—in "Some Aspects of Whitehead's Metaphysics," in *Explorations,* eds. Ford and Kline, pp. 35–40—has provided an account of the succession of phases that is in some respects similar to the one I am advancing here. But important differences between Christian's interpretation and mine still remain.

27. The equation of extrinsic supersession with temporal supersession must not be taken to imply that extrinsic supersession is in physical time. Neither extrinsic, nor intrinsic, supersession is in physical time; but the former can, whereas the latter cannot, be correlated with the generation of an occasion's finite extensive quantum and, hence, with physical time and chronometrical relations. Unless the context indicates otherwise, whenever I speak of the temporal relations of actual entities, I mean their relations of extrinsic supersession.

28. Christian, *Interpretation,* pp. 155–56, 119.

29. Ibid. pp. 119, 155–56.
30. Ibid. pp. 119, 156, 77.
31. Ibid. p. 77.
32. Ibid. p. 139.
33. Ibid. pp. 141–42.
34. Ibid. pp. 130–31, 134–35.
35. The single most important exception to this generalization is found in Stephen David Ross, *Perspective in Whitehead's Metaphysics* (Albany: State University of New York Press, 1983). Ross' main theme is the role played in Whitehead's philosophy by the principle that all being is perspectival. Thus, Ross is concerned with the notion of connexity in its broadest sense (see note 1 of this chapter). Accordingly, he has much to say about the solidarity of actual entities and about the role played, in that respect, by the extensive continuum. A comparison of his view and mine cannot be undertaken here, but the two views should prove to be mutually illuminating.

Chapter Two: The Principle of Relativity

1. Richard M. Rorty is a notable exception. He takes Whitehead literally, or almost so, in two excellent articles discussing, among other things, the possible link between a concrete entity's being *knowable* and its being *repeatable* ("Matter and Event," in *The Concept of Matter*, ed. E. McMullin, Notre Dame University Press, 1963; and "The Subjectivist Principle and the Linguistic Turn," in *Alfred North Whitehead: Essays on His Philosophy*, ed. George L. Kline, Prentice-Hall, 1963). Unfortunately, Rorty's insight into Whitehead's intended use of the doctrine of repeatable particulars is clouded by his misunderstanding of other relevant Whiteheadian principles. He is thus led to reject Whitehead's doctrine as both untenable and unnecessary. Since I am not concerned here with issues of adequacy or tenability but only with showing that Whitehead did indeed hold that completed actualities are repeatable, I have no reason to discuss Rorty's views at this time. But I believe that no complete account of this aspect of Whitehead's philosophy can afford to ignore what Rorty has had to say about it.
2. Whitehead's conception of God as one actual entity that is always becoming, and hence never complete, raises an interesting problem. For if God is never completely determinate, he is never a being; yet God does fall under the principle of relativity, does function as an object for all other actualities. I will deal with this problem in Chapter Four. Suffice it to say, for now, that God is an object for other actualities only in respect to those aspects of himself that are completely determinate.
3. The relativity principle is necessary, but not sufficient, for the complete intelligibility of the thesis of solidarity. It cannot by itself explain the sense in which occasions contemporary with, or later than, a given occasion are at once without and within that occasion.
4. The considerations presented so far in this chapter, and also a few of those presented in the next, appear, with slight modifications, in my "Whitehead's Principle of Relativity," *Process Studies*, 8 (1978), 1–20. To date, the only explicit

attempt to repudiate my contention that actual occasions are repeatable appears in a brief note by Paul F. Schmidt, "Nobo's Thesis on the Repeatability of Actual Occasions," *Process Studies*, 11 (1981), 104–06.

5. It should be noted that, in the organic philosophy, the terms 'given' and 'datum', like the term 'actual world', are also systematically ambiguous, and are so precisely for the same reason—the twofold reality of every completed actuality. In a more general sense, the systematic ambiguity of all these terms results from the systematic ambiguity of 'object', which may mean 'an object as a transcendent capacity' or an 'object as a realized, immanent determinant' (PR 366–67). In fact, the ambiguity attaches to every entity of every category of existence; for the principle of relativity means, in effect, that "to exist is to function, and to possess a capacity for functioning beyond any particular actual exemplification" (ESP 313). The capacity to function resides in the original self of whatever entity is in question, and each exemplification of that capacity is the entity itself *as reproduced* in some actual entity.

6. A hybrid physical feeling is defined by Whitehead as "the prehension by one subject of a conceptual prehension, or of an 'impure' prehension, belonging to the mentality of another subject" (PR 163).

7. It should be noted, in this regard, that an occasion's hybrid physical feeling of another temporal occasion may introduce into its conceptual experience eternal objects which are not physically realized in its temporal world, but which were conceptually entertained by the earlier occasion. The occasion's hybrid physical feeling of God, on the other hand, is the only feeling that can introduce into its conceptual experience eternal objects that are neither physically, nor conceptually, exemplified in its temporal world. Thus, ultimately, all conceptual originality in the temporal world is derived from God's primordial conceptual experience.

8. For a recent instance of attributing the activity of objectification and conformation to the autonomous subject, see William J. Garland, "Whitehead's Theory of Causal Objectification," *Process Studies*, 12 (1982), 180–91.

9. Christian, *An Interpretation of Whitehead's Metaphysics*, pp. 130–44.

10. Ibid. p. 141.

11. Ibid. pp. 130–31, 134.

12. Ibid. pp. 131, 134–39, 143.

13. Ibid. p.131.

14. Ibid.

15. Ibid. p. 134.

16. Ibid. pp. 141–42.

17. See: Christian, *Interpretation*, pp. 141–42; Johnson, *Whitehead's Theory of Reality*, pp. 30–31; Leclerc, *Whitehead's Metaphysics*, pp. 158–59; Paul F. Schmidt, *Perception and Cosmology in Whitehead's Philosophy* (New Brunswick: Rutgers University Press, 1967), p. 124; Sherburne, *Whitehead's Metaphysics*, p. 48.

18. See: Charles Hartshorne, *Creative Synthesis and Philosophic Method* (La Salle: The Open Court Publishing Co., 1970), pp. 117–21; Sheilah O' Flynn Brennan, "Substance Within Substance," *Process Studies*, 7 (1977), 14–26; Nancy Frankenberry, "The Power of the Past," *Process Studies*, 13 (1983), 132–42; William J. Garland, "Whitehead's Theory of Causal Objectification," (see note 8, above). In "Whitehead's Principle of Relativity," I cited Victor Lowe as holding this view (see his *Understanding Whitehead*, The Johns Hopkins Press, Baltimore, 1966, pp.

359–60). But, in a very generous letter of 17 January 1980, Lowe has expressed his general agreement with all my published views on Whitehead's philosophy. In that letter, Lowe informed me that Whitehead once said to him that the notion of repetition ought to have been given an explicit place in the categoreal scheme.

19. The process of transition produces, in addition, the initial conformal feelings and the initial conceptual reproductions. But our concern now is limited to the causal objectifications that are its first productions.

Chapter Three: The Principles of Ontology and Creativity

1. Christian's interpretation of the organic philosophy, for example, is vitiated by the adoption of this mistaken view; see *Interpretation*, pp. 319–30.
2. See note 18 to Chapter Two.
3. See note 17 to Chapter Two.
4. In regard to Hume's adumbration of the principle of relativity, see PR 198–227, particularly 206: "The first point to notice is that Hume's philosophy is pervaded by the notion of 'repetition', and that memory is a particular example of this character of experience, that in some sense there is entwined in its fundamental nature the fact that it is repeating something."
5. See, for example, the formulation of the ontological principle appearing in the categoreal scheme, PR 36–37. Also, see PR 327.
6. This last statement needs to be qualified. In truth, creativity is one aspect of the ultimate reality grounding each particular case of the many becoming one and being increased by one. Other aspects of this ultimate reality, I shall argue in the text, are envisagement and extensiveness. Later I shall refer to this reality as 'the extenso-creative matrix', or as 'the Creative Receptacle', or as 'the existential matrix'. In any coherent development of the organic philosophy, this ultimate reality is the reason why the Category of the Ultimate expresses a *de jure*, and not a mere *de facto*, regularity. In this respect, Whiteheadians need to take seriously the criticisms of the Category of the Ultimate raised by Robert C. Neville in *Creativity and God: A Challenge to Process Theology* (New York: The Seabury Press, 1980), pp. 40–46, and in "Whitehead on the One and the Many," *Explorations*, eds. Ford and Kline, pp. 257–71.

I believe that my efforts in this essay provide the basis for a satisfactory answer to Neville's criticisms, but only to the extent that I develop the organic theory of the ultimate beyond the chaotic state in which Whitehead left it. Thus, my efforts make evident the need to develop systematically a coherent organic theory of the existential matrix. I go a long way in that direction in this essay, but I leave for another time a more systematic treatment of the topic.

7. Compare Archie Graham, "Metaphysical Principles and the Category of the Ultimate," *Process Studies*, 7 (1977), 108–111; and David L. Schindler, "Whitehead's Challenge to Thomism on the Problem of God: The Metaphysical Issues," *International Philosophical Quarterly*, 19 (1979), 285–99; F. Bradford Wallack, *The Epochal Nature of Process in Whitehead's Metaphysics* (Albany: State University of New York Press, 1980), pp. 68–72.

8. The neglect of transition should be fairly evident to anyone familiar with the major book-length interpretations of Whitehead's philosophy.

9. Charles Michael Johnson's "On Prehending the Past" (*Process Studies*, 6 {1976}, 255–69) is an important and recent exception to this trend. But Johnson's interpretation of transition differs markedly from mine.

10. London: George Allen and Unwin Ltd., 1958; New York: The Macmillan Company, 1958.

11. Leclerc, *Whitehead's Metaphysics*, pp. 68–71, 82.

12. Ibid. pp. 82, 171.

13. Ibid. pp. 81.

14. New Haven: Yale University Press, 1961, pp. 21–23.

15. For example, George L. Kline, in his "Form, Concrescence and Concretum: A Neo-Whiteheadian Analysis" (*The Southern Journal of Philosophy*, 7 {1969-70}, 357), finds it extremely puzzling that Whitehead should speak so often of the objectification of a superject *for* a subject in concrescence. Why not, he wants to know, *by* the concrescence? If the answer escapes Kline, it is because, as he admits, he can find no ontological difference between transition and concrescence (ibid. p. 351, note 1; also p. 360). But transition is the process *whereby* the superjects are objectified *for* the subject.

A revised and expanded version of Kline's article appears in *Explorations*, eds. Ford and Kline, pp. 104–46. In this updated version, Kline acknowledges my attempts to distinguish transition from concrescence, but, without arguing the point, he states that he remains unconvinced (pp. 140–41). The arguments which Kline finds unconvincing appeared in my "Transition in Whitehead: A Creative Process Distinct from Concrescence," *International Philosophical Quarterly*, 19 (1979), 265–83, and are repeated here, with substantial revisions and additions, in Sections 11, 12 and 13 of the present chapter. For other reactions to my article on transition, see: Joseph A. Bracken, S.J., "Substance-Society-Natural Systems: A Creative Rethinking of Whitehead's Cosmology," *International Philosophical Quarterly*, 25 (1985), 3–13; W. Norris Clarke, S.J., *The Philosophical Approach to God: A Neo-Thomistic Perspective*, (Winston-Salem, N.C.: Wake Forest University Publications, 1979), p. 81; Nancy Frankenberry, "The Power of the Past," *Process Studies*, 13 (1983), 132–42; William J. Garland, "Whitehead's Theory of Causal Objectification," *Process Studies*, 12 (1982), 180–91; George R. Lucas, "The Compositional History of Whitehead's Writings," *International Philosophical Quarterly*, 24 (1984), 313–25; David L. Schindler, "Whitehead's Inability to Affirm a Universe of Value," *Process Studies*, 13 (1983), 117–31; and John R. Stacer, S.J. "Integrating Thomistic and Whiteheadian Perspectives on God," *International Philosophical Quarterly*, 21 (1981), 355–77.

16. Thus, for Locke, "It is evident the internal constitution, whereon their properties depend, is unknown to us," *An Essay Concerning Human Understanding*, Vol. 2, Book III, Ch. VI, Article 9.

17. Locke, Vol. 1, Book II, Ch. XIV, Article 1.

18. Locke, Vol. 1, Book II, Ch. XXI, Article 2.

19. This becomes evident if one reads with care Chapter X of Part II of PR and the abstract of that chapter appearing on PR 62. Also relevant to this issue are PR 135 and 428.

20. The relation between the creativity of transition and the creativity of

concrescence will be gradually explained in the text. Suffice it to say for now that the creativity of transition is the creativity of the universe as in the very process of individualizing itself into a new occasion under conditions imposed by the already completed actualities. The creativity of concrescence, on the other hand, is the creativity of the universe as already individualized and as belonging to the occasion embodying it. The actuality in concrescence is transcended by the transition which begot it, is transcended in a way analogous to that in which an individual product is transcended by the process of its production.

21. The statement that the transcendent creativity objectifies the completed occasion according to the occasion's physical purposes should be qualified with the phrase "conditions permitting." The conditions are the other actual entities (God included) to be objectified and the requirement that, as objectified in a novel occasion, the past occasions must be compatible for aesthetic synthesis in the novel occasion's experience of them (PR 101, 173, 227, 321). I return to this topic at various places in the text.

22. See Chapter One, Section 10 above.

23. Propositions, contrasts, and multiplicities are organic categories of existence. Propositions, roughly speaking, are real, non-eternal possibilities of the data of certain physical feelings being integrated with the data of certain conceptual feelings. Contrasts are best understood as particular modes of synthesis of entities in one prehension. Finally, multiplicities are best construed as pure disjunctions of diverse entities.

Chapter Four: Creativity, Eternal Objects, and God

1. The views presented here regarding the reality of creativity, together with the considerations of the previous chapter concerning the principle of creativity and the ontological principle, and those in later chapters respecting the relationship between creativity and the extensive continuum, should be compared and contrasted with those presented on the same topics by William J. Garland in "The Ultimacy of Creativity," *Explorations*, eds. Ford and Kline, pp. 212–38. Garland's excellent article substantially revises and enlarges the article of the same title appearing in *The Southern Journal of Philosophy*, 7 (1969), 361–76. The similarities between Garland's views and mine are remarkable. We differ significantly only in respect to the greater role that I attribute to extensiveness as an aspect of the Ultimate and to transition as the process of efficient causation.

2. To call an actual entity, or individualized embodiment of the creativity, an 'accident' is needlessly misleading, particularly when it leads Whitehead to say that God is a 'primordial accident' of the creativity. The term 'attribute', which Whitehead used in SMW, would have been better. For the organic conception of the universe, it is no accident that there are actual entities, though no specified actual entity, other than God, is necessary. In other words, no particular actual occasion is necessary, but it is necessary that there be actual occasions.

3. The views presented here on eternal objects and God invite comparison with those of William A. Christian. See his *An Interpretation of Whitehead's Metaphysics*, Parts Two and Three. Also compare: Ivor Leclerc, "The Structure of Form,"

Revue Internationale de Philosophie, 15 (1961), 185–203, and "Whitehead and the Theory of Form," *Process and Divinity: Philosophical Essays Presented to Charles Hartshorne*, eds. William L. Reese and Eugene Freeman (La Salle, Illinois: Open Court Publishing Co., 1964), 127–137; John W. Lango, "The Relatedness of Eternal Objects in Whitehead's *Process and Reality*," *Process Studies*, 1 (1971), 124–28.

4. Compare Marjorie Suchocki, "The Metaphysical Ground of the White-headian God," *Process Studues*, 5 (1975), 237–46; see, in particular, the last page of this excellent article: "We maintain that it is determinateness which allows causal efficacy, rather than the pastness of concrescence as such. . . . Since determinateness is necessary for objectification, there is no categoreal reason why God may not be prehended by an occasion, despite the fact that his concrescence is everlasting, and hence 'with' all occasions."

5. I shall return to this topic in Chapters Six and Seven.

6. Compare Villard Alan White, "Sensa and Patterns," *Process Studies*, 10 (1980), 39–43.

7. See Whitehead's letter of 2 January 1936 to Charles Hartshorne, as reproduced in Kline's *Whitehead: Essays on His Philosophy*, pp. 198–99.

Chapter Five: The Extensive Continuum

1. For the identical meaning of 'world' and 'cosmic epoch' see PR 303.

2. See also PR 52–53, 464.

3. This does not mean that pure extension is without properties; it means that it can gain additional properties by the ingression of eternal objects. It is formless, but it can gain forms.

4. See also SMW 130, and MT 212.

5. See also SMW 179.

6. See also MT 212.

7. The relevant discussion is in PR 141–47.

8. See also PR 507–08 in respect to the inheritance of the geometrical system by which our cosmic epoch is defined.

9. For example, William Christian holds that "extension, and with it the notions of space, time, and regions, is derivative by abstraction from the nature of feelings" (*Interpretation*, p. 156). Christian also holds that "the continuum itself is constituted by actual occasions" (*Ibid.*, p. 394). A. H. Johnson, to give another example, denies that the extensive continuum is any sort of underlying entity; nevertheless, he is aware "that Whitehead apparently has a different and contradictory meaning for the term *extensive continuum*" (*Whitehead's Theory of Reality*, pp. 57; also 185). I believe my interpretation resolves the 'contradiction' to which Johnson refers. For other examples of the failure to distinguish extension from actualized extension see: Rasvihary Das, *The Philosophy of Whitehead* (New York: Russell & Russell, 1928, 1964), pp. 77–78; and Robert Palter, *Whitehead's Philosophy of Science* (Chicago: The University of Chicago Press, 1960), p. 112. See also Ivor Leclerc, "Whitehead and the Problem of Extension" *Journal of Philosophy*, 58 (1961), 559–565.

More recent accounts of Whitehead's theory of extension display an increasing awareness of its systematic importance in Whitehead's metaphysical thought but fall way short of clearly distinguishing between the eternal extensive continuum and the realized spatio-temporal continuum constituted by the extensive standpoints of the actual occasions in our cosmic epoch. None of these more recent accounts catches on to the fact that eternal extension and eternal creativity are aspects of the ultimate reality underlying the becoming, the being, and the solidarity of actual antities. See: Elizabeth M. Kraus, *The Metaphysics of Experience: A Companion to Whitehead's Process and Reality* (New York: Fordham University Press, 1979), pp. 58–60, 127–57; Stephen David Ross, *Perspectives in Whitehead's Metaphysics*, pp. 169–218, 267, 271; and F. Bradford Wallack, *The Epochal Nature of Process in Whitehead's Metaphysics*, pp. 271–312. See also John B. Cobb, Jr. and Donald W. Sherburne, "Regional Inclusion and the Extensive Continuum," *Process Studies*, 2 (1972), 277–95.

10. In one sense, $a*/C*$, $b*/C*$, and $c*/C*$ are shorthand notations for $(a*/C*)**$, $(b*/C*)**$, and $(c*/C*)**$, respectively; for those regions might have served as standpoints for actual entities, but in fact they do not. They are not proper regions, but potential regions that might have become proper regions. In another sense, however, $a*/C*$, $b*/C*$, and $c*/C*$ may be construed as *proper subregions*, since they are modal aspects of proper regions. In other words, because each mirrors the boundary and extensive structure of a proper region, each has a derivative boundary and structure (except for $c*/C*$, which mirrors the structure of $C*$ potentially, not actually; but more about this later). The same complex pattern determining the structure and boundary of the original proper region also determines the structure and boundary of the mirroring modal subregion (except in the case of $c*/C*$, or of self-aspects in general). Of course, the pattern of the modal subregion is a subordinate component of the more complex pattern determining the boundary and structure of the proper region within which the modal subregion is found (again, the self-aspect excepted). For that reason, the simpler pattern differentiates, but does not separate, the modal subregion from the rest of the parent region. In addition, by reason of the prehensiveness of extension, or so I will argue in the text, each proper region is the integral, indissoluble unity of its own intrinsic modal differentiations. Thus, the subordinate functioning of a modal subregion's pattern, and the prehensive character of the subregion's parent region, jointly attenuate the boundedness of the modal subregion, but not so much as to prohibit construing the modal subregion as a proper subregion. In any case, the notation used to denote modal subregions is adequate for our purposes because what is of interest to us is the modal property of these regions, and not their character of being regions that might have functioned as proper regions.

11. PR 303, 146–47, MT 100.

12. Assuming that $B*$ and $C*$ are contemporaries, their relationship would be mirrored in $A*$ by $c**/pr**/\&**/b*/A*$ and $b**/pr**/\&**/c*/A*$.

13. It should be noted that Whitehead holds that this character of simple location is assumed both by classical and by relativity physics (SMW 70, 81).

14. The latter portion of this passage was quoted a few pages back. It is repeated here for emphasis and clarity.

15. Notice that Whitehead is not using the notation which I use.

16. The field of presentational immediacy, it should be noted, is part of the

continuum as thus included. This field presents itself for perception and cognition as a spatio-temporal continuum with almost negligible temporal duration. This field is yet another signification of 'extensive continuum'. Its relevance will be studied in Chapter Eight.

17. For example, the contiguity of b^*/C^* and c^*/C^* would represent the contiguity, or immediate external connection, of B^* and C^*. Similarly, the contiguity of $a^*/b^*/C^*$ and $b^*/b^*/C^*$ would represent the contiguity of A^* and B^*. The four modal subregions in question would also be representing the mediate external connection of A^* and C^*.

18. My views on the epochal theory of time presuppose my interpretation of the category of supersession (Chapter One, Section 11). I hope to devote a book to the further elucidation of this theory. Compare Jerome Ashmore, "Diverse Currents in Whitehead's View of Time," *Process Studies*, 2 (1972), 193–200; Bowman L. Clarke, "Process, Time, and God," *Process Studies*, 13 (1983), 245–59; Richard W. Field, "William James and the Epochal Theory of Time," ibid., 260–74; Robert Neville, "Genetic Succession, Time, and Becoming," *Process Studies*, 1 (1971), 194–98; Lewis S. Ford, "Genetic and Coordinate Division Correlated," ibid., 199–209; William W. Hammerschmidt, *Whitehead's Philosophy of Time* (1947; rpt. New York: Russell & Russell, 1975); and F. Bradford Wallack, *The Epochal Nature of Process in Whitehead's Metaphysics*, especially the last three chapters.

Chapter Six: Objectification, Position, and Self-Identity

1. See, for example, Johnson in *Whitehead's Theory of Reality*: "Thus, the extensive continuum is not an underlying or all-inclusive entity. The term refers to the fact that data are available in a definite complex fashion. It must be admitted that Whitehead apparently has a different and contradictory meaning for the term *extensive continuum*. On occasion he refers to something apart from actual entities" (p. 57). Later, in his evaluational chapter, Johnson says that Whitehead's "discussion of the extensive continuum also issues in apparent confusion. It is referred to as *both* (a) a distinct entity, real in its own right and (b) a relational characteristic of other realities" (p. 185). A more recent example is afforded by Ross in his *Perspective in Whitehead's Metaphysics*: "I have noted that the extensive continuum in its full generality is a defining condition for the perspectivity and togetherness of all occasions in one universe. It is presupposed by every becoming, and in this sense does not seem to be a consequence of becoming or a special condition of our cosmic epoch. An alternative is that there are different senses of extensive continuity in Whitehead's theory, one of greater generality than the other" (p. 170). See also his remarks in pp. 267–68, 271.

2. The relevant passages are as follows. For the first similarity: PR 46–47; AI 155–56, 171–72, 192. For the second: PR 46–47, 103; AI 156, 171–72, 192; see also S 36. For the third: PR 30, 47, 104–05, 129–30, 134–35, 249, 344, 362; AI 171. For the fourth: PR 10–11, 43–44, 97–98, 104–05, 113; SMW 148. For the fifth: SMW 174–75; PR 104–05. For the sixth and last: SMW 99–102, 207; PR 124.

3. In his letter to Charles Hartshorne of January 2nd, 1936, Whitehead writes: "There is one point as to which you—and everyone—misconstrue me—obviously

my usual faults of exposition are to blame. I mean my doctrine of *eternal objects*." In this letter Whitehead identifies both SMW and PR as the *loci* where he has treated the doctrine of eternal objects. I find this interesting because I am convinced that nearly everything said about eternal objects in PR presupposes the reader's understanding of what was said about them in SMW. Yet few readers, and not too many Whiteheadian scholars, ever have SMW in mind when they interpret PR in respect to the doctrine of eternal objects. For a slightly edited version of Whitehead's letter see George L. Kline (ed.), *Alfred North Whitehead: Essays on His Philosophy*, pp. 198–99.

4. It should be noted that it cannot be absolutely necessary that B's immediate descendant occupy, or embody, C^{**}; but B's immediate descendant will necessarily occupy C^{**} *provided* that this fact be compatible with the claims laid on the future by B's contemporaries. Thus if Q anticipates that its immediate descendant will occupy R^{**}, and if R indeed occupies R^*, and if R^* overlaps with C^{**}, then it would follow that the immediate descendant of B could not possibly embody C^{**}. It would still remain true, however, that wherever the immediate descendant of B came into being, B would be modally present in it. But it would then be the case that the modal presence of the extensive region that B's immediate descendant actually came to embody had not played a relevant role in the experience enjoyed by B. In other words, it would be the case that the modal presence of that region had not been relevantly differentiated from the rest of $fu^{**}/\&^{**}/B^*$.

5. In the passage quoted, Whitehead is discussing a nexus; but, as I will go on to show in the text, the position of a nexus is derivative from the position of its component actualities. Actual entities are the primary entities exhibiting position as an essential component of their respective natures. They are dated and located in relation to each other.

6. In this context, Whitehead says that "the abstract essence is a complex eternal object" (PR 94). But this is at odds with the systematic terminology introduced elsewhere in his writings, and which I have discussed in Chapter Four. The set of eternal objects having unrestricted ingression in an actual entity constitutes a definite contrast and not a complex eternal object. The *manner* of the contrast is a complex eternal object; but the contrast is the joint realization of its *manner* and its *matter*. The matter of the contrast is a set of simple eternal objects and a set of complex eternal objects of less complexity than the manner itself. The first set cannot be empty; the second may.

7. See also SMW 207; MT 147.

8. The theory of the indicative scheme, and with it the notion of position, plays an indispensable, if mostly implicit, role in the development and cogency of Whitehead's metaphysical views on propositions, propositional feelings, and judgments. The examination of those views is beyond the scope of the present essay. For Whitehead's non-metaphysical treatment of indication, see his "Indication, Classes, Numbers, Validation," *Mind*, 43 (1934), 281–97. This article was included in the 1947 Philosophical Library hardback edition of Whitehead's *Essays in Science and Philosophy* (pp. 313–31), but was dropped from all subsequent editions.

9. For a brief statement of the empirical or cosmological version of this doctrine see R 23. But notice that in that book 'position' becomes the 'essential relations' of a factor, and that 'definiteness' becomes the contigent or 'adjectival relations' of a factor.

To miss the significance of the distinction between aboriginal position and acquired definiteness is to undermine the freedom of self-determination that Whitehead attributes to every actual entity. For a sustained attack on the cogency of Whitehead's doctrine of freedom, see Edward Pols, *Whitehead's Metaphysics: A Critical Examination of Process and Reality* (Carbondale and Edwardsville: Southern Illinois University Press, 1967).

10. See also: S 26; PR 233, 250, 323; AI 332.

11. This statement occurs in Part III of PR. Whenever it was written, Whitehead had yet to distinguish clearly between the total *determinateness* of an occasion, which includes the occasion's position, and the *definiteness* of the occasion, which is primarily that part of the occasion's determinateness that results from the occasion's autonomous self-causation. This is one of many reasons why I would argue, Lewis Ford in *Emergence* to the contrary, that most of PR's Part III was written *before* most of Parts I and II.

12. Notice that this principle is a reformulation of the principle of solidarity as given in Whitehead's Harvard lectures of 1926–27.

13. In the organic philosophy, 'change' is defined as 'the difference between actual occasions constituting successive moments in the history of a social nexus or enduring object' (PR 114, 123, 124–25).

14. PR 29–30, 32, 76 (footnote 9), 86–87, 239.

Chapter Seven: Extensional Solidarity and the Dative Phase

1. PR 112, 118, 470–71; AI 171–72, 240–41, 258–59.

2. See also SMW 98–101 and MT 95.

3. As used in this context, the term 'transmission' should not be taken to mean that a numerically self-same entity travels from one region of the extensive continuum to another. In the continuum there is no locomotion. The reproduction, in one locus, of what already exists in another locus is what Whitehead means by *transmission* whenever he uses that term in a strictly metaphysical sense. This qualification applies both to transmission through objectification and to transmission through conformation. Compare Richard W. Field, "Transmission, Inheritance, and Efficient Causation," *Process Studies*, 14 (1984), 44–46.

4. This is the main reason why Whitehead contends that everything is in the experience of an actual entity. If it is not in the entity's experience, it is not in its universe. It is also the reason why Whitehead says that the "ontological principle can be expressed as: All real togetherness is togetherness in the formal constitution of an actuality" (PR 48). But to take this statement literally is to court interpretative disaster. For one thing, stipulative definitions aside, disjunctive diversities are each a species of togetherness. For another, each causal objectification abstracts from the full definiteness of the actuality being objectified. Thus, there are disjunctive diversities without, as well as conjunctive diversities within, the experience of an actual entity. Thus, too, there is more in the extrinsic universe of an actuality than is found in the intrinsic universe of that same actuality. In short, we must not forget that the world within experience is numerically different from, and qualitatively less definite than, the world without experience. But, in respect

to the self-identity of things, the world within and the world without *are two and the same*. The neglect of this doctrine, it seems to me, vitiates many interpretations of Whitehead's philosophy. For a recent example of this neglect, see F. Bradford Wallack's *The Epochal Nature of Process in Whitehead's Metaphysics*, particularly pages 40 through 46.

5. Some of these new attained actualities will be contemporaries of *B*, and will be comtemporaries of *C*, since they are not causally objectified in *C*, nor *C* in them.

6. For example, this confusion vitiates Lewis Ford's recent efforts in *The Emergence of Whitehead's Metaphysics*. See chapters 8 through 10 of that book, but particularly pages 199 through 207. What is peculiar about Ford's position is that he takes Whitehead to have held, but also to have abandoned, the view of transition for which I have been arguing.

Chapter Eight: Solidarity and Individuality

1. By phenomenology, in this context, I understand a description of all that appears in and for conscious experience. I believe it is impossible for such a description to be presuppositionless. On the other hand, I believe that a preliminary critique of metaphysical notions enables the overcoming of many metaphysical, epistemic, and linguistic biases and prejudices that might otherwise be brought to the descriptive task. Moreover, insofar as metaphysical presuppositions are unavoidable, I hold that they should function overtly in the description. However, it is one goal of phenomenology, thus conceived, to keep metaphysical presuppositions to a categoreally coherent minimum. In the end, I take phenomenology to both suggest and test some of the categories and principles of metaphysics.

2. Notice that I have taken the liberty of substituting the *B* and *C* of my example for the *A* and *B*, respectively, of Whitehead's example.

3. The use of single quotation marks around the initial instances of *transmission*, *transmitted*, *accompanies*, and *passes* is intended to remind the reader that in the present context those words are not to be taken in their more literal senses. For example, there is a numerical difference between the eternal object at b^*/C^* and the same eternal object at c^*/C^*. The *endurance* of the quality from concrete moment to concrete moment is the *reiteration* or re-enactment of the quality in each concrete moment (SMW 186). See note 3 to the previous chapter.

4. Whitehead's references to concrescence as *microscopic* and to transition as *macroscopic* have caused considerable speculation as to his intended meaning. My suggestion is that the words are intended to be taken in their original etymological senses. Thus, it is not the size of the process that determines its label; rather, the relative size of the cosmos taken into account—*viewed*, if you will—by the process is what determines its characterization as either microscopic or macroscopic. Concrescence is microscopic because it contemplates the universe writ small—that is, the universe as reproduced; transition is macroscopic because it envisages the universe writ large—that is, the universe in itself. Notice, moreover, that there can be no difference in the size of the two processes; both occur within, and are

concerned with the determination of, the occasion's extensive standpoint. Notice also that, in transition, the macrocosmos begets a new microcosmos, whereas, in concrescence, the microcosmos completes itself. For a good overview of the issue, see Wallack, *The Epochal Nature of Process*, pp. 76–80. In this respect, her views and mine are very similar.

5. See also AI 246–51.

6. The terminological carelessness with which Whitehead presents his views on the subjectivist doctrine and the subjectivist principle is truly incredible (PR 238–54, 288–94). Two resolute attempts to make sense of it are: James E. Lindsey, Jr., "The Subjectivist Principle and the Linguistic Turn Revisited," *Process Studies*, 6 (1976), 97–102; and David Ray Griffin, "The Subjectivist Principle and Its Reformed and Unreformed Versions," *Process Studies*, 7 (1977), 27–36. I have benefitted from both discussions.

7. How could the subject experience change within the solipsism of the present moment? Without memory and cumulative phases of experience, there can be no perception of change.

8. For example, in *Symbolism* Whitehead writes that "the conception of the world here adopted is that of functional activity. By this I mean that every actual thing is something by reason of its activity; whereby its nature consists in its relevance to other things, and its individuality consists in its synthesis of other things so far as they are relevant to it. In enquiring about any one individual we must ask how other individuals enter 'objectively' into the unity of its own experience. This unity of its own experience is that individual existing *formally*. We must also enquire how it enters into the 'formal' existence of other things; and this entrance is that individual existing *objectively*, that is to say—existing abstractly, exemplifying only some elements in its formal content" (S 26–27). Later, Whitehead says that the doctrine of a direct experience of an external world, which he maintains, drives one's "philosophical construction to a conception of the world as an interplay of functional activity whereby each concrete individual thing arises from its determinate relativity to the settled world of other concrete individuals, at least so far as the world is past and settled" (S 29).

Notice, in this same regard, the frequency with which the notion of function appears in the categoreal scheme of PR. Notice, too, the recasting of the principle of relativity in terms of the concept of function (PR 336; ESP 313).

9. I use 'itself', rather than 'himself' or 'herself', because I am primarily concerned with an occasion of human subjectivity, rather than with an enduring human being or person.

10. In respect to the prehensions constitutive of C, for example, the public side of each prehension has its locus somewhere in $\mathcal{C}/C^*$, whereas the private side has its locus somewhere in c^*/C^*.

11. Another reason for not discussing the solidarity of the universe in God is that I do not find Whitehead's account of it particularly cogent.

Selected Bibliography

Alston, William P. "Internal Relatedness and Pluralism in Whitehead." *Review of Metaphysics* 5 (1952): 535–558.

Alston, William P. "Simple Location." *Review of Metaphysics* 8 (1954–1955): 334–341.

Alston, William P. "Whitehead's Denial of Simple Location." *Journal of Philosophy* 48 (1951): 713–721.

Ashmore, Jerome. "Diverse Currents in Whitehead's View of Time." *Process Studies* 2 (1972): 193–200.

Blyth, John W. *Whitehead's Theory of Knowledge*. 1941. Reprint. New York: Kraus Reprint Corporation, 1967.

Bohm, David. *Causality and Chance in Modern Physics*. London: Routledge & Kegan Paul, 1957.

Bohm, David. *Quantum Theory*. Englewood Cliffs, N.J.: Prentice-Hall, 1951.

Bohm, David. *Wholeness and the Implicate Order*. London: Routledge & Kegan Paul, 1980.

Bracken, Joseph A., S.J. "Substance-Society-Natural Systems: A Creative Rethinking of Whitehead's Cosmology." *International Philosophical Quarterly* 25 (1985): 3–13.

Brennan, Sheilah O'Flynn. "Substance Within Substance." *Process Studies* 7 (1977): 14–26.

Briggs, John P., and Peat, F. David. *Looking Glass Universe: The Emerging Science of Wholeness*. New York: Simon & Schuster, Inc., Cornerstone Library, 1984.

Burch, George Bosworth. "Whitehead's Harvard Lectures, 1926–27." Edited by Dwight C. Stewart. *Process Studies* 4 (1974): 199–206.

Burgess, J.M. *Experience and Conceptual Activity: A Philosophical Essay Based Upon the Writings of A. N. Whitehead*. Cambridge: The M.I.T. Press, 1965.

Capra, Fritjof. *The Tao of Physics: An Exploration of the Parallels Between Modern Physics and Eastern Mysticism*. New York: Bantam Books, 1977.

Carr, H. Wildon. "The Interaction of Body and Mind." *Proceedings of the Aristotelian Society, 1917–18*: 1–37.

Christian, William A. *An Interpretation of Whitehead's Metaphysics*. 1959. Reprint. New Haven: Yale University Press, 1967.

Christian, William A. "Some Aspects of Whitehead's Metaphysics." *Explorations in Whitehead's Philosophy*. Edited by Lewis S. Ford and George L. Kline. New York: Fordham University Press, 1983: 31–44.

Clarke, Bowman L. "Process, Time, and God." *Process Studies* 13 (1982): 245–59.

Clarke, Norris W., S.J. *The Philosophical Approach to God: A Neo-Thomistic Perspective*. Winston-Salem, N.C.: Wake Forest University Publications, 1979.

Cobb, John B., Jr. "Freedom in Whitehead's Philosophy: A Response to Edward Pols." *Southern Journal of Philosophy* 7 (1969): 409–13.

Cobb, John B., Jr., and Griffin, David Ray. *Mind in Nature: Essays on the Interface of Science and Philosophy*. Washington: University Press of America, 1977.

Cobb, John B., Jr., and Griffin, David Ray. *Process Theology: An Introductory Exposition*. Philadelphia: Westminster Press, 1976.

Cobb, John B., Jr., and Sherburne, Donald W. "Regional Inclusion and the Extensive Continuum." *Process Studies* 2 (1972): 277–95.

Das, Rasvihary. *The Philosophy of Whitehead*. 1938. Reprint. New York: Russell & Russell, 1928.

Fancher, Robert. "Of Time, the Self, and Rem Edwards," *Process Studies* 7 (1977): 40–43.

Field, Richard W. "Transmission, Inheritance, and Efficient Causation." *Process Studies* 14 (1984): 44–46.

Field, Richard W. "William James and the Epochal Theory of Time." *Process Studies* 13 (1983): 260–74.

Folse, Henry J., Jr. "Complementarity, Bell's Theorem, and the Framework of Process Metaphysics." *Process Studies*, 11 (1981): 242–58.

Ford, Lewis S. "The Concept of Process: From Transition to Concrescence." *Whitehead und der Prozessbegriff*. Edited by Harold Holz and Ernest Wolf-Gazo. Freiburg and Munich: Verlag Karl Alber, 1984: 73–101.

Ford, Lewis S. *The Emergence of Whitehead's Metaphysics, 1925–1929*. Albany: State University of New York Press, 1984.

Ford, Lewis S. "Genetic and Coordinate Division Correlated." *Process Studies* 1 (1971): 199–209.

Ford, Lewis S. "Some Proposals Concerning the Composition of Process and Reality." *Process Studies* 8 (1978): 145–56.

Ford, Lewis S., and Kline, George L. *Explorations in Whitehead's Philosophy*. New York: Fordham University Press, 1983.

Frankenberry, Nancy. "The Power of the Past." *Process Studies* 13 (1983): 132–42.

Garland, William J. "The Ultimacy of Creativity." *The Southern Journal of Philosophy* 7 (1969): 361–76.

Garland, William J. "The Ultimacy of Creativity" *Explorations in Whitehead's Philosophy*. Edited by Lewis S. Ford and George L. Kline. New York: Fordham University Press, 1983: 212–38.

Garland, William J. "Whitehead's Theory of Causal Objectification." *Process Studies* 12 (1982): 180–91.

Graham, Archie. "Metaphysical Principles and the Category of the Ultimate." *Process Studies* 7 (1977): 108–11.

Griffin, David Ray. "Rupert Sheldrake. *A New Science of Life: The Hypothesis of Formative Causation*." *Process Studies* 12 (1982): 34–40.

Griffin, David Ray. "The Subjectivist Principle and Its Reformed and Unreformed Versions." *Process Studues* 7 (1977): 27–36.

Hall, David L. *The Civilization of Experience: A Whiteheadian Theory of Culture*. New York: Fordham University Press, 1973.

Hammerschmidt, William W. *Whitehead's Philosophy of Time*. 1947. Reprint. New York: Russell & Russell, 1975.

Hartshorne, Charles. "Bell's Theorem and Stapp's Revised View of Space-Time." *Process Studies* 7 (1977): 183–91.

Hartshorne, Charles. *Creative Synthesis and Philosophic Method*. La Salle, Illinois: Open Court Publishing Co., 1970.

Hartshorne, Charles. *Insights and Oversights of Great Thinkers: An Evaluation of Western Philosophy*. Albany: State University of New York Press, 1983.

Hartshorne, Charles. "Whitehead's Novel Intuition." *Alfred North Whitehead: Essays on His Philosophy*. Edited by George Kline. New Jersey: Prentice-Hall, 1963: 18–26.

Hartshorne, Charles. "Whitehead and Ordinary Language." *Southern Journal of Philosophy* 7 (1969): 437–45.

Hartshorne, Charles. *Whitehead's Philosophy: Selected Essays, 1935–1970*. Lincoln: University of Nebraska Press, 1972.

Holz, Harold and Wolf-Gazo, Ernest. *Whitehead und der Prozessbegriff*. Frieburg and Munich: Verlag Karl Alber, 1984.

Johnson, A.H. *Whitehead's Theory of Reality*. 1952. Reprint. New York: Dover Publications, Inc., 1962.

Johnson, Charles Michael. "On Prehending the Past." *Process Studies* 6 (1976): 255–69.

Jones, William B. "Bell's Theorem, H.P. Stapp, and Process Theism." *Process Studies* 7 (1977): 250–61.

Kline, George L., *Alfred North Whitehead: Essays on His Philosophy*. Englewood Cliffs, N.J.: Prentice-Hall, Spectrum Book, 1963.

Kline, George L. "Form, Concrescence and Concretum." *Explorations in*

Whitehead's Philosophy. Edited by Lewis S. Ford and George L. Kline. New York: Fordham University Press, 1983: 104–46.

Kraus, Elizabeth M. *The Metaphysics of Experience: A Companion to Whitehead's Process and Reality*. New York: Fordham University Press, 1979.

Lango, John W. "The Relatedness of Eternal Objects in Whitehead's *Process and Reality*." *Process Studies* 1 (1971): 124–28.

Leclerc, Ivor. "The Structure of Form." *Revue Internationale de Philosophie*. 15 (1961): 185–203.

Leclerc, Ivor. *Whitehead's Metaphysics: An Introductory Exposition*. London: George Allen and Unwin, 1958.

Leclerc, Ivor. "Whitehead and the Problem on Extension." *Journal of Philosophy* 58 (1961): 559–65.

Leclerc, Ivor. "Whitehead and the Theory of Form." *Process and Divinity: Philosophical Essays Presented to Charles Hartshorne*. Edited by William L. Reese and Eugene Freeman. La Salle, Illinois: Open Court Publishing Co., 1964: 127–37.

LeShan, Lawrence, and Margenau, Henry. *Einstein's Space and Van Gogh's Sky: Physical Reality and Beyond*. New York: Macmillan Publishing Company, 1982.

Lindsey, James E., Jr. "The Subjectivist Principle and the Linguistic Turn Revisited." *Process Studies* 6 (1976): 97–102.

Locke, John. *An Essay Concerning Human Understanding*. 2 vols. Reprint. New York: Dover Publications, Inc., 1959.

Lovejoy, Arthur O. *The Revolt Against Dualism: An Inquiry Concerning the Existence of Ideas*. 2nd ed. La Salle, Illinois: Open Court Publishing Company, 1960.

Lowe, Victor. *Understanding Whitehead*. Baltimore: Johns Hopkins Press, 1966.

Lowe, Victor. "Whitehead's Gifford Lectures." *The Southern Journal of Philosophy* 7 (1969): 329–338.

Lucas, George R., Jr. "The Compositional History of Whitehead's Writings." *International Philosophical Quarterly*. 24 (1984): 312–25.

Lucas, George R., Jr. *The Genesis of Modern Process Thought: A Historical Outline with Bibliography*. Metuchen, N.J. and London: The Scarecrow Press and American Theological Library Association, 1983.

Lucas, George R., Jr. *Two Views of Freedom in Process Thought: A Study of Hegel and Whitehead*. Missoula, Montana: Scholars Press, 1979.

McMullin, E., ed. *The Concept of Matter*. Indiana: Notre Dame University Press, 1963.

Neisser, Ulric. *Cognitive Psychology*. New York: Meredith Publishing Co., 1967.

Neville, Robert C. *Creativity and God: A Challenge to Process Theology*. New York: Seabury Press, 1980.

Neville, Robert C. "Genetic Succession, Time, and Becoming." *Process Studies* 1 (1971): 194–98.

Neville, Robert C. "Whitehead on the One and the Many." *Explorations in Whitehead's Philosophy*. Edited by Lewis S. Ford and George L. Kline. New York: Fordham University Press, (1983): 257–71.

Nobo, Jorge L. "Transition in Whitehead: A Creative Process Distinct from Concrescence." *International Philosophical Quarterly* 19 (1979): 265–83.

Nobo, Jorge L. "Whitehead's Principle of Process." *Process Studies* 4 (1974): 275–84.

Nobo, Jorge L. "Whitehead's Principle of Relativity." *Process Studies* 8 (1978): 1–20.

Odin, Steve. *Process Metaphysics and Hua-yen Buddhism. A Critical Study of Cumulative Penetration vs. Interpenetration*. Albany: State University of New York Press, 1982.

Palter, Robert M. *Whitehead's Philosophy of Science*. Chicago: University of Chicago Press, 1960.

Pribram, Karl H., ed. *On the Biology of Learning*. New York: Harcourt, Brace & World, Inc., 1969.

Prigogine, Ilya, and Stengers, Isabelle. *Order Out of Chaos: Man's New Dialogue with Nature*. Toronto and New York: Bantam Books, 1984.

Pols, Edward. *Whitehead's Metaphysics: A Critical Examination of Process and Reality*. Carbondale and Edwardsville: Southern Illinois University Press, 1967.

Reese, William L., and Freeman, Eugene. *Process and Divinity, Philosophical Essays Presented to Charles Hartshorne*. La Salle, Illinois: Open Court Publishing Co., 1964.

Rorty, Richard M. "Matter and Event." *The Concept of Matter*. Edited by E. McMullin. Indiana: Notre Dame University Press, 1963.

Rorty, Richard M. "The Subjectivist Principle and the Linguistic Turn." *Alfred North Whitehead: Essays on His Philosophy*. Edited by George L. Kline. Englewood Cliffs, N.J.: Prentice-Hall, 1963: 134–57.

Ross, Stephen David. *Perspective in Whitehead's Metaphysics*. Albany: State University of New York Press, 1983.

Schindler, David L. "Whitehead's Challenge to Thomism on the Problem of God: The Metaphysical Issues." *International Philosophical Quarterly* 19 (1979): 285–99.

Schindler, David L. "Whitehead's Inability to Affirm a Universe of Value." *Process Studies* 13 (1983): 117–31.

Schmidt, Paul F. "Nobo's Thesis on the Repeatability of Actual Occasions." *Process Studies* 11 (1981): 104–06.

Schmidt, Paul F. *Perception and Cosmology in Whitehead's Philosophy*. New Brunswick, N.J.: Rutgers University Press, 1967.

Sheldrake, Rupert. *A New Science of Life: The Hypothesis of Formative Causation*. Los Angeles: J.P. Tarcher, Inc., 1981.

Sherburne, Donald W. *A Key to Whitehead's Process and Reality*. New York: Macmillan Co., 1966.

Sherburne, Donald W. *A Whiteheadian Aesthetic*. New Haven: Yale University Press, 1961.

Stacer, John R., S.J. "Integrating Thomistic and Whiteheadian Perspectives on God." *International Philosophical Quarterly* 21 (1981): 355–77.

Suchocki, Marjorie. "The Metaphysical Ground of the Whiteheadian God." *Process Studies* 5 (1975): 237–46.

Thorpe, W.H. *Purpose in a World of Chance: A Biologist's View*. Oxford: Oxford University Press, 1978.

Trickett, David G. "David Bohm. *Wholeness and the Implicate Order*." *Process Studies* 12 (1982): 50–54.

Wallack, F. Bradford *The Epochal Nature of Process in Whitehead's Metaphysics*. Albany: State University of New York Press, 1980.

Weiss, Paul. *Modes of Being*. Carbondale and Edwardsville: Southern Illinois University Press, 1958.

Weiss, Paul. *Reality*. 1938. Reprint. Carbondale and Edwardsville: Southern Illinois University Press, 1967.

Wilber, Ken, ed. *The Holographic Paradigm and Other Paradoxes: Exploring the Leading Edge of Science*. Boulder and London: Shambhala Publications, 1982.

White, Villard Alan. "Sensa and Patterns." *Process Studies* 10 (1980): 39–43.

Whitehead, Alfred North. *Adventures of Ideas*. New York: The Macmillan Company, 1933.

Whitehead, Alfred North. *The Concept of Nature*. Cambridge: Cambridge University Press, 1964.

Whitehead, Alfred North. *An Enquiry Concerning the Principles of Natural Knowledge*. 1925. Reprint. New York: Dover Publications, Inc., 1982.

Whitehead, Alfred North. *Essays in Science and Philosophy*. New York: Philosophical Library, 1947.

Whitehead, Alfred North. *The Function of Reason*. 1929. Reprint. Boston: Beacon Press, 1958.

Whitehead, Alfred North. "Indication, Classes, Numbers, Validation." *Mind* 43 (1934): 281–97.

Whitehead, Alfred North. *The Interpretation of Science: Selected Essays*. Indianapolis: Bobbs-Merrill Company, 1961.

Whitehead, Alfred North. *Modes of Thought*. New York: The Macmillan Company, 1938.

Whitehead, Alfred North. *Process and Reality: An Essay in Cosmology*. New York: The Macmillan Company, 1929.

Whitehead, Alfred North. *Process and Reality: An Essay in Cosmology*. Corrected Edition. Edited by David Ray Griffin and Donald W. Sherburne. New York: The Free Press, 1978.

Whitehead, Alfred North. *The Principle of Relativity with Applications to Physical Science*. Cambridge: Cambridge University Press, 1922.

Whitehead, Alfred North. *Religion in the Making*. New York: The Macmillan Company, 1926.

Whitehead, Alfred North. *Science and the Modern World*. New York: The Macmillan Company, 1925.

Whitehead, Alfred North. *Symbolism: Its Meaning and Effect*. 1927. Reprint. New York: G.P. Putnam's Sons, Capricorn Books, 1959.

Index

Individuality (*continued*)
  deepened, 285, 287, 390; independent, 390; full, 285, 287–88, 357,
  382; fully-clothed, 285–86, 289, 302;
  minimal, 285, 287, 356; senses of,
  286–88
Individualization, 117, 119–20, 130–31,
  161–62, 168, 256, 286–89, 356–57;
  minimal, 287; deepened, 287
Induction, 372
Information, 323, 327–29, 339, 341–42,
  362
Inheritance, 21, 120, 356, 358, 362, 410
Intentionality, 342. *See also* Reference,
  transcendental
Intersubjective agreement, 388
Intrinsic (or formal) reality (of actual entity), 259–67, 298, 300–02, 315,
  319, 348, 353, 355, 397. *See also*
  Self-immanent existence
Isolation of eternal objects, principle of,
  92, 177

Johnson, A. H., 400, 402, 406, 410, 412
Johnson, Charles Michael, 403, 408
Jones, William B., 401
Judgement, 276–77, 329, 413

Kline, George L., 400, 403, 408
Knower, 387
Knowledge, 303, 329–30, 349, 358, 366–
  68, 371–72, 375, 377–79, 386–87,
  405
Kraus, Elizabeth M., 411

Lango, John W., 410
Leclerc, Ivor, 112, 139–40, 151, 402,
  406, 408–10
Leibniz, Gottfried Wilhelm, 236, 371
Lindsey, James E., Jr., 416
Location, 225, 307, 314; absolute, 276,
  301; correlative, 275–76, 278–81;
  multiple, 262–72, 276–78, 280–81,
  301, 355–56; self-immanent, 270,
  277; self-transcendent, 270, 277
Locke, John, 142, 143, 144, 145, 148,
  408
Locus (or loci), 240, 267, 355–56, 366–
  67
Lowe, Victor, 2, 400, 406–07
Lucas, George R., Jr., 403, 408
Lure, objective, 120, 184–85

Macrocosmos, 358, 415–16
Macroscopic process. *See* Creative process
  and Transition
Manifold reality, 270
Manner of a pattern, 176
Many, the, 103, 131, 135, 162–63, 202,
  241, 249, 276, 312, 376–77, 395,
  407; as accumulated, 103–05, 131,
  134–35; as conjunctive, 131–135,
  305–06, 376; as disjunctive, 131–35,
  305–06, 309; as reproduced, 103–05,
  131, 134–35. *See also* Diversity
Matter (Aristotelian), 170–71, 331
Meaning, 366–67
Memory, 62, 363, 372, 375, 401, 407;
  physical, 80, 363–65, 375. *See also*
  Perception, in the pure mode of
  causal efficacy *and* Experience,
  mnemonic
Mental pole, 85–87, 90–91, 98–99, 124,
  146, 148–50, 155, 186–88, 191, 357,
  359, 392
Metaphysical, 324, 346–47; analysis, 343;
  chronology, 327; hologram, 327–29;
  topology, 327
Metaphysics, 243–47, 286, 330, 344,
  369, 383, 387, 415; and cosmology,
  344; and phenomenology, 387, 415;
  definition of, 6–7, 401
Microcosmos, 315, 358, 415–16
Microscopic process. *See* Creative process
  and Concrescence
Miller, David L., xv
Modal differentiation, 228–29, 232, 271,
  311, 336, 353, 362, 378, 411, 413;
  potential, 31
Modal economy, principle of. *See* Modal
  presence, transitivity of
Modal mirroring, 224–28, 231, 235–36,
  241–43, 262–65, 267, 271, 275, 277,
  280, 307, 311–13, 334–35, 346, 411;
  potential, 313
Modal presence (or immanence), 225–26,
  233, 237, 239–43, 248, 271, 274,
  315, 326–28, 333–35, 344, 348, 366,
  373, 378–79; potential, 313; transitivity of, 228–29, 261, 274, 301
Modal scheme (or structure), 225, 242–
  43, 274–78, 280, 301, 311–15, 319,
  323, 327, 333, 335–37, 339–48, 354,
  366–67, 370, 378, 398; actual (or
  real), 311, 313, 327, 335; crystallization of, 313, 324, 327, 335, 378–79;

Relative extensive order, 274–76
Relative genetic order, 274–75
Relativity physics, 46, 53, 279, 411
Repetition, 58, 61–69, 92–93, 113, 134,
137, 179, 191–93, 200, 240, 268–69,
300, 318, 327, 377, 407; and the
Category of the Ultimate, 134–35;
and the ontological principle, 113;
and the principle of relativity, 34,
61–69, 75, 105, 407; and transition,
29–32, 102, 150, 353–56; in the conformal phase (or in conformation),
31, 70–73, 77–78, 95–99, 146, 198,
353–56. *See also* Conformation; in
the dative phase (or in causal objectification), 18–20, 54–55, 67, 70–76,
95–99, 146. *See also* Objectification,
causal; in the integrative phases, 90–
93; in the mental phases, 31, 84–87;
of actual entities (or particulars), 18–
20, 55, 57, 61–62, 66–67, 75, 81,
93, 96, 99–105, 134, 137–38, 163–
64, 179, 373, 377–79, 397, 405–06;
of contrasts, 192; of eternal objects
(or universals), 56–57, 61, 78, 84–
85, 91–93, 96, 137–38, 179, 191–
92, 200, 353–56; of world or universe, 112–14, 137, 327
Representation, 362–63, 369–70
Reproduction. *See* Objectification, causal,
Conformation, Reenactment, *and*
Repetition
Responsive phase. *See* Phases of becoming, conformal physical feeling
Rorty, Richard M., 405
Ross, Stephen David, 405, 411–12

Satisfaction. *See* Phases of becoming *and*
Superject
Scheme of extensive order, 242, 246. *See
also* Extensive scheme of division,
Indicative scheme, *and* Modal
scheme
Schindler, David L., 403, 407–08
Science, 243–45
Self, 114, 130, 134, 150, 382, 385, 393,
395
Self-definition, 350, 357
Self-determination, 115, 159
Self-diversity, 58, 137, 259, 289, 292,
295–97, 302, 394
Self-identity, 18, 58, 67, 81, 100, 135,

137, 201, 251, 259, 270, 273, 278–
81, 283–84, 289, 291–92, 295–302,
314, 341, 355, 374, 378, 388, 392,
397, 402
Self-immanent existence, 259–68, 270–
71, 277, 281, 289, 299–301. *See also*
Intrinsic reality
Self-realization, 159, 173, 299
Self-revelation, 143, 298, 317, 319, 379–
80. *See also* Objectification *and* Universalization
Self-transcendent existence, 101–02, 110,
259–67, 271, 277, 289, 299–301,
319, 397. *See also* Extrinsic reality
Sensationalist doctrine, 372, 377
Sensationalist principle, 371–72, 377,
380, 391–92
Sherburne, Donald W., 112, 139–40,
151, 402, 406, 411
Significance, 367–68, 370; for others,
293; for self, 292–94
Simple location, 236–38, 240, 267–70,
411; fallacy of, 236
Solidarity (or connectedness), 1, 5–6, 20,
23, 31, 33, 58, 62, 110, 113, 132,
136, 166–67, 179, 187, 198–203,
246, 268, 289–90, 300, 317, 325–26,
328, 380–81, 398–99, 402, 405; and
the categoreal scheme, xiii, 4, 6–9,
32, 205; and the Category of the Ultimate, 8, 131–37, 163; and eternal
objects, 25, 179, 198–202, 311–12,
399; and extension, xiv, 9, 20, 22–
23, 50–58, 205–07, 219–22, 248–49,
311–12, 346–48, 379, 397; and extenso-creative matrix, 54, 328; and
individuality, 5–6, 220, 290, 302–
03, 317, 348–49, 358, 380–96; and
the ontological principle, 8, 33, 161,
163–64; and the organic working hypothesis, 5; and the principle of creativity, 33, 161, 163; and the
principle of process, 33; and the
principle of relativity, 8, 33, 69,
161, 163–64; divine, 202–03, 397,
416; extensional, 59, 303–04, 346–
48, 378–79, 381; functional, 59,
303, 380–92, 395–96, 416; objective,
59, 303, 378–80, 396; of actual entity and world (or universe), 3–4,
19–20, 348, 358, 399; of actualities,
1–4, 7, 31, 50–51, 53–54, 95, 100,
103, 107–08, 133, 135, 160, 163,